LONGINUS ON THE SUBLIME

CAMBRIDGE UNIVERSITY PRESS WAREHOUSE,

C. F. CLAY, Manager.

London: FETTER LANE, E.C.

Glasgow: 50, WELLINGTON STREET.

Leipzig: F. A. BROCKHAUS.

New York: G. P. PUTNAM'S SONS.

Bombay and Calcutta: MACMILLAN AND CO., Ltd.

LONGINUS
ON THE SUBLIME

THE GREEK TEXT EDITED AFTER THE PARIS
MANUSCRIPT

WITH

*INTRODUCTION, TRANSLATION, FACSIMILES
AND APPENDICES*

By

W. RHYS ROBERTS

Litt.D. (Camb.), Hon. LL.D. (St Andrews);
Professor of Classics in the University of Leeds; formerly
Professor of Greek in the University College of North Wales, Bangor

SECOND EDITION

Cambridge :
at the University Press
1907

Cambridge:

PRINTED BY JOHN CLAY, M.A.

AT THE UNIVERSITY PRESS.

VIRO REVERENDO

EDWINO ABBOTT ABBOTT

SCHOLAE CIVITATIS LONDINENSIS QVONDAM
ARCHIDIDASCALO

QVI

ET ANIMI SVBLIMITATE ET SCRIPTORVM

INSIGNE ILLVD COMPROBAVIT DICTVM

ὕψος μεγαλοφροσύνης ἀπήχημα

HANC EDITIONEM GRATO ANIMO DEDICAT

DISCIPVLVS

PREFACE

It is 60 years since the publication of the last English edition of Longinus on the Sublime. The edition of D. B. Hickie appeared in 1836, having had many English predecessors, not the least interesting of which was that published more than a century earlier (in 1724) by Zachary Pearce, Fellow of Trinity College, Cambridge, and afterwards Bishop of Bangor.

An editor who resumes the task to-day finds that, if he takes due account of the investigations of continental scholars, he will probably seem to be issuing not so much a new edition as a new book. The application to this treatise (as to other remains of classical antiquity) of the scientific method has not only produced an altered text, but has changed our entire conception of the scope of the work and of its historical background. Some appearance of paradox is the inevitable result. The modern editor must devote the two halves of his Introduction to a criticism of the traditional title of the book. He must challenge the ascription and explain the description. He must point out that the author is probably not the historical Longinus, while the subject is not 'the Sublime' in the ordinary acceptation of that term.

In view of many prevalent misconceptions, an attempt has been made in the Introduction (pp. 23—37) to indicate the spirit in which the author of the treatise approaches those

*questions of style and literary criticism with which he is chiefly
concerned.   His book is so happily conceived that professed
students of Greek literature will find it most interesting and
suggestive, while men of letters generally may perhaps judge it
worthy of a place on the shelves of that Library for Critics
which it is sometimes said that every modern writer might do
well to form.   It is not difficult to imagine that a man of literary
tastes who had never chanced to read the book would be pleasantly
surprised were he to open it.   He might possibly expect to find a
dry philosophical disquisition on sublimity in the more exalted
sense of the term.   Instead of this, he would discover a very
fresh and living book in which a genial Greek critic discourses
to a young Roman friend, or pupil, on those problems of literary
criticism and of style which Greek literature freely suggested
now that it was studied (as it were) from outside.   He would
find that he had before him quite an anthology, culled from the
Greek writers, of choice passages in prose and verse, together
with some specimens of faulty or vicious style.   He would
observe that the critic makes and applies his selections much in
the same way as does Matthew Arnold in our own day.
Matthew Arnold's method has, as we all know, been attacked;
but subjective as it is, it cannot fail to be interesting and instructive when employed by a master with whom criticism is,
to use the words of the treatise, 'the last and crowning fruit of
long experience.'   And the actual judgments which these two
mature literary critics of the ancient and the modern world
pronounce are remarkably and reassuringly similar owing to
the fact that, in their maturity, they have both arrived at the
conclusion that the test of really great literature is its* ὕψος, *or
(in Matthew Arnold's words)* 'the high seriousness which
comes from absolute sincerity.'

    The reader of literary tastes to whom reference has just been

*made will, it is hoped, find the present edition of some service to
him. It has been planned in a somewhat novel way in order
that those who so desire may confine themselves to the text only
or to the text and translation only, while those who require
further help may find it (by means of the indices or otherwise)
in the introduction or the appendices, where it is offered separately
and in an ordered form. With regard to the book generally,
the editor can only express the hope that something like the due
balance has been maintained as between the literary and the
scientific side of his work; that the frequent quotations from
foreign authorities may be excused as proper in themselves and
as giving incidentally that air of cosmopolitanism which is so
appropriate to the treatise; that the text possesses at least the
merit of close adherence to the best surviving manuscript; and
that the translation may be exact enough to serve to some
extent in place of a formal commentary, while it may also to
some extent suggest the tone and manner of the original.*

*It may be permissible to add that this edition has been in
preparation for some years in connexion with a larger undertaking,*—A **History of Greek Literary Criticism,** *or* **An
Account of the Literary Opinions of the Greeks during
the Classical, the Alexandrian, and the Graeco-Roman
Periods.** *With a view to the better accomplishment of this
undertaking, the editor has, he may mention, prepared a number
of preliminary literary-historical studies (one of which he has
published) of Greek life at various epochs and at various centres
both within and beyond Greece itself,—centres such as Boeotia,
Sicily, Alexandria, Rome. For published articles of his own
which bear upon the book now edited, he desires to refer to
the Bibliographical Appendix, p. 257.*

*The Bibliography forms a record of the editor's obligations
to his predecessors in the same field. But special and personal*

thanks are due to his colleague Mr E. V. Arnold, and to his former colleague Mr G. B. Mathews, for kind and valuable assistance rendered while the book has been passing through the press.

*   *   *   *   *   *   *

The whole of the verse translations in this volume (with the exception of the late Mr J. A. Symonds' rendering of the Ode of Sappho) are from the hand of Mr A. S. Way. Mr Way has generously allowed the use not only of his published versions of Homer and Euripides but also of his unpublished versions of Aeschylus and Sophocles. And more than that, he has specially translated for this edition the remaining lines which occur in the treatise. For this accumulated kindness the editor feels that he is indebted to Mr Way in no ordinary measure.

UNIVERSITY COLLEGE OF NORTH WALES,
   BANGOR.
      January 17, 1899.

Some changes of detail have been made in the second edition. But in substance the book remains the same ; and I have seen no reason to withdraw or modify my views upon the vexed question of Authorship.

W. R. R.

THE UNIVERSITY,
   LEEDS.
      August 21, 1907.

CONTENTS

		PAGE
INTRODUCTION. I.	Authorship of the Treatise . . .	1
II.	Contents and Character of the Treatise	23
TEXT and TRANSLATION	. . . .	40
APPENDICES. Appendix A.	Textual. With Critical Notes .	163
Appendix B.	Linguistic. With a Select Glossary chiefly of Rhetorical Terms	186
Appendix C.	Literary. With a List of Authors and Quotations . . .	211
Appendix D.	Bibliographical. With a Glance at the Influence of the Treatise in Modern Times .	247
INDICES. I.	Index Rerum	263
II.	Index Nominum	265
III.	Index Graecitatis	269
Facsimiles of P 2036	*To precede Introduction*	

† ἈΡΙCΤΟΤΕΛΟΥC ΦΥCΙΚꞶΝ ΠΡΟΒΛΗΜΑΤꞶΝ ΕΙΔΟC
CΥΝΑΓꞶΓΗC :

† ΔΙΟΝΥΣΙΟΥ   ΛΟΓΓΙΝΟΥ   ΠΕΡΙ ΥΨΟΥC : †

+ ΔΙΟΝΥΣΙΟΥ Η ΛΟΓΓΙΝΟΥ ΠΕΡΙ ΥΨΟΥΣ

ιθ	ὅσα περὶ τὰ θερμὰ ὕδατα	κδ
κα	ὅσα περὶ τὸν ἀέρα	κε
ξα	ὅσα περὶ ἀνέμους	κς
ια	ὅσα περὶ Ἀλεξανδρείαν	κζ
	ὅσα περὶ σωφροσύνην καὶ ἀκολασίαν	κη
η	ὅσα περὶ δικαιοσύνην καὶ ἀδικίαν	κθ
ιγ	ὅσα περὶ φρόνησιν καὶ σοφίαν	λ
κθ	ὅσα περὶ φαῦλον	λα
ιζ	ὅσα περὶ ὦτα	λβ
ιη	ὅσα περὶ μυκτῆρα	λγ
ιδ	ὅσα περὶ στόμα	λδ
ι	ὅσα τινὰ φθην	λε
ς	ὅσα περὶ πρόσωπον	λς
ια	ὅσα περὶ χρόαν	λζ

P. 2036. fol. 1v.   Vide p. 4.

INTRODUCTION.

I. AUTHORSHIP OF THE TREATISE.

When Francis Robortello at Basle, in the year 1554, issued the *editio princeps* of the Greek Treatise on the Sublime, he attributed the work to 'Dionysius Longinus.' Διονυσίου Λογγίνου ῥήτορος περὶ ὕψους βιβλίον are the words found upon his title-page. In this ascription he was followed by Paul Manutius, who in the next year (1555) published an edition at Venice. The fashion thus set by the earliest editors became universal. Edition followed edition in quick succession, and translations made the book known in almost every European country. But in every issue of text or rendering Longinus was assumed to be the author. It was the same with the foremost critics and writers of France and of England. Boileau was in this matter at one with the rest of the translators. His acquiescence in the general view was shared by Fénelon, Rollin, and Laharpe, and in England by Addison, Hume, and Hurd. Pope, in a well-known passage, speaks of the 'bold Longinus,' whose 'own example strengthens all his laws.' And even the severely scientific Gibbon refers, with some hesitation possibly in the choice of the adjective but with no hesitation in the choice of the name, to the 'sublime Longinus.'

An ascription so firmly rooted in the tradition of two centuries was not easily shaken, and even now it finds, here and there, unquestioning acceptance. But since the first doubt was raised at the commencement of the present century, the tendency of critical opinion has been, with some fluctuations, increasingly adverse to the old view. In the present edition, although the traditional heading appears for the sake of convenience upon the title-page, an endeavour will be made to establish, in the light of the most recent research, two main propositions : (1) that the external evidence in favour of attribution to the historical Longinus is of a highly dubious character, and (2) that the internal evidence seems to point to the first century rather than the third as the period within which the treatise was probably written. In presenting the facts under the two headings *A. External Evidence*, and *B. Internal Evidence*, it will be convenient in each case to treat first of the negative indications (viz. arguments drawn from silence, from omissions, etc.), and afterwards of the positive.

A.—EXTERNAL EVIDENCE.

(*a*) NEGATIVE. It is a remarkable fact that the Treatise on the Sublime is not quoted or mentioned by any writer of antiquity. So complete is the silence with regard to it that some have conjectured that it was written for private circulation only. Publication, they think, was deliberately avoided by its author, who was influenced either by modesty or by prudential motives. Its epistolary form may possibly be held to give some colour to this view[1]. At all events, the obscurity which surrounded it until it was printed was great, as great as its subsequent celebrity. The silence extends—and this brings us face to face with the problem before us—to those lists of the works of Longinus which we owe to Porphyry, Suidas, and others. The *De Sublimitate* is not by any of these authorities mentioned among the writings of Longinus, and the omission is the more striking that the treatise is no ordinary one. The seriousness of the difficulty has long been recognised by those who have regarded Longinus as the author. But the ingenuity of scholars has, as usual, proved equal to the occasion. They suggest that the περὶ ὕψους

---

[1] Cp. G. Buchenau, *De Scriptore Libri* Περὶ Ὕψους, p. 66, and A. Jannarakis, Εἰς τὸ Περὶ Ὕψους λεγόμενον βιβλίον Κριτικαὶ Σημειώσεις, p. 8.

formed part of οἱ φιλόλογοι (or αἱ φιλόλογοι ὁμιλίαι, as the title is also given), one of the attested works of Longinus. But while the possibility of this explanation cannot be denied, it should be remarked that it does not find any very obvious support in the character of the surviving fragments of οἱ φιλόλογοι, or in the character of the περὶ ὕψους itself. The latter, to all appearance, occupies a position of its own as a polemical essay directed against the work of a writer who is named in its opening sentence. It may be added that in certain passages (viii. 1, xxxix. 1, xliv. 12) of the *De Sublimitate* the author seems to intimate that he had written, or intended to write, about Xenophon, about composition (σύνθεσις λόγων), and about the passions (τὰ πάθη) ; but these subject-headings, also, fail to appear in the lists of the works of Longinus.

(β) POSITIVE. The absence of the treatise from the accredited lists of Longinus' works, although it was felt to require explanation, caused no great uneasiness till the beginning of this century (1808), when the Italian scholar Amati made an important discovery. He found that a Vatican MS. (no. 285) of the *De Sublimitate* contained the following inscription : Διονυσίου ἢ Λογγίνου περὶ ὕψους. Hitherto it had been taken for granted (by Robortello himself, no doubt, as well as by those who followed him) that all the manuscripts attributed the book to 'Dionysius Longinus'; it was disconcerting, therefore, to find that one of them indicated 'Dionysius *or* Longinus' as the author. But this was not all. Once curiosity had been aroused by Amati, another discovery followed. It was found that the same alternative was offered by the Paris MS. 2036, which dates from the tenth century and is beyond comparison the best of the existing codices of the *De Sublimitate*. True, the other title was also given in that MS. ; but the new point noticed was that, immediately after the index of the 'Physical Problems of Aristotle,' the words Διονυσίου ἢ Λογγίνου occurred. They occurred also, it was found, in MS. 985 of the Bibliothèque Nationale[1]. And

---

[1] The present editor has recently had an opportunity of examining P. 2036 and P. 985 in the Bibliothèque Nationale. In P. 2036 the περὶ ὕψους follows the

last of all, it was discovered (and for this final discovery we return from France to Italy) that a manuscript at Florence had, as the inscription on its cover, ἀνωνύμου περὶ ὕψους. The most surprising thing, perhaps, about all this new information, was that it had not been obtained earlier. But the treatise was so implicitly believed to be the work of Longinus that any hints to the contrary passed almost unheeded. Indeed, the variation in Codex Parisinus 2036 had been noted, a considerable time before Amati announced his discovery in the Vatican Library, by the German scholar Rostgaard ; but nothing came of Rostgaard's observation.

However, once it had been fairly opened, the question could not again be closed. A wide field for speculation was presented. The names of 'Longinus' and 'Dionysius,' without further specification, lent themselves to numerous conjectures. And even if, as seemed most probable, the names were to be understood of their two most famous bearers in the literary domain, the uncertainty became, in reality, not less but greater. For when a free choice is allowed between two men who stand more than a couple of centuries apart, we feel justified in conjecturing that we have before us nothing more than the guess of some late Byzantine authority who was himself in doubt and therefore named, alternatively, the two

---

Problems of Aristotle which occupy the greater part of the manuscript. The Problems are prefaced by an index or table of contents (forming fol. 1, *r.* and *v.*). At the end of the index are added the words :

$$+ \quad ΔΙΟΝΥϹΙΟΥ \quad Η \quad ΛΟΓΓΙΝΟΥ \quad \overset{E}{Π} \quad ΥΨΟΥϹ \quad +$$

At the beginning of the text of the treatise the heading is :

$$+ \quad ΔΙΟΝΥϹΙΟΥ \quad ΛΟΓΓΙΝΟΥ \quad ΠΕΡΙΥΨΟΥϹ \quad : \quad +$$

This title is distinguished from the other by the absence of the ἤ, but it is also distinguished (and this appears to have escaped even Vahlen's careful scrutiny) from it by the fact that a considerable space separates the first word from the second and the second from the third, while the third and fourth are run together. It would almost seem as if (notwithstanding the absence of the ἤ) the reader were still offered his choice between Dionysius and Longinus. The same absence and presence of the ἤ, and the same separation and non-separation, are to be observed in P. 985, on f. 222 *v.* (beginning of the treatise) and f. 79 *v.* (index) respectively. The facsimile specimens of P. 2036 which have been inserted in this edition give a more exact representation of the two titles.

most eminent critics known to him[1]. On this interpretation, the title might have run, as some one has suggested, Διονυσίου ἢ Λογγίνου ἢ ἄλλου τινός. It might, in fact, have been compressed into a single word, the ἀνωνύμου of the Codex Laurentianus.

And here, while the question of the name or names found in the manuscripts is under review, it may be pointed out that the traditional ascription of the treatise to Longinus had been felt to present a special difficulty on the score of nomenclature. But the difficulty, instead of encouraging a healthy scepticism, had led once more to a display of that ready ingenuity which is certainly no less characteristic of the conservative than of the innovator. The full name of Zenobia's minister, as given by more than one ancient authority, was Cassius Longinus. How, then, account for 'Dionysius Longinus,' which at best is a somewhat rare combination of a Greek and a Latin name? The answer was ready to hand. Longinus in his youth had borne the Greek name of Dionysius, but later he adopted that of Cassius Longinus, in honour of some powerful Roman patron of that name : his full and proper designation, therefore, was Dionysius Cassius Longinus. And that designation he bore until the discovery of the real inscription came to remind those interested in the matter that there were absolutely no facts upon which to base this elaborate theory.

It has already been said that the Treatise on the Sublime is not quoted or mentioned by 'any writer of antiquity.' From that statement there is no occasion to recede ; but before we leave the consideration of the external evidence, allusion should be made to certain passages from an external source which have sometimes been supposed to show a knowledge of the book. The source in question is the commentator John of Sicily ('Ιωάννης Σικελιώτης). The references which

---

[1] H. Usener (*Rheinisches Museum*, xxviii. 412) has adduced a Byzantine passage which is much to the point : ἡμεῖς δὲ πῶς τὸ ταπεινὸν ὑψηλῶς φράσαιμεν <ἄν> καὶ τὸ ἀμελῶς κατευγλωττισμένον, καὶ τῷ γοργῷ τὸ ἀνειμένον συμμίξαιμεν καὶ τὴν χάριν τῷ διηρμένῳ πρὸς μέγεθος ; καὶ τί ποιήσαιμεν πρὸς τὰς κρίσεις Λογγίνου, πρὸς τὸ Διονυσίου πολυμαθές, πρὸς τὸ εὐφυὲς Ἑρμογένους τοῦ Κίλικος; (Cramer, *Anecd. Oxon.*, iii. 159, 4).

John of Sicily has been thought to make to the treatise are
vague and disputable.   But even if we were to assume for the
sake of argument that they were definite and unmistakable,
they would be of little importance; and for this reason.   The
date assigned by Walz to John of Sicily is the thirteenth
century.   Now, as we have seen, the Paris MS. 2036 of the
De Sublimitate is supposed to belong to the tenth century.
Accordingly John may have drawn any ideas he entertained
with regard to the authorship of the treatise from that manuscript of it.   He cannot, therefore, be safely regarded as in
any sense an original and independent authority[1].

B.—INTERNAL EVIDENCE.

(*a*) NEGATIVE.   The treatise on the Sublime abounds in
references to Greek authors and in quotations from them.
Catholic alike in praise and blame, it ranges the centuries for
its illustrations of good style or of bad.   Bards of the pre-
historic days of Greece, writers of its Attic prime, erudite
poets of the Alexandrian era, rhetoricians of the Augustan
age,—all figure in its pages.   But notwithstanding the great
number of its references to writings of an earlier date, the
Treatise (or so much of it as we now possess) makes no
mention of any rhetorician, philosopher, or other writer
belonging to the second or to the third century A.D.   Here
again the supporters of the traditional view that Cassius
Longinus was the author are confronted by a grave difficulty.
The gap is a truly remarkable one.   How comes it that
no reference is made to the rhetorician Hermogenes, who
flourished during the reign of Marcus Aurelius Antoninus,
and whose shortcomings (rather than those of Caecilius)
might have provided an opening for a book?   How is it that

---

[1] How precarious these arguments connected with John of Sicily are may be
inferred from the fact that Émile Egger, who urged them in the first edition of his
Histoire de la Critique chez les Grecs (pp. 531–533), silently abandons them in his
second edition and in the *Journal des Savants* (Mai 1884).   Further details, if
desired, may be found in Vaucher, *Études Critiques sur le Traité du Sublime*,
pp. 57, 58, 62, 63, and in Canna, *Della Sublimità: libro attribuito a Cassio
Longino*, pp. 39, 40.

Longinus, who was the centre of a wide circle, makes no mention of his companions in the schools or of his friends? How is it, lastly and above all, that he makes no mention of his enemies, some of whom presumably had written books? For, granted that his taste may have been too fastidious to find examples of excellence in the writings of his contemporaries or of his more immediate predecessors, yet the task he set himself was the exemplification not only of the elevated manner but also of its opposite. And to go back for instances of defective style to Alexandrian times or to a period earlier still, instead of attacking living offenders, would have entailed the sacrifice of much obvious point and piquancy.

(β) POSITIVE. The internal evidence of a positive character is various in its nature and unequal in its value. It will be convenient to examine first that portion of it which relates to the names of persons. The evidential bearings of the *prosopographia*, so to say, of the treatise are considerable.

I. PROSOPOGRAPHIA. Under this head let us, following the example of the author in his book, start with Caecilius.

(1) *Caecilius.* The book opens thus: τὸ μὲν τοῦ Κεκιλίου συγγραμμάτιον, ὃ περὶ ὕψους συνετάξατο, ἀνασκοπουμένοις ἡμῖν ὡς οἶσθα κοινῇ, Ποστούμιε † Φλωρεντιανὲ φίλτατε, ταπεινότερον ἐφάνη τῆς ὅλης ὑποθέσεως, κ.τ.λ. It is clear from these words that Caecilius had composed an essay on the sublime, and that our author is dissatisfied with it. Now Caecilius was a rhetorician contemporary with Dionysius of Halicarnassus, of whom in fact he was a close friend[1]. The question, therefore, arises whether it is probable that in the third century a writer would follow, so closely as our author appears to do, the treatment which his chosen subject had met with in the reign of Augustus. To such a question, as to other similar questions here propounded, one who entertains the gravest doubts as to the third-century authorship will nevertheless think it fair to reply that, though not likely, it is not

---

[1] For further particulars reference may be made to the Literary Appendix under *Caecilius*.

impossible. For, to borrow an illustration from another field, did not seventy years pass before a reply was made, by Origen, to the *True Word* of Celsus?   And on the fiery battle-ground of religious controversy one might expect that polemic would know no lengthy pause.   A treatise need not, therefore, follow very closely in the train of one that suggested it.   But on the other hand it cannot be denied that this particular treatise is written with all the earnestness and ardour of a writer who is refuting the errors of a contemporary or a near predecessor. Hermogenes might have provoked a third-century antagonist to this display of zeal, but hardly Caecilius.

(2) *Moses.* Moses is not expressly named in the *De Sublimitate*, but he is unambiguously indicated in the well-known words of c. ix. 9.   It is sometimes contended that the reference to Moses tells in precisely the opposite direction to the mention of Caecilius; it makes the third century more likely than the first.   But even if this be admitted (and we can hardly admit any implication that such a reference to Genesis is out of the question in a Graeco-Roman author of the first century), there is still open to us the plausible suggestion that we should seek a connecting link in Caecilius himself.   The author of the *De Sublimitate* may have had no direct knowledge of the Old Testament, but may have drawn this illustration from the tractate of Caecilius, who was 'in faith a Jew[1].' The fact that the citation is not an exact one may be held, so far, to confirm the conjecture.

(3) *Ammonius.* At one time the occurrence in the treatise of this name seemed not only to supply a definite post-Augustan reference, but also to create a strong presumption that Longinus was the author.   For it is recorded of Longinus that when a young man he had travelled widely, and that at Alexandria he had attended the classes of the leading Neo-platonists, and among them of Ammonius surnamed Saccas. But Ammonius, standing by itself, was, as F. A. Wolf cautiously observed, not an <u>uncommon</u> name, and identification must not be too hasty ; further inquiry must be made before Ammonius Saccas, or any other Ammonius, was supposed necessarily to

---

[1] Reference may be made to the Literary Appendix—under *Moses*.

be meant. Some time after this useful word of warning and exhortation had been dropped, G. Roeper made an interesting discovery which he communicated in the year 1846 to the first volume of Schneidewin and Leutsch's *Philologus*. Searching the Venice scholia to the Iliad, he found that an earlier Ammonius, a successor of Aristarchus at Alexandria, had written περὶ τῶν ὑπὸ Πλάτωνος μετενηνεγμένων ἐξ Ὁμήρου[1]. These words accord so well with the reference to Ammonius in the *De Sublimitate* (xiii. 3) that there can be little, if any, doubt that this is the Ammonius in question.

(4) *Theodorus.* Theodorus is mentioned in the third chapter: 'A third, and closely allied, kind of defect in matters of passion is that which Theodorus used to call *parenthyrsus*[2].' Here the imperfect tense (ἐκάλει) may possibly imply that the writer had attended the lectures of this Theodorus, who can hardly be other than Theodorus of Gadara (or 'of Rhodes,' as he preferred to be called), who taught rhetoric to the emperor Tiberius, and who is often quoted by Quintilian[3]. The way in which his name is introduced, without further preface or addition, seems to imply that its bearer was a recent, and (like Theodorus of Gadara) a well-known authority.

(5) *Cicero.* The treatise contains (xii. 4) a set comparison between Cicero and Demosthenes, introduced by the words: 'And it is in these same respects, my dear Terentianus, that it seems to me (supposing always that we as Greeks are allowed to have an opinion upon the point) that Cicero differs from Demosthenes in elevated passages. For the latter is

---

[1] SCHOL. A HOMERI IL. IX. 540: ἔρδεσκεν· Ἀμμώνιος ἐν τῷ περὶ τῶν ὑπὸ Πλάτωνος μετενηνεγμένων ἐξ Ὁμήρου διὰ τοῦ ϛ προφέρεται ἔρεϛεν. SUIDAS: Ἀμμώνιος Ἀμμωνίου Ἀλεξανδρεύς, Ἀλεξάνδρου γνώριμος, ὃς καὶ διεδέξατο τὴν σχολὴν Ἀριστάρχου πρὸ τοῦ μοναρχῆσαι τὸν Αὔγουστον.

[2] iii. 5: τούτῳ παράκειται τρίτον τι κακίας εἶδος ἐν τοῖς παθητικοῖς, ὅπερ ὁ Θεόδωρος παρένθυρσον ἐκάλει.

[3] Quintilian, *Inst. Or.*, iii. 1, 17: 'Theodorus Gadareus, qui se dici maluit Rhodium, quem studiose audisse, cum in eam insulam secessisset, dicitur Tiberius Caesar.' Suetonius, *Tib.*, 57: 'saeva ac lenta natura ne in puero quidem latuit: quam Theodorus Gadareus rhetoricae praeceptor et perspexisse primus sagaciter et assimilasse aptissime visus est, subinde in obiurgando appellans eum πηλὸν αἵματι πεφυραμένον.'

characterised by sublimity which is for the most part rugged,
Cicero by profusion,' etc. We are not concerned here with
the substance of this comparison ; its main interest for us lies
in the fact that it was instituted at all. With regard to its
bearing upon the date of composition, two considerations
present themselves : (1) references to Cicero in the Greek
rhetoricians are excessively rare, and it would be hard to
find a parallel to this passage of the *De Sublimitate* in any
extant Greek work ; (2) the passage had not only a parallel,
but a precedent, in the lost dissertation (συγγραμμάτιον) of
Caecilius. Plutarch is our authority for the statement that
'the all-accomplished Caecilius......had the temerity to publish
a comparison between Demosthenes and Cicero[1].'

(6) *Terentianus.* About the identification of the Terentianus to whom the treatise is addressed, and whose name
occurs in the passage just quoted and in several others, it will
be convenient to inquire a little later.

(7) Πυγμαῖοι, Κολοσσός, Πυθία. Lastly, a few miscellaneous names may be added to the personal names already
given. The Pygmies are referred to in a curious passage of
c. xliv., where the pertinent point is that the exhibition of
them seems to be regarded by the author as a novelty (εἴ γε
τοῦτο πιστὸν ἀκούω xliv. 5). This would, it appears, apply
best to the period of the early Caesars ; afterwards the thing
became more common. But manifestly an argument of this
nature cannot be pressed. The gaps in our information are
too formidable to allow us to draw, without hesitation, such
inferences as the one just suggested, or the allied one that the
author must have been living at a distance from the capital
when he wrote the passage. Still more precarious are any
arguments based on 'the faulty Colossus' (xxxvi. 3), or on the
Pythia (xiii. 2). It has been maintained that by 'the faulty
Colossus' must be meant, not the Colossus of Rhodes, but
that of Nero, which was renovated under Vespasian ; and it
has been pointed out that the Pythian priestess ceased to give
oracles under Domitian, resumed her activity under Hadrian,

---

[1] Plutarch, *Demosth.* 3 : ὁ περιττὸς ἐν ἅπασι Κεκίλιος...ἐνεανιεύσατο σύγκρισιν
τοῦ Δημοσθένους καὶ Κικέρωνος ἐξενεγκεῖν.

and became finally silent under Caracalla. Pieces of evidence so indecisive as these are added rather in the hope of making the review complete than of supporting any special thesis[1].

II. STYLE AND VOCABULARY. Arguments drawn from style and vocabulary are notoriously insecure, and to be of any value at all they must be based upon an adequate analysis, such as will more conveniently find a place in the Linguistic Appendix. Here it need only be said, by way of anticipation and with all due reserve, that a study of its language would seem on the whole to suggest that the book was not produced by Longinus in the third century, but is rather an isolated work of the first century. It is well, however, to lay no special stress on conclusions which, from the nature of the case, are exceedingly tentative and precarious. They are, therefore, mentioned here simply for what they are worth, and with the object of making the most of every possible aid towards the settlement of the problem.

III. GENERAL AFFINITIES. This heading is still more vague than the last. It may nevertheless be useful to inquire whether the writer's habits of thought and intellectual stand-point seem to be those of the first or those of the third century, and with which of the two centuries (as far as we are acquainted with them) he stands in closer literary and spiritual relationship.

His subject is elevation (ὕψος) of style, and this, he holds, depends ultimately upon elevation of character. 'Sublimity is the echo of a great soul' (ὕψος μεγαλοφροσύνης ἀπήχημα, ix. 2). The breadth of view, here displayed and elsewhere prominent, is a distinctive feature of his treatise, and seems, as we shall see in a moment, to ally him rather with the Roman writers of the first century than with any Greek writers whether of the first century or the third.

A word must, however, first be said about the narrower or

---

[1] Further information on the above points will be found in Buchenau, *De Scriptore Libri* Περὶ Ὕψους, pp. 34 ff.; in Vaucher, *Études Critiques*, pp. 55, 56; and in *Hermes* ii. pp. 238, 239 (Otto Jahn).

more scholastic side of the treatise. This offers more obvious—
we must again make every allowance for possible defects in
our information—points of contact with the Greek and Roman
rhetoricians of the first century than with those of the third.
In his rhetorical terminology, and it may be added in his
literary judgments, the author is distinctly at variance with
the views implied in the surviving fragments of Longinus,
whereas on a similar book by Caecilius our treatise is in a
certain sense based, and it would seem to follow that essay more
closely than its combative tone might on a first reading suggest[1].

Between the *De Sublimitate* and Quintilian, again, the
points of resemblance, especially where the rhetorical figures
are concerned, are many and unmistakable[2]. So remarkable,
indeed, are they that some have thought that both the author
and Quintilian must be drawing on Caecilius[3]. But the whole
problem of the exact relation in which Caecilius, Dionysius
of Halicarnassus and Quintilian stand to one another and to
the *De Sublimitate*, though highly interesting, seems with our
present data hopelessly insoluble[4]. The important point at
present is to observe the fact of the existence of coincidences
afforded by these works, as also by the *Dialogus de Oratoribus*,
to which treatise reference will be made immediately.

But besides its decided Roman affinities, the treatise sends
out its roots in other directions also. That it has points of
contact with the Jews has already appeared. But here direct
reference may be made to passages in two first-century Graeco-
Jewish writers, Josephus and Philo. The passage of Josephus
(*Antiqq. Iud.*, ad init.) is : ἤδη τοίνυν τοὺς ἐντευξομένους τοῖς
βιβλίοις παρακαλῶ τὴν γνώμην θεῷ προσανέχειν, καὶ δοκι-
μάζειν τὸν ἡμέτερον νομοθέτην, εἰ τήν τε φύσιν αὐτοῦ ἀξίως
κατενόησε καὶ τῇ δυνάμει πρεπούσας ἀεὶ τὰς πράξεις ἀνέθηκεν.

---

[1] Cp. Vaucher pp. 73 seqq., and Canna pp. 23–26, for Longinus; for Caecilius
see the Literary Appendix and the dissertations of Martens and Coblentz named
in the Bibliographical Appendix.

[2] Vaucher pp. 45 n., 85, 201 ; Canna pp. 21, 22.

[3] Coblentz pp. 54, 58, 59.

[4] The more we investigate, the more certain we are as to the existence, and
the less certain as to the particular origin, of a vast floating mass of literary
criticism contained in the rhetorical writings of the first century.

That of Philo (*De Ebrietate*, 198 ; vol. ii., p. 208, in Cohn and Wendland's edition, 1896–97) is : ἐγὼ δ᾽ οὐ τεθαύμακα, εἰ πεφορημένος καὶ μιγὰς ὄχλος, ἐθῶν καὶ νόμων τῶν ὁπωσοῦν εἰσηγμένων ἀκλεὴς δοῦλος, ἀπ᾽ αὐτῶν ἔτι σπαργάνων ὑπακούειν ὡς ἂν δεσποτῶν ἢ τυράννων ἐκμαθών, κατακεκονδυλισμένος τὴν ψυχὴν καὶ μέγα καὶ νεανικὸν φρόνημα λαβεῖν μὴ δυνάμενος, πιστεύει τοῖς ἅπαξ παραδοθεῖσι καὶ τὸν νοῦν ἐάσας ἀγύμναστον ἀδιερευνήτοις καὶ ἀνεξετάστοις συναινέσεσί τε καὶ ἀρνήσεσι χρῆται. If these two passages be compared, the first with *De Subl.* ix. 9, and the second with *De Subl.* xliv. 3, 4, the close parallelism will assuredly cause surprise. But of course such parallelisms do not furnish any demonstration of a first-century authorship ; on the contrary, they would be consistent with the claims of the historical Longinus. The same may be said of certain resemblances between the treatise and the writings of Plutarch, resemblances which often have their origin in a common admiration of Plato. Traces of Stoicism, also, or of Alexandrian influences, are in themselves little to go upon ; nor can we safely build an argument upon the analogies drawn from the realm of art with which the treatise (cp. xvii. 2, xxxvi. 3) illustrates and enforces its literary precepts, though we are at liberty to point out that such analogies are very frequently employed by writers of the first century[1].

More is perhaps to be expected from an examination of those speculations with regard to the causes of the decline of eloquence which are found in c. xliv. of the treatise. If that remarkable chapter is read with care, its drift becomes plain. The decline of eloquence, it is intimated, may be traced to the decay of liberty, or it may be traced to the spread of wealth and luxury. The lament of liberty appears (so some have thought) to be uttered with a certain timidity, and is placed in another's mouth. It seems to be implied more than once that the servitude may be a just servitude[2].

---

[1] For these analogies reference may be made to E. Bertrand, *De Pictura et Sculptura apud Veteres Rhetores*, and to the appendix to Brzoska's dissertation *De Canone Decem Oratorum Atticorum Quaestiones*.

[2] 'Longinus was forced to enervate them (sc. his noble ideas as to liberty),

But the main point is that the lament should be made at all. Anything of the kind will hardly be found in similar writings subsequent to the first century—in Lucian, or Aristeides, or Maximus of Tyre. In the first century, on the other hand, the topic was a commonplace (ἐκεῖνο τὸ θρυλούμενον, xliv. 2) of Roman literature, and as such doubtless it is reflected in our treatise[1].

Much the same may be said of the reference to the evil influence of riches. With ἤδη νοσοῦμεν in xliv. 6 Cobet aptly compares Livy's '*nuper* divitiae avaritiam et abundantes voluptates desiderium per luxum atque libidinem pereundi perdendique omnia invexere.' It is doubtful whether Longinus could have so written of his contemporaries as the author does in the words which (xliv. 9) follow those just quoted. As Cobet asks, 'Num Longinus aut Graeci aut Syri accipiebant pecuniam ob rem iudicandam aut mortibus alienis inhiabant aut malis artibus heredipetarum utebantur? Romana haec sunt vitia et flagitia[2].'

CONCLUSION.

We take it, then, that in the Treatise we hear the voice of a dying liberty, not of a liberty long since dead. We seem to catch the accents of a Tacitus. Those words ἅπασαν δουλείαν, κἂν ᾖ δικαιοτάτη, timidly uttered though they may possibly be, recall the bitter sarcasm of the *Annals* (vi. 8): 'tibi summum rerum iudicium di dedere; nobis obsequii gloria relicta est.' The phrase ἡ τῆς οἰκουμένης εἰρήνη reminds us

not only by the term δικαιοτάτη, which he takes care to apply twice to the present despotism; but by employing the stale pretence of putting his own thoughts into the mouth of a nameless philosopher.' Edward Gibbon, *Journal*, October 25, 1762.

[1] For various references to the degeneracy and its causes, see Seneca, *Ep.* 114; Pliny, *Hist. Nat.* xiv. 1; Plin. iun. *Ep.* viii. 14; Tac. *Dial. de Orat.* xxix. xxxvi. xxxvii.; Vell. Paterc. *Hist. Rom.* i. 17; Petronius, *Satyr.* lxxxviii.; Quintil. *Inst. Orat.* ii. 10, 3 seqq. Quintilian further wrote a separate treatise, now lost, on the decay of prose composition, *De Causis Corruptae Eloquentiae:* cp. A. Reuter, *De Quintiliani libro qui fuit De Causis Corruptae Eloquentiae*, Vratislaviae, 1887.

[2] *Mnemosyne*, N.S., vii. 421.

of the *Dialogus* (xxxviii.): 'postquam longa temporum quies
et continuum populi otium et adsidua senatus tranquillitas et
maxima principis disciplina ipsam quoque eloquentiam sicut
omnia depacaverat[1].'

The parallelism, seen not in the point just mentioned only
but in many others, between the *Dialogus* and the *De Sublimitate*, might well form the subject of a separate inquiry.
The opening sentence of the *Dialogus* breathes the very tone
and spirit of the Treatise on the Sublime: 'Saepe ex me
requiris, Iuste Fabi, cur, cum priora saecula tot eminentium
oratorum ingeniis gloriaque floruerint, nostra potissimum
aetas deserta et laude eloquentiae orbata vix nomen ipsum
oratoris retineat; neque enim ita appellamus nisi antiquos,
horum autem temporum diserti causidici et advocati et patroni
et quidvis potius quam oratores vocantur.' Both inquirers—
both the Roman and the Greek—agree in the answer they
would give to this question: they hold that the literary decline
is due to deep-seated moral causes. It is this elevation of
view that raises their works so far above the standpoint of
the ordinary handbooks of rhetoric.

Among minor and more accidental points of resemblance
may be reckoned the fact that both books have been preserved
in a more or less fragmentary form, and that both alike lay
for centuries in complete obscurity without a hint, from any
quarter, of their existence. Possibly both were intended for
private (perhaps for secret) circulation rather than for publication in the ordinary way. Around both, again, an extensive
controversy with regard to authorship has arisen, but with
marked differences in its circumstances and its results. The
manuscript ascription of the *Dialogus* to Tacitus is definite
and unimpeachable. The book was, therefore, naturally included in the editio princeps of Tacitus' then known works,
that issued by Vendelin de Spira at Venice in 1470. The
great attack upon its authenticity was made by Justus Lipsius
a century later, an attack resting principally (like those
which have followed it) upon grounds of style. But although

---

[1] Compare also chapters xxxvi., xxxvii., ibid.

scepticism began much earlier in the case of the *Dialogus* than in that of the *De Sublimitate,* the Tacitean ascription has fared better than the Longinian.   For while a few critics still suspend their judgment, the majority (and among them its latest editors in America and England, Gudeman and Peterson) hold that the Dialogue is an early work of Tacitus. With the *De Sublimitate* it is, as we have seen, otherwise. The claims of Longinus are upheld by few. And although the evidence is not absolutely conclusive, we must perforce admit that the balance inclines strongly in favour of the first century and against the third. The equivocal testimony of the manuscripts ; the absence of direct references in ancient authors ; the names included in the treatise or absent from it ; the writer's affinities in style, in thought, and in general standpoint ; such considerations, when taken singly, cause hesitation, and when taken together raise the most serious doubts as to the truth of the traditional view.

The alternative—the highly probable alternative—is to regard the first century as the period of composition and an unknown author as the writer. An 'unknown author,' because the various attempts at identification have failed to carry conviction; they still remain conjectures, nothing more. With regard to *Longinus*, indeed, the issue is the simple one of the adoption or rejection of a single claimant, no other Longinus than the Longinus of history having been at any time suggested as a possible author of the treatise. It is different with *Dionysius*, the optional name given in the manuscript inscription. This name has produced a plentiful crop of guesses : Dionysius of Halicarnassus, Aelius Dionysius of Halicarnassus, Dionysius Atticus of Pergamus, Dionysius of Miletus. But the claims advanced on behalf of these writers are advanced either without evidence or in the face of evidence. It is the same if the conjectures take a wider range. W. Christ suggests the name of *Theon*, who wrote a treatise περὶ συντά-ξεως λόγου[1]. But this is avowedly pure guesswork. Vaucher's advocacy of *Plutarch*, on the other hand, is supported by much argument and a considerable array of facts. But the

---

[1] W. Christ, *Gesch. d. gr. Litt.* (third edition, 1898), p. 758.

theory is surrounded by so many difficulties of its own that it is now practically abandoned[1]. On the whole it seems best frankly to confess our ignorance, and while recognising the high probability of a first-century authorship to think of the author himself as AVCTOR IGNOTVS. We had best inscribe the work ἈΝѠΝΎΜΟΥ, thus following the reading of the Florence manuscript. This may seem an inconclusive conclusion, but it is the only one at present within our reach, and it is safer to marshal evidence than to propound theories.

But while it is good science to refuse to hazard any conjecture which our information does not warrant, it is good science also to decline to follow some critics in abandoning all hope of ever seeing a solution of this knotty problem. Let us rather recognise that we are confronted with one of those stimulating and fruitful uncertainties which classical research so often presents to its votaries,—uncertainties which are stimulating because there is some possibility of removing them, and fruitful because in any case they lead to the more thorough investigation of the obscurer by-ways of history and literature. Two directions from which light might possibly come in the present case may here be mentioned.

(1) Best of all would be the discovery of a fresh MS. of the *De Sublimitate*, free from the lacunae which at present disfigure the treatise. It is to be remembered that the gaps amount to something like one-third of the whole work, the approximate extent of the loss being ascertainable from the leaves missing in P. 2036. In these lost parts there may have been references which would help to fix more nearly the date of the book. An ounce of definite fact of this kind inspires more confidence than a ton of loose speculation upon supposed variations of style. It is men like Amati and Roeper that

---

[1] For *Plutarch* reference may be made to Vaucher 93–119; Canna 15, 16; Winkler 19; Brigh. 37. For *Dionys. of Halic.*, see Vaucher 44, 45, 50, 54, 90; Canna 11. *Ael. Dionys. of Halic.*, Vaucher 91; Egger, *Longini quae supersunt*, lvi. *Dionys. Att. of Perg.*, Vaucher 46, 90; Canna 12–14; Pessonneaux 292; Blass, *Griech. Bereds.*, 158. *Dionys. of Miletus*, Vaucher 91; Pess. 292. [Full titles of the books here indicated by the authors' names will, where not already given, be found in the Bibliographical Appendix.]

have really advanced matters, and this because they have kept their eyes open to hard facts within and without the treatise, and have recognised that even the most trivial fact may become luminous and instructive when duly correlated with others. Very welcome, in particular, would be the discovery of any such correspondence between the treatise and some other writing as that coincidence between the *Dialogus de Oratoribus* and Pliny's Epistles which was first noticed by A. G. Lange. In c. ix. of the *Dialogus* occur the words : *adice quod poetis...in nemora et lucos, id est in solitudinem, secedendum est* (cp. ibid. c. xii. ad init.). Lange pointed out that Pliny (Ep. ix. 10), addressing Tacitus and referring to the pursuit of poetry, says *poemata...tu inter nemora et lucos commodissime perfici putas.* This, though it may not be proof positive, is at least a remarkable resemblance, and one cannot wonder that much is made of it by the supporters of the view that Tacitus wrote the *Dialogus.* Our own problem furnishes, as we have seen, some similar coincidences, but we could wish for something more precise and definite than we at present have. The missing portions of the treatise, should they be discovered, might possibly supply our want. And in view of some pleasant recent surprises, who shall venture to say that such a discovery is an impossibility ?

(2) The second possible side-light is the identification of the Terentianus to whom the treatise is addressed[1]. This question deserves, perhaps, a fuller consideration than it has hitherto received.

Let us first collect the particulars as to Terentianus which are provided, directly or indirectly, by the treatise itself. At its commencement he is addressed as Ποστούμιε † Φλωρεντιανὲ φίλτατε. The other forms of address have been classified as

---

[1] In continuation of a parallelism already mentioned, it may be noted that the Fabius Iustus to whom the *Dialogus* is addressed was probably Pliny the Younger's friend, Consul Suffectus in 102 A.D. The person addressed is, therefore, in the one case as well as in the other, a factor in the determination of the date.—Again, a question arises in both cases as to the precise signification of *iuvenis* or νεανίας. Tacitus (or whoever the author was) speaks of himself as ' iuvenis admodum ' at the time of the Dialogue. In the *De Sublimitate*, on the other hand, it is Terentianus that is addressed in the words ὦ νεανία.

follows in the interesting Swedish edition of Elias Janzon (Upsala, 1894) : Τερεντιανὲ φίλτατε (xxix. 2 ; xliv. 1), φίλτατε Τερεντιανέ (xii. 40), Τερεντιανὲ ἥδιστε (i. 4 ; iv. 3), ὦ νεανία (xv. 1: altered by the editors to ὦ Τερεντιανέ, against the best manuscript authority, and against the usage of the author, who elsewhere couples some endearing epithet with the name Τερεντιανέ), ὦ φίλος (vi.), ὦ ἑταῖρε (xxvi. 2), ἑταῖρε (i. 2 ; ix. 6; ix. 10), κράτιστε (xxxix. 1), φίλτατε (i. 3 ; vii. 1; xiii. 2 ; xvii. 1). It is clear from these expressions that a close friendship existed between the two men. By the form of allocution ὦ νεανία, and by such expressions as ἕνεκα τῆς σῆς χρηστομα-θείας in xliv. 1 (cp. the didactic tone of τοῦ μαθεῖν χάριν and ὅπως ἦ σοι γνώριμον in ix. 10 and 15, as well as the words ἀνεγνωκὼς τὰ ἐν τῇ Πολιτείᾳ τὸν τύπον οὐκ ἀγνοεῖς in xiii. 1), it may or may not be implied that the two friends stood, or had stood, to one another in the relation of master to pupil ; probably it is. Certainly they had examined the work of Caecilius together (i. 1), and they may have been associated in the study of Xenophon (viii. 1). It is, moreover, implied in the treatise that Terentianus was a cultured Roman with some experience of public life (xii. 4 ; i. 2, 3, 4). The author seems to wish it to be understood that his book consists of jottings only (ὑπομνηματίσασθαι i. 2, ὑπομνήματος xxxvi. 4), and that it is designed specially, if not exclusively, for the delectation of the person to whom it is addressed (i. 2).

The particulars thus collected are interesting, but they cannot be said to be precise. If we chose to designate the author as the AVCTOR AD TERENTIANVM, that designation would not at present mean anything more than AVCTOR INCERTVS or AVCTOR IGNOTVS. Probably we need fresh material from within or from without the treatise before we can hope for an actual identification. But meanwhile we must make the most of every fragment of evidence we possess. And from this point of view it cannot be considered satis-factory that so little attention should have been paid to the reading of P. 2036 at the beginning of the treatise. P. gives Φλωρεντιανέ, for which the editors, following Manutius, have with one accord substituted Τερεντιανέ, in order to bring the address into line with those found elsewhere in the treatise. Probably this change is right as far as it goes, but it does not go far enough to account for what, if unexplained, must seem a strange aberration in so excellent a manuscript as P.[1] A possible explanation may be suggested tentatively and with all reserve. It is that, in its original form, the address ran thus : Ποστούμιε Μαῦρε Τερεντιανὲ φίλτατε. At a comparatively early period in the history of the text doubt may have arisen as to Μαῦρε, it may have been changed into Φλῶρε, and finally a ' conflation' of Φλῶρε and Τερεντιανέ may have yielded Φλωρεντιανέ. Μαῦρε might well be doubted on grounds of : (1) rarity, (2) order, (3) superfluity. To take the points one by one. (1) *Rarity.* 'Maurus,' as a personal name or affix, is not common in Latin, and still less common in Greek, where its transliterated form may have been none the more pleasing because of its close resemblance to μῶρος. But the form itself is, of course, well attested both in manuscripts and in inscriptions such as this :—

AM
ΛΡΟCΜ
ΤωΖΗ
΄8Ϥ

Μαῦρος Μηζώτρου.

(Kaibel, *Inscrr. Gr. Sic. et It.*, 2412, 31.)

(2) *Order.* The inversion in the order of Τερεντιανέ and Μαῦρε may have caused difficulty to a copyist. But this inversion is not uncommon, in writers of the imperial period at any rate. Incidentally an instance (' Iuste Fabi') has already been quoted from the *Dialogus*, and 'Afro Domitio' may be added from c. xiii. of the same book. In Greek we find instances as early as Dionys. Halic. (e.g. Βάρρων Τερέντιος = Terentius Varro, *Antiqq. Rom.*, i. 14). The usage is rarer when the praenomen, as well as the nomen and cognomen, is used (the full array of the ' tria nomina' is itself

---

[1] The exact reading of P. is φλωρεντιανὲ. ' φλ puncto notatum ut suspectum,' as the editors say.

rare) ; but it is hardly unexampled in the Latin of this period. Considerations of rhythm or euphony (to which our author pays great attention) might here suggest the order *Postumius Maurus Terentianus*, the same explanation probably holding good in the case of the Tacitean *Afro Domitio* already quoted. (3) *Superfluity.* A long-suffering scribe would be prone to think that one of these names might easily be spared, and he may therefore have dropped the Μαῦρε altogether as some of the MSS. have done, or preserved only a scanty vestige of it in Φλωρεντιανέ. But it is possible that our author of set purpose gave the name in full at the commencement of his treatise, and there only ; he wished to be specially formal at the beginning. His first sentence, even as it stands, is of an astonishing amplitude, and he would probably have regarded an additional word as an advantage rather than the contrary. Whatever the name may be which has disappeared, —whether it be Μαῦρε, or Φλῶρε, or Φλώρηνς, or Φλωρεντῖνε, or Φλ. = (Φλάβιε or Φλαούιε),—it may confidently be conjectured that *some* name has been lost, and that this is the key to the reading of the best MSS. For it must be remembered that they show no variation when Τερεντιανέ occurs, as it does occur five several times, in other passages of the treatise.

If the name lost were assumed to be Μαῦρε, then it would be easy to go one step further and to suggest the identification of the person actually addressed with Terentianus Maurus, the writer on prosody. But this is to embark on still more precarious speculations. The practical point is that, whether or no the Terentianus of the *De Sublimitate* has any direct connexion with Terentianus Maurus and with Africa, we shall not fail to notice that the writer of the Treatise has some points of contact with Alexandria. In certain respects the Nile (to which he refers with admiration) seems to be nearer to him than Rome itself. He sometimes writes as if, when writing, he knew of things in the capital by hearsay rather than by actual experience. He can speak in general terms of Roman vices, but he does not appear (as has been already seen) to possess the knowledge of a resident with regard to definite, though perhaps trivial circumstances, such as the confinement of the Pygmies.　But the very theme of his book, as well as its specific points of contact with Philo, with Josephus, with Caecilius, with the Hebrew scriptures, seems to associate him, in spirit if not in residence, with Alexandria, the great meeting-place of Jew and Greek.

The hypothesis that the book was produced at a distance from Rome, or sent to a friend at a distance from Rome, might help to account for the fact that it seems to have been little known in antiquity.　If that friend was also in an official position, there might seem double reason for secrecy with regard to a work which might be held to embody seditious sentiments.　A book designed for private circulation would naturally not be multiplied to any extent, and this would explain the paucity of independent copies of the treatise.

One final word with regard to the person addressed.　Some may feel inclined to regard the Terentianus of the treatise as an entirely fictitious person, the offspring of the literary convention which conducted such discussions in the form of dialogue or epistle.　But so extreme a view, though it might be put forward, could hardly be successfully defended.　For apart from the fact that the general practice was to introduce real personages into such letters and dialogues, there is a special reality and intimacy about the references to Terentianus in the *De Sublimitate*.　One of the chief impressions, in fact, which we form upon internal evidence with regard to our anonymous author is that, whatever else he may have been, he was at least a warm-hearted friend and an enthusiastic teacher.　Internal evidence also assures us that he was a Greek, who had some acquaintance with Latin and even with Hebrew literature ; that he was conversant, to some extent, with art as well as with literature ; that in his general view of things, as well as in his diction, he had been influenced greatly by Plato ; and that he had written on other subjects than his present one[1].

---

[1] The following passages seem to contain references to other writings of his : viii. 1, ὡς κἂν τοῖς περὶ Ξενοφῶντος (if this is a reference to a separate work) ὡρισά-μεθα. ix. 2, γέγραφά που καὶ ἑτέρωθι τὸ τοιοῦτον · ὕψος μεγαλοφροσύνης ἀπήχημα. xxiii. 3, καὶ τὸ Πλατωνικόν, ὃ καὶ ἑτέρωθι παρετεθείμεθα, ἐπὶ τῶν Ἀθηναίων · 'οὐ γὰρ

The personal details afforded by the Περὶ Ὕψους are, thus, few in number. But the work as a whole constitutes a remarkable revelation of personality, and it may be said to be its author's best biography and monument. An account of its contents and an estimate of its character will, therefore, fittingly continue and conclude this introduction.

II. CONTENTS AND CHARACTER OF THE TREATISE.

The contents and character of the treatise will be found to be admirably indicated in the traditional Greek title Περὶ Ὕψους, and in its accepted English equivalent *On the Sublime*, if only the words ὕψος and *sublime* be correctly understood.

The English equivalent has, no doubt, often caused misconception. The treatise has been thought to be at once more ambitious in purpose, and more narrow in scope, than it really is. But the Greek title Περὶ Ὕψους, 'Concerning Height or Elevation,' does not convey that idea of abnormal altitude which is often associated with the word *sublime*. The object of the author rather is to indicate broadly the essentials of a noble and impressive style. In fact, if we were to describe the treatise as one on style, or even on literary criticism generally, we should be nearer the mark than if we connected it solely with the idea of 'sublimity' in the narrower sense. The author's own words make this plain, for early in his book (i. 3) he remarks that the friend whom he is addressing is too well versed in literary studies to need the reminder that sublimity is a certain distinction and excellence in expression, and that it is from no other source than this that the greatest authors have derived their eminence and gained an immortality of renown. A cursory review of the

Πέλοπες,' κ.τ.λ. xxxix. 1...ἡ διὰ τῶν λόγων αὐτὴ ποιὰ σύνθεσις. ὑπὲρ ἧς ἐν δυσὶν ἀποχρώντως ἀποδεδωκότες συντάγμασιν...xliv. 12...τὰ πάθη, περὶ ὧν ἐν ἰδίῳ προηγουμένως ὑπεσχόμεθα γράψειν ὑπομνήματι...

contents of the book will suffice to show the width of its range and to indicate its true character.

At the outset the author, after offering the definition of sublimity just given, proceeds to ask whether there is such a thing as an art of the sublime. His answer is that, though elevation of tone is innate, yet art can regulate the use of natural gifts. It is, he says, with diction as with life. A man favoured by fortune ought to know how to use his advantages; a writer of genius ought to profit by the help of art. In order to show that a systematic treatise can effect much in the way of warning as well as by means of precept, he gives a short account of defects of style which are opposed to sublimity. He describes and illustrates the vices of tumidity, puerility, misplaced passion, and frigidity. This done, he further characterises the true sublime, and shows how it may be distinguished from false imitations. Next he enumerates five sources of the sublime. The first and most important of these is grandeur of thought—the power of forming great conceptions. This power is founded on nobility of character. Elevated thoughts are also, we are told, the result of the imitation of great models, of imaginative power, and of the choice and grouping of the most striking circumstances. The second source is vehement and inspired passion. While affirming that there is no tone so lofty as that of genuine passion, the author does not treat of this topic in detail, but reserves it for a separate work. Third in order come figures of speech, such as adjuration, rhetorical question, asyndeton, and lastly hyperbaton or inverted order. The writer makes the general remark that a figure is at its best when the very fact that it is a figure escapes attention. The fourth source of sublimity is noble phrasing or diction. The chief element in this is the choice of proper and striking words, a choice which, he says, wonderfully attracts and enthralls the hearer, and breathes into dead things a kind of living voice[1]. Other elements are metaphors, and similes, and hyperbole. Fifthly and finally comes elevation in the arrangement of words. Of this examples are given, and some remarks are added on

[1] xxx. 1.

such specific vices of style as arise from the use of too few
words or too many, of too much rhythm or too little. The
author concludes with the notable passage in which he en-
deavours to trace the causes of the dearth of great literature
in his own day[1].

This short sketch of the contents of the treatise is designed
to indicate its relation to the general subject of style. When
we come to particulars, this relation is seen to be still more
intimate, and yet to imply no narrowness of view on the
author's part. His hints with regard to thought and expression are shrewd and helpful, all the more so that he is too
broad-minded to have any superstitious faith in such formal
Rules of Style as used to be popular in England a generation
or two ago under the shadow of his name. A few examples
of his illuminative observations may be given here in anticipation. Speaking of Demosthenes, he remarks how that
orator shows us that even in the revels of the imagination
sobriety is required[2]. His good sense is seen in his praise of
familiar language when used in season. A homely expression,
he says, is sometimes much more telling than elegant diction,
for it is understood at once since it is drawn from common
life, and the fact that it is familiar makes it only the more convincing[3]. Of tumidity, or bombast, we are told that it seeks
to transcend the sublime, and that it is a fault which seems
particularly hard to avoid, but that if examined in the light of
day, it fades away from the awe-inspiring into the contemptible[4].
An over-rhythmical style is condemned on the ground that it
does not communicate to its hearers the emotion conveyed by
the words, but that conveyed by the rhythm. The author is
the determined enemy of conceits and puerilities of all kinds,
and he remarks that men fall into these errors because, while
they aim at the uncommon and elaborate, and most of all at

---

[1] A fuller analysis of the contents of the treatise will be found in the Literary
Appendix. For the word ὕψος—its history, signification, and modern equivalents
—the Linguistic Appendix may be consulted.

[2] xvi. 4 : διδάσκων ὅτι κἂν βακχεύμασι νήφειν ἀναγκαῖον. Cp. Hamlet to the
Players (iii. 2); 'for in the very torrent, and, as I may say, the whirlwind of
passion, you must acquire and beget a temperance that may give it smoothness.'

[3] xxxi. 1.   [4] iii. 1, 3, 4.

the attractive, they find that they have drifted into the tawdry and affected[1]. He expressly denounces that 'pursuit of novelty in the expression of ideas which may be regarded as the fashionable craze of the day[2].' 'Art is perfect,' he says in one place, 'when it seems to be nature, and nature attains her end when she contains art hidden within her'; and again, 'We should employ art as in every way an aid to nature, for the conjunction of the two may be held to constitute perfection[3].' In this spirit he makes the remark, with reference to Demosthenes, that the tricks of rhetoric are hidden away in the blaze of the noontide splendour of sublimity and passion. 'By what means,' he asks, 'has the orator here concealed the figure? Clearly, by the very excess of light. For just as all dim lights are extinguished in the glare of the sun, so do the artifices of rhetoric fade from view when bathed in the pervading splendour of sublimity[4].' Evidently with the critic who writes thus the judgment of style was, to quote his own words, 'the last and crowning fruit of long experience[5].' Everywhere the man's sincerity of purpose and clearness of vision are manifest, and a book written in this earnest and enlightened spirit does not soon fall out of date.

Furthermore, the treatise may be regarded as a disquisition not only on the formation of style, but on literary criticism generally. In proof of this, it is only necessary to add to the foregoing description of its contents the reminder that it is a veritable storehouse of quotations illustrating excellences and defects both of manner and of matter, both of form and of spirit. Reference is made to as many as fifty Greek writers, whose dates range over something like a thousand years. Some of these are quoted repeatedly, Homer oftenest of all, and next after him Herodotus, Plato, and Demosthenes. The author's quality as a critic is most decisively seen in his preference of the best. The second-rate writers of Alexandria, though nearer in time, are not suffered to eclipse the true classics of Greece; they are quoted rather in illustration of defects than of merits. But in Homer we are bidden to admire such passages as speak of Ossa and Pelion; of Strife,

---

[1] iii. 4 and iv. [2] v. [3] xxii. 1, xxxvi. 4. [4] xvii. 2. [5] vi.

'with her head in the skies and her feet on the earth'; of the
Battle of the Gods; of the earth-shaking Poseidon; of the
cry of Ajax to Father Zeus 'to slay, if slay he must, *in the
light*,' and of the yet more impressive silence of the same hero
in the shades[1]. Nowhere is the critic's skilful touch better
seen than where he treats of Homer. In drawing, for instance,
a comparison between the Iliad and the Odyssey, he assigns
the former poem to the poet's vigorous manhood when he was
at the height of his inspiration, the latter to his mellower age.
'In the Odyssey Homer may be likened to a sinking sun,
whose grandeur remains without its intensity.' But he is
careful to add, 'If I speak of old age, it is nevertheless the old
age of Homer[2].' Again, he has the rather happy remark that
Homer 'has made, as far as lay within his power, gods of the
men concerned in the Siege of Troy, and men of the gods[3].'
Altogether, it is refreshing to see how often and with what
sympathy a critic in the late evening of Greece reverts to the
poet of its earliest dawn. His admiration for noble literature
has incidentally accomplished even more for Sappho than for
Homer, though the former is but once mentioned by him.
In his tenth chapter, as an example of the proper choice and
grouping of the most striking circumstances, he adduces, and
in so doing has preserved for posterity, a fragment of Sappho's
poetry. The gist of his comment on the wonderful love-ode
in question is that we see depicted in it not one passion only
but a concourse of the passions. His critical acumen is, moreover, seen in the illustrations given, up and down his work,
not only of sublimity but of its opposite. The treatment in
x. 5, 6 of Aratus, the Alexandrian poet, is a neat instance of
his critical method. Besides Aratus, other minor writers, such
as Timaeus and Theopompus, are made to furnish examples
of faults which should be shunned by those who wish to write
in the elevated manner. But the author is of too fearless a
nature to strike only at the lesser men. He assails the great
writers, such as Herodotus and Aeschylus, where they seem
to him to offend against the canons of good taste. He has
the courage to say that Demosthenes is too austere to be

---

[1] viii., ix.   [2] ix. 13, 14.   [3] ix. 7.

graceful and witty, and that when he forces himself into jocularity, he does not excite laughter, but rather becomes the subject of it[1]. And he makes bold to affirm with regard to Euripides, the idol of the rhetorician, that he is by nature anything but elevated, and that it is only by force put upon his natural disposition that he appears to rise to tragic heights[2]. In such comments as these, whether we agree with them or not, we recognise pieces of genuine literary criticism, and the literary critic stands equally revealed in the note of pleasant egotism which makes itself heard now and again during the course of the treatise, and in such general maxims as that the poet must himself see what he would have others see,—must, in fact, have his 'eye upon the object.'

Nor are such now familiar topics of criticism as *correctness*, the *standard of taste*, and the *comparative method*, neglected by the author. Upon the question of correctness he shows a breadth of view which is in marked contrast with the opinions commonly held (and by his professed admirers, strange to say) in England for a century or more from the time of the Restoration. He is no believer in what is faultily faultless ; he is a supreme believer in fervour and inspiration. Elevation with some flaws is, he cannot doubt, to be preferred to uniform correctness without elevation. His attitude in the matter is defined in some striking passages of chapters xxxiii. and xxxvi. To the often-asked question whether there is any trustworthy test of the sublime—any sure standard of taste in literature—he returns (vii. 3, 4) an answer which seems surprisingly modern because it is so permanently true. No modern critic could formulate more precisely, in relation to literature, the *quod semper, quod ubique* principle.

Modern in many ways, the author is in nothing more modern than in foreshadowing, in the passage just mentioned and in others, the application of the comparative method to the study of literature. It is easy to scoff at specific literary comparisons, and no doubt there is often much that is puerile and inept about them. But, as M. Ferdinand Brunetière has pointed out, the ridicule comes with ill grace from those who

---

[1] xxxiv. 3. [2] xv. 3.

celebrate so loudly the triumphs in our own day of comparative anatomy, comparative physiology, and comparative
philology. In a sense science may be said to begin in comparison, in the effort to distinguish things that differ and
thereby to bring out the true nature of each and all. At
the same time it is well to remember the necessary limitations
of the comparative method where literature is concerned. It
is utterly out of place and futile, if its object is to place the
great writers in an order of merit, and to establish a sort
of literary hierarchy. And even where the aim is simply
to bring out the distinctive points of contrasted authors, it
should not be forgotten that the methods of the laboratory
can never fully be applied to the analysis of the finest products
of the human mind. In this matter it may not unfairly be
claimed that our author assumes a judicious attitude. The
comparison, in the tenth chapter, of a passage in Homer with
a passage in Aratus is distinctly happy. And so, in its way,
is the comparison between Homer in the Iliad and Homer in
the Odyssey. And so, again, is the section in which he compares, not the same poet in different works, but two orators of
different countries, Demosthenes and Cicero. Speaking with
due diffidence as a Greek addressing a Roman, he ventures the
opinion that it is in profusion that Cicero chiefly differs from
Demosthenes. The latter is like a thunderbolt or flash of
lightning ; the former resembles a widespread conflagration
which rolls on with all-devouring flames[1].

In his use, however limited it may be, of the comparative
method the author has the advantage over his great predecessors Plato and Aristotle, neither of whom knew any
literature except his own. It is interesting to observe in
what general features he agrees with, or differs from, these
masters of literary criticism. With both he has this in
common, that he may often seem unduly verbal and philological,—may often seem to attach excessive importance to
rhythm, to figures, and to questions of form generally. Not
that it is so in reality. Rather, attention to such matters

------

[1] xii. 4.

must be the backbone of criticism, and especially of early criticism. In other points the author resembles Plato more nearly than he resembles Aristotle. He breathes the spirit of the *Ion* rather than of the Poetics. He is subjective rather than objective. He is an enthusiast rather than an analyst. He is better fitted to fire the young than to convince the maturely sceptical. He speaks rather of 'transport' or 'inspiration' than of 'purgation' or 'the universal.' He was not a man of deep and penetrating intellect like Aristotle, but he was nevertheless a critic of keen artistic sensibilities. His book does not offer the great luminous definitions contained in the Poetics, nor is it marked by the cool and searching scientific analysis by which that work is distinguished. Yet it may be that it supplies something of its own. Aristotle but seldom makes us feel that there sometimes dwells in words a beauty which defies analysis because it is the direct expression of a human spirit and is charged with emotion as well as controlled by reason. Our author's chief aim is, on the other hand, aesthetic rather than purely scientific. This difference in standpoint has had at least one noteworthy indirect effect. Let us suppose for a moment that every vestige of ancient Greek literature had disappeared with the exception of the Poetics which is a fragment, or with the exception of the Treatise on the Sublime which is also incomplete. In the latter case we should at least possess the better anthology; we should be in a better position to form some conception of the supreme excellence of Homer, and Sappho, and other Greek poets. And this result would be due to the fact that the author's method is much less rigorous than that of Aristotle in the Poetics, and allows greater copiousness of quotation.

His catholicity has led him still further. While Aristotle, notwithstanding his encyclopaedic learning, knew no literature beyond his own, it is an interesting fact that our author in his treatise refers not only to Latin literature but to Hebrew. Among the many literary critics from Aristophanes to the Alexandrians and Dionysius of Halicarnassus, and from Cicero to Quintilian and the author of the *Dialogus de Oratoribus*,

he is distinguished by the account he takes of three several
literatures. It is not impossible that he had been anticipated
in this respect by the Caecilius to whom he so often refers.
But we cannot tell. All we know is that, when discoursing
on noble thought as inspired by nobility of soul, our author
writes : ' The legislator of the Jews, no ordinary man, having
formed and expressed a worthy conception of the might of
the Godhead, writes in the very beginning of his Laws, " God
said—what ? Let there be light, and there was light ; let there
be land, and there was land[1]." '

And here a word may fitly be said as to the connexion of
sublimity, in the more restricted and more usual sense of the
English term, with Hebrew influences. It has sometimes
been maintained that sublimity, in this sense, is the peculiar
possession of the Hebrew race and is unknown to the Greek
classic writers. The contention is suggestive, but too absolute.
The highest possible examples of sublimity, it may be urged,
are to be found in such Hebrew writers as Isaiah. Moderns
like Milton, it may be further advanced, owe much of their
sublimity, directly or indirectly, to Hebrew sources. But on
the other hand we can hardly deny the quality, however
rigorous may be our definition of it, to early Greek writers
such as Homer and Aeschylus, and to the early phases of
some of the more modern literatures. Are we, then, to look
everywhere for Oriental influences, and not rather to seek the
clue in the brooding wonder of primitive man wherever
found ? The whole question is too large and vague for
summary treatment. In France, for instance, an eminent
critic has suggested that the reason why the literature of his
country is deficient in sublimity is that the French translation
of the Bible is a poor one and has never taken possession of
the popular mind, while the English version is magnificent
and has influenced English literary style for centuries. But
surely the cause lies deeper than this. We must not forget
that in French there is no essential difference between the
vocabulary of prose and that of poetry. We cannot forget,

[1] ix. 9.

either, Voltaire's comment on the 'darkness visible' of Milton
and on a similar expression in Spanish : ' Ce n'est pas assez
que l'on puisse excuser la licence de ces expressions, l'exactitude française n'admet rien qui ait besoin d'excuse[1].'   That is
quite an intelligible attitude to assume, but it is one which at
once puts sublimity out of the question.   We can imagine
that Aristotle might have assumed it ; so completely does he
sometimes seem to regard poetry from the logician's point of
view.   But such an attitude we should feel to be quite alien
to the author of the Greek Treatise on the Sublime, and
equally alien, we may add, to the author of the English
treatise on the Sublime and Beautiful.   Burke's admirable
work is notable, among many other things, for its striking
quotations from the Old Testament and from Milton, and for
its insistence upon the truth that sublimity is closely connected with a sense of uncertainty, obscurity, infinity.   ' A
clear idea,' he says, ' is another name for a little idea,' and then
proceeds to quote from the Book of Job a passage whose
amazing sublimity he considers to be principally due to the
terrible uncertainty of the thing described.   Sublimity belongs, in fact, to the region of vastness and mystery.   In a
pregnant sentence Aristotle declares that a good style must
be clear without being mean ; lucidity is, from this point of
view, the first essential.   But when sublimity is in question,
the order is reversed.   First and foremost stands grandeur of
conception, even if a certain obscurity of expression should
follow in its train.

   It has been seen that the word *sublimity* is, in its modern
acceptation, too limited in scope to cover our author's meaning.   Shall we, then, do better to think of him as an exponent
of what is sometimes called the *grand style* ?   This term is
less restricted than the other, and therein it has the advantage.
But it has also disadvantages of its own.   It is not free
from the suggestion of bombast and excessive elaboration.
Against such vices our author strongly protests, and he would
have been the last to eulogize a style whose brilliance may
dazzle the eyes of one generation, but whose disappearance

[1] *Œuvres de Voltaire* (Paris, 1828), xiii. 441.

awakens satisfaction rather than regret in the mind of the next. His admiration is reserved for something much more permanent, a classic excellence. His attitude is that of one who cares little whether or no the grand style disappears if only the great style remains. And his view of the elements of a great style is at once discriminating and lofty. He is too sound a verbal critic to overlook the importance of the more technical or scholastic side. But he is also too broad-minded to forget that greatness of style must ultimately rest on a much wider basis than that afforded by technical rules. His double standpoint is worthy of attention because it must have been rare in his own time and it cannot be said to be common in ours.

As a critic he sees that care and study are needed in the formation of a great style. And if proof of this fact were required, it would be necessary only to point to specific instances in ancient and in modern times. Writers like Virgil and Tennyson perhaps bear the marks of elaboration upon them, and it would therefore be superfluous to refer to their known habits of work. But such carefulness has often characterised those authors whose seeming naturalness and spontaneity afford but little trace of it. Recent inquiries have shown what pains Burns and Keats lavished on their poetry. In antiquity there was a well-known story of the immense trouble taken by Plato in writing the exordium, so simple in appearance, of his *Republic*. It is perhaps inappropriate to link the name of any modern prose-writer with that of the greatest of all writers of prose, but whether we think of Plato's translator Jowett, or of Newman or of Matthew Arnold, the same law of minute attention to the art of expression might be proved to hold good. Even where there is simplicity, it is usually a studied simplicity; where there is ease, it is elaborate ease.

As to our author's own style we sometimes feel, as perhaps might be expected from his theme, that he fails to show that business-like directness of exposition which is so effective when information or instruction is to be imparted, and which is so foreign to the atmosphere of a leisurely seclusion. Of succinct expression he has little to say in this treatise; it does not belong directly to his present subject, and possibly he had already dealt with it elsewhere. But whether he had done so or not, we feel that he would not have desired to conceal any limitations or shortcomings which could fairly be alleged against himself. His book leaves upon the mind the agreeable impression that he would have been quite ready to allow that there might well be defects in his own style and in his treatment of his subject. In his style he sometimes shows the faults of the period at which he wrote, faults such as diffuseness and poetical phraseology. Similarly, in his treatment of his subject, he is apt to be too minute and to lose himself occasionally in technicalities. In fact, he does not escape the characteristic defect of the teacher who has to deal with pupils of all grades of intellectual apprehension; now and then he appears to be unduly didactic and to verge upon tediousness.

But these are trifling blemishes, and we scarcely heed them in the presence of his deeply earnest purpose and his breadth of view. As his fourth chapter shows, no one could entertain less respect than he for mere bookishness. Nor could any one discern more clearly how mistaken is the view of those who regard style as an end in itself or talk glibly of 'art for art's sake.' Like the author of the *Dialogue on Oratory*, he sees in literature not a convention, not a matter of form, but the reflexion of a national life; a great style is evoked by great surroundings and great events. His lofty conception of individual and of national morality, and his view of the relation of both to literature, are clearly seen in such passages as ix. 3; xliv. 1, 6, 8; xxxv. 2, 3. About a man who can write as he here writes there is something of the profound moral gravity and the lofty eloquence which mark a Demosthenes or a Burke. The ethical fervour of the author's style calls to mind his own often-quoted saying that 'sublimity is the echo of a great soul[1].' He is himself a man of great moral endowments; the misfortune was that he had fallen upon evil days. The heroic age was in the far past, and the present

[1] ix. 2.

was, to him, a time of spiritual destitution, when men loved
show and comfort, and were no longer earnest in the pursuit
of perfection.

Such is the man as we view him in his book, and we feel
that—historical evidence apart—he might well have lived the
life of that Longinus of the third century who was famous for
his learning and his gifts as a critic ; who at Alexandria had
been the brilliant pupil of the Neoplatonists ; who at Athens
gained celebrity as the teacher of young men ambitious of
philosophical and literary culture ; who at Palmyra, as the
minister of Zenobia, inspired the defiant reply sent by the
queen to the letter of the emperor Aurelian which demanded
her submission ; who met his death in the spirit of a hero.

But sentiment cannot take the place of proof, and the
treatise must henceforward stand upon its own merits, as it can
well afford to do. Nor is it clear that it does not gain as
much in general interest by being assigned to the first century
rather than the third, as it loses in personal interest by being
dissociated from the fascinating name of Longinus. At the
same time it must be admitted that this uncertainty with
regard to its authorship has undoubtedly been one of the chief
causes of its recent neglect. Other reasons have been the not
unnatural reaction from the extravagant deference—bordering
on superstition—paid to it in France and England during the
eighteenth century ; the philosophical tendency of criticism,
and the ultra-scientific tendency of scholarship, in Germany ;
the purely fastidious objections to a late and unfamiliar style
entertained by many students of the classics, and the more
substantial difficulties felt with regard to the constitution of
the text and the interpretation of vexed passages, the Greek
having been pronounced unusually hard by a judge so
supremely able as Edward Gibbon; and (in England especially)
that absence of a critical edition which may be regarded, not
only as a cause of the neglect, but also as a result of some of
the other causes just recited. Of late, however, signs of a
fresh reaction have shown themselves even in the smaller
European countries. Within the last few decades, for example,
versions of the treatise have appeared in Spain, where Castilian

illustrations of its precepts are freely offered ; in Italy, where
the traditional interest in literary criticism, and in this book
in particular, has produced excellent fruit ; and in Sweden,
where the vigorous modern school of Scandinavian literature
thus connects itself with the past.

The merits, in virtue of which the treatise makes this
enduring appeal to various countries and successive centuries,
are—as we have seen—manifold. Taken as a whole, it is the
most striking single piece of literary criticism produced by
any Greek writer posterior to Aristotle. It further claims our
respect and admiration by its noble tone ; by its apt precepts
with respect to style ; by its judicious attitude towards funda-
mental questions such as those of the errors of genius, the
standard of taste, the relation of art to nature and of literature
to life ; by its value as a treasury of extracts, and of happy
appreciations destined to be confirmed by every fresh discovery of Hyperides or Bacchylides ; and lastly, by its
historical interest as one of the earliest essays in comparative
criticism, and as an aesthetic treatise which has had some
degree of influence upon almost every European literature.

For the modern world it is perhaps specially valuable in
two respects. At a time when criticism is apt to be superficial
and to lack width of outlook, it reminds us, by the admitted
justice in the main of its censure and its praise, that there is
a real continuity in the principles of criticism,—a firm and
abiding foundation for the judgments of taste. And in the
second place it is well adapted to form an aid to the systematic
study of Greek literature; and that from a most suggestive
and stimulating point of view. By no work that has come
down to us from antiquity is a deeper impression produced
of the enjoyment of Greek literature than by this. It is an
enjoyment so keen that we might be tempted to describe it
as Epicurean (in the popular sense) were it not tinged with
Stoic seriousness and Platonic ardour. Above all, it is a
contagious enjoyment. The writer loves Greek literature
and can make others love it. And his love rests upon
knowledge. His view is comprehensive. He has studied
his subject in every period of its history and in every

phase of its development. And he not only knows Greek literature, but he knows it from a more detached standpoint than was possible to Aristotle or even to the Alexandrian critics. He is writing under the Roman empire, and at a time when new nations and new religions were in the making. He is an ancient studying the ancients, and yet he stands at the central point of the world's history. Addressing himself to a Roman, he recognises that Greek literature was fitted to command the interest of mankind at large, and that the distinctive feature to which it owed and would owe its supremacy was its elevation ($ὕψος$). His deep humanity and his broad sympathies have helped him, as they have helped Plutarch, to interpret the spirit of antiquity to the modern mind, and have given him a permanent place in the history of literature as the last great critic of ancient Greece and (in some sense) the first international critic of a wider world.

INCERTI CVIVSDAM AVCTORIS

DE SVBLIMITATE COMMENTARIVS

AD FIDEM POTISSIMVM CODICIS ANTIQVISSIMI

PARISINI 2036 (P)

EDITVS

ET IN SERMONEM ANGLICVM CONVERSVS.

ΠΕΡΙ ΥΨΟΥΣ.

I

Τὸ μὲν τοῦ Κεκιλίου συγγραμμάτιον, ὃ περὶ ὕψους P. 178v
συνετάξατο, ἀνασκοπουμένοις ἡμῖν ὡς οἶσθα κοινῇ, Ποστούμιε †Φλωρεντιανὲ φίλτατε, ταπεινότερον ἐφάνη τῆς ὅλης ὑποθέσεως καὶ ἥκιστα τῶν καιρίων ἐφαπτόμενον, οὐ πολλήν τε ὠφέλειαν, ἧς μάλιστα δεῖ στοχάζεσθαι τὸν γράφοντα, περιποιοῦν τοῖς ἐντυγχάνουσιν, εἴγ’ ἐπὶ πάσης τεχνολογίας δυεῖν ἀπαιτουμένων, προτέρου μὲν τοῦ δεῖξαι, τί τὸ ὑποκείμενον, δευτέρου δὲ τῇ τάξει, τῇ δυνάμει δὲ κυριωτέρου, πῶς ἂν ἡμῖν αὐτὸ τοῦτο καὶ δι’ ὧν τινων μεθόδων κτητὸν γένοιτο, ὅμως ὁ Κεκίλιος, ποῖον μέν τι ὑπάρχει τὸ ὑψηλόν, διὰ μυρίων ὅσων ὡς ἀγνοοῦσι πειρᾶται δεικνύναι, τὸ δὲ δι’ ὅτου τρόπου τὰς ἑαυτῶν φύσεις προάγειν ἰσχύοιμεν ἂν εἰς ποσὴν μεγέθους ἐπίδοσιν, οὐκ οἶδ’ ὅπως ὡς οὐκ ἀναγκαῖον παρέλιπεν· 2. πλὴν ἴσως τουτονὶ μὲν τὸν ἄνδρα οὐχ οὕτως αἰτιᾶσθαι τῶν ἐκλελειμμένων, ὡς αὐτῆς τῆς ἐπινοίας καὶ σπουδῆς ἄξιον ἐπαινεῖν. ἐπεὶ δ’ ἐνεκελεύσω καὶ ἡμᾶς
τι πε|ρὶ ὕψους πάντως εἰς σὴν ὑπομνηματίσασθαι χάριν, 179r
φέρε, εἴ τι δὴ δοκοῦμεν ἀνδράσι πολιτικοῖς τεθεωρηκέναι χρήσιμον, ἐπισκεψώμεθα. αὐτὸς δ’ ἡμῖν, ἑταῖρε, τὰ ἐπὶ

3 †Φλωρεντιανὲ] Vide Append. A, infra. 7 εἴτ’ P, corr. Spengelius, εἶτ’ Manutius. 13 ἰ*|σχύοιμεν P. 20 ἑτ**ρε P ἑταῖρε P.

ON THE SUBLIME.

I

You will remember, my dear Postumius Terentianus[1],
that when we examined together the treatise of Caecilius
on the Sublime, we found that it fell below the dignity of
the whole subject, while it failed signally to grasp the
essential points, and conveyed to its readers but little of
that practical help which it should be a writer's principal
aim to give. In every systematic treatise two things are
required. The first is a statement of the subject; the other,
which although second in order ranks higher in importance, is
an indication of the methods by which we may attain our end.
Now Caecilius seeks to show the nature of the sublime
by countless instances as though our ignorance demanded
it, but the consideration of the means whereby we may
succeed in raising our own capacities to a certain pitch of
elevation he has, strangely enough, omitted as unnecessary.
2. However, it may be that the man ought not so much
to be blamed for his shortcomings as praised for his happy
thought and his enthusiasm. But since you have urged
me, in my turn, to write a brief essay on the sublime
for your special gratification, let us consider whether the
views I have formed contain anything which will be of use
to public men. You will yourself, my friend, in accordance

---

[1] Probably this name (together with another which has disappeared) underlies
the reading of P. See Introduction (pp. 19, 20) and Appendix A (p. 170).

μέρους, ὡς πέφυκας καὶ καθήκει, συνεπικρινεῖς ἀλη-
θέστατα· εὖ γὰρ δὴ ὁ ἀποφηνάμενος τί θεοῖς ὅμοιον
ἔχομεν, 'εὐεργεσίαν' εἶπας 'καὶ ἀλήθειαν.' 3. γράφων
δὲ πρὸς σέ, φίλτατε, τὸν παιδείας ἐπιστήμονα, σχεδὸν
5 ἀπήλλαγμαι καὶ τοῦ διὰ πλειόνων προϋποτίθεσθαι, ὡς
ἀκρότης καὶ ἐξοχή τις λόγων ἐστὶ τὰ ὕψη, καὶ ποιητῶν
τε οἱ μέγιστοι καὶ συγγραφέων οὐκ ἄλλοθεν ἢ ἐνθένδε
ποθὲν ἐπρώτευσαν καὶ ταῖς ἑαυτῶν περιέβαλον εὐκλείαις
τὸν αἰῶνα.   4. οὐ γὰρ εἰς πειθὼ τοὺς ἀκροωμένους
10 ἀλλ' εἰς ἔκστασιν ἄγει τὰ ὑπερφυᾶ· πάντη δέ γε σὺν
ἐκπλήξει τοῦ πιθανοῦ καὶ τοῦ πρὸς χάριν ἀεὶ κρατεῖ τὸ
θαυμάσιον, εἴγε τὸ μὲν πιθανὸν ὡς τὰ πολλὰ ἐφ' ἡμῖν,
ταῦτα δὲ δυναστείαν καὶ βίαν ἄμαχον προσφέροντα
παντὸς ἐπάνω τοῦ ἀκροωμένου καθίσταται. καὶ τὴν
15 μὲν ἐμπειρίαν τῆς εὑρέσεως καὶ τὴν τῶν πραγμάτων
τάξιν καὶ οἰκονομίαν οὐκ ἐξ ἑνὸς οὐδ' ἐκ δυεῖν, ἐκ δὲ
τοῦ ὅλου τῶν λόγων ὕφους μόλις ἐκφαινομένην ὁρῶμεν,
ὕψος δέ που καιρίως ἐξενεχθὲν τά τε πράγματα δίκην
σκηπτοῦ πάντα διεφόρησεν καὶ τὴν τοῦ ῥήτορος εὐθὺς
20 ἀθρόαν ἐνεδείξατο δύναμιν. ταῦτα γὰρ οἶμαι καὶ τὰ
παραπλήσια, Τερεντιανὲ | ἥδιστε, κἂν αὐτὸς ἐκ πείρας 179ᵛ
ὑφηγήσαιο.

II

Ἡμῖν δ' ἐκεῖνο διαπορητέον ἐν ἀρχῇ, εἰ ἔστιν ὕψους
τις ἢ βάθους τέχνη, ἐπεί τινες ὅλως οἴονται διηπατῆσθαι
25 τοὺς τὰ τοιαῦτα ἄγοντας εἰς τεχνικὰ παραγγέλματα.
γεννᾶται γάρ, φησί, τὰ μεγαλοφυῆ καὶ οὐ διδακτὰ παρα-
γίνεται, καὶ μία τέχνη πρὸς αὐτὰ τὸ πεφυκέναι· χείρω τε
τὰ φυσικὰ ἔργα, ὡς οἴονται, καὶ τῷ παντὶ δειλότερα καθίσταται ταῖς τεχνολογίαις κατασκελετευόμενα.   2. ἐγὼ

1 πέφυκασ P.   3 εἶπας, in margine ἀντὶ τοῦ εἰπών P.   8 περιέβαλο*ν P.
24 οἴοντ** P οἴονται P.

with your nature and with what is fitting, join me in
appraising each detail with the utmost regard for truth;
for he answered well who, when asked in what qualities
we resemble the Gods, declared that we do so in benevo-
lence and truth[1]. 3. As I am writing to you, my good friend,
who are well versed in literary studies, I feel almost ab-
solved from the necessity of premising at any length that
sublimity is a certain distinction and excellence in expression, and that it is from no other source than this that the
greatest poets and writers have derived their eminence and
gained an immortality of renown. 4. The effect of elevated
language upon an audience is not persuasion but transport.
At every time and in every way imposing speech, with
the spell it throws over us, prevails over that which aims
at persuasion and gratification. Our persuasions we can
usually control, but the influences of the sublime bring
power and irresistible might to bear, and reign supreme
over every hearer. Similarly, we see skill in invention,
and due order and arrangement of matter, emerging as
the hard-won result not of one thing nor of two, but of
the whole texture of the composition, whereas Sublimity
flashing forth at the right moment scatters everything before
it like a thunderbolt, and at once displays the power of
the orator in all its plenitude. But enough; for these reflexions, and others like them, you can, I know well, my dear
Terentianus, yourself suggest from your own experience.

II

First of all, we must raise the question whether there is
such a thing as an art of the sublime or lofty. Some hold
that those are entirely in error who would bring such matters
under the precepts of art. A lofty tone, says one, is innate,
and does not come by teaching; nature is the only art that
can compass it. Works of nature are, they think, made worse
and altogether feebler when wizened by the rules of art.

[1] See Appendix C (p. 244), *Scriptor Incertus* (3).

δὲ ἐλεγχθήσεσθαι τοῦθ᾽ ἑτέρως ἔχον φημί, εἰ ἐπισκέψαιτό
τις, ὅτι ἡ φύσις, ὥσπερ τὰ πολλὰ ἐν τοῖς παθητικοῖς καὶ
διηρμένοις αὐτόνομον, οὕτως οὐκ εἰκαῖόν τι κἀκ παντὸς
ἀμέθοδον εἶναι φιλεῖ, καὶ ὅτι αὕτη μὲν πρῶτόν τι καὶ
5 ἀρχέτυπον γενέσεως στοιχεῖον ἐπὶ πάντων ὑφέστηκεν,
τὰς δὲ ποσότητας καὶ τὸν ἐφ᾽ ἑκάστου καιρόν, ἔτι δὲ τὴν
ἀπλανεστάτην ἄσκησίν τε καὶ χρῆσιν ἱκανὴ παρορίσαι
καὶ συνενεγκεῖν ἡ μέθοδος, καὶ ὡς ἐπικινδυνότερα, αὐτὰ
ἐφ᾽ αὑτῶν δίχα ἐπιστήμης, ἀστήρικτα καὶ ἀνερμάτιστα
10 ἐαθέντα τὰ μεγάλα, ἐπὶ μόνῃ τῇ φορᾷ καὶ ἀμαθεῖ τόλμῃ
λειπόμενα· δεῖ γὰρ αὐτοῖς ὡς κέντρου πολλάκις, οὕτω δὲ
καὶ χαλινοῦ. 3. ὅπερ γὰρ ὁ Δημοσθένης ἐπὶ τοῦ κοινοῦ
τῶν ἀνθρώπων ἀποφαίνεται βίου, μέγιστον μὲν εἶναι τῶν
ἀγαθῶν τὸ εὐτυχεῖν, δεύτερον δὲ καὶ οὐκ ἔλαττον τὸ εὖ
15 βουλεύεσθαι, ὅπερ οἷς ἂν μὴ παρῇ συναναιρεῖ πάντως καὶ
θάτερον, τοῦτ᾽ ἂν καὶ ἐπὶ τῶν λόγων εἴποιμεν, ὡς ἡ μὲν
φύσις τὴν τῆς εὐτυχίας τάξιν ἐπέχει, ἡ τέχνη δὲ τὴν τῆς
εὐβουλίας. τὸ δὲ κυριώτατον, ὅτι καὶ αὐτὸ τὸ εἶναί τινα
τῶν ἐν λόγοις ἐπὶ μόνῃ τῇ φύσει οὐκ ἄλλοθεν ἡμᾶς ἢ
20 παρὰ τῆς τέχνης ἐκμαθεῖν δεῖ. εἰ ταῦθ᾽, ὡς ἔφην, ἐπιλο-
γίσαιτο καθ᾽ ἑαυτὸν ὁ τοῖς χρηστομαθοῦσιν ἐπιτιμῶν, οὐκ
ἂν ἔτι, ἐμοὶ δοκεῖ, περιττὴν καὶ ἄχρηστον τὴν ἐπὶ τῶν
προκειμένων ἡγήσαιτο θεωρίαν...

DESVNT DVO FOLIA

7 παρορίσαι, in marg. γρ. πορίσαι P.

16 ὡς ἡ μὲν] cum his verbis desinit folium versum III quaternionis ΚΔ (179ᵛ),
deinde desunt duo folia (IV et V). quae sequuntur verba φύσις—θεωρίαν om. P,
edidit primus Tollius ex Vaticano cod. 285. eadem leguntur verba in cod. Parisino
985, ex quo Vaticanum descriptum esse verisimile est. 18 κυριώτατον ὅτι]
Pearcius, κυριώτατόν τε Vat. 285 et Par. 985. 22 ἐμοὶ δοκεῖ] Spengelius,
μοι δοκῶ Vat. 285 et Par. 985. 23 ἡγήσαιτο] Boivinus : ......σαιτο (m.
alt. κομίσαιτο) Par. 985, κομίσαιτο Vat. 285.

2. But I maintain that this will be found to be otherwise if it be observed that, while nature as a rule is free and independent in matters of passion and elevation, yet is she wont not to act at random and utterly without system. Further, nature is the original and vital underlying principle in all cases, but system can define limits and fitting seasons, and can also contribute the safest rules for use and practice. Moreover, the expression of the sublime is more exposed to danger when it goes its own way without the guidance of knowledge, —when it is suffered to be unstable and un-ballasted,—when it is left at the mercy of mere momentum and ignorant audacity. It is true that it often needs the spur, but it is also true that it often needs the curb[1]. 3. Demosthenes expresses the view, with regard to human life in general, that good fortune is the greatest of blessings, while good counsel, which occupies the second place, is hardly inferior in importance, since its absence contributes inevitably to the ruin of the former[2]. This we may apply to diction, nature occupying the position of good fortune, art that of good counsel. Most important of all, we must remember that the very fact that there are some elements of expression which are in the hands of nature alone, can be learnt from no other source than art. If, I say, the critic of those who desire to learn were to turn these matters over in his mind, he would no longer, it seems to me, regard the discussion of the subject as superfluous or useless...

---

[1] Appendix C, *Scr. Inc.* (10).   [2] Demosth. *c. Aristocr.* 113.

III

* * καὶ καμίνου σχῶσι μάκιστον σέλας.   180ʳ
εἰ γάρ τιν᾽ ἑστιοῦχον ὄψομαι μόνον,
μίαν παρείρας πλεκτάνην χειμάρροον,
στέγην πυρώσω καὶ κατανθρακώσομαι·
5   νῦν δ᾽ οὐ κέκραγά πω τὸ γενναῖον μέλος.

οὐ τραγικὰ ἔτι ταῦτα, ἀλλὰ παρατράγῳδα, αἱ πλεκτάναι,
καὶ τὸ πρὸς οὐρανὸν ἐξεμεῖν, καὶ τὸ τὸν Βορέαν αὐλητὴν
ποιεῖν, καὶ τὰ ἄλλα ἑξῆς· τεθόλωται γὰρ τῇ φράσει καὶ
τεθορύβηται ταῖς φαντασίαις μᾶλλον ἢ δεδείνωται, κἂν
10 ἕκαστον αὐτῶν πρὸς αὐγὰς ἀνασκοπῇς, ἐκ τοῦ φοβεροῦ
κατ᾽ ὀλίγον ὑπονοστεῖ πρὸς τὸ εὐκαταφρόνητον. ὅπου δ᾽
ἐν τραγῳδίᾳ, πράγματι ὀγκηρῷ φύσει καὶ ἐπιδεχομένῳ
στόμφον, ὅμως τὸ παρὰ μέλος οἰδεῖν ἀσύγγνωστον, σχολῇ
γ᾽ ἂν οἶμαι λόγοις ἀληθινοῖς ἁρμόσειεν. 2. ταύτῃ καὶ
15 τὰ τοῦ Λεοντίνου Γοργίου γελᾶται γράφοντος ʽΞέρξης ὁ
τῶν Περσῶν Ζεύς,᾽ καὶ ʽΓῦπες ἔμψυχοι τάφοι,᾽ καί τινα
τῶν Καλλισθένους ὄντα οὐχ ὑψηλὰ ἀλλὰ μετέωρα, καὶ ἔτι
μᾶλλον τὰ Κλειτάρχου· φλοιώδης γὰρ ἀνὴρ καὶ φυσῶν
κατὰ τὸν Σοφοκλέα,

20   μικροῖς μὲν αὐλίσκοισι, φορβειᾶς δ᾽ ἄτερ.

τά γε μὴν Ἀμφικράτους τοιαῦτα καὶ Ἡγησίου καὶ Μά-
τριδος· πολλαχοῦ γὰρ ἐνθουσιᾶν ἑαυτοῖς δοκοῦντες οὐ
βακχεύουσιν ἀλλὰ παίζουσιν. 3. ὅλως δ᾽ ἔοικεν εἶναι
τὸ οἰδεῖν ἐν τοῖς μάλιστα δυσφυλακτότατον. φύσει γὰρ
25 ἅπαντες οἱ μεγέθους ἐφιέμενοι, φεύγοντες ἀσθενείας καὶ
ξηρότητος κατάγνωσιν, οὐκ οἶδ᾽ ὅπως ἐπὶ τοῦθ᾽ ὑποφέ-
ρονται, πειθόμενοι τῷ ʽμεγάλων ἀπολισθαίνειν ὅμως

1—5 versus metricos hic et alibi continue scribit P, notis hisce (> > > > >) in
margine plerumque adpositis ubi laudantur verba sive poetae sive scriptoris
pedestris. 3 χειμάρρον P.   11 ὑπονοστεῖ, in marg. ἀντὶ τοῦ χωρισθῆναι
δυνήσεταί σοι P.   13 σχολῇ P.   18 ἀνήρ] ἀνὴρ P.   26 ὅ*πως P.
27 μεγάλων] μεγάλω P.

III

Quell they the oven's far-flung splendour-glow!
Ha, let me but one hearth-abider mark—
One flame-wreath torrent-like I'll whirl on high;
I'll burn the roof, to cinders shrivel it!—
Nay, now my chant is not of noble strain[1].

Such things are not tragic but pseudo-tragic—'flame-wreaths,' and 'belching to the sky,' and Boreas represented as a 'flute-player,' and all the rest of it. They are turbid in expression and confused in imagery rather than the product of intensity, and each one of them, if examined in the light of day, sinks little by little from the terrible into the contemptible. But since even in tragedy, which is in its very nature stately and prone to bombast, tasteless tumidity is unpardonable, still less, I presume, will it harmonise with the narration of fact. 2. And this is the ground on which the phrases of Gorgias of Leontini are ridiculed when he describes Xerxes as the 'Zeus of the Persians' and vultures as 'living tombs.' So is it with some of the expressions of Callisthenes which are not sublime but high-flown, and still more with those of Cleitarchus, for the man is frivolous and blows, as Sophocles has it,

On pigmy hautboys: mouthpiece have they none[2].

Other examples will be found in Amphicrates and Hegesias and Matris, for often when these writers seem to themselves to be inspired they are in no true frenzy but are simply trifling. 3. Altogether, tumidity seems particularly hard to avoid. The explanation is that all who aim at elevation are so anxious to escape the reproach of being weak and dry that they are carried, as by some strange law of nature, into the opposite extreme. They put their trust in the maxim that

---

[1] Appendix C, *Aeschylus.*—Translated by A. S. Way : see Preface.
[2] Appendix C, *Sophocles.*—Translated by A. S. Way : see Preface.

εὐγενὲς ἁ|μάρτημα.' 4. κακοὶ δὲ ὄγκοι καὶ ἐπὶ σωμάτων 180ᵛ
καὶ λόγων, οἱ χαῦνοι καὶ ἀναλήθεις καὶ μήποτε περιστάντες
ἡμᾶς εἰς τοὐναντίον· οὐδὲν γάρ φασι ξηρότερον ὑδρωπικοῦ. ἀλλὰ τὸ μὲν οἰδοῦν ὑπεραίρειν βούλεται τὰ ὕψη,
5 τὸ δὲ μειρακιῶδες ἄντικρυς ὑπεναντίον τοῖς μεγέθεσι·
ταπεινὸν γὰρ ἐξ ὅλου καὶ μικρόψυχον καὶ τῷ ὄντι κακὸν
ἀγεννέστατον. τί ποτ' οὖν τὸ μειρακιῶδές ἐστιν; ἢ δῆλον
ὡς σχολαστικὴ νόησις, ὑπὸ περιεργασίας λήγουσα εἰς
ψυχρότητα; ὀλισθαίνουσι δ' εἰς τοῦτο τὸ γένος ὀρεγό-
10 μενοι μὲν τοῦ περιττοῦ καὶ πεποιημένου καὶ μάλιστα τοῦ
ἡδέος, ἐποκέλλοντες δὲ εἰς τὸ ῥωπικὸν καὶ κακόζηλον.
5. τούτῳ παράκειται τρίτον τι κακίας εἶδος ἐν τοῖς
παθητικοῖς, ὅπερ ὁ Θεόδωρος παρένθυρσον ἐκάλει. ἔστι
δὲ πάθος ἄκαιρον καὶ κενὸν ἔνθα μὴ δεῖ πάθους, ἢ ἄμετρον
15 ἔνθα μετρίου δεῖ. πολλὰ γὰρ ὥσπερ ἐκ μέθης τινὲς εἰς
τὰ μηκέτι τοῦ πράγματος, ἴδια ἑαυτῶν καὶ σχολικὰ
παραφέρονται πάθη· εἶτα πρὸς οὐδὲν πεπονθότας ἀκροατὰς
ἀσχημονοῦσιν, εἰκότως, ἐξεστηκότες πρὸς οὐκ ἐξεστη-
κότας· πλὴν περὶ μὲν τῶν παθητικῶν ἄλλος ἡμῖν ἀπό-
20 κειται τόπος.

IV

Θατέρου δὲ ὧν εἴπομεν, λέγω δὲ τοῦ ψυχροῦ, πλήρης
ὁ Τίμαιος, ἀνὴρ τὰ μὲν ἄλλα ἱκανὸς καὶ πρὸς λόγων
ἐνίοτε μέγεθος οὐκ ἄφορος, πολυΐστωρ, ἐπινοητικός· πλὴν
ἀλλοτρίων μὲν ἐλεγκτικώτατος ἁμαρτημάτων, ἀνεπαίσθη-
25 τος δὲ ἰδίων, ὑπὸ δὲ ἔρωτος τοῦ ξένας νοήσεις ἀ|εὶ κινεῖν 181ʳ
πολλάκις ἐκπίπτων εἰς τὸ παιδαριωδέστατον. 2. παρα-
θήσομαι δὲ τἀνδρὸς ἓν ἢ δύο, ἐπειδὴ τὰ πλείω προέλαβεν

---

2 ἀναλήθ***σ P ἀναλήθεισ P.   ****ιστάντεσ P περιστάντες libri
deteriores.   6 ἐξ ὅλου, in marg. ἀντὶ τοῦ διόλου P.   8 περιεργασίασ P
περιεργίασ (superscripto γι ab eadem manu) P.   11 ῥωπικὸν] Is. Vossius,
ῥοπικὸν P.

'failure in a great attempt is at least a noble error[1].' 4. But evil are the swellings, both in the body and in diction, which are inflated and unreal, and threaten us with the reverse of our aim ; for nothing, say they, is drier than a man who has the dropsy. While tumidity desires to transcend the limits of the sublime, the defect which is termed puerility is the direct antithesis of elevation, for it is utterly low and mean and in real truth the most ignoble vice of style. What, then, is this puerility ? Clearly, a pedant's thoughts, which begin in learned trifling and end in frigidity. Men slip into this kind of error because, while they aim at the uncommon and elaborate and most of all at the attractive, they drift unawares into the tawdry and affected. 5. A third, and closely allied, kind of defect in matters of passion is that which Theodorus used to call *parenthyrsus*. By this is meant unseasonable and empty passion, where no passion is required, or immoderate, where moderation is needed. For men are often carried away, as if by intoxication, into displays of emotion which are not caused by the nature of the subject, but are purely personal and wearisome. In consequence they seem to hearers who are in no wise affected to act in an ungainly way. And no wonder ; for they are beside themselves, while their hearers are not. But the question of the passions we reserve for separate treatment.

IV

Of the second fault of which we have spoken—frigidity— Timaeus supplies many examples. Timaeus was a writer of considerable general ability, who occasionally showed that he was not incapable of elevation of style. He was learned and ingenious, but very prone to criticise the faults of others while blind to his own. Through his passion for continually starting novel notions, he often fell into the merest childishness. 2. I will set down one or two examples only of his manner, since the greater number have been already appropriated by

---

[1] Appendix C, *Scr. Inc.* (7).

ὁ Κεκίλιος. ἐπαινῶν Ἀλέξανδρον τὸν μέγαν, 'ὃς τὴν
Ἀσίαν ὅλην' φησίν ' ἐν ἐλάττοσι παρέλαβεν, ἢ ὅσοις
τὸν ὑπὲρ τοῦ πρὸς Πέρσας πολέμου πανηγυρικὸν λόγον
Ἰσοκράτης ἔγραψεν.' θαυμαστή γε τοῦ Μακεδόνος ἡ
5 πρὸς τὸν σοφιστὴν σύγκρισις· δῆλον γάρ, ὦ Τίμαιε, ὡς
οἱ Λακεδαιμόνιοι διὰ τοῦτο πολὺ τοῦ Ἰσοκράτους κατ'
ἀνδρίαν ἐλείποντο, ἐπειδὴ οἱ μὲν τριάκοντα ἔτεσι Μεσ-
σήνην παρέλαβον, ὁ δὲ τὸν πανηγυρικὸν ἐν μόνοις δέκα
συνετάξατο. 3. τοῖς δὲ Ἀθηναίοις ἁλοῦσι περὶ Σικελίαν
10 τίνα τρόπον ἐπιφωνεῖ; ὅτι ' εἰς τὸν Ἑρμῆν ἀσεβήσαντες
καὶ περικόψαντες αὐτοῦ τὰ ἀγάλματα, διὰ τοῦτ' ἔδωκαν
δίκην, οὐχ ἥκιστα δι' ἕνα ἄνδρα, ὃς ἀπὸ τοῦ παρανομη-
θέντος διὰ πατέρων ἦν, Ἑρμοκράτη τὸν Ἕρμωνος.' ὥστε
θαυμάζειν με, Τερεντιανὲ ἥδιστε, πῶς οὐ καὶ εἰς Διονύσιον
15 γράφει τὸν τύραννον· ' ἐπεὶ γὰρ εἰς τὸν Δία καὶ τὸν
Ἡρακλέα δυσσεβὴς ἐγένετο, διὰ τοῦτ' αὐτὸν Δίων καὶ
Ἡρακλείδης τῆς τυραννίδος ἀφείλοντο.' 4. τί δεῖ περὶ
Τιμαίου λέγειν, ὅπου γε καὶ οἱ ἥρωες ἐκεῖνοι, Ξενοφῶντα
λέγω καὶ Πλάτωνα, καίτοιγε ἐκ τῆς Σωκράτους ὄντες παλαί-
20 στρας, ὅμως διὰ τὰ οὕτως μικροχαρῆ ποτε ἑαυτῶν ἐπιλαν-
θάνονται; ὁ μέν γε ἐν τῇ Λακεδαιμονίων γράφει πολιτείᾳ·
' ἐκείνων μὲν γοῦν ἧττον μὲν ἂν φωνὴν ἀκούσαις ἢ τῶν
λιθίνων, ἧττον δ' ἂν ὄμματα στρέψαις ἢ τῶν χαλκῶν,
αἰ|δημονεστέρους δ' ἂν αὐτοὺς ἡγήσαιο καὶ αὐτῶν τῶν ἐν 181ᵛ
25 τοῖς ὀφθαλμοῖς παρθένων.' Ἀμφικράτει καὶ οὐ Ξενοφῶντι
ἔπρεπε τὰς ἐν τοῖς ὀφθαλμοῖς ἡμῶν κόρας λέγειν παρθένους
αἰδήμονας. οἷον δὲ Ἡράκλεις τὸ τὰς ἁπάντων ἑξῆς κόρας
αἰσχυντηλὰς εἶναι πεπεῖσθαι, ὅπου φασὶν οὐδενὶ οὕτως
ἐνσημαίνεσθαι τήν τινων ἀναίδειαν ὡς ἐν τοῖς ὀφθαλμοῖς.

---

2 παρέλαβεν∗P.   5 πρ P.   6 ἰ∗σοκράτους P.   7 ἀνδρ∗ίαν P.
μεσήνην P σ addidit m. rec. P.   13 ἦν] Manutius, ἀν P.   22 γ' οὖν
(sic ubique) P.   τοῦτο ξενοφῶντος in marg. P.   29 τήν τινων ἀναίδειαν
ὡς ἐν τοῖσ ὀφθαλμοῖσ ἰταμόν· οἰνοβαρέσ· P.—delendum ἰταμὸν tanquam glossema.
Vide Append. A.

removed in 1st para.

unfortunate comparison

Caecilius. In the course of a eulogy on Alexander the Great, he describes him as 'the man who gained possession of the whole of Asia in fewer years than it took Isocrates to write his *Panegyric* urging war against the Persians[1].' Strange indeed is the comparison of the man of Macedon with the rhetorician. How plain it is, Timaeus, that the Lacedaemonians, thus judged, were far inferior to Isocrates in prowess, for they spent thirty years in the conquest of Messene, whereas he composed his *Panegyric* in ten. 3. Consider again the way in which he speaks of the Athenians who were captured in Sicily. 'They were punished because they had acted impiously towards Hermes and mutilated his images, and the infliction of punishment was chiefly due to Hermocrates the son of Hermon, who was descended, in the paternal line, from the outraged god[1].' I am surprised, beloved Terentianus, that he does not write with regard to the despot Dionysius that 'Dion and Heracleides deprived him of his sovereignty because he had acted impiously towards Zeus and Heracles.' 4. But why speak of Timaeus when even those heroes of literature, Xenophon and Plato, though trained in the school of Socrates, nevertheless sometimes forget themselves for the sake of such paltry pleasantries? Xenophon writes in the *Polity of the Lacedaemonians* : 'You would find it harder to hear their voice than that of busts of marble, harder to deflect their gaze than that of statues of bronze ; you would deem them more modest than the very maidens in their eyes[2].'

It was worthy of an Amphicrates and not of a Xenophon to call the pupils of our eyes 'modest maidens.' Good heavens, how strange it is that the pupils of the whole company should be believed to be modest notwithstanding the common saying that the shamelessness of individuals is indicated by nothing so much as the eyes! 'Thou sot, that hast the eyes

---

[1] Appendix C, *Timaeus.*   [2] Xen. *de Rep. Laced.* III. 5.

4—2

'οἰνοβαρές, κυνὸς ὄμματ' ἔχων' φησίν. 5. ὁ μέντοι
Τίμαιος, ὡς φωρίου τινὸς ἐφαπτόμενος, οὐδὲ τοῦτο Ξενοφῶντι τὸ ψυχρὸν κατέλιπεν. φησὶ γοῦν ἐπὶ τοῦ Ἀγαθο-
κλέους καὶ τὸ 'τὴν ἀνεψιὰν ἑτέρῳ δεδομένην ἐκ τῶν
5 ἀνακαλυπτηρίων ἁρπάσαντα ἀπελθεῖν· ὃ τίς ἂν ἐποίησεν
ἐν ὀφθαλμοῖς κόρας, μὴ πόρνας ἔχων;' 6. τί δέ; ὁ τἆλλα
θεῖος Πλάτων τὰς δέλτους θέλων εἰπεῖν 'γράψαντες'
φησὶν 'ἐν τοῖς ἱεροῖς θήσουσι κυπαριττίνας μνήμας.' καὶ
πάλιν 'περὶ δὲ τειχῶν, ὦ Μέγιλλε, ἐγὼ ξυμφεροίμην ἂν τῇ
10 Σπάρτῃ τὸ καθεύδειν ἐᾶν ἐν τῇ γῇ κατακείμενα τὰ τείχη,
καὶ μὴ ἐπανίστασθαι.' 7. καὶ τὸ Ἡροδότειον οὐ πόρρω,
τὸ φάναι τὰς καλὰς γυναῖκας 'ἀλγηδόνας ὀφθαλμῶν.'
καίτοιγε ἔχει τινὰ παραμυθίαν, οἱ γὰρ παρ' αὐτῷ ταυτὶ
λέγοντές εἰσιν οἱ βάρβαροι καὶ ἐν μέθῃ, ἀλλ' οὐδ' ἐκ
15 τοιούτων προσώπων διὰ μικροψυχίαν καλὸν ἀσχημονεῖν
πρὸς τὸν αἰῶνα.

V

Ἅπαντα μέντοι τὰ οὕτως ἄσεμνα διὰ μίαν ἐμφύεται
τοῖς λόγοις αἰτίαν, διὰ τὸ περὶ τὰς νοήσεις καινόσπουδον,
περὶ ὃ δὴ μάλιστα κορυβαντιῶσιν οἱ νῦν· ἀφ' ὧν γὰρ
20 ἡμῖν τἀγαθά, σχεδὸν ἀπ' αὐτῶν τούτων καὶ τὰ κακὰ 182ʳ
γεννᾶσθαι φιλεῖ. ὅθεν ἐπίφορον εἰς συνταγμάτων κατόρ-
θωσιν τά τε κάλλη τῆς ἑρμηνείας καὶ τὰ ὕψη καὶ πρὸς
τούτοις αἱ ἡδοναί· καὶ αὐτὰ ταῦτα καθάπερ τῆς ἐπιτυχίας,
οὕτως ἀρχαὶ καὶ ὑποθέσεις καὶ τῶν ἐναντίων καθίστανται.
25 τοιοῦτόν πως καὶ αἱ μεταβολαὶ καὶ ὑπερβολαὶ καὶ τὰ
πληθυντικά· δείξομεν δ' ἐν τοῖς ἔπειτα τὸν κίνδυνον,
ὃν ἔχειν ἐοίκασι. διόπερ ἀναγκαῖον ἤδη διαπορεῖν καὶ

---

6 τ' ἄλλα P.   7 περὶ Πλάτωνος in marg. P.   11 περὶ ἡροδότου
in marg. P.   14 μέθει P.   21 φι*λεῖ P.   ἐπίφρον (o superscripto a m. rec.) P.   22 κάλλει corr. κάλλη P.

of a dog,' as Homer has it[1]. 5. Timaeus, however, has not
left even this piece of frigidity to Xenophon, but clutches it
as though it were hid treasure. At all events, after saying
of Agathocles that he abducted his cousin, who had been
given in marriage to another man, from the midst of the
nuptial rites, he asks, 'Who could have done this had he not
had wantons, in place of maidens, in his eyes?' 6. Yes,
and Plato (usually so divine) when he means simply *tablets*
says, 'They shall write and preserve *cypress memorials* in the
temples[2].'

And again, 'As touching walls, Megillus, I should hold
with Sparta that they be suffered to lie asleep in the earth and
not summoned to arise[3].' 7. The expression of Herodotus
to the effect that beautiful women are 'eye-smarts' is not
much better[4]. This, however, may be condoned in some
degree since those who use this particular phrase in his
narrative are barbarians and in their cups, but not even in the
mouths of such characters is it well that an author should
suffer, in the judgment of posterity, from an unseemly exhibition of triviality.

V

All these ugly and parasitical growths arise in literature
from a single cause, that pursuit of novelty in the expression
of ideas which may be regarded as the fashionable craze
of the day. Our defects usually spring, for the most part,
from the same sources as our good points. Hence, while
beauties of expression and touches of sublimity, and charming
elegances withal, are favourable to effective composition, yet
these very things are the elements and foundation, not only of
success, but also of the contrary. Something of the kind is
true also of variations and hyperboles and the use of the plural
number, and we shall show subsequently the dangers to which
these seem severally to be exposed. It is necessary now to

---

[1] *Iliad* I. 225.   [2] Plato, *Legg.* V. 741 C.
[3] Plato, *Legg.* VI. 778 D.   [4] Herod. V. 18.

ὑποτίθεσθαι, δι' ὅτου τρόπου τὰς ἀνακεκραμένας κακίας
τοῖς ὑψηλοῖς ἐκφεύγειν δυνάμεθα.

VI

„ Ἔστι δέ, ὦ φίλος, εἴ τινα περιποιησαίμεθ' ἐν πρώτοις
καθαρὰν τοῦ κατ' ἀλήθειαν ὕψους ἐπιστήμην καὶ ἐπίκρισιν.
5 καίτοι τὸ πρᾶγμα δύσληπτον· ἡ γὰρ τῶν λόγων κρίσις
πολλῆς ἐστι πείρας τελευταῖον ἐπιγέννημα· οὐ μὴν ἀλλ',
ὡς εἰπεῖν ἐν παραγγέλματι, ἐντεῦθέν ποθεν ἴσως τὴν
διάγνωσιν αὐτῶν οὐκ ἀδύνατον πορίζεσθαι.

VII

Εἰδέναι χρή, φίλτατε, διότι, καθάπερ κἂν τῷ κοινῷ
10 βίῳ οὐδὲν ὑπάρχει μέγα, οὗ τὸ καταφρονεῖν ἐστι μέγα,
οἷον πλοῦτοι τιμαὶ δόξαι τυραννίδες, καὶ ὅσα δὴ ἄλλα
ἔχει πολὺ τὸ ἔξωθεν προστραγῳδούμενον, οὐκ ἂν τῷ γε
φρονίμῳ δόξειεν ἀγαθὰ ὑπερβάλλοντα, ὧν αὐτὸ τὸ
περιφρονεῖν ἀγαθὸν οὐ μέτριον· θαυμάζουσι γοῦν τῶν
15 ἐχόντων αὐτὰ μᾶλλον τοὺς δυναμένους ἔχειν καὶ διὰ
μεγαλοψυχίαν ὑπερορῶντας· τῇδέ που καὶ ἐπὶ τῶν διηρ-
μένων ἐν ποιήμασι καὶ λόγοις ἐπισκεπτέον, μή τινα
μεγέθους φαντασίαν ἔχοι τοιαύτην, ᾗ πο|λὺ πρόσκειται 182ᵛ
τὸ εἰκῆ προσαναπλαττόμενον, ἀναπτυττόμενα δὲ ἄλλως
20 εὑρίσκοιτο χαῦνα, ὧν τοῦ θαυμάζειν τὸ περιφρονεῖν
εὐγενέστερον.   2. φύσει γάρ πως ὑπὸ τἀληθοῦς ὕψους
ἐπαίρεταί τε ἡμῶν ἡ ψυχὴ καὶ γαῦρόν τι ἀνάστημα
λαμβάνουσα πληροῦται χαρᾶς καὶ μεγαλαυχίας, ὡς αὐτὴ
γεννήσασα ὅπερ ἤκουσεν.   3. ὅταν οὖν ὑπ' ἀνδρὸς
25 ἔμφρονος καὶ ἐμπείρου λόγων πολλάκις ἀκουόμενόν τι
πρὸς μεγαλοφροσύνην τὴν ψυχὴν μὴ συνδιατιθῇ, μηδ'

18   τοαύτη P, correxit m. rec.   22   ἀνάστημα] libri deteriores, ἀνάθημα P.

seek and to suggest means by which we may avoid the defects
which attend the steps of the sublime.

VI

The best means would be, my friend, to gain, first of all, clear
knowledge and appreciation of the true sublime. The enter-
prise is, however, an arduous one. For the judgment of style
is the last and crowning fruit of long experience. None the
less, if I must speak in the way of precept, it is not impossible
perhaps to acquire discrimination in these matters by attention
to some such hints as those which follow.

VII

You must know, my dear friend, that it is with the sublime
as in the common life of man. In life nothing can be considered great which it is held great to despise. For instance,
riches, honours, distinctions, sovereignties, and all other things
which possess in abundance the external trappings of the
stage, will not seem, to a man of sense, to be supreme blessings,
since the very contempt of them is reckoned good in no small
degree, and in any case those who could have them, but are
high-souled enough to disdain them, are more admired than
those who have them. So also in the case of sublimity in
poems and prose writings, we must consider whether some
supposed examples have not simply the appearance of
elevation with many idle accretions, so that when analysed
they are found to be mere vanity—objects which a noble
nature will rather despise than admire. 2. For, as if in-
stinctively, our soul is uplifted by the true sublime; it takes a
proud flight, and is filled with joy and vaunting, as though it
had itself produced what it has heard. 3. When, therefore, a
thing is heard repeatedly by a man of intelligence, who is well
versed in literature, and its effect is not to dispose the soul to

ἐγκαταλείπῃ τῇ διανοίᾳ πλεῖον τοῦ λεγομένου τὸ ἀναθεω-
ρούμενον, πίπτῃ δ᾽, ἂν εὖ τὸ συνεχὲς ἐπισκοπῇς, εἰς
ἀπαύξησιν, οὐκ ἂν ἔτ᾽ ἀληθὲς ὕψος εἴη μέχρι μόνης τῆς
ἀκοῆς σῳζόμενον. τοῦτο γὰρ τῷ ὄντι μέγα, οὗ πολλὴ
5 μὲν ἡ ἀναθεώρησις, δύσκολος δέ, μᾶλλον δ᾽ ἀδύνατος ἡ
κατεξανάστασις, ἰσχυρὰ δὲ ἡ μνήμη καὶ δυσεξάλειπτος.
4. ὅλως δὲ καλὰ νόμιζε ὕψη καὶ ἀληθινὰ τὰ διὰ παντὸς
ἀρέσκοντα καὶ πᾶσιν. ὅταν γὰρ τοῖς ἀπὸ διαφόρων
ἐπιτηδευμάτων βίων ζήλων ἡλικιῶν λόγων ἕν τι καὶ ταὐτὸν
10 ἅμα περὶ τῶν αὐτῶν ἅπασι δοκῇ, τόθ᾽ ἡ ἐξ ἀσυμφώνων
ὡς κρίσις καὶ συγκατάθεσις τὴν ἐπὶ τῷ θαυμαζομένῳ
πίστιν ἰσχυρὰν λαμβάνει καὶ ἀναμφίλεκτον.

VIII

Ἐπεὶ δὲ πέντε, ὡς ἂν εἴποι τις, πηγαί τινές εἰσιν αἱ τῆς
ὑψηγορίας γονιμώταται, προϋποκειμένης ὥσπερ ἐδάφους
15 τινὸς κοινοῦ ταῖς πέντε ταύταις ἰδέαις τῆς ἐν τῷ λέγειν
δυνάμεως, ἧς ὅλως χωρὶς οὐδέν, πρῶτον μὲν καὶ κράτιστον
τὸ περὶ τὰς νοήσεις ἀδρεπήβολον, ὡς κἂν τοῖς περὶ
Ξενοφῶντος ὡρισάμεθα· δεύτερον δὲ τὸ σφοδρὸν καὶ
ἐνθουσιαστικὸν πάθος· ἀλλ᾽ αἱ μὲν δύο αὗται τοῦ ὕψους
20 κατὰ τὸ πλέον αὐθιγενεῖς συστάσεις, αἱ λοιπαὶ δ᾽ ἤδη καὶ
διὰ τέχνης, ἥ τε ποιὰ τῶν σχημάτων πλάσις (δισσὰ δέ
που ταῦτα τὰ μὲν νοήσεως, θάτερα δὲ λέξεως), ἐπὶ δὲ
τούτοις ἡ γενναία φράσις, ἧς μέρη πάλιν ὀνομάτων τε
ἐκλογὴ καὶ ἡ τροπικὴ καὶ πεποιημένη λέξις· πέμπτη δὲ
25 μεγέθους αἰτία καὶ συγκλείουσα τὰ πρὸ ἑαυτῆς ἅπαντα, ἡ

1 ἐγκαταλίπηι P ἐγκαταλείπηι P.   2 ἂν εὖ τὸ] Reiskius, ἄνευ|** τὸ P.
4 σωζόμενον P.   14 γο*νιμώταται P.   προ|ϋποκειμένησ (η corr. in ras.) P.
17 ἀδρεπήβολον] cum hac voce desinit f. 182ᵛ. totum qui sequitur ab ὡς ad
ἰδέσθαι p. 64. 15 locum om. P, cuius in margine imo adscriptum est a manu
recenti : λείπει desunt folia octo seu quaternio ΚΕ. quaternionis huius folia duo
exteriora (p. 56. 17 ὡς—p. 60. 17 ἠρκέσθην et p. 60. 18 τὸ ἐπ᾽ οὐρανὸν—p. 64. 15
ἰδέσθαι), in codd. dett. hodie servata, ex P iam Victorii aetate (anno 1568) ex-
ciderant.   25 πρὸ ἑαυτῆς] codd. praeter Par. 2960 qui πρὸς αὐτῆς praebet.
πρὸ αὐτῆς Spengelius, Iahnius.

cp. Keats.

high thoughts, and it does not leave in the mind more food for reflexion than the words seem to convey, but falls, if examined carefully through and through, into disesteem, it cannot rank as true sublimity because it does not survive a first hearing. For that is really great which bears a repeated examination, and which it is difficult or rather impossible to withstand, and the memory of which is strong and hard to efface. 4. In general, consider those examples of sublimity to be fine and genuine which please all and always. For when men of different pursuits, lives, ambitions, ages, languages, hold identical views on one and the same subject, then that verdict which results, so to speak, from a concert of discordant elements makes our faith in the object of admiration strong and unassailable.

VIII

There are, it may be said, five principal sources of elevated language. Beneath these five varieties there lies, as though it were a common foundation, the gift of discourse, which is indispensable. First and most important is the power of forming great conceptions, as we have elsewhere explained in our remarks on Xenophon. Secondly, there is vehement and inspired passion. These two components of the sublime are for the most part innate. Those which remain are partly the product of art. The due formation of figures deals with two sorts of figures, first those of thought and secondly those of expression. Next there is noble diction, which in turn comprises choice of words, and use of metaphors, and elaboration of language. The fifth cause of elevation—one which is the fitting conclusion of all that have preceded it—is dignified

ἐν ἀξιώματι καὶ διάρσει σύνθεσις· φέρε δὴ τὰ ἐμπεριεχόμενα καθ᾽ ἑκάστην ἰδέαν τούτων ἐπισκεψώμεθα, τοσοῦτον
προειπόντες, ὅτι τῶν πέντε μορίων ὁ Κεκίλιος ἔστιν ἃ
παρέλιπεν, ὡς καὶ τὸ πάθος ἀμέλει. 2. ἀλλ᾽ εἰ μὲν ὡς
5 ἕν τι ταῦτ᾽ ἄμφω, τό τε ὕψος καὶ τὸ παθητικόν, καὶ ἔδοξεν
αὐτῷ πάντη συνυπάρχειν τε ἀλλήλοις καὶ συμπεφυκέναι,
διαμαρτάνει· καὶ γὰρ πάθη τινὰ διεστῶτα ὕψους καὶ
ταπεινὰ εὑρίσκεται, καθάπερ οἶκτοι λῦπαι φόβοι, καὶ
ἔμπαλιν πολλὰ ὕψη δίχα πάθους, ὡς πρὸς μυρίοις ἄλλοις
10 καὶ τὰ περὶ τοὺς Ἀλωάδας τῷ ποιητῇ παρατετολμημένα,

Ὄσσαν ἐπ᾽ Οὐλύμπῳ μέμασαν θέμεν· αὐτὰρ ἐπ᾽ Ὄσσῃ
Πήλιον εἰνοσίφυλλον, ἵν᾽ οὐρανὸς ἄμβατος εἴη·

καὶ τὸ τούτοις ἔτι μεῖζον ἐπιφερόμενον,

καί νύ κεν ἐξετέλεσσάν.

15 3. παρά γε μὴν τοῖς ῥήτορσι τὰ ἐγκώμια καὶ τὰ πομπικὰ
καὶ ἐπιδεικτικὰ τὸν μὲν ὄγκον καὶ τὸ ὑψηλὸν ἐξ ἅπαντος
περιέχει, πάθους δὲ χηρεύει κατὰ τὸ πλεῖστον, ὅθεν ἥκιστα
τῶν ῥητόρων οἱ περιπαθεῖς ἐγκωμιαστικοὶ ἢ ἔμπαλιν
οἱ ἐπαινετικοὶ περιπαθεῖς. 4. εἰ δ᾽ αὖ πάλιν ἐξ ὅλου
20 μὴ ἐνόμισεν ὁ Κεκίλιος τὸ ἐμπαθὲς <ἐς> τὰ ὕψη ποτὲ
συντελεῖν, καὶ διὰ τοῦτ᾽ οὐχ ἡγήσατο μνήμης ἄξιον, πάνυ
διηπάτηται· θαρρῶν γὰρ ἀφορισαίμην ἄν, ὡς οὐδὲν οὕτως
ὡς τὸ γενναῖον πάθος, ἔνθα χρή, μεγαληγόρον, ὥσπερ
ὑπὸ μανίας τινὸς καὶ πνεύματος ἐνθουσιαστικῶς ἐκπνέον
25 καὶ οἱονεὶ φοιβάζον τοὺς λόγους.

IX

Οὐ μὴν ἀλλ᾽ ἐπεὶ τὴν κρατίστην μοῖραν ἐπέχει τῶν
ἄλλων τὸ πρῶτον, λέγω δὲ τὸ μεγαλοφυές, χρὴ κἀνταῦθα,

---

20 ἐς] Faber, Vahlenus, om. libri. Cp. xxxix. 1 τῶν συντελουσῶν εἰς τὸ ὕψος.
post ἐμπαθὲς facile excidisse potest ἐς.   23 μεγαλήγορον] El. Robortellus,
μεγαλήτορον libri ceteri.

and elevated composition. Come now, let us consider what is involved in each of these varieties, with this one remark by way of preface, that Caecilius has omitted some of the five divisions, for example, that of passion. 2. Surely he is quite mistaken if he does so on the ground that these two, sublimity and passion, are a unity, and if it seems to him that they are by nature one and inseparable. For some passions are found which are far removed from sublimity and are of a low order, such as pity, grief and fear ; and on the other hand there are many examples of the sublime which are independent of passion, such as the daring words of Homer with regard to the Aloadae, to take one out of numberless instances,

Yea, Ossa in fury they strove to upheave on Olympus on high,
With forest-clad Pelion above, that thence they might step to the
    sky[1].

And so of the words which follow with still greater force :—

    Ay, and the deed had they done[2].

3. Among the orators, too, eulogies and ceremonial and occasional addresses contain on every side examples of dignity and elevation, but are for the most part void of passion. This is the reason why passionate speakers are the worst eulogists, and why, on the other hand, those who are apt in encomium are the least passionate. 4. If, on the other hand, Caecilius thought that passion never contributes at all to sublimity, and if it was for this reason that he did not deem it worthy of mention, he is altogether deluded. I would affirm with confidence that there is no tone so lofty as that of genuine passion, in its right place, when it bursts out in a wild gust of mad enthusiasm and as it were fills the speaker's words with frenzy.

IX

Now the first of the conditions mentioned, namely elevation of mind, holds the foremost rank among them all. We must,

---

[1] *Odyss.* XI. 315, 316.
[2] *Odyss.* XI. 317.

καὶ εἰ δωρητὸν τὸ πρᾶγμα μᾶλλον ἢ κτητόν, ὅμως καθ'
ὅσον οἷόν τε τὰς ψυχὰς ἀνατρέφειν πρὸς τὰ μεγέθη, καὶ
ὥσπερ ἐγκύμονας ἀεὶ ποιεῖν γενναίου παραστήματος.
2. τίνα, φήσεις, τρόπον ; γέγραφά που καὶ ἑτέρωθι τὸ
5 τοιοῦτον· ὕψος μεγαλοφροσύνης ἀπήχημα. ὅθεν καὶ
φωνῆς δίχα θαυμάζεταί ποτε ψιλὴ καθ' ἑαυτὴν ἡ ἔννοια
δι' αὐτὸ τὸ μεγαλόφρον, ὡς ἡ τοῦ Αἴαντος ἐν Νεκυίᾳ
σιωπὴ μέγα καὶ παντὸς ὑψηλότερον λόγου. 3. πρῶτον
οὖν τὸ ἐξ οὗ γίνεται προϋποτίθεσθαι πάντως ἀναγκαῖον,
10 ὡς ἔχειν δεῖ τὸν ἀληθῆ ῥήτορα μὴ ταπεινὸν φρόνημα
καὶ ἀγεννές. οὐδὲ γὰρ οἷόν τε μικρὰ καὶ δουλοπρεπῆ
φρονοῦντας καὶ ἐπιτηδεύοντας παρ' ὅλον τὸν βίον θαυμαστόν τι καὶ τοῦ παντὸς αἰῶνος ἐξενεγκεῖν ἄξιον· μεγάλοι
δὲ οἱ λόγοι τούτων, κατὰ τὸ εἰκός, ὧν ἂν ἐμβριθεῖς ὦσιν
15 αἱ ἔννοιαι. 4. ταύτῃ καὶ εἰς τοὺς μάλιστα φρονηματίας
ἐμπίπτει τὰ ὑπερφυᾶ· ὁ γὰρ τῷ Παρμενίωνι φήσαντι,
' ἐγὼ μὲν ἠρκέσθην' . . . .

DESVNT SEX FOLIA

. . . . τὸ ἐπ' οὐρανὸν ἀπὸ γῆς διάστημα· καὶ τοῦτ' ἂν
εἴποι τις οὐ μᾶλλον τῆς Ἔριδος ἢ Ὁμήρου μέτρον.
20 5. ᾧ ἀνόμοιόν γε τὸ Ἡσιόδειον ἐπὶ τῆς Ἀχλύος, εἴγε
Ἡσιόδου καὶ τὴν Ἀσπίδα θετέον·

τῆς ἐκ μὲν ῥινῶν μύξαι ῥέον·

οὐ γὰρ δεινὸν ἐποίησε τὸ εἴδωλον, ἀλλὰ μισητόν. ὁ δὲ
πῶς μεγεθύνει τὰ δαιμόνια ;

25
ὅσσον δ' ἠεροειδὲς ἀνὴρ ἴδεν ὀφθαλμοῖσιν,
ἥμενος ἐν σκοπιῇ, λεύσσων ἐπὶ οἴνοπα πόντον·
τόσσον ἐπιθρώσκουσι θεῶν ὑψηχέες ἵπποι.

τὴν ὁρμὴν αὐτῶν κοσμικῷ διαστήματι καταμετρεῖ. τίς

17 ἂν ἠρκέσθην libri deteriores excepto P 2960 cuius pr. m. ἀνηρκέ dat, supplet
m. rec. σθην.   19 εἴποι] Manutius, εἰπεῖν libri.

therefore, in this case also, although we have to do rather
with an endowment than with an acquirement, nurture our
souls (as far as that is possible) to thoughts sublime, and
make them always pregnant, so to say, with noble inspiration.
2. In what way, you may ask, is this to be done ? Elsewhere
I have written as follows : 'Sublimity is the echo of a great
soul.' Hence also a bare idea, by itself and without a spoken
word, sometimes excites admiration just because of the
greatness of soul implied. Thus the silence of Ajax in the
Underworld is great and more sublime than words[1]. 3. First,
then, it is absolutely necessary to indicate the source of this
elevation, namely, that the truly eloquent must be free from
low and ignoble thoughts. For it is not possible that men with
mean and servile ideas and aims prevailing throughout their
lives should produce anything that is admirable and worthy
of immortality. Great accents we expect to fall from the lips
of those whose thoughts are deep and grave. 4. Thus it is that
stately speech comes naturally to the proudest spirits. [You
will remember the answer of] Alexander to Parmenio when
he said ' For my part I had been well content[2] '.........

......the distance from earth to heaven ; and this might
well be considered the measure of Homer no less than of
Strife. 5. How unlike to this the expression which is used
of Sorrow by Hesiod, if indeed the *Shield* is to be attributed
to Hesiod :

> Rheum from her nostrils was trickling[3].

The image he has suggested is not terrible but rather loath-
some. Contrast the way in which Homer magnifies the higher
powers :

And far as a man with his eyes through the sea-line haze may
  discern,
On a cliff as he sitteth and gazeth away o'er the wine-dark deep,
So far at a bound do the loud-neighing steeds of the Deathless
  leap[4].

He makes the vastness of the world the measure of their

---

[1] *Odyss.* XI. 543.   [2] Appendix C, p. 215 (quotation from Arrian).
[3] Hesiod, *Scut.* 267.   [4] *Il.* V. 770.

οὖν οὐκ ἂν εἰκότως διὰ τὴν ὑπερβολὴν τοῦ μεγέθους
ἐπιφθέγξαιτο, ὅτι ἂν δὶς ἐξῆς ἐφορμήσωσιν οἱ τῶν θεῶν
ἵπποι, οὐκέθ' εὑρήσουσιν ἐν κόσμῳ τόπον; 6. ὑπερφυᾶ
καὶ τὰ ἐπὶ τῆς θεομαχίας φαντάσματα·

5   ἀμφὶ δ' ἐσάλπιγξεν μέγας οὐρανὸς Οὔλυμπός τε.
    ἔδδεισεν δ' ὑπένερθεν ἄναξ ἐνέρων Ἀϊδωνεύς,
    δείσας δ' ἐκ θρόνου ἆλτο καὶ ἴαχε, μή οἱ ἔπειτα
    γαῖαν ἀναρρήξειε Ποσειδάων ἐνοσίχθων,
    οἰκία δὲ θνητοῖσι καὶ ἀθανάτοισι φανείη,
10   σμερδαλέ᾽, εὐρώεντα, τά τε στυγέουσι θεοί περ.

ἐπιβλέπεις, ἑταῖρε, ὡς ἀναρρηγνυμένης μὲν ἐκ βάθρων
γῆς, αὐτοῦ δὲ γυμνουμένου ταρτάρου, ἀνατροπὴν δὲ ὅλου
καὶ διάστασιν τοῦ κόσμου λαμβάνοντος, πάνθ' ἅμα,
οὐρανὸς ᾅδης, τὰ θνητὰ τὰ ἀθάνατα, ἅμα τῇ τότε συμπο-
15 λεμεῖ καὶ συγκινδυνεύει μάχῃ; 7. ἀλλὰ ταῦτα φοβερὰ
μέν, πλὴν ἄλλως, εἰ μὴ κατ' ἀλληγορίαν λαμβάνοιτο,
παντάπασιν ἄθεα καὶ οὐ σῴζοντα τὸ πρέπον. Ὅμηρος
γάρ μοι δοκεῖ παραδιδοὺς τραύματα θεῶν στάσεις τιμω-
ρίας δάκρυα δεσμὰ πάθη πάμφυρτα τοὺς μὲν ἐπὶ τῶν
20 Ἰλιακῶν ἀνθρώπους, ὅσον ἐπὶ τῇ δυνάμει, θεοὺς πε-
ποιηκέναι, τοὺς θεοὺς δὲ ἀνθρώπους. ἀλλ' ἡμῖν μὲν
δυσδαιμονοῦσιν ἀπόκειται λιμὴν κακῶν ὁ θάνατος, τῶν
θεῶν δ' οὐ τὴν φύσιν ἀλλὰ τὴν ἀτυχίαν ἐποίησεν αἰώνιον.
8. πολὺ δὲ τῶν περὶ τὴν θεομαχίαν ἀμείνω τὰ ὅσα
25 ἄχραντόν τι καὶ μέγα τὸ δαιμόνιον ὡς ἀληθῶς καὶ ἄκρατον
παρίστησιν, οἷα (πολλοῖς δὲ πρὸ ἡμῶν ὁ τόπος ἐξείργασται) τὰ ἐπὶ τοῦ Ποσειδῶνος,

    τρέμε δ' οὔρεα μακρὰ καὶ ὕλη
  καὶ κορυφαὶ Τρώων τε πόλις καὶ νῆες Ἀχαιῶν

---

4 καὶ τὰ] Manutius, καὶ vel τὰ om. libri.

leap. The sublimity is so overpowering as naturally to prompt the exclamation that if the divine steeds were to leap thus twice in succession they would pass beyond the confines of the world. 6. How transcendent also are the images in the Battle of the Gods :—

Far round wide heaven and Olympus echoed his clarion of thunder ;
And Hades, king of the realm of shadows, quaked thereunder.
And he sprang from his throne, and he cried aloud in the dread
    of his heart
Lest o'er him earth-shaker Poseidon should cleave the ground
    apart,
And revealed to Immortals and mortals should stand those awful
    abodes,
Those mansions ghastly and grim, abhorred of the very Gods[1].

You see, my friend, how the earth is torn from its foundations, Tartarus itself is laid bare, the whole world is upturned and parted asunder, and all things together—heaven and hell, things mortal and things immortal—share in the conflict and the perils of that battle !

7. But although these things are awe-inspiring, yet from another point of view, if they be not taken allegorically, they are altogether impious, and violate our sense of what is fitting. Homer seems to me, in his legends of wounds suffered by the gods, and of their feuds, reprisals, tears, bonds, and all their manifold passions, to have made, as far as lay within his power, gods of the men concerned in the Siege of Troy, and men of the gods. But whereas we mortals have death as the destined haven of our ills if our lot is miserable, he portrays the gods as immortal not only in nature but also in misfortune. 8. Much superior to the passages respecting the Battle of the Gods are those which represent the divine nature as it really is—pure and great and undefiled ; for example, what is said of Poseidon in a passage fully treated by many before ourselves :

Her far-stretching ridges, her forest-trees, quaked in dismay,
And her peaks, and the Trojans' town, and the ships of Achaia's
    array,

---

[1] *Il.* XXI. 388, XX. 61—65.

ποσσὶν ὑπ' ἀθανάτοισι Ποσειδάωνος ἰόντος.
βῆ δ' ἐλάαν ἐπὶ κύματ', ἄταλλε δὲ κήτε' ὑπ' αὐτοῦ
πάντοθεν ἐκ κευθμῶν, οὐδ' ἠγνοίησεν ἄνακτα.
γηθοσύνῃ δὲ θάλασσα διίστατο, τοὶ δὲ πέτοντο.

5 9. ταύτῃ καὶ ὁ τῶν Ἰουδαίων θεσμοθέτης, οὐχ ὁ τυχὼν
ἀνήρ, ἐπειδὴ τὴν τοῦ θείου δύναμιν κατὰ τὴν ἀξίαν ἐχώρησε
κἀξέφηνεν, εὐθὺς ἐν τῇ εἰσβολῇ γράψας τῶν νόμων ' εἶπεν
ὁ Θεός ' φησί· τί ; 'γενέσθω φῶς, καὶ ἐγένετο· γενέσθω
γῆ, καὶ ἐγένετο.' 10. οὐκ ὀχληρὸς ἂν ἴσως, ἑταῖρε,
10 δόξαιμι, ἓν ἔτι τοῦ ποιητοῦ καὶ τῶν ἀνθρωπίνων παρα-
θέμενος τοῦ μαθεῖν χάριν, ὡς εἰς τὰ ἡρωϊκὰ μεγέθη
συνεμβαίνειν ἐθίζει. ἀχλὺς ἄφνω καὶ νὺξ ἄπορος αὐτῷ
τὴν τῶν Ἑλλήνων ἐπέχει μάχην· ἔνθα δὴ ὁ Αἴας ἀμηχανῶν,

Ζεῦ πάτερ, φησίν, ἀλλὰ σὺ ῥῦσαι ὑπ' ἠέρος υἷας Ἀχαιῶν,
15 ποίησον δ' αἴθρην, δὸς δ' ὀφθαλμοῖσιν ἰδέσθαι· |
ἐν δὲ φάει καὶ ὄλεσσον.

183ʳ

ἔστιν ὡς ἀληθῶς τὸ πάθος Αἴαντος, οὐ γὰρ ζῆν εὔχεται
(ἦν γὰρ τὸ αἴτημα τοῦ ἥρωος ταπεινότερον), ἀλλ' ἐπειδὴ
ἐν ἀπράκτῳ σκότει τὴν ἀνδρίαν εἰς οὐδὲν γενναῖον εἶχε
20 διαθέσθαι, διὰ ταῦτ' ἀγανακτῶν ὅτι πρὸς τὴν μάχην ἀργεῖ,
φῶς ὅτι τάχιστα αἰτεῖται, ὡς πάντως τῆς ἀρετῆς εὑρήσων
ἐντάφιον ἄξιον, κἂν αὐτῷ Ζεὺς ἀντιτάττηται. 11. ἀλλὰ
γὰρ Ὅμηρος μὲν ἐνθάδε οὔριος συνεμπνεῖ τοῖς ἀγῶσιν,
καὶ οὐκ ἄλλο τι αὐτὸς πέπονθεν ἢ

25 μαίνεται, ὡς ὅτ' Ἄρης ἐγχέσπαλος ἢ ὀλοὸν πῦρ
οὔρεσι μαίνηται, βαθέης ἐνὶ τάρφεσιν ὕλης,
ἀφλοισμὸς δὲ περὶ στόμα γίγνεται·

δείκνυσι δ' ὅμως διὰ τῆς Ὀδυσσείας (καὶ γὰρ ταῦτα

---

5 ταύτῃ—9 ἐγένετο] de hoc loco, quem uncis inclusit Spengelius, vide sis
Append. C, s. n. Moses. θεσμοθέτης] libri omnes excepto cod. El. qui
θεσμοδείτης praestat. θεσμοδότης (aetatis recentioris vocabulum) in textum recipiunt
Robortellus et nuper Spengelius. 19 ἀνδρ*ίαν P. 25 ἐγχεσπάλοσ P.
27 ἀφλυσμὸσ P.

Beneath his immortal feet, as onward Poseidon strode.
Then over the surges he drave: leapt sporting before the God
Sea-beasts that uprose all round from the depths, for their king
    they knew,
And for rapture the sea was disparted, and onward the car-steeds
    flew[1].

9. Similarly, the legislator of the Jews, no ordinary man,
having formed and expressed a worthy conception of the
might of the Godhead, writes at the very beginning of his
Laws, 'God said'—what? 'Let there be light, and there
was light; let there be land, and there was land[2].' 10. Perhaps I shall not seem tedious, my friend, if I bring forward one
passage more from Homer—this time with regard to the
concerns of *men*—in order to show that he is wont himself to
enter into the sublime actions of his heroes. In his poem the
battle of the Greeks is suddenly veiled by mist and baffling
night. Then Ajax, at his wits' end, cries:

Zeus, Father, yet save thou Achaia's sons from beneath the gloom,
And make clear day, and vouchsafe unto us with our eyes to see!
So it be but in light, destroy us[3]!

That is the true attitude of an Ajax. He does not pray for
life, for such a petition would have ill beseemed a hero. But
since in the hopeless darkness he can turn his valour to no
noble end, he chafes at his slackness in the fray and craves
the boon of immediate light, resolved to find a death worthy
of his bravery, even though Zeus should fight in the ranks
against him. 11. In truth, Homer in these cases shares the
full inspiration of the combat, and it is neither more nor less
than true of the poet himself that

Mad rageth he as Arês the shaker of spears, or as mad flames
    leap
Wild-wasting from hill unto hill in the folds of a forest deep,
And the foam-froth fringeth his lips[4].

He shows, however, in the Odyssey (and this further

---

[1] *Il.* XIII. 18, XX. 60, XIII. 19, XIII. 27—29.
[2] Appendix C, *Moses*.   [3] *Il.* XVII. 645—647.
[4] *Il.* XV. 605—607.

R.   5

πολλῶν ἕνεκα προσεπιθεωρητέον), ὅτι μεγάλης φύσεως
ὑποφερομένης ἤδη ἴδιόν ἐστιν ἐν γήρᾳ τὸ φιλόμυθον.
12. δῆλος γὰρ ἐκ πολλῶν τε ἄλλων συντεθεικὼς ταύτην
δευτέραν τὴν ὑπόθεσιν, ἀτὰρ δὴ κἀκ τοῦ λείψανα τῶν
5 Ἰλιακῶν παθημάτων διὰ τῆς Ὀδυσσείας ὡς ἐπεισόδιά
τινα τοῦ Τρωϊκοῦ πολέμου προσεπεισφέρειν, καὶ νὴ Δί᾽
ἐκ τοῦ τὰς ὀλοφύρσεις καὶ τοὺς οἴκτους ὡς πάλαι που
προεγνωσμένους τοῖς ἥρωσιν ἐνταῦθα προσαποδιδόναι.
οὐ γὰρ ἀλλ᾽ ἢ τῆς Ἰλιάδος ἐπίλογός ἐστιν ἡ Ὀδύσσεια·
10 ἔνθα μὲν Αἴας κεῖται ἀρήϊος, ἔνθα δ᾽ Ἀχιλλεύς,
ἔνθα δὲ Πάτροκλος, θεόφιν μήστωρ ἀτάλαντος·
ἔνθα δ᾽ ἐμὸς φίλος υἱός.

13. ἀπὸ δὲ τῆς αὐτῆς αἰτίας, οἶμαι, τῆς μὲν Ἰλιάδος
γραφομένης ἐν ἀκμῇ πνεύματος ὅλον τὸ σωμάτιον δρα-
15 ματικὸν ὑπεστήσατο | καὶ ἐναγώνιον, τῆς δὲ Ὀδυσσείας 183ᵛ
τὸ πλέον διηγηματικόν, ὅπερ ἴδιον γήρως. ὅθεν ἐν τῇ
Ὀδυσσείᾳ παρεικάσαι τις ἂν καταδυομένῳ τὸν Ὅμηρον
ἡλίῳ, οὗ δίχα τῆς σφοδρότητος παραμένει τὸ μέγεθος.
οὐ γὰρ ἔτι τοῖς Ἰλιακοῖς ἐκείνοις ποιήμασιν ἴσον ἐνταῦθα
20 σῴζει τὸν τόνον, οὐδ᾽ ἐξωμαλισμένα τὰ ὕψη καὶ ἱζήματα
μηδαμοῦ λαμβάνοντα, οὐδὲ τὴν πρόχυσιν ὁμοίαν τῶν
ἐπαλλήλων παθῶν, οὐδὲ τὸ ἀγχίστροφον καὶ πολιτικὸν
καὶ ταῖς ἐκ τῆς ἀληθείας φαντασίαις καταπεπυκνωμένον·
ἀλλ᾽ οἷον ὑποχωροῦντος εἰς ἑαυτὸν Ὠκεανοῦ καὶ περὶ
25 τὰ ἴδια μέτρα ἐρημουμένου τὸ λοιπὸν φαίνονται τοῦ
μεγέθους ἀμπώτιδες κἂν τοῖς μυθώδεσι καὶ ἀπίστοις
πλάνος. 14. λέγων δὲ ταῦτ᾽ οὐκ ἐπιλέλησμαι τῶν ἐν
τῇ Ὀδυσσείᾳ χειμώνων καὶ τῶν περὶ τὸν Κύκλωπα καί
τινων ἄλλων, ἀλλὰ γῆρας διηγοῦμαι, γῆρας δ᾽ ὅμως
30 Ὁμήρου· πλὴν ἐν ἅπασι τούτοις ἑξῆς τοῦ πρακτικοῦ
κρατεῖ τὸ μυθικόν. παρεξέβην δ᾽ εἰς ταῦθ᾽, ὡς ἔφην, ἵνα

observation deserves attention on many grounds) that, when
a great genius is declining, the special token of old age is the
love of marvellous tales. 12. It is clear from many indications
that the Odyssey was his second subject. A special proof is
the fact that he introduces in that poem remnants of the
adventures before Ilium as episodes, so to say, of the Trojan
War. And indeed, he there renders a tribute of mourning
and lamentation to his heroes as though he were carrying out
a long-cherished purpose. In fact, the Odyssey is simply an
epilogue to the Iliad :—

There lieth Ajax the warrior wight, Achilles is there,
There is Patroclus, whose words had weight as a God he were;
There lieth mine own dear son[1].

13. It is for the same reason, I suppose, that he has made
the whole structure of the Iliad, which was written at the
height of his inspiration, full of action and conflict, while the
Odyssey for the most part consists of narrative, as is characteristic of old age. Accordingly, in the Odyssey Homer may be
likened to a sinking sun, whose grandeur remains without its
intensity. He does not in the Odyssey maintain so high a
pitch as in those poems of Ilium. His sublimities are not
evenly sustained and free from the liability to sink ; there is
not the same profusion of accumulated passions, nor the
supple and oratorical style, packed with images drawn from
real life. You seem to see henceforth the ebb and flow of
greatness, and a fancy roving in the fabulous and incredible,
as though the ocean were withdrawing into itself and were
being laid bare within its own confines. 14. In saying this
I have not forgotten the tempests in the Odyssey and the
story of the Cyclops and the like. If I speak of old age, it is
nevertheless the old age of Homer. The fabulous element,
however, prevails throughout this poem over the real. The
object of this digression has been, as I said, to show how

----

[1] *Odyss.* III. 109—111.

δείξαιμι, ὡς εἰς λῆρον ἐνίοτε ῥᾷστον κατὰ τὴν ἀπακμὴν τὰ
μεγαλοφυῆ παρατρέπεται οἷα τὰ περὶ τὸν ἀσκὸν καὶ τοὺς
ἐκ Κίρκης συοφορβουμένους, οὓς ὁ Ζωΐλος ἔφη χοιρίδια
κλαίοντα, καὶ τὸν ὑπὸ τῶν πελειάδων ὡς νεοσσὸν παρα-
5 τρεφόμενον Δία καὶ τὸν ἐπὶ τοῦ ναυαγίου δέχ᾽ ἡμέρας
ἄσιτον τά τε περὶ τὴν μνηστηροφονίαν ἀπίθανα. τί
γὰρ ἂν ἄλλο φήσαιμεν ταῦτα ἢ τῷ ὄντι τοῦ Διὸς ἐνύπνια;
15. δευτέρου δὲ εἵνεκα προσιστορείσθω τὰ κατὰ τὴν
Ὀδύσσειαν, ὅπως ᾖ σοι γνώριμον, ὡς ἡ ἀπα|κμὴ τοῦ 184ʳ
10 πάθους ἐν τοῖς μεγάλοις συγγραφεῦσι καὶ ποιηταῖς εἰς
ἦθος ἐκλύεται. τοιαῦτα γάρ που τὰ περὶ τὴν τοῦ Ὀδυσ-
σέως ἠθικῶς αὐτῷ βιολογούμενα οἰκίαν, οἱονεὶ κωμῳδία
τίς ἐστιν ἠθολογουμένη.

X

Φέρε νῦν, εἴ τι καὶ ἕτερον ἔχοιμεν ὑψηλοὺς ποιεῖν
15 τοὺς λόγους δυνάμενον, ἐπισκεψώμεθα. οὐκοῦν ἐπειδὴ
πᾶσι τοῖς πράγμασι φύσει συνεδρεύει τινὰ μόρια ταῖς
ὕλαις συνυπάρχοντα, ἐξ ἀνάγκης γένοιτ᾽ ἂν ἡμῖν ὕψους
αἴτιον τὸ τῶν ἐμφερομένων ἐκλέγειν ἀεὶ τὰ καιριώτατα
καὶ ταῦτα τῇ πρὸς ἄλληλα ἐπισυνθέσει καθάπερ ἕν τι
20 σῶμα ποιεῖν δύνασθαι. ὃ μὲν γὰρ τῇ ἐκλογῇ τὸν ἀκροατὴν
τῶν λημμάτων, ὃ δὲ τῇ πυκνώσει τῶν ἐκλελεγμένων
προσάγεται. οἷον ἡ Σαπφὼ τὰ συμβαίνοντα ταῖς ἐρωτι-
καῖς μανίαις παθήματα ἐκ τῶν παρεπομένων καὶ ἐκ τῆς
ἀληθείας αὐτῆς ἑκάστοτε λαμβάνει. ποῦ δὲ τὴν ἀρετὴν
25 ἀποδείκνυται; ὅτε τὰ ἄκρα αὐτῶν καὶ ὑπερτεταμένα δεινὴ
καὶ ἐκλέξαι καὶ εἰς ἄλληλα συνδῆσαι.

---

1 ἀπακμὴν] Manutius, ἀκμὴν P.   18 ἐμφερομένων] Tollius, ἐκφερομένων P.
20, 21 ὃ μὲν—ὃ δὲ] Pearcius, ὁ μὲν—ὁ δὲ P.

easily great natures in their decline are sometimes diverted into absurdity, as in the incident of the wine-skin and of the men who were fed like swine by Circe (*whining porkers*, as Zoilus called them), and of Zeus like a nestling nurtured by the doves, and of the hero who was without food for ten days upon the wreck, and of the incredible tale of the slaying of the suitors[1]. For what else can we term these things than veritable dreams of Zeus? 15. These observations with regard to the Odyssey should be made for another reason— in order that you may know that the genius of great poets and prose-writers, as their passion declines, finds its final expression in the delineation of character. For such are the details which Homer gives, with an eye to characterisation, of life in the home of Odysseus; they form as it were a comedy of manners.

X

Let us next consider whether we can point to anything further that contributes to sublimity of style. Now, there inhere in all things by nature certain constituents which are part and parcel of their substance. It must needs be, therefore, that we shall find one source of the sublime in the systematic selection of the most important elements, and the power of forming, by their mutual combination, what may be called one body. The former process attracts the hearer by the choice of the ideas, the latter by the aggregation of those chosen. For instance, Sappho everywhere chooses the emotions that attend delirious passion from its accompaniments in actual life. Wherein does she demonstrate her supreme excellence? In the skill with which she selects and binds together the most striking and vehement circumstances of passion :—

---

[1] *Odyss.* IX. 182, X. 17, X. 237, XII. 62, XII. 447, XXII. 79.

2. φαίνεταί μοι κῆνος ἴσος θεοῖσιν
ἔμμεν ὡνήρ, ὅστις ἐναντίος τοι
ἰζάνει, καὶ πλησίον ἁδὺ φωνεύσας ὑπακούει

5 καὶ γελαίσας ἰμερόεν, τό μοι μὰν
καρδίαν ἐν στήθεσιν ἐπτόασεν.
ὥς σε γὰρ ἴδω βροχέως με φωνᾶς
οὐδὲν ἔτ᾽ εἴκει·

ἀλλὰ κὰμ μὲν γλῶσσα ἔαγε· λεπτὸν δ᾽
10 αὐτίκα χρῷ πῦρ ὑπαδεδρόμακεν·
ὀππάτεσσι δ᾽ οὐδὲν ὄρημ᾽, ἐπιρρόμ-
βεισι δ᾽ ἄκουαι·

κὰδ δέ μ᾽ ἱδρὼς κακχέεται, τρόμος δὲ
παῖσαν ἀγρεῖ, χλωροτέρα δὲ ποίας
15 ἐμμί· τεθνάκην δ᾽ ὀλίγω | ᾽πιδεύην   184ᵛ
φαίνομαι.

ἀλλὰ πᾶν τολματόν, ἐπεὶ καὶ πένητα

3. οὐ θαυμάζεις, ὡς ὑπὸ τὸ αὐτὸ τὴν ψυχὴν τὸ σῶμα
τὰς ἀκοὰς τὴν γλῶσσαν τὰς ὄψεις τὴν χρόαν, πάνθ᾽ ὡς
20 ἀλλότρια διοιχόμενα ἐπιζητεῖ καὶ καθ᾽ ὑπεναντιώσεις ἅμα
ψύχεται κάεται, ἀλογιστεῖ φρονεῖ; ἢ γὰρ φοβεῖται ἢ
παρ᾽ ὀλίγον τέθνηκεν· ἵνα μὴ ἕν τι περὶ αὐτὴν πάθος
φαίνηται, παθῶν δὲ σύνοδος. πάντα μὲν τοιαῦτα γίνεται
περὶ τοὺς ἐρῶντας, ἡ λῆψις δ᾽ ὡς ἔφην τῶν ἄκρων καὶ ἡ
25 εἰς ταὐτὸ συναίρεσις ἀπειργάσατο τὴν ἐξοχήν· ὅνπερ
οἶμαι καὶ ἐπὶ τῶν χειμώνων τρόπον ὁ ποιητὴς ἐκλαμβάνει

1—17 In P continue scripta sunt Sapphus verba hunc in modum : φαίνεταί
μοι|κῆνοσϊσοσθεοῖσινἔμμενωνἤρο＊στισἐναντίοστοιζά|νεικαὶπλησίονἁδύφων· σαῖσὑπακούει
καὶγελᾶ＊ισὶ|μερόεντὸμὴἐμὰνκαρδίᾱνἐνστήθεσινἐπτόασεν · ὡσ|γὰρσῖδωβρόχεώσμεφωνᾶσ
οὐδὲνἔτ᾽εἴκει · ἀλλὰκᾶν|μὲνγλῶσσαἔαγελεπτὸνδ᾽αὐτίκαχρῷπῦρὑπαδεδρό|μακενὸππάτεσιδ᾽
οὐδὲνόρῆμἠἐπιρομβεῖσιδ᾽ἄκουε᾽|ἐκαδεμὶἱδρῶσϕυχρὸσκὰκχέεταιτρόμοσδὲπᾶ＊σὰ|ναγρεῖχλω-
ροτέραδὲποίασἔμμιτεθνάκηνδ᾽ὀλίγω|πιδεύσηνφαίνομαι · ἀλλὰπαντόλμα＊τονἐπεὶκαὶπέ|νη-
τα. Vide Append. A.   18 θαυμάζεις] Robortellus, θαυμάζοισ P.   ὑπὸ τὸ]
Spengelius (in proleg.), ὑπ᾽ P.   21 κάεται P.   ἀλογιστεῖ] Manutius,
ἀλογιστὶ P.   25 ὅνπερ] Manutius, ὅπερ P.   26 τῶν superscr. τὸν P.

2.   Peer of Gods he seemeth to me, the blissful
Man who sits and gazes at thee before him,
Close beside thee sits, and in silence hears thee
    Silverly speaking,

Laughing love's low laughter.   Oh this, this only
Stirs the troubled heart in my breast to tremble !
For should I but see thee a little moment,
    Straight is my voice hushed ;

Yea, my tongue is broken, and through and through me
'Neath the flesh impalpable fire runs tingling ;
Nothing see mine eyes, and a noise of roaring
    Waves in my ear sounds ;

Sweat runs down in rivers, a tremor seizes
All my limbs, and paler than grass in autumn,
Caught by pains of menacing death, I falter,
    Lost in the love-trance[1].

3.   Are you not amazed how at one instant she summons,
as though they were all alien from herself and dispersed, soul,
body, ears, tongue, eyes, colour ?   Uniting contradictions, she
is, at one and the same time, hot and cold, in her senses and
out of her mind, for she is either terrified or at the point
of death.   The effect desired is that not one passion only
should be seen in her, but a concourse of the passions.   All
such things occur in the case of lovers, but it is, as I said, the
selection of the most striking of them and their combination
into a single whole that has produced the singular excellence
of the passage.   In the same way Homer, when describing

[1] Appendix C, *Sappho.*

τῶν παρακολουθούντων τὰ χαλεπώτατα. 4. ὁ μὲν γὰρ
τὰ Ἀριμάσπεια ποιήσας ἐκεῖνα οἴεται δεινά·

θαῦμ' ἡμῖν καὶ τοῦτο μέγα φρεσὶν ἡμετέρῃσιν.
ἄνδρες ὕδωρ ναίουσιν ἀπὸ χθονὸς ἐν πελάγεσσι·
5 δύστηνοί τινές εἰσιν, ἔχουσι γὰρ ἔργα πονηρά,
ὄμματ' ἐν ἄστροισι, ψυχὴν δ' ἐνὶ πόντῳ ἔχουσιν.
ἦ που πολλὰ θεοῖσι φίλας ἀνὰ χεῖρας ἔχοντες
εὔχονται σπλάγχνοισι κακῶς ἀναβαλλομένοισι.

παντὶ οἶμαι δῆλον, ὡς πλέον ἄνθος ἔχει τὰ λεγόμενα ἢ
10 δέος. 5. ὁ δὲ Ὅμηρος πῶς; ἓν γὰρ ἀπὸ πολλῶν λε-
γέσθω·

ἐν δ' ἔπεσ', ὡς ὅτε κῦμα θοῇ ἐν νηΐ πέσῃσι
λάβρον ὑπαὶ νεφέων ἀνεμοτρεφές, ἡ δέ τε πᾶσα
ἄχνῃ ὑπεκρύφθη, ἀνέμοιο δὲ δεινὸς ἀήτης
15 ἱστίῳ ἐμβρέμεται, τρομέουσι δέ τε φρένα ναῦται
δειδιότες· τυτθὸν γὰρ ὑπὲκ θανάτοιο φέρονται.

6. ἐπεχείρησε καὶ ὁ Ἄρατος τὸ αὐτὸ τοῦτο μετενεγκεῖν,

ὀλίγον δὲ διὰ ξύλον ἄϊδ' ἐ|ρύκει· 185ʳ

πλὴν μικρὸν αὐτὸ καὶ γλαφυρὸν ἐποίησεν ἀντὶ φοβεροῦ·
20 ἔτι δὲ παρώρισε τὸν κίνδυνον, εἰπών, 'ξύλον ἄϊδ' ἀπείργει.'
οὐκοῦν ἀπείργει. ὁ δὲ ποιητὴς οὐκ εἰς ἅπαξ παρορίζει τὸ
δεινόν, ἀλλὰ τοὺς ἀεὶ καὶ μόνον οὐχὶ κατὰ πᾶν κῦμα
πολλάκις ἀπολλυμένους εἰκονογραφεῖ. καὶ μὴν τὰς προ-
θέσεις ἀσυνθέτους οὔσας συναναγκάσας παρὰ φύσιν καὶ
25 εἰς ἀλλήλας συμβιασάμενος 'ὑπὲκ θανάτοιο' τῷ μὲν
συνεμπίπτοντι πάθει τὸ ἔπος ὁμοίως ἐβασάνισεν, τῇ δὲ

---

2 ἀρ*ιμάσπεια P.   3 θαῦμ' *μιν P θαῦμ' ἡμῖν P.   4 ναίουσιν (αι
corr. in litura) P.   4 πελάγεσι P σ addidit m. rec. P.   7 ἤπου P, corr.
Manutius.   9 παντὶ* P.   10 ἢ δέος] Victorius, ἡδέως P.   16 δεδιό-
τεσ P.   16 τυτθὸν P τ addidit m. rec. P.   23 ἀπολυμμένουσ P.

tempests, picks out the most appalling circumstances. 4. The
author of the *Arimaspeia* thinks to inspire awe in the following
way :—

A marvel exceeding great is this withal to my soul—
Men dwell on the water afar from the land, where deep seas roll.
Wretches are they, for they reap but a harvest of travail and
    pain,
Their eyes on the stars ever dwell, while their hearts abide in
    the main.
Often, I ween, to the Gods are their hands upraised on high,
And with hearts in misery heavenward-lifted in prayer do they cry[1].

It is clear, I imagine, to everybody that there is more
elegance than terror in these words. 5. But what says
Homer? Let one instance be quoted from among many :—

And he burst on them like as a wave swift-rushing beneath black
    clouds,
Heaved huge by the winds, bursts down on a ship, and the wild
    foam shrouds
From the stem to the stern her hull, and the storm-blast's terrible
    breath
Roars in the sail, and the heart of the shipmen shuddereth
In fear, for that scantly upborne are they now from the clutches
    of death[2].

6. Aratus has attempted to convert this same expression
to his own use :—

And a slender plank averteth their death[3].

Only, he has made it trivial and neat instead of terrible.
Furthermore, he has put bounds to the danger by saying
A plank keeps off death. After all, it *does* keep it off. Homer,
however, does not for one moment set a limit to the terror of
the scene, but draws a vivid picture of men continually in peril
of their lives, and often within an ace of perishing with each
successive wave. Moreover, he has in the words ὑπὲκ θανάτοιο,
forced into union, by a kind of unnatural compulsion, prepositions not usually compounded. He has thus tortured his

---

[1] Appendix C, *Aristeas*.   [2] *Il.* xv. 624—628.
[3] Appendix C, *Aratus*.

τοῦ ἔπους συνθλίψει τὸ πάθος ἄκρως ἀπεπλάσατο καὶ
μόνον οὐκ ἐνετύπωσε τῇ λέξει τοῦ κινδύνου τὸ ἰδίωμα
' ὑπὲκ θανάτοιο φέρονται.' 7. οὐκ ἄλλως ὁ Ἀρχίλοχος
ἐπὶ τοῦ ναυαγίου, καὶ ἐπὶ τῇ προσαγγελίᾳ ὁ Δημοσθένης·
5 ' ἑσπέρα μὲν γὰρ ἦν,' φησίν· ἀλλὰ τὰς ἐξοχὰς ὡς ἂν
εἴποι τις ἀριστίνδην ἐκκαθήραντες ἐπισυνέθηκαν, οὐδὲν
φλοιῶδες ἢ ἄσεμνον ἢ σχολικὸν ἐγκατατάττοντες διὰ
μέσου. λυμαίνεται γὰρ ταῦτα τὸ ὅλον ὡσανεὶ ψύγματα
ἢ ἀραιώματα ἐμποιοῦντα <ἐς> μεγέθη συνοικονομούμενα
10 τῇ πρὸς ἄλληλα σχέσει συντετειχισμένα.

XI

Σύνεδρός ἐστι ταῖς προεκκειμέναις ἀρετὴ καὶ ἣν καλοῦ-
σιν αὔξησιν, ὅταν δεχομένων τῶν πραγμάτων καὶ ἀγώνων
κατὰ περιόδους ἀρχάς τε πολλὰς καὶ ἀναπαύλας ἕτερα
ἑτέροις ἐπεισκυκλούμενα μεγέθη συνεχῶς ἐπεισάγηται
15 κατ' ἐπίβασιν. 2. τοῦτο δὲ εἴτε διὰ τοπηγορίαν, εἴτε
δείνωσιν, ἢ πραγμάτων ἢ κατασκευῶν ἐπίρρωσιν, εἴτ'
ἐποικονομίαν ἔργων ἢ παθῶν | (μυρίαι γὰρ ἰδέαι τῶν 185ᵛ
αὐξήσεων) γίνοιτο, χρὴ ˙γινώσκειν ὅμως τὸν ῥήτορα,
ὡς οὐδὲν ἂν τούτων καθ' αὑτὸ συσταίη χωρὶς ὕψους
20 τέλειον, πλὴν εἰ μὴ ἐν οἴκτοις ἄρα, νὴ Δία, ἢ ἐν εὐτε-
λισμοῖς, τῶν δ' ἄλλων αὐξητικῶν ὅτου περ ἂν τὸ ὑψηλὸν
ἀφέλῃς, ὡς ψυχὴν ἐξαιρήσεις σώματος· εὐθὺς γὰρ ἀτονεῖ
καὶ κενοῦται τὸ ἔμπρακτον αὐτῶν μὴ τοῖς ὕψεσι συνεπιρ-
ρωννύμενον. 3. ᾗ μέντοι διαφέρει τοῦ ἀρτίως εἰρημένου
25 τὰ νῦν παραγγελλόμενα (περιγραφὴ γάρ τις ἦν ἐκεῖνο

---

2 μόνονοὐκ corr. in μονονοὐκ P. 3 φέρονται] Manutius, φέροντα P.
5 ἦν P corr. P. ὡς ἂν] Ruhnkenius, ὡς P. 6 ἀριστ*∗δην P ἀριστίνδην P.
7 διαμέσου P. 9 αι P ῇ superscripsit m. rec. P. <ἐς> vide Append. A.
10 συντετειχι∗σμένα P. 15 **τε διὰ P εἴτε διὰ P. 18 γίνοιτο (post
parenthesin) Morus: γίνοιντο P. γινώ∗|σκειν P. 23 συνεπιρρωνύμενον P.
24 διαφέρει P διαφέρῃ P.

line into the similitude of the impending calamity, and by
constriction of the verse has excellently figured the disaster,
and almost stamped upon the expression the very form and
pressure of the danger, ὑπὲκ θανάτοιο φέρονται. 7. This
is true also of Archilochus in his account of the shipwreck,
and of Demosthenes in the passage which begins 'It was
evening,' where he describes the bringing of the news[1]. The
salient points they selected, one might say, according to
merit and massed them together, inserting in the midst nothing
frivolous, mean, or trivial. For these faults mar the effect
of the whole, just as though they introduced chinks or fissures
into stately and co-ordered edifices, whose walls are com-
pacted by their reciprocal adjustment.

XI

An allied excellence to those already set forth is that
which is termed *amplification.* This figure is employed when
the narrative or the course of a forensic argument admits, from
section to section, of many starting-points and many pauses,
and elevated expressions follow, one after the other, in an
unbroken succession and in an ascending order. 2. And
this may be effected either by way of the rhetorical treatment
of commonplaces, or by way of intensification (whether events
or arguments are to be strongly presented), or by the orderly
arrangement of facts or of passions ; indeed, there are innumerable kinds of amplification. Only, the orator must in
every case remember that none of these methods by itself,
apart from sublimity, forms a complete whole, unless indeed
where pity is to be excited or an opponent to be disparaged.
In all other cases of amplification, if you take away the
sublime, you will remove as it were the soul from the body.
For the vigour of the amplification at once loses its intensity
and its substance when not resting on a firm basis of the
sublime. 3. Clearness, however, demands that we should
define concisely how our present precepts differ from the

[1] Demosth. *De Cor.*, 169.

τῶν ἄκρων λημμάτων καὶ εἰς ἑνότητα σύνταξις), καὶ τίνι
καθόλου τῶν αὐξήσεων παραλλάττει τὰ ὕψη, τῆς σαφηνείας
αὐτῆς ἕνεκα συντόμως διοριστέον.

XII

Ὁ μὲν οὖν τῶν τεχνογράφων ὅρος ἔμοιγ' οὐκ ἀρεστός.
5 αὔξησίς ἐστι, φασί, λόγος μέγεθος περιτιθεὶς τοῖς ὑπο-
κειμένοις· δύναται γὰρ ἀμέλει καὶ ὕψους καὶ πάθους καὶ
τρόπων εἶναι κοινὸς οὗτος ὁ ὅρος, ἐπειδὴ κἀκεῖνα τῷ λόγῳ
περιτίθησι ποιόν τι μέγεθος. ἐμοὶ δὲ φαίνεται ταῦτα
ἀλλήλων παραλλάττειν, ᾗ κεῖται τὸ μὲν ὕψος ἐν διάρματι,
10 ἡ δ' αὔξησις καὶ ἐν πλήθει· διὸ κεῖνο μὲν κἂν νοήματι
ἑνὶ πολλάκις, ἡ δὲ πάντως μετὰ ποσότητος καὶ περιουσίας
τινὸς ὑφίσταται. 2. καὶ ἔστιν ἡ αὔξησις, ὡς τύπῳ
περιλαβεῖν, συμπλήρωσις ἀπὸ πάντων τῶν ἐμφερομένων
τοῖς πράγμασι μορίων καὶ τόπων, ἰσχυροποιοῦσα τῇ
15 ἐπιμονῇ τὸ κατεσκευασμένον, ταύτῃ τῆς πίστεως διεστῶσα,
ὅτι ἡ μὲν τὸ ζητούμενον ἀποδεί[κνυσιν . . .

DESVNT DVO FOLIA

. . . | πλουσιώτατα, καθάπερ τι πέλαγος, εἰς ἀναπεπτα- 186ʳ
μένον κέχυται πολλαχῇ μέγεθος. 3. ὅθεν, οἶμαι, κατὰ
λόγον ὁ μὲν ῥήτωρ ἅτε παθητικώτερος πολὺ τὸ διάπυρον
20 ἔχει καὶ θυμικῶς ἐκφλεγόμενον, ὁ δὲ καθεστὼς ἐν ὄγκῳ
καὶ μεγαλοπρεπεῖ σεμνότητι, οὐκ ἔψυκται μέν, ἀλλ' οὐχ
οὕτως ἐπέστραπται. 4. οὐ κατ' ἄλλα δέ τινα ἢ ταῦτα,
ἐμοὶ δοκεῖ, φίλτατε Τερεντιανέ, (λέγω δέ, εἰ καὶ ἡμῖν ὡς
Ἕλλησιν ἐφεῖταί τι γινώσκειν) καὶ ὁ Κικέρων τοῦ Δημο-
25 σθένους ἐν τοῖς μεγέθεσι παραλλάττει· ὁ μὲν γὰρ ἐν ὕψει
τὸ πλέον ἀποτόμῳ, ὁ δὲ Κικέρων ἐν χύσει, καὶ ὁ μὲν

---

2 παραλάττει P.   4 ὅρος αὐξήσεως in marg. P.   7 ὁ add. Manutius.
14 πράγμασι μορίων] Portus, πράγμασινορίων P.   16 ἀποδείκνυσιν] Manutius, ἀποδεί P : desunt folia quartum et quintum quaternionis Kϛ.   23 εἰ add.
Manutius.   25 τίνι παραλάτει Κικέρων Δημοσθένους in marg. P.

point under consideration a moment ago, namely the marking-out of the most striking conceptions and the unification of them; and wherein, generally, the sublime differs from amplification.

XII

Now the definition given by the writers on rhetoric does not satisfy me. Amplification is, say they, discourse which invests the subject with grandeur[1]. This definition, however, would surely apply in equal measure to sublimity and passion and figurative language, since they too invest the discourse with a certain degree of grandeur. The point of distinction between them seems to me to be that sublimity consists in elevation, while amplification embraces a multitude of details. Consequently, sublimity is often comprised in a single thought, while amplification is universally associated with a certain magnitude and abundance. 2. Amplification (to sum the matter up in a general way) is an aggregation of all the constituent parts and topics of a subject, lending strength to the argument by dwelling upon it, and differing herein from proof that, while the latter demonstrates the matter under investigation………

With his vast riches Plato swells, like some sea, into a greatness which expands on every side. 3. Wherefore it is, I suppose, that the orator[2] in his utterance shows, as one who appeals more to the passions, all the glow of a fiery spirit. Plato, on the other hand, firm-planted in his pride and magnificent stateliness, cannot indeed be accused of coldness, but he has not the same vehemence. 4. And it is in these same respects, my dear friend Terentianus, that it seems to me (supposing always that we Greeks are allowed to have an opinion upon the point) that Cicero differs from Demosthenes in elevated passages. For the latter is characterised by sublimity which is for the most part rugged, Cicero by

---

[1] Appendix C, *Scr. Inc.* (4).   [2] Sc. Demosthenes.

ἡμέτερος διὰ τὸ μετὰ βίας ἕκαστα, ἔτι δὲ τάχ⬤ς ῥώμης
δεινότητος οἷον καίειν τε ἅμα καὶ διαρπάζειν, σκηπτῷ τινι
παρεικάζοιτ᾽ ἂν ἢ κεραυνῷ, ὁ δὲ Κικέρων ὡς ἀμφιλαφής
τις ἐμπρησμὸς οἶμαι πάντη νέμεται καὶ ἀνειλεῖται, πολὺ
5 ἔχων καὶ ἐπίμονον ἀεὶ τὸ καῖον, καὶ διακληρονομούμενον
ἄλλοτ᾽ ἀλλοίως ἐν αὑτῷ καὶ κατὰ διαδοχὰς ἀνατρεφόμενον.
5. ἀλλὰ ταῦτα μὲν ὑμεῖς ἂν ἄμεινον ἐπικρίνοιτε, καιρὸς
δὲ τοῦ Δημοσθενικοῦ μὲν ὕψους καὶ ὑπερτεταμένου ἔν τε
ταῖς δεινώσεσι καὶ τοῖς σφοδροῖς πάθεσι, καὶ ἔνθα δεῖ
10 τὸν ἀκροατὴν τὸ σύνολον ἐκπλῆξαι, τῆς δὲ χύσεως, ὅπου
χρὴ καταντλῆσαι· τοπηγορίαις τε γὰρ καὶ ἐπιλόγοις κατὰ
τὸ πλέον καὶ παραβάσεσι καὶ τοῖς φραστικοῖς ἅπασι καὶ
ἐπιδεικτικοῖς, ἱστορίαις τε καὶ φυσιολογίαις, καὶ οὐκ
ὀλίγοις ἄλλοις μέρεσιν ἁρμόδιος.

XIII

15 Ὅτι μέντοι ὁ Πλάτων (ἐπάνειμι γάρ) τοιούτῳ τινὶ
χεύματι ἀψοφητὶ ῥέων | οὐδὲν ἧττον μεγεθύνεται, ἀνεγνω- 186ᵛ
κὼς τὰ ἐν τῇ Πολιτείᾳ τὸν τύπον οὐκ ἀγνοεῖς. ΄οἱ ἄρα
φρονήσεως᾽ φησὶ ΄καὶ ἀρετῆς ἄπειροι εὐωχίαις δὲ καὶ
τοῖς τοιούτοις ἀεὶ συνόντες κάτω ὡς ἔοικε φέρονται καὶ
20 ταύτῃ πλανῶνται διὰ βίου, πρὸς δὲ τὸ ἀληθὲς ἄνω οὔτ᾽
ἀνέβλεψαν πώποτε οὔτ᾽ ἀνηνέχθησαν οὐδὲ βεβαίου τε καὶ
καθαρᾶς ἡδονῆς ἐγεύσαντο, ἀλλὰ βοσκημάτων δίκην κάτω
ἀεὶ βλέποντες καὶ κεκυφότες εἰς γῆν καὶ εἰς τραπέζας
βόσκονται χορταζόμενοι καὶ ὀχεύοντες, καὶ ἕνεκα τῆς
25 τούτων πλεονεξίας λακτίζοντες καὶ κυρίττοντες ἀλλήλους
σιδηροῖς κέρασι καὶ ὁπλαῖς ἀποκτιννύουσι δι᾽ ἀπληστίαν.᾽
2. Ἐνδείκνυται δ᾽ ἡμῖν οὗτος ἀνήρ, εἰ βουλοίμεθα

---

4 ἐμπρησμὸσ P ἐμπρισμὸσ P.   5 διακληρονομ**μενον P διακληρονο-
μούμενον P.   8 δημο*‖σθενικοῦ P.   μούμενον P.   10 ἀκρο‖ατὴν (ο corr. in ras.) P.
14 ἁρμόδιο*σ P.   17 πολι*τείαι P.   25 ἀλλήλουσ] codices Platonis,
ἀλλήλοισ P.   27 ἀνὴρ P.

profusion. Our orator[1], owing to the fact that in his vehemence,—aye, and in his speed, power and intensity,—he can
as it were consume by fire and carry away all before him, may
be compared to a thunderbolt or flash of lightning. Cicero, on
the other hand, it seems to me, after the manner of a widespread conflagration, rolls on with all-devouring flames, having
within him an ample and abiding store of fire, distributed now
at this point now at that, and fed by an unceasing succession.
5. This, however, you[2] will be better able to decide ; but the
great opportunity of Demosthenes' high-pitched elevation
comes where intense utterance and vehement passion are in
question, and in passages in which the audience is to be
utterly enthralled. The profusion of Cicero is in place where
the hearer must be flooded with words, for it is appropriate to
the treatment of commonplaces, and to perorations for the
most part and digressions, and to all descriptive and declamatory passages, and to writings on history and natural science,
and to many other departments of literature.

XIII

To return from my digression. Although Plato thus flows
on with noiseless stream, he is none the less elevated. You
know this because you have read the *Republic* and are familiar
with his manner. 'Those,' says he, 'who are destitute of
wisdom and goodness and are ever present at carousals and
the like are carried on the downward path, it seems, and
wander thus throughout their life. They never look upwards
to the truth, nor do they lift their heads, nor enjoy any pure
and lasting pleasure, but like cattle they have their eyes ever
cast downwards and bent upon the ground and upon their
feeding-places, and they graze and grow fat and breed, and
through their insatiate desire of these delights they kick and
butt with horns and hoofs of iron and kill one another in
their greed[3].'

2. This writer shows us, if only we were willing to pay

---

[1] Sc. Demosthenes.   [2] Sc. 'you Romans.'   [3] Pl. *Rep.* IX. 586 A.

μὴ κατολιγωρεῖν, ὡς καὶ ἄλλη τις παρὰ τὰ εἰρημένα ὁδὸς
ἐπὶ τὰ ὑψηλὰ τείνει. ποία δὲ καὶ τίς αὕτη; ἡ τῶν
ἔμπροσθεν μεγάλων συγγραφέων καὶ ποιητῶν μίμησίς
τε καὶ ζήλωσις. καί γε τούτου, φίλτατε, ἀπρὶξ ἐχώμεθα
5 τοῦ σκοποῦ· πολλοὶ γὰρ ἀλλοτρίῳ θεοφοροῦνται πνεύματι
τὸν αὐτὸν τρόπον, ὃν καὶ τὴν Πυθίαν λόγος ἔχει τρίποδι
πλησιάζουσαν, ἔνθα ῥῆγμά ἐστι γῆς ἀναπνεῖν ὥς φασιν
ἀτμὸν ἔνθεον, αὐτόθεν ἐγκύμονα τῆς δαιμονίου καθιστα-
μένην δυνάμεως παραυτίκα χρησμῳδεῖν κατ᾽ ἐπίπνοιαν.
10 οὕτως ἀπὸ τῆς τῶν ἀρχαίων μεγαλοφυΐας εἰς τὰς τῶν
ζηλούντων ἐκείνους ψυχὰς ὡς ἀπὸ ἱερῶν στομίων ἀπόρροιαί
τινες φέρονται, ὑφ᾽ ὧν ἐπι|πνεόμενοι καὶ οἱ μὴ λίαν 187
φοιβαστικοὶ τῷ ἑτέρων συνενθουσιῶσι μεγέθει.　3. μόνος
Ἡρόδοτος Ὁμηρικώτατος ἐγένετο; Στησίχορος ἔτι πρό-
15 τερον ὅ τε Ἀρχίλοχος, πάντων δὲ τούτων μάλιστα ὁ
Πλάτων ἀπὸ τοῦ Ὁμηρικοῦ κείνου νάματος εἰς αὐτὸν
μυρίας ὅσας παρατροπὰς ἀποχετευσάμενος. καὶ ἴσως
ἡμῖν ἀποδείξεων ἔδει, εἰ μὴ τὰ ἐπ᾽ εἴδους καὶ οἱ περὶ
Ἀμμώνιον ἐκλέξαντες ἀνέγραψαν.　4. ἔστι δ᾽ οὐ κλοπὴ
20 τὸ πρᾶγμα, ἀλλ᾽ ὡς ἀπὸ καλῶν εἰδῶν ἢ πλασμάτων ἢ
δημιουργημάτων ἀποτύπωσις. καὶ οὐδ᾽ ἂν ἐπακμάσαι
μοι δοκεῖ τηλικαῦτά τινα τοῖς τῆς φιλοσοφίας δόγμασι,
καὶ εἰς ποιητικὰς ὕλας πολλαχοῦ συνεμβῆναι καὶ φράσεις
εἰ μὴ περὶ πρωτείων νὴ Δία παντὶ θυμῷ πρὸς Ὅμηρον,
25 ὡς ἀνταγωνιστὴς νέος πρὸς ἤδη τεθαυμασμένον, ἴσως μὲν
φιλονεικότερον καὶ οἱονεὶ διαδορατιζόμενος, οὐκ ἀνωφελῶς
δ᾽ ὅμως διηριστεύετο· ᾽ἀγαθὴ᾽ γὰρ κατὰ τὸν Ἡσίοδον
᾽ἔρις ἥδε βροτοῖσι.᾽ καὶ τῷ ὄντι καλὸς οὗτος καὶ ἀξιονι-
κότατος εὐκλείας ἀγών τε καὶ στέφανος, ἐν ᾧ καὶ τὸ
30 ἡττᾶσθαι τῶν προγενεστέρων οὐκ ἄδοξον.

2 ἡ] Manutius, om. P.　　4 φίλ*τατε P.　　　ἐχόμεθα P ἐχώμεθα P.
15 ὅ τε] Manutius, ὅ γε P.　　16 αὐτὸν P, corr. Faber.　　18 ἐπ᾽ εἴδους]
Faber, ἐπ᾽ ινδοῦσ P, item p. 154. 5 ἐπιδούσ.　　20 εἰδῶν] Tollius, ἠθῶν P.
22 τοῖς om. P superscr. m. rec. P.　　28 ἀξιονικό*τατοσ P.

him heed, that another way (beyond anything we have mentioned) leads to the sublime. And what, and what manner of
way, may that be? It is the imitation and emulation of
previous great poets and writers. And let this, my dear
friend, be an aim to which we steadfastly apply ourselves. For
many men are carried away by the spirit of others as if
inspired, just as it is related of the Pythian priestess when she
approaches the tripod, where there is a rift in the ground which
(they say) exhales divine vapour. By heavenly power thus
communicated she is impregnated and straightway delivers
oracles in virtue of the afflatus. Similarly from the great
natures of the men of old there are borne in upon the souls of
those who emulate them (as from sacred caves) what we may
describe as *effluences*, so that even those who seem little likely
to be possessed are thereby inspired and succumb to the spell
of the others' greatness.   3.   Was Herodotus alone a devoted
imitator of Homer? No, Stesichorus even before his time,
and Archilochus, and above all Plato, who from the great
Homeric source drew to himself innumerable tributary streams.
And perhaps we should have found it necessary to prove this,
point by point, had not Ammonius and his followers selected
and recorded the particulars.   4.   This proceeding is not
plagiarism; it is like taking an impression from beautiful forms
or figures or other works of art. And it seems to me that
there would not have been so fine a bloom of perfection on
Plato's philosophical doctrines, and that he would not in many
cases have found his way to poetical subject-matter and
modes of expression, unless he had with all his heart and
mind struggled with Homer for the primacy, entering the lists
like a young champion matched against the man whom all
admire, and showing perhaps too much love of contention
and breaking a lance with him as it were, but deriving some
profit from the contest none the less. For, as Hesiod says,
'This strife is good for mortals[1].' And in truth that struggle
for the crown of glory is noble and best deserves the victory
in which even to be worsted by one's predecessors brings
no discredit.

[1] Hes. *Op. et D.* 24.

R.   6

XIV

Οὐκοῦν καὶ ἡμᾶς, ἡνίκ' ἂν διαπονῶμεν ὑψηγορίας τι
καὶ μεγαλοφροσύνης δεόμενον, καλὸν ἀναπλάττεσθαι ταῖς
ψυχαῖς, πῶς ἂν εἰ τύχοι ταὐτὸ τοῦθ' Ὅμηρος εἶπεν, πῶς δ'
ἂν Πλάτων ἢ Δημοσθένης ὕψωσαν ἢ ἐν ἱστορίᾳ Θουκυ-
5 δίδης. προσπίπτοντα γὰρ ἡμῖν κατὰ ζῆλον ἐκεῖνα τὰ
πρόσωπα καὶ οἷον | διαπρέποντα, τὰς ψυχὰς ἀνοίσει πως 187
πρὸς τὰ ἀνειδωλοποιούμενα μέτρα·   2. ἔτι δὲ μᾶλλον, εἰ
κἀκεῖνο τῇ διανοίᾳ προσυπογράφοιμεν, πῶς ἂν τόδε τι ὑπ'
ἐμοῦ λεγόμενον παρὼν Ὅμηρος ἤκουσεν ἢ Δημοσθένης,
10 ἢ πῶς ἂν ἐπὶ τούτῳ διετέθησαν· τῷ γὰρ ὄντι μέγα τὸ
ἀγώνισμα, τοιοῦτον ὑποτίθεσθαι τῶν ἰδίων λόγων δικαστήριον καὶ θέατρον, καὶ ἐν τηλικούτοις ἥρωσι κριταῖς τε
καὶ μάρτυσιν ὑπέχειν τῶν γραφομένων εὐθύνας πεπαῖχθαι.
3. πλέον δὲ τούτων παρορμητικόν, εἰ προστιθείης, πῶς
15 ἂν ἐμοῦ ταῦτα γράψαντος ὁ μετ' ἐμὲ πᾶς ἀκούσειεν αἰών;
εἰ δέ τις αὐτόθεν φοβοῖτο, μὴ τοῦ ἰδίου βίου καὶ χρόνου
φθέγξαιτό τι ὑπερήμερον, ἀνάγκη καὶ τὰ συλλαμβανόμενα
ὑπὸ τῆς τούτου ψυχῆς ἀτελῆ καὶ τυφλὰ ὥσπερ ἀμβλοῦσθαι, πρὸς τὸν τῆς ὑστεροφημίας ὅλως μὴ τελεσφορούμενα
20 χρόνον.

XV

Ὄγκου καὶ μεγαληγορίας καὶ ἀγῶνος ἐπὶ τούτοις, ὦ
νεανία, καὶ αἱ φαντασίαι παρασκευαστικώταται· οὕτω
γοῦν εἰδωλοποιίας αὐτὰς ἔνιοι λέγουσι· καλεῖται μὲν γὰρ
κοινῶς φαντασία πᾶν τὸ ὁπωσοῦν ἐννόημα γεννητικὸν
25 λόγου παριστάμενον· ἤδη δ' ἐπὶ τούτων κεκράτηκε τοῦ-
νομα, ὅταν ἃ λέγεις ὑπ' ἐνθουσιασμοῦ καὶ πάθους βλέπειν

---

5 προσπίπτοντα] Manutius, προπίπτοντα P.   10 τοῦτο P τούτω P.
13 πεπ**χθαι P πεπαῖχθαι P.   Vide Append. A.   26 λέγησ P, corr.
Spengelius.

XIV

continuation of imitation

Accordingly, it is well that we ourselves also, when elaborating anything which requires lofty expression and elevated conception, should shape some idea in our minds as to how perchance Homer would have said this very thing, or how it would have been raised to the sublime by Plato or Demosthenes or by the historian Thucydides. For those personages, presenting themselves to us and inflaming our ardour and as it were illumining our path, will carry our minds in a mysterious way to the high standards of sublimity which are imaged within us. 2. Still more effectual will it be to suggest this question to our thoughts, 'What sort of hearing would Homer, had he been present, or Demosthenes have given to this or that when said by me, or how would they have been affected by the other?' For the ordeal is indeed a severe one, if we presuppose such a tribunal and theatre for our own utterances, and imagine that we are undergoing a scrutiny of our writings before these great heroes, acting as judges and witnesses. 3. A greater incentive still will be supplied if you add the question, 'In what spirit will each succeeding age listen to me who have written thus?' But if one shrinks from the very thought of uttering aught that may transcend the term of his own life and time, the conceptions of his mind must necessarily be incomplete, blind, and as it were untimely born, since they are by no means brought to the perfection needed to ensure a futurity of fame.

XV

Images, moreover, contribute greatly, my young friend, to dignity, elevation, and power as a pleader. In this sense some call them mental representations. In a general way the name of *image* or *imagination* is applied to every idea of the mind, in whatever form it presents itself, which gives birth to speech. But at the present day the word is predominantly used in cases where, carried away by enthusiasm and passion,

δοκῇς καὶ ὑπ' ὄψιν τιθῇς τοῖς ἀκούουσιν. 2. ὡς δ'
ἕτερόν τι ἡ ῥητορικὴ φαντασία βούλεται καὶ ἕτερον ἡ
παρὰ ποιηταῖς, οὐκ ἂν λάθοι σε, οὐδ' ὅτι τῆς | μὲν ἐν   188
ποιήσει τέλος ἐστὶν ἔκπληξις, τῆς δ' ἐν λόγοις ἐνάργεια.
5 ἀμφότεραι δ' ὅμως τό τε < παθητικὸν > ἐπιζητοῦσι καὶ τὸ
συγκεκινημένον.

    ὦ μῆτερ ἱκετεύω σε, μὴ 'πίσειέ μοι
    τὰς αἱματωποὺς καὶ δρακοντώδεις κόρας·
    αὗται γάρ, αὗται πλησίον θρώσκουσί μου.
10 καὶ

    οἴμοι, κτανεῖ με· ποῖ φύγω;

ἐνταῦθ' ὁ ποιητὴς αὐτὸς εἶδεν Ἐρινύας· ὃ δὲ ἐφαντάσθη,
μικροῦ δεῖν θεάσασθαι καὶ τοὺς ἀκούοντας ἠνάγκασεν. 3.
ἔστι μὲν οὖν φιλοπονώτατος ὁ Εὐριπίδης δύο ταυτὶ
15 πάθη, μανίας τε καὶ ἔρωτας, ἐκτραγῳδῆσαι, κἀν τούτοις
ὡς οὐκ οἶδ' εἴ τισιν ἑτέροις ἐπιτυχέστατος, οὐ μὴν ἀλλὰ
καὶ ταῖς ἄλλαις ἐπιτίθεσθαι φαντασίαις οὐκ ἄτολμος.
ἥκιστά γέ τοι μεγαλοφυὴς ὢν ὅμως τὴν αὐτὸς αὑτοῦ
φύσιν ἐν πολλοῖς γενέσθαι τραγικὴν προσηνάγκασεν,
20 καὶ παρ' ἕκαστα ἐπὶ τῶν μεγεθῶν, ὡς ὁ ποιητής,

    οὐρῇ δὲ πλευράς τε καὶ ἰσχίον ἀμφοτέρωθεν
    μαστίεται, ἑὲ δ' αὐτὸν ἐποτρύνει μαχέσασθαι.

4. τῷ γοῦν Φαέθοντι παραδιδοὺς τὰς ἡνίας ὁ Ἥλιος,

    ἔλα δὲ μήτε Λιβυκὸν αἰθέρ' εἰσβαλών·
25   κρᾶσιν γὰρ ὑγρὰν οὐκ ἔχων, ἀψῖδα σὴν
    κάτω διήσει,

φησίν, εἶθ' ἑξῆς,

2 ἢ παρὰ P.   3 λάθοι* P.   ἐμποιήσει* P.   5 τό τε] P, παθη-
τικὸν add. Kayserus.   12 ὁ P, corr. Manutius.   16 ἑτέ*|ροισ P.
22 ἑὲ] codd. Homeri, ἐ P.   μαχέσασθαι] codd. Homeri, μάχεσθαι P.
25 ἀψίδας ἣν P, corr. Faber.   26 δίεισι P, corr. Faber.

you think you see what you describe, and you place it before
the eyes of your hearers. 2. Further, you will be aware of
the fact that an image has one purpose with the orators and
another with the poets, and that the design of the poetical
image is enthralment, of the rhetorical—vivid description.
Both, however, seek to stir the passions and the emotions.

> Mother!—'beseech thee, hark not thou on me
> Yon maidens gory-eyed and snaky-haired!
> Lo there!—lo there!—they are nigh—they leap on me[1]!

And:

> Ah! she will slay me! whither can I fly[2]?

In these scenes the poet himself saw Furies, and the image
in his mind he almost compelled his audience also to behold.
3. Now, Euripides is most assiduous in giving the utmost
tragic effect to these two emotions—fits of love and madness.
Herein he succeeds more, perhaps, than in any other respect,
although he is daring enough to invade all the other regions
of the imagination. Notwithstanding that he is by nature
anything but elevated, he forces his own genius, in many
passages, to tragic heights, and everywhere in the matter of
sublimity it is true of him (to adopt Homer's words) that

The tail of him scourgeth his ribs and his flanks to left and to
  right,
And he lasheth himself into frenzy, and spurreth him on to the
  fight[3].

4. When the Sun hands the reins to Phaethon, he says

> 'Thou, driving, trespass not on Libya's sky,
> Whose heat, by dews untempered, else shall split
> Thy car asunder.'

And after that,

---

[1] Eurip. *Orest.* 255.   [2] Eurip. *Iph. in T.* 291.
[3] *Il.* XX. 170, 1.

ἵει δ' ἐφ' ἑπτὰ Πλειάδων ἔχων δρόμον.
τοσαῦτ' ἀκούσας εἶτ' ἔμαρψεν ἡνίας·
κρούσας δὲ πλευρὰ πτεροφόρων ὀχημάτων
μεθῆκεν, αἱ δ' ἔπταντ' ἐπ' αἰθέρος πτύχας.
5 πατὴρ δ' ὄπισθε νῶτα Σειρίου βεβὼς
ἵππευε, παῖδα νουθετῶν· ἐκεῖσ' ἔλα,
τῇδε στρέφ' ἅρμα, τῇδε.

ἆρ' οὐκ ἂν εἴποις, ὅτι ἡ ψυχὴ τοῦ γράφοντος συνε|πιβαίνει 188
τοῦ ἅρματος, καὶ συγκινδυνεύουσα τοῖς ἵπποις συνεπτέ-
10 ρωται; οὐ γὰρ ἄν, εἰ μὴ τοῖς οὐρανίοις ἐκείνοις ἔργοις
ἰσοδρομοῦσα ἐφέρετο, τοιαῦτ' ἄν ποτε ἐφαντάσθη. ὅμοια
καὶ τὰ ἐπὶ τῆς Κασσάνδρας αὐτῷ,

ἀλλ', ὦ φίλιπποι Τρῶες.

5. τοῦ δ' Αἰσχύλου φαντασίαις ἐπιτολμῶντος ἡρωϊκω-
15 τάταις, ὥσπερ καὶ οἱ Ἑπτὰ ἐπὶ Θήβας παρ' αὐτῷ,

ἄνδρες (φησὶν) ἑπτὰ θούριοι λοχαγέται,
ταυροσφαγοῦντες εἰς μελάνδετον σάκος,
καὶ θιγγάνοντες χερσὶ ταυρείου φόνου,
Ἄρη τ' Ἐννὼ καὶ φιλαίματον Φόβον
20 ὁρκωμότησαν,

τὸν ἴδιον αὐτῶν πρὸς ἀλλήλους δίχα οἴκτου συνομνύμενοι
θάνατον, ἐνίοτε μέντοι ἀκατεργάστους καὶ οἱονεὶ ποκοειδεῖς
τὰς ἐννοίας καὶ ἀμαλάκτους φέροντος, ὅμως ἑαυτὸν ὁ
Εὐριπίδης κἀκείνοις ὑπὸ φιλοτιμίας τοῖς κινδύνοις προσ-
25 βιβάζει. 6. καὶ παρὰ μὲν Αἰσχύλῳ παραδόξως τὰ τοῦ
Λυκούργου βασίλεια κατὰ τὴν ἐπιφάνειαν τοῦ Διονύσου

---

2   τοσαῦ*|τ' (τ posterius a m. rec.) P—ex τόσαῦτ' | videlicet.   εἶτ'] Manutius,
τις P, παῖς Grotio auctore Vahlenus.   4 ἔπταντο P.   5 ὄπισθεν ὦτα P,
corr. Manutius.   6, 7 ἐκεῖσ' ἔλα, τῇδε στρέφ'] Portus, ἐκεῖσε ἐλατῆρα ἔστρεφ' P.
9 σ**κινδυνεύουσα P συγκινδυνεύουσα P.   15 οἱ] Morus, om. P.   18 θιγγάνοντες
χερσὶ] Robortellus, θιγγάνοντισ χερσὶ P.   21 αὐτῶν P.   22 ποκοειδέσ in
marg. P.   23 ἀμαλάκτους φέροντοσ] Manutius, ἀναλάκτουσ φέροντασ P.
24 φιλ***|μίασ P φιλοτι|μίας P.   25 αἰ*|σχύλω P.

'Speed onward toward the Pleiads seven thy course.'
Thus far the boy heard; then he snatched the reins :
He lashed the flanks of that wing-wafted team ;
Loosed rein ; and they through folds of cloudland soared.
Hard after on a fiery star his sire
Rode, counselling his son—'Ho ! thither drive !
Hither thy car turn—hither[1] !'

Would you not say that the soul of the writer enters the chariot at the same moment as Phaethon and shares in his dangers and in the rapid flight of his steeds? For it could never have conceived such a picture had it not been borne in no less swift career on that journey through the heavens. The same is true of the words which Euripides attributes to his Cassandra :—

O chariot-loving Trojans[2].

5.   Aeschylus, too, ventures on images of a most heroic stamp. An example will be found in his *Seven against Thebes*, where he says

For seven heroes, squadron-captains fierce,
Over a black-rimmed shield have slain a bull,
And, dipping in the bull's blood each his hand,
By Ares and Enyo, and by Panic
Lover of blood, have sworn[3].

In mutual fealty they devoted themselves by that joint oath to a relentless doom.   Sometimes, however, he introduces ideas that are rough-hewn and uncouth and harsh ; and Euripides, when stirred by the spirit of emulation, comes perilously near the same fault, even in spite of his own natural bent.   6.   Thus in Aeschylus the palace of Lycurgus

---

[1] Appendix C, *Euripides*.   [2] Appendix C, *Euripides*.
[3] Aesch. *S. c. Th.* 42.

θεοφορεῖται,

ἐνθουσιᾷ δὴ δῶμα, βακχεύει στέγη·

ὁ δ᾽ Εὐριπίδης τὸ αὐτὸ τοῦθ᾽ ἑτέρως ἐφηδύνας ἐξεφώνησε,

πᾶν δὲ συνεβάκχευ᾽ ὄρος.

5 7. ἄκρως δὲ καὶ ὁ Σοφοκλῆς ἐπὶ τοῦ θνήσκοντος Οἰδίπου
καὶ ἑαυτὸν μετὰ διοσημείας τινὸς θάπτοντος πεφάντασται,
καὶ κατὰ τὸν ἀπόπλουν τῶν Ἑλλήνων ἐπὶ τἀχιλλέως
προφαινομένου τοῖς ἀναγομένοις ὑπὲρ τοῦ τάφου, ἣν οὐκ
οἶδ᾽ εἴ τις ὄψιν ἐναργέστερον εἰδωλοποίησε Σιμωνίδου·
10 πάντα δ᾽ ἀμήχανον παρατίθεσθαι. 8. οὐ μὴν ἀλλὰ τὰ
μὲν παρὰ τοῖς ποιηταῖς μυθικωτέ|ραν ἔχει τὴν ὑπερέκπτω- 189
σιν, ὡς ἔφην, καὶ πάντη τὸ πιστὸν ὑπεραίρουσαν, τῆς δὲ
ῥητορικῆς φαντασίας κάλλιστον ἀεὶ τὸ ἔμπρακτον καὶ
ἐνάληθες. δειναὶ δὲ καὶ ἔκφυλοι αἱ παραβάσεις, ἡνίκ᾽
15 ἂν ᾖ ποιητικὸν τοῦ λόγου καὶ μυθῶδες τὸ πλάσμα καὶ
εἰς πᾶν προσεκπῖπτον τὸ ἀδύνατον, ὡς ἤδη νὴ Δία καὶ οἱ
καθ᾽ ἡμᾶς δεινοὶ ῥήτορες, καθάπερ οἱ τραγῳδοί, βλέπουσιν
Ἐρινύας, καὶ οὐδὲ ἐκεῖνο μαθεῖν οἱ γενναῖοι δύνανται, ὅτι
ὁ λέγων Ὀρέστης

20   μέθες, μί᾽ οὖσα τῶν ἐμῶν Ἐρινύων
       μέσον μ᾽ ὀχμάζεις, ὡς βάλῃς ἐς τάρταρον,

φαντάζεται ταῦθ᾽ ὅτι μαίνεται. 9. τί οὖν ἡ ῥητορικὴ
φαντασία δύναται; πολλὰ μὲν ἴσως καὶ ἄλλα τοῖς λόγοις
ἐναγώνια καὶ ἐμπαθῆ προσεισφέρειν, κατακιρναμένη
25 μέντοι ταῖς πραγματικαῖς ἐπιχειρήσεσιν οὐ πείθει τὸν
ἀκροατὴν μόνον, ἀλλὰ καὶ δουλοῦται. 'καὶ μὴν εἴ τις,'
φησὶν 'αὐτίκα δὴ μάλα κραυγῆς ἀκούσειε πρὸ τῶν δικα-
στηρίων, εἶτ᾽ εἴποι τις, ὡς ἀνέῳκται τὸ δεσμωτήριον, οἱ

---

1 θεοφ*ρεῖται P θεοφορεῖται P.   4 συνεβάκχευ᾽] Porsonus, συνεβάκχευεν P,
συνεβάκχευσ᾽ codd. Euripidis.   5 θνήσκοντος P.   οἰδ**που P οἰδίπου P.
7 ἔπειτ᾽ ἀχιλλέωσ P, corr. Manutius.   16 ἀδύνατον] Manutius, δυνατὸν P.
21 τάρτ|*ον P τάρτα|ρον P.   28 εἶτ᾽ P.

at the coming of Dionysus is strangely represented as *possessed* :—

> A frenzy thrills the hall; the roofs are bacchant
> With ecstasy[1] :

an idea which Euripides has echoed, in other words, it is true, and with some abatement of its crudity, where he says :—

> The whole mount shared their bacchic ecstasy[2].

7. Magnificent are the images which Sophocles has conceived of the death of Oedipus, who makes ready his burial amid the portents of the sky[3]. Magnificent, too, is the passage where the Greeks are on the point of sailing away and Achilles appears above his tomb to those who are putting out to sea— a scene which I doubt whether anyone has depicted more vividly than Simonides[4]. But it is impossible to cite all the examples that present themselves. 8. It is no doubt true that those which are found in the poets contain, as I said, a tendency to exaggeration in the way of the fabulous and that they transcend in every way the credible, but in oratorical imagery the best feature is always its reality and truth. Whenever the form of a speech is poetical and fabulous and breaks into every kind of impossibility, such digressions have a strange and alien air. For example, the clever orators forsooth of our day, like the tragedians, see Furies, and— fine fellows that they are—cannot even understand that Orestes when he cries

> Unhand me !—of mine Haunting Fiends thou art—
> Dost grip my waist to hurl me into hell[5]!

has these fancies because he is mad. 9. What, then, can oratorical imagery effect? Well, it is able in many ways to infuse vehemence and passion into spoken words, while more particularly when it is combined with the argumentative passages it not only persuades the hearer but actually makes him its slave. Here is an example. 'Why, if at this very moment,' says Demosthenes, 'a loud cry were to be heard in front of the courts, and we were told that the prison-house

---

[1] Appendix C, *Aeschylus*.   [2] Eurip. *Bacchae*, 726.
[3] Soph. *Oed. Col.* 1586.   [4] Appendix C, *Simonides*.   [5] Eurip. *Orest.* 264.

δὲ δεσμῶται φεύγουσιν, οὐθεὶς οὕτως οὔτε γέρων οὔτε
νέος ὀλίγωρός ἐστιν, ὃς οὐχὶ βοηθήσει, καθ' ὅσον δύναται·
εἰ δὲ δή τις εἴποι παρελθών, ὡς ὁ τούτους ἀφεὶς οὗτός
ἐστιν, οὐδὲ λόγου τυχὼν παραυτίκ' ἂν ἀπόλοιτο.' 10. ὡς
5 νὴ Δία καὶ ὁ Ὑπερίδης κατηγορούμενος, ἐπειδὴ τοὺς
δούλους μετὰ τὴν ἧτταν ἐλευθέρους ἐψηφίσατο, τοῦτο τὸ
ψήφισμα, εἶπεν, οὐχ ὁ ῥήτωρ ἔγραψεν ἀλλ' ἡ ἐν Χαιρωνείᾳ
μάχη. ἅμα γὰρ τῷ πραγματικῷ ἐπιχειρεῖν ὁ ῥήτωρ
πεφάντασται, διὸ καὶ τὸν τοῦ πείθειν ὅρον ὑπερ|βέβηκε 189ᵛ
10 τῷ λήμματι. 11. φύσει δέ πως ἐν τοῖς τοιούτοις ἅπασιν
ἀεὶ τοῦ κρείττονος ἀκούομεν, ὅθεν ἀπὸ τοῦ ἀποδεικτικοῦ
περιελκόμεθα εἰς τὸ κατὰ φαντασίαν ἐκπληκτικόν, ᾧ τὸ
πραγματικὸν ἐγκρύπτεται περιλαμπόμενον. καὶ τοῦτ'
οὐκ ἀπεικότως πάσχομεν· δυεῖν γὰρ συνταττομένων ὑφ'
15 ἓν ἀεὶ τὸ κρεῖττον εἰς ἑαυτὸ τὴν θατέρου δύναμιν περισπᾷ.

12. Τοσαῦτα περὶ τῶν κατὰ τὰς νοήσεις ὑψηλῶν
καὶ ὑπὸ μεγαλοφροσύνης μιμήσεως ἢ φαντασίας ἀπο-
γεννωμένων ἀρκέσει.

XVI

Αὐτόθι μέντοι καὶ ὁ περὶ σχημάτων ἐφεξῆς τέτακται
20 τόπος· καὶ γὰρ ταῦτ', ἂν ὃν δεῖ σκευάζηται τρόπον, ὡς
ἔφην, οὐκ ἂν ἡ τυχοῦσα μεγέθους εἴη μερίς. οὐ μὴν ἀλλ'
ἐπεὶ τὸ πάντα διακριβοῦν πολύεργον ἐν τῷ παρόντι,
μᾶλλον δ' ἀπεριόριστον, ὀλίγα τῶν ὅσα μεγαληγορίας
ἀποτελεστικὰ τοῦ πιστώσασθαι τὸ προκείμενον ἕνεκα
25 καὶ δὴ διέξιμεν. 2. ἀπόδειξιν ὁ Δημοσθένης ὑπὲρ τῶν
πεπολιτευμένων εἰσφέρει· τίς δ' ἦν ἡ κατὰ φύσιν χρῆσις
αὐτῆς; 'οὐχ ἡμάρτετε, ὦ τὸν ὑπὲρ τῆς τῶν Ἑλλήνων
ἐλευθερίας ἀγῶνα ἀράμενοι· ἔχετε δὲ οἰκεῖα τούτου

---

7 χ**ρωνεία P χαιρωνεία P.   8 πραγματικῶι P, πραγματικῶς Morus
Vahlenus.   9 ὑπερ|βέβηκε* P.   19 περὶ σχημάτων in marg. P.

22 πολυεργον P.   25 διέξ*μεν P διέξιμεν P.   27 ὦ] P Spengelius,
ἄνδρες Ἀθηναῖοι addit Manutio auctore Vahlenus.

lies open and the prisoners are in full flight, no one, whether he be old or young, is so heedless as not to lend aid to the utmost of his power; aye, and if any one came forward and said that yonder stands the man who let them go, the offender would be promptly put to death without a hearing[1].' 10. In the same way, too, Hyperides on being accused, after he had proposed the liberation of the slaves subsequently to the great defeat, said 'This proposal was framed, not by the orator, but by the battle of Chaeroneia[2].' The speaker has here at one and the same time followed a train of reasoning and indulged a flight of imagination. He has, therefore, passed the bounds of mere persuasion by the boldness of his conception. 11. By a sort of natural law in all such matters we always attend to whatever possesses superior force; whence it is that we are drawn away from demonstration pure and simple to any startling image within whose dazzling brilliancy the argument lies concealed. And it is not unreasonable that we should be affected in this way, for when two things are brought together, the more powerful always attracts to itself the virtue of the weaker. 12. It will be enough to have said thus much with regard to examples of the sublime in thought, when produced by greatness of soul, imitation, or imagery.

XVI

Here, however, in due order comes the place assigned to Figures; for they, if handled in the proper manner, will contribute, as I have said, in no mean degree to sublimity. But since to treat thoroughly of them all at the present moment would be a great, or rather an endless task, we will now, with the object of proving our proposition, run over a few only of those which produce elevation of diction. 2. Demosthenes is bringing forward a reasoned vindication of his public policy. What was the natural way of treating the subject? It was this. 'You were not wrong, you who engaged in the struggle for the freedom of Greece. You have

---

[1] Demosth. *c. Timocr.* 208.   [2] Appendix C, *Hyperides*.

παραδείγματα· οὐδὲ γὰρ οἱ ἐν Μαραθῶνι ἥμαρτον οὐδ᾽ οἱ
ἐν Σαλαμῖνι οὐδ᾽ οἱ ἐν Πλαταιαῖς·᾽ ἀλλ᾽ ἐπειδὴ καθάπερ
ἐμπνευσθεὶς ἐξαίφνης ὑπὸ θεοῦ καὶ οἱονεὶ φοιβόληπτος
γενόμενος, τὸν τῶν ἀριστέων τῆς Ἑλλάδος ὅρκον ἐξεφώ-
5 νησεν ʽ οὐκ ἔστιν ὅπως ἡμάρτετε, μὰ τοὺς ἐν Μαραθῶνι
προκινδυνεύσαντας,᾽ φαίνεται δι᾽ ἑνὸς τοῦ ὀμοτικοῦ σχή- 190
ματος, ὅπερ ἐνθάδε ἀποστροφὴν ἐγὼ καλῶ, τοὺς μὲν
προγόνους ἀποθεώσας, ὅτι δεῖ τοὺς οὕτως ἀποθανόντας
ὡς θεοὺς ὀμνύναι παριστάνων, τοῖς δὲ κρίνουσι τὸ τῶν
10 ἐκεῖ προκινδυνευσάντων ἐντιθεὶς φρόνημα, τὴν δὲ τῆς
ἀποδείξεως φύσιν μεθεστακὼς εἰς ὑπερβάλλον ὕψος καὶ
πάθος καὶ ξένων καὶ ὑπερφυῶν ὅρκων ἀξιοπιστίαν, καὶ
ἅμα παιώνειόν τινα καὶ ἀλεξιφάρμακον εἰς τὰς ψυχὰς
τῶν ἀκουόντων καθιεὶς λόγον, ὡς κουφιζομένους ὑπὸ τῶν
15 ἐγκωμίων μηδὲν ἔλαττον τῇ μάχῃ τῇ πρὸς Φίλιππον ἢ
ἐπὶ τοῖς κατὰ Μαραθῶνα καὶ Σαλαμῖνα νικητηρίοις παρί-
στασθαι φρονεῖν· οἷς πᾶσι τοὺς ἀκροατὰς διὰ τοῦ σχημα-
τισμοῦ συναρπάσας ᾤχετο. 3. καίτοι παρὰ τῷ Εὐπόλιδι
τοῦ ὅρκου τὸ σπέρμα φασὶν εὑρῆσθαι·

20   οὐ γὰρ μὰ τὴν Μαραθῶνι τὴν ἐμὴν μάχην,
          χαίρων τις αὐτῶν τοὐμὸν ἀλγυνεῖ κέαρ.

ἔστι δ᾽ οὐ τὸ ὁπωσοῦν τινα ὀμόσαι μέγα, τὸ δὲ ποῦ καὶ
πῶς καὶ ἐφ᾽ ὧν καιρῶν καὶ τίνος ἕνεκα. ἀλλ᾽ ἐκεῖ μὲν
οὐδέν ἐστ᾽ εἰ μὴ ὅρκος, καὶ πρὸς εὐτυχοῦντας ἔτι καὶ οὐ
25 δεομένους παρηγορίας τοὺς Ἀθηναίους, ἔτι δ᾽ οὐχὶ τοὺς
ἄνδρας ἀπαθανατίσας ὁ ποιητὴς ὤμοσεν, ἵνα τῆς ἐκείνων
ἀρετῆς τοῖς ἀκούουσιν ἐντέκῃ λόγον ἄξιον, ἀλλ᾽ ἀπὸ τῶν
προκινδυνευσάντων ἐπὶ τὸ ἄψυχον ἀπεπλανήθη, τὴν μάχην.
παρὰ δὲ τῷ Δημοσθένει πεπραγμάτευται πρὸς ἡττημέ-
30 νους ὁ ὅρκος, ὡς μὴ Χαιρώνειαν ἔτ᾽ Ἀθηναίοις ἀτύχημα

domestic warrant for it. For the warriors of Marathon did no wrong, nor they of Salamis, nor they of Plataea[1].' When, however, as though suddenly inspired by heaven and as it were frenzied by the God of Prophecy, he utters his famous oath by the champions of Greece ('assuredly ye did no wrong; I swear it by those who at Marathon stood in the forefront of the danger'), in the public view by this one Figure of Adjuration, which I here term *Apostrophe*, he deifies his ancestors. He brings home the thought that we ought to swear by those who have thus nobly died as we swear by Gods, and he fills the mind of the judges with the high spirit of those who there bore the brunt of the danger, and he has transformed the natural course of the argument into transcendent sublimity and passion and that secure belief which rests upon strange and prodigious oaths. He instils into the minds of his hearers the conviction—which acts as a medicine and an antidote—that they should, uplifted by these eulogies, feel no less proud of the fight against Philip than of the triumph at Marathon and Salamis. By all these means he carries his hearers clean away with him through the employment of a single figure.

3. It is said, indeed, that the germ of the oath is found in Eupolis:—

> For, by the fight I won at Marathon,
> No one shall vex my soul and rue it not[2].

But it is not sublime to swear by a person in any chance way; the sublimity depends upon the place and the manner and the circumstances and the motive. Now in the passage of Eupolis there is nothing but the mere oath, addressed to the Athenians when still prosperous and in no need of comfort. Furthermore, the poet in his oath has not made divinities of the men in ord... ...eate in his hearers a worthy conception of their val... who stood in the t... thing—the fight. In D... ...ned for van quished men, with the intention that Chaeroneia should no longer appear a failure to the Athenians. He gives them at

---

[1] Cp. Dem. *de Cor.* 208.   [2] Appendix C, *Eupolis*.

φαίνεσθαι, καὶ | ταὐτόν, ὡς ἔφην, ἅμα ἀπόδειξίς ἐστι τοῦ 190ᵛ
μηδὲν ἡμαρτηκέναι παράδειγμα ὅρκων πίστις ἐγκώμιον
προτροπή. 4. κἀπειδήπερ ὑπήντα τῷ ῥήτορι· 'λέγεις
ἧτταν πολιτευσάμενος, εἶτα νίκας ὀμνύεις,' διὰ ταῦθ' ἑξῆς
5 κανονίζει καὶ δι' ἀσφαλείας ἄγει καὶ ὀνόματα, διδάσκων
ὅτι κἂν βακχεύμασι νήφειν ἀναγκαῖον· 'τοὺς προκινδυνεύσαντας' φησὶ 'Μαραθῶνι καὶ τοὺς Σαλαμῖνι καὶ
ἐπ' Ἀρτεμισίῳ ναυμαχήσαντας, καὶ τοὺς ἐν Πλαταιαῖς
παραταξαμένους.' οὐδαμοῦ 'νικήσαντας' εἶπεν, ἀλλὰ
10 πάντη τὸ τοῦ τέλους διακέκλοφεν ὄνομα, ἐπειδήπερ ἦν
εὐτυχὲς καὶ τοῖς κατὰ Χαιρώνειαν ὑπεναντίον. διόπερ
καὶ τὸν ἀκροατὴν φθάνων εὐθὺς ὑποφέρει· 'οὓς ἅπαντας
ἔθαψε δημοσίᾳ' φησὶν 'ἡ πόλις, Αἰσχίνη, οὐχὶ τοὺς
κατορθώσαντας μόνους.'

XVII

15   Οὐκ ἄξιον ἐπὶ τούτου τοῦ τόπου παραλιπεῖν ἕν τι τῶν
ἡμῖν τεθεωρημένων, φίλτατε, ἔσται δὲ πάνυ σύντομον,
ὅτι φύσει πως συμμαχεῖ τε τῷ ὕψει τὰ σχήματα καὶ
πάλιν ἀντισυμμαχεῖται θαυμαστῶς ὑπ' αὐτοῦ. πῇ δὲ καὶ
πῶς, ἐγὼ φράσω. ὕποπτόν ἐστιν ἰδίως τὸ διὰ σχημάτων
20 πανουργεῖν καὶ προσβάλλον ὑπόνοιαν ἐνέδρας ἐπιβουλῆς
παραλογισμοῦ. καὶ ταῦθ' ὅταν ᾖ πρὸς κριτὴν κύριον ὁ
λόγος, μάλιστα δὲ πρὸς τυράννους βασιλέας ἡγεμόνας
ἐν ὑπεροχαῖς· ἀγανακτεῖ γὰρ εὐθύς, εἰ ὡς παῖς ἄφρων
ὑπὸ τεχνίτου ῥήτορος σχηματίοις κατασοφίζεται, καὶ εἰς
25 καταφρό|νησιν ἑαυτοῦ λαμβάνων τὸν παραλογισμὸν ἐνίοτε 191ʳ
μὲν ἀποθηριοῦται τὸ σύνολον, κἂν ἐπικρατήσῃ δὲ τοῦ
θυμοῦ, πρὸς τὴν πειθὼ τῶν λόγων πάντως ἀντιδιατίθεται.
διόπερ καὶ τότε ἄριστον δοκεῖ τὸ σχῆμα, ὅταν αὐτὸ τοῦτο
διαλανθάνῃ ὅτι σχῆμά ἐστιν. 2. τὸ τοίνυν ὕψος καὶ

---

3 λέγεις] Robortellus, λέγεισ λέγεισ P.   17 συμμαχεῖ τε] Schurzfleischius,
συμμαχεῖται (poster. a in ras.) P.   24 σχημάτιον in marg. P.   28 ὅταν—
σχῆμα om. P, addidit in marg. eadem manus.

one and the same time, as I remarked, a demonstration that
they have done no wrong, an example, the sure evidence of
oaths, a eulogy, an exhortation.   4. And since the orator was
likely to be confronted with the objection, 'You are speaking
of the *defeat* which has attended your administration, and
yet you swear by *victories*,' in what follows he consequently
measures even individual words, and chooses them unerringly,
showing that even in the revels of the imagination sobriety
is required. 'Those,' he says, 'who stood in the forefront
of the danger at Marathon, and those who fought by sea at
Salamis and Artemisium, and those who stood in the ranks
at Plataea.' Nowhere does he use the word 'conquered,' but
at every turn he has evaded any indication of the result, since
it was fortunate and the opposite of what happened at
Chaeroneia. So he at once rushes forward and carries his
hearer off his feet. 'All of whom,' says he, 'were accorded
a public burial by the state, Aeschines, and not *the successful
only*.'

XVII

I ought not, my dear friend, to omit at this point an
observation of my own, which shall be most concisely stated.
It is that, by a sort of natural law, figures bring support to
the sublime, and on their part derive support in turn from it
in a wonderful degree. Where and how, I will explain. The
cunning use of figures is peculiarly subject to suspicion, and
produces an impression of ambush, plot, fallacy. This is so
when the plea is addressed to a judge with absolute powers,
and particularly to despots, kings, and leaders in positions of
superiority. Such an one at once feels resentment if, like a
foolish boy, he is tricked by the paltry figures of the oratorical
craftsman. Construing the fallacy into a personal affront, sometimes he becomes quite wild with rage, or if he controls his
anger, steels himself utterly against persuasive words. Wherefore a figure is at its best when the very fact that it is a figure
escapes attention.   2. Accordingly, sublimity and passion

πάθος τῆς ἐπὶ τῷ σχηματίζειν ὑπονοίας ἀλέξημα καὶ
θαυμαστή τις ἐπικουρία καθίσταται, καί πως παραληφθεῖσα ἡ τοῦ πανουργεῖν τέχνη τοῖς κάλλεσι καὶ μεγέθεσι
τὸ λοιπὸν δέδυκε καὶ πᾶσαν ὑποψίαν ἐκπέφευγεν. ἱκανὸν
5 δὲ τεκμήριον τὸ προειρημένον ‘μὰ τοὺς ἐν Μαραθῶνι.’
τίνι γὰρ ἐνταῦθ᾽ ὁ ῥήτωρ ἀπέκρυψε τὸ σχῆμα; δῆλον ὅτι
τῷ φωτὶ αὐτῷ. σχεδὸν γὰρ ὥσπερ καὶ τἀμυδρὰ φέγγη
ἐναφανίζεται τῷ ἡλίῳ περιαυγούμενα, οὕτω τὰ τῆς ῥητορικῆς
σοφίσματα ἐξαμαυροῖ περιχυθὲν πάντοθεν τὸ μέγεθος.
10 3. οὐ πόρρω δ᾽ ἴσως τούτου καὶ ἐπὶ τῆς ζωγραφίας τι συμ-
βαίνει· ἐπὶ γὰρ τοῦ αὐτοῦ κειμένων ἐπιπέδου παραλλήλων
ἐν χρώμασι τῆς σκιᾶς τε καὶ τοῦ φωτός, ὅμως προϋπαντᾷ
τε τὸ φῶς ταῖς ὄψεσι καὶ οὐ μόνον ἔξοχον ἀλλὰ καὶ
ἐγγυτέρω παρὰ πολὺ φαίνεται. οὐκοῦν καὶ τῶν λόγων
15 τὰ πάθη καὶ τὰ ὕψη ταῖς ψυχαῖς ἡμῶν ἐγγυτέρω κείμενα
διά τε φυσικήν τινα συγγένειαν καὶ διὰ λαμπρότητα, ἀεὶ
τῶν σχημάτων προεμφανίζεται καὶ τὴν τέχνην αὐτῶν
ἀποσκιάζει καὶ οἷον ἐν κατακαλύψει τηρεῖ.

XVIII

Τί δ᾽ ἐκεῖνα φῶμεν, τὰς πεύσεις τε καὶ ἐρωτήσεις; ἆρα
20 οὐκ αὐταῖς ταῖς τῶν σχημάτων | εἰδοποιίαις παρὰ πολὺ 191
ἐμπρακτότερα καὶ σοβαρώτερα συντείνει τὰ λεγόμενα;
‘ἢ βούλεσθε εἰπέ μοι περιιόντες ἀλλήλων πυνθάνεσθαι·
λέγεταί τι καινόν; τί γὰρ ἂν γένοιτο τούτου καινότερον
ἢ Μακεδὼν ἀνὴρ καταπολεμῶν τὴν Ἑλλάδα; τέθνηκε
25 Φίλιππος; οὐ μὰ Δί᾽ ἀλλ᾽ ἀσθενεῖ. τί δ᾽ ὑμῖν διαφέρει;
καὶ γὰρ ἂν οὗτός τι πάθῃ, ταχέως ὑμεῖς ἕτερον Φίλιππον
ποιήσετε.’ καὶ πάλιν ‘πλέωμεν ἐπὶ Μακεδονίαν’ φησί.
‘ποῖ δὴ προσορμιούμεθα, ἤρετό τις. εὑρήσει τὰ σαθρὰ
τῶν Φιλίππου πραγμάτων αὐτὸς ὁ πόλεμος.’ ἦν δὲ ἁπλῶς

---

2 παραληφθεῖσα ἡ] Tollius, παραληφθεῖσαν P.   8 παυγῶ in marg. P.

13 καὶ οὐ μόνον] Victorius, καιόμενον P.

form an antidote and a wonderful help against the mistrust which attends upon the use of figures. The art which craftily employs them lies hid and escapes all future suspicion, when once it has been associated with beauty and sublimity. A sufficient proof is the passage already adduced, 'By the men of Marathon I swear.' By what means has the orator here concealed the figure? Clearly, by the very excess of light. For just as all dim lights are extinguished in the blaze of the sun, so do the artifices of rhetoric fade from view when bathed in the pervading splendour of sublimity. 3. Something like this happens also in the art of painting. For although light and shade, as depicted in colours, lie side by side upon the same surface, light nevertheless meets the vision first, and not only stands out, but also seems far nearer. So also with the manifestations of passion and the sublime in literature. They lie nearer to our minds through a sort of natural kinship and through their own radiance, and always strike our attention before the figures, whose art they throw into the shade and as it were keep in concealment.

XVIII

But what are we next to say of questions and interrogations? Is it not precisely by the visualizing qualities of these figures that Demosthenes strives to make his speeches far more effective and impressive? 'Pray tell me,—tell me, you sir,—do you wish to go about and inquire of one another, Is there any news? Why, what greater news could there be than this, that a Macedonian is subduing Greece? Is Philip dead? No; but he is ill. Dead or ill, what difference to you? Should anything happen to him, you will speedily create another Philip[1].' Again he says, 'Let us sail against Macedonia. Where shall we find a landing-place? someone asks. The war itself will discover the weak places in Philip's position[2].' All this, if stated plainly

---

[1] Dem. *Philipp.* I. 10.   [2] Dem. *Philipp.* I. 44.

ῥηθὲν τὸ πρᾶγμα τῷ παντὶ καταδεέστερον, νυνὶ δὲ τὸ
ἔνθουν καὶ ὀξύρροπον τῆς πεύσεως καὶ ἀποκρίσεως καὶ
τὸ πρὸς ἑαυτὸν ὡς πρὸς ἕτερον ἀνθυπαντᾶν οὐ μόνον
ὑψηλότερον ἐποίησε τῷ σχηματισμῷ τὸ ῥηθὲν ἀλλὰ καὶ
5 πιστότερον. 2. ἄγει γὰρ τὰ παθητικὰ τότε μᾶλλον,
ὅταν αὐτὰ φαίνηται μὴ ἐπιτηδεύειν αὐτὸς ὁ λέγων ἀλλὰ
γεννᾶν ὁ καιρός, ἡ δ' ἐρώτησις ἡ εἰς ἑαυτὸν καὶ ἀπόκρισις
μιμεῖται τοῦ πάθους τὸ ἐπίκαιρον. σχεδὸν γὰρ ὡς οἱ ὑφ'
ἑτέρων ἐρωτώμενοι παροξυνθέντες ἐκ τοῦ παραχρῆμα πρὸς
10 τὸ λεχθὲν ἐναγωνίως καὶ ἀπ' αὐτῆς τῆς ἀληθείας ἀνθυ-
παντῶσιν, οὕτως τὸ σχῆμα τῆς πεύσεως καὶ ἀποκρίσεως
εἰς τὸ δοκεῖν ἕκαστον τῶν ἐσκεμμένων ἐξ ὑπογύου κεκινῆ-
σθαί τε καὶ λέγεσθαι τὸν ἀκροατὴν ἀπάγον καὶ παρα-
λογίζεται. ἔτι τοίνυν (ἐν γάρ τι τῶν ὑψηλοτάτων τὸ
15 Ἡροδότειον πεπίστευται) εἰ οὕτως ἔ| . . . .

DESVNT DVO FOLIA

XIX

. . . . |πλοκα ἐκπίπτει καὶ οἱονεὶ προχεῖται τὰ λεγόμενα, 19
ὀλίγου δεῖν φθάνοντα καὶ αὐτὸν τὸν λέγοντα. ' καὶ συμ-
βαλόντες' φησὶν ὁ Ξενοφῶν 'τὰς ἀσπίδας ἐωθοῦντο
ἐμάχοντο ἀπέκτεινον ἀπέθνησκον.' 2. καὶ τὰ τοῦ Εὐρυ-
20 λόχου,

ἤλθομεν ὡς ἐκέλευες, ἀνὰ δρυμά, φαίδιμ' Ὀδυσσεῦ.
εἴδομεν ἐν βήσσῃσι τετυγμένα δώματα καλά.

τὰ γὰρ ἀλλήλων διακεκομμένα καὶ οὐδὲν ἧσσον κατεσπευ-
σμένα φέρει τῆς ἀγωνίας ἔμφασιν ἅμα καὶ ἐμποδιζούσης

---

8 ὡς οἱ] Faber, ὅσον P, ὅσοι Petra. 9 παροξυνθέντες] Morus, παροξύ-
νοντεσ P. 13 ἀπά*ον P ἀπάγον P. 15 desunt folia quartum
et quintum quaternionis ΚΖ. 16 ἄπλοκα Manutius. 29 ἀπέθνησκον P.
22 *ίδομεν P εὔρομεν in marg. P εὔρομεν codd. Homeri. βήσσησιν P.

and directly, would have been altogether weaker. As it is, the excitement, and the rapid play of question and answer, and the plan of meeting his own objections as though they were urged by another, have by the help of the figure made the language used not only more elevated but also more convincing. 2. For an exhibition of passion has a greater effect when it seems not to be studied by the speaker himself but to be inspired by the occasion ; and questions asked and answered by oneself simulate a natural outburst of passion. For just as those who are interrogated by others experience a sudden excitement and answer the inquiry incisively and with the utmost candour, so the figure of question and answer leads the hearer to suppose that each deliberate thought is struck out and uttered on the spur of the moment, and thus beguiles his reason. We may further quote that passage of Herodotus which is regarded as one of the most elevated : 'if thus.......'

XIX

The words issue forth without connecting links and are poured out as it were, almost outstripping the speaker himself. 'Locking their shields,' says Xenophon, 'they thrust fought slew fell[1].' 2. And so with the words of Eurylochus :—

We passed, as thou badst, Odysseus, midst twilight of oak-trees round.
There amidst of the forest-glens a beautiful palace we found[2].

For the lines detached from one another, but none the less hurried along, produce the impression of an agitation which interposes obstacles and at the same time adds impetuosity.

---

[1] Xen. *Hellen.* IV. 3, 19.   [2] *Odyss.* X. 251, 2.

τι καὶ συνδιωκούσης. τοιαῦθ' ὁ ποιητὴς ἐξήνεγκε διὰ
τῶν ἀσυνδέτων.

XX

Ἄκρως δὲ καὶ ἡ ἐπὶ ταὐτὸ σύνοδος τῶν σχημάτων
εἴωθε κινεῖν, ὅταν δύο ἢ τρία οἷον κατὰ συμμορίαν
5 ἀνακιρνάμενα ἀλλήλοις ἐρανίζῃ τὴν ἰσχὺν τὴν πειθὼ τὸ
κάλλος, ὁποῖα καὶ τὰ εἰς τὸν Μειδίαν, ταῖς ἀναφοραῖς
ὁμοῦ καὶ τῇ διατυπώσει συναναπεπλεγμένα τὰ ἀσύνδετα.
'πολλὰ γὰρ ἂν ποιήσειεν ὁ τύπτων, ὧν ὁ παθὼν ἔνια οὐδ'
ἂν ἀπαγγεῖλαι δύναιτο ἑτέρῳ, τῷ σχήματι τῷ βλέμματι
10 τῇ φωνῇ.' 2. εἶθ' ἵνα μὴ ἐπὶ τῶν αὐτῶν ὁ λόγος ἰὼν
στῇ (ἐν στάσει γὰρ τὸ ἠρεμοῦν, ἐν ἀταξίᾳ δὲ τὸ πάθος,
ἐπεὶ φορὰ ψυχῆς καὶ συγκίνησίς ἐστιν), εὐθὺς ἐπ' ἄλλα
μεθήλατο ἀσύνδετα καὶ ἐπαναφοράς· 'τῷ σχήματι τῷ
βλέμματι τῇ φωνῇ, ὅταν ὡς ὑβρίζων, ὅταν ὡς ἐχθρός, ὅταν
15 κονδύλοις, ὅταν ὡς δοῦλον.' οὐδὲν ἄλλο διὰ τούτων ὁ
ῥήτωρ ἢ ὅπερ ὁ τύπτων ἐργάζεται, τὴν διάνοιαν τῶν
δικαστῶν τῇ ἐπαλλήλῳ πλήττει φορᾷ. 3. εἶτ' ἐντεῦθεν
πάλιν ὡς αἱ καταιγίδες, ἄλλην ποιούμενος ἐμβολὴν 'ὅταν
κονδύλοις, | ὅταν ἐπὶ κόρρης' φησί· 'ταῦτα, κινεῖ, ταῦτα 192ᵛ
20 ἐξίστησιν ἀνθρώπους, ἀήθεις ὄντας τοῦ προπηλακίζεσθαι·
οὐδεὶς ἂν ταῦτα ἀπαγγέλλων δύναιτο τὸ δεινὸν παρα-
στῆσαι.' οὐκοῦν τὴν μὲν φύσιν τῶν ἐπαναφορῶν καὶ
ἀσυνδέτων πάντη φυλάττει τῇ συνεχεῖ μεταβολῇ· οὕτως
αὐτῷ καὶ ἡ τάξις ἄτακτον καὶ ἔμπαλιν ἡ ἀταξία ποιὰν
25 περιλαμβάνει τάξιν.

XXI

Φέρε οὖν, πρόσθες τοὺς συνδέσμους, εἰ θέλοις, ὡς ποι-
οῦσιν οἱ Ἰσοκράτειοι· 'καὶ μὴν οὐδὲ τοῦτο χρὴ παραλιπεῖν,

---

1 συνδιωκούσης] Faber, συνδιοικούσησ P.   4 συμμορίαν] Manutius, συμμορίασ P.
5 ἐρανίζ** P ἐρανίζηι P.   15 ὅταν ὡς δοῦλον] P, ὅταν ἐπὶ κόρρης libri Demosthenis,
quos sequuntur Manutius et Spengelius deleto ὡς δοῦλον. sed auctor verba suo more
libere laudat.   21 ἂν om. P, add. libri deteriores.   26 συνδ. in marg. P.

This result Homer has produced by the omission of conjunctions.

XX

A powerful effect usually attends the union of figures for a common object, when two or three mingle together as it were in partnership, and contribute a fund of strength, persuasiveness, beauty. Thus, in the speech against Meidias, examples will be found of *asyndeton*[1] interwoven with instances of *anaphora*[2] and *diatyposis*[3]. 'For the smiter can do many things (some of which the sufferer cannot even describe to another) by attitude, by look, by voice[4].' 2. Then, in order that the narrative may not, as it advances, continue in the same groove (for continuance betokens tranquillity, while passion—the transport and commotion of the soul—sets order at defiance), straightway he hurries off to other *Asyndeta* and *Repetitions*. 'By attitude, by look, by voice, when he acts with insolence, when he acts like an enemy, when he smites with his fists, when he smites you like a slave.' By these words the orator produces the same effect as the assailant—he strikes the mind of the judges by the swift succession of blow on blow. 3. Starting from this point again, as suddenly as a gust of wind, he makes another attack. 'When smitten with blows of fists,' he says, 'when smitten upon the cheek. These things stir the blood, these drive men beyond themselves, when unused to insult. No one can, in describing them, convey a notion of the indignity they imply.' So he maintains throughout, though with continual variation, the essential character of the *Repetitions* and *Asyndeta*. In this way, with him, order is disorderly, and on the other hand disorder contains a certain element of order.

XXI

Come now, add, if you please, in these cases connecting particles after the fashion of the followers of Isocrates. Furthermore, this fact too must not be overlooked that the

---

[1] *Broken sentences.* [2] *Repetition of words.*
[3] *Vivid description.* [4] Demosth. *in Mid.* 72.

ὡς πολλὰ ἂν ποιήσειεν ὁ τύπτων, πρῶτον μὲν τῷ σχήματι, εἶτα δὲ τῷ βλέμματι, εἶτά γε μὴν αὐτῇ τῇ φωνῇ,·
καὶ εἴσῃ κατὰ τὸ ἑξῆς οὕτως παραγράφων, ὡς τοῦ πάθους
τὸ συνδεδιωγμένον καὶ ἀποτραχυνόμενον, ἐὰν τοῖς συν-
5 δέσμοις ἐξομαλίσῃς εἰς λειότητα, ἄκεντρόν τε προσπίπτει
καὶ εὐθὺς ἔσβεσται. 2. ὥσπερ γὰρ εἴ τις συνδήσειε
τῶν θεόντων τὰ σώματα τὴν φορὰν αὐτῶν ἀφῄρηται,
οὕτως καὶ τὸ πάθος ὑπὸ τῶν συνδέσμων καὶ τῶν ἄλλων
προσθηκῶν ἐμποδιζόμενον ἀγανακτεῖ· τὴν γὰρ ἐλευθερίαν
10 ἀπολλύει τοῦ δρόμου καὶ τὸ ὡς ἀπ' ὀργάνου τινὸς ἀφίεσθαι.

XXII

Τῆς δὲ αὐτῆς ἰδέας καὶ τὰ ὑπερβατὰ θετέον. ἔστι δὲ
λέξεων ἢ νοήσεων ἐκ τοῦ κατ' ἀκολουθίαν κεκινημένη
τάξις καὶ οἱονεὶ χαρακτὴρ ἐναγωνίου πάθους ἀληθέστατος.
ὡς γὰρ οἱ τῷ ὄντι ὀργιζόμενοι ἢ φοβούμενοι ἢ ἀγανακ-
15 τοῦντες ἢ ὑπὸ ζηλοτυπίας ἢ ὑπὸ ἄλλου τινὸς (πολλὰ
γὰρ καὶ ἀναρίθμητα πάθη καὶ οὐδ' ἂν εἰπεῖν τις ὁπόσα
δύναιτο), ἑκάστοτε παραπίπτοντες ἄλλα προθέμενοι πολ- 193
λάκις ἐπ' ἄλλα μεταπηδῶσι, μέσα τινὰ παρεμβαλόντες
ἀλόγως, εἶτ' αὖθις ἐπὶ τὰ πρῶτα ἀνακυκλοῦντες καὶ πάντη
20 πρὸς τῆς ἀγωνίας, ὡς ὑπ' ἀστάτου πνεύματος, τῇδε κἀκεῖσε
ἀγχιστρόφως ἀντισπώμενοι τὰς λέξεις τὰς νοήσεις τὴν
ἐκ τοῦ κατὰ φύσιν εἱρμοῦ παντοίως πρὸς μυρίας τροπὰς
ἐναλλάττουσι τάξιν· οὕτω παρὰ τοῖς ἀρίστοις συγγραφεῦσι διὰ τῶν ὑπερβατῶν ἡ μίμησις ἐπὶ τὰ τῆς φύσεως
25 ἔργα φέρεται. τότε γὰρ ἡ τέχνη τέλειος, ἡνίκ' ἂν φύσις
εἶναι δοκῇ, ἡ δ' αὖ φύσις ἐπιτυχής, ὅταν λανθάνουσαν
περιέχῃ τὴν τέχνην· ὥσπερ λέγει ὁ Φωκαεὺς Διονύσιος
παρὰ τῷ Ἡροδότῳ· 'ἐπὶ ξυροῦ γὰρ ἀκμῆς ἔχεται ἡμῖν

---

10 ἀπολλύει] Finckhius Vahlenus, ἀπολύει P.   1·1 περὶ ὑπερβατῶν ὅρος
ὑπερβατοῦ in marg. P.   18 μέσ*α P.   19 ἀλ*όγωσ P.   πάντηι P.

smiter may do many things, first by attitude, then by look,
then again by the mere voice.' You will feel, if you transcribe
the passage in this orderly fashion, that the rugged impetuosity
of passion, once you make it smooth and equable by adding
the copulatives, falls pointless and immediately loses all its
fire. 2. Just as the binding of the limbs of runners deprives
them of their power of rapid motion, so also passion, when
shackled by connecting links and other appendages, chafes
at the restriction, for it loses the freedom of its advance and
its rapid emission as though from an engine of war.

realistic imitation
of what happens
in life

XXII

Hyperbata, or *inversions*, must be placed under the same
category. They are departures in the order of expressions
or ideas from the natural sequence; and they bear, it may
be said, the very stamp and impress of vehement emotion.
Just as those who are really moved by anger, or fear, or
indignation, or jealousy, or any other emotion (for the passions
are many and countless, and none can give their number), at
times turn aside, and when they have taken one thing as their
subject often leap to another, foisting in the midst some
irrelevant matter, and then again wheel round to their original
theme, and driven by their vehemence, as by a veering wind,
now this way now that with rapid changes, transform their
expressions, their thoughts, the order suggested by a natural
sequence, into numberless variations of every kind ; so also
among the best writers it is by means of *hyperbaton* that
imitation approaches the effects of nature. For art is perfect
when it seems to be nature, and nature hits the mark when
she contains art hidden within her. We may illustrate by
the words of Dionysius of Phocaea in Herodotus. 'Our
fortunes lie on a razor's edge, men of Ionia ; for freedom or

τὰ πράγματα, ἄνδρες Ἴωνες, εἶναι ἐλευθέροις ἢ δούλοις,
καὶ τούτοις ὡς δραπέτῃσιν. νῦν ὦν ὑμεῖς ἢν μὲν βούλησθε
ταλαιπωρίας ἐνδέχεσθαι, παραχρῆμα μὲν πόνος ὑμῖν, οἷοί
τε δὲ ἔσεσθε ὑπερβαλέσθαι τοὺς πολεμίους.' 2. ἐνταῦθ'
5 ἦν τὸ κατὰ τάξιν· 'ὦ ἄνδρες Ἴωνες, νῦν καιρός ἐστιν ὑμῖν
πόνους ἐπιδέχεσθαι· ἐπὶ ξυροῦ γὰρ ἀκμῆς ἔχεται ἡμῖν τὰ
πράγματα.' ὁ δὲ τὸ μὲν ' ἄνδρες Ἴωνες ' ὑπερεβίβασεν·
προεισέβαλεν οὖν εὐθὺς ἀπὸ τοῦ φόβου, ὡς μηδ' ἀρχὴν
φθάνων πρὸς τὸ ἐφεστὼς δέος προσαγορεῦσαι τοὺς ἀκού-
10 οντας· ἔπειτα δὲ τὴν τῶν νοημάτων ἀπέστρεψε τάξιν.
πρὸ γὰρ τοῦ φῆσαι ὅτι αὐτοὺς δεῖ πονεῖν (τοῦτο γάρ ἐστιν
ὃ παρακελεύεται), ἔμπροσθεν ἀποδίδωσι τὴν αἰτίαν, δι' ἣν
πονεῖν δεῖ, ' ἐπὶ ξυροῦ ἀκμῆς ' φήσας ' ἔχεται ἡμῖν τὰ
πράγματα·' ὡς μὴ δοκεῖν ἐσκεμμένα λέγειν, ἀλλ' ἠναγκα-
15 σμένα. 3. ἔτι δὲ μᾶλλον ὁ Θουκυδίδης καὶ τὰ φύσει
πάντως ἡνωμένα καὶ ἀδιανέμητα ὅμως ταῖς ὑπερβάσεσιν
ἀπ' ἀλλήλων ἄγειν δεινότατος. ὁ δὲ Δημοσθένης οὐχ
οὕτως μὲν αὐθάδης ὥσπερ οὗτος, πάντων δ' ἐν τῷ γένει
τούτῳ κατακορέστατος, καὶ πολὺ τὸ ἀγωνιστικὸν ἐκ τοῦ
20 ὑπερβιβάζειν καὶ ἔτι νὴ Δία τὸ ἐξ ὑπογύου λέγειν συνεμ-
φαίνων, καὶ πρὸς τούτοις εἰς τὸν κίνδυνον τῶν μακρῶν
ὑπερβατῶν τοὺς ἀκούοντας συνεπισπώμενος· 4. πολλάκις
γὰρ τὸν νοῦν, ὃν ὥρμησεν εἰπεῖν, ἀνακρεμάσας καὶ μεταξὺ
ὡς εἰς ἀλλόφυλον καὶ ἀπεοικυῖαν τάξιν, ἀλλ' ἐπ' ἄλλοις διὰ
25 μέσου καὶ ἔξωθέν ποθεν ἐπεισκυκλῶν, εἰς φόβον ἐμβαλὼν
τὸν ἀκροατὴν ὡς ἐπὶ παντελεῖ τοῦ λόγου διαπτώσει, καὶ
συναποκινδυνεύειν ὑπ' ἀγωνίας τῷ λέγοντι συναναγκάσας,
εἶτα παραλόγως διὰ μακροῦ τὸ πάλαι ζητούμενον εὐκαίρως
ἐπὶ τέλει που προσαποδούς, αὐτῷ τῷ κατὰ τὰς ὑπερβάσεις

---

2 δραπέτῃσιν νῦν· ὦν P.   ἡμεῖσ P.   3 ταλαιπωρίαισ P, corr. Manutius.
8 προ*εισέβαλεν P.   ἂν superscripto οὖν P, οὖν ἂν Robortellus, γὰρ Manutius.
ἀρχὴ P, corr. Robortellus.   27 ὑπογωνία P, ὑπ' ἀγωνίασ in margine praebet
eadem manus.

for bondage, and that the bondage of runaway slaves. Now, therefore, if you choose to submit to hardships, you will have toil for the moment, but you will be able to overcome your foes[1].' 2. Here the natural order would have been : 'Men of Ionia, now is the time for you to meet hardships; for our fortunes lie on a razor's edge.' But the speaker postpones the words 'Men of Ionia.' He starts at once with the danger of the situation, as though in such imminent peril he had no time at all to address his hearers. Moreover, he inverts the order of ideas. For instead of saying that they ought to endure hardships, which is the real object of his exhortation, he first assigns the reason because of which they ought to endure hardships, in the words 'our fortunes lie on a razor's edge.' The result is that what he says seems not to be premeditated but to be prompted by the necessities of the moment. 3. In a still higher degree Thucydides is most bold and skilful in disjoining from one another by means of transpositions things that are by nature intimately united and indivisible. Demosthenes is not so masterful as Thucydides, but of all writers he most abounds in this kind of figure, and through his use of hyperbata makes a great impression of vehemence, yes and of unpremeditated speech, and moreover draws his hearers with him into all the perils of his long inversions. 4. For he will often leave in suspense the thought which he has begun to express, and meanwhile he will heap, into a position seemingly alien and unnatural, one thing upon another parenthetically and from any external source whatsoever, throwing his hearer into alarm lest the whole structure of his words should fall to pieces, and compelling him in anxious sympathy to share the peril of the speaker; and then unexpectedly, after a long interval, he adds the long-awaited conclusion at the right place, namely the end, and produces a far greater effect by this very use, so

---

[1] Herod. VI. 11.

παραβόλῳ καὶ ἀκροσφαλεῖ πολὺ μᾶλλον ἐκπλήττει. φειδὼ
δὲ τῶν παραδειγμάτων ἔστω διὰ τὸ πλῆθος.

XXIII

Τά γε μὴν πολύπτωτα λεγόμενα, ἀθροισμοὶ καὶ μεταβολαὶ καὶ κλίμακες, πάνυ ἀγωνιστικά, ὡς οἶσθα, κόσμου
5 τε καὶ παντὸς ὕψους καὶ πάθους συνεργά. τί δέ; αἱ τῶν
πτώσεων χρόνων προσώπων ἀριθμῶν γενῶν ἐναλλάξεις
πῶς ποτε καταποικίλλουσι καὶ ἐπεγείρουσι τὰ ἑρμηνευ-
τικά; 2. φημὶ δὲ τῶν κα|τὰ τοὺς ἀριθμοὺς οὐ μόνα ταῦτα 194ʳ
κοσμεῖν, ὁπόσα τοῖς τύποις ἑνικὰ ὄντα τῇ δυνάμει κατὰ
10 τὴν ἀναθεώρησιν πληθυντικὰ εὑρίσκεται·

αὐτίκα, φησί, λαὸς ἀπείρων
θύννον ἐπ᾽ ἠϊόνεσσι διϊστάμενοι κελάδησαν·

ἀλλ᾽ ἐκεῖνα μᾶλλον παρατηρήσεως ἄξια, ὅτι ἔσθ᾽ ὅπου
προσπίπτει τὰ πληθυντικὰ μεγαλορρημονέστερα καὶ αὐτῷ
15 δοξοκοποῦντα τῷ ὄχλῳ τοῦ ἀριθμοῦ. 3. τοιαῦτα παρὰ
τῷ Σοφοκλεῖ τὰ ἐπὶ τοῦ Οἰδίπου·

ὦ γάμοι, γάμοι,
ἐφύσαθ᾽ ἡμᾶς καὶ φυτεύσαντες πάλιν
ἀνεῖτε ταὐτὸ σπέρμα κἀπεδείξατε
20 πατέρας ἀδελφοὺς παῖδας, αἷμ᾽ ἐμφύλιον,
νύμφας, γυναῖκας, μητέρας τε χὠπόσα
αἴσχιστ᾽ ἐν ἀνθρώποισιν ἔργα γίγνεται.

πάντα γὰρ ταῦτα ἓν ὄνομά ἐστιν, Οἰδίπους, ἐπὶ δὲ θατέρου
Ἰοκάστη, ἀλλ᾽ ὅμως χυθεὶς εἰς τὰ πληθυντικὰ ὁ ἀριθμὸς
25 συνεπλήθυσε καὶ τὰς ἀτυχίας, καὶ ὡς ἐκεῖνα πεπλεόνασται

ἐξῆλθον Ἕκτορές τε καὶ Σαρπηδόνες·

1 φειδῶσ P.   3 πολύπτωτα κλίμακες ἀθροισμοί μεταβολαί in marg. P.
12 θύννον] Vahlenus, θύννων P.   ἠιόνεσι P.   14 μεγαλορημονέστερα P.
15 δοξοκοπῶ in marg. P.   22 αἴσχι∗|στ᾽ P.   γίνεται P.

bold and hazardous, of hyperbaton. Examples may be spared because of their abundance.

XXIII

The figures which are termed *polyptota*—accumulations, and variations, and climaxes—are excellent weapons of public oratory, as you are aware, and contribute to elegance and to every form of sublimity and passion. Again, how greatly do changes of cases, tenses, persons, numbers, genders, diversify and enliven exposition. 2. Where the use of numbers is concerned, I would point out that style is not adorned only or chiefly by those words which are, as far as their forms go, in the singular but in meaning are, when examined, found to be plural: as in the lines

> A countless crowd forthright
> Far-ranged along the beaches were clamouring 'Thunny in sight[1]!'

The fact is more worthy of observation that in certain cases the use of the plural (for the singular) falls on the ear with still more imposing effect and impresses us by the very sense of multitude which the number conveys. . 3. Such are the words of Oedipus in Sophocles :

> O nuptials, nuptials,
> Ye gendered me, and, having gendered, brought
> To light the selfsame seed, and so revealed
> Sires, brothers, sons, in one—all kindred blood !—
> Brides, mothers, wives, in one !—yea, whatso deeds
> Most shameful among humankind are done[2].

The whole enumeration can be summed up in a single proper name—on the one side Oedipus, on the other Jocasta. None the less, the expansion of the number into the plural helps to pluralise the misfortunes as well. There is a similar instance of multiplication in the line :—

> Forth Hectors and Sarpedons marching came[3],

---

[1] Appendix C, *Scr. Inc.* (8).   [2] Soph. *Oed. T.* 1403.
[3] Appendix C, *Scr. Inc.* (5).

καὶ τὸ Πλατωνικόν, ὃ καὶ ἑτέρωθι παρετεθείμεθα, ἐπὶ
τῶν Ἀθηναίων· 4. ʻοὐ γὰρ Πέλοπες οὐδὲ Κάδμοι οὐδʼ
Αἴγυπτοί τε καὶ Δαναοὶ οὐδʼ ἄλλοι πολλοὶ φύσει βάρβαροι
συνοικοῦσιν ἡμῖν, ἀλλʼ αὐτοὶ Ἕλληνες, οὐ μιξοβάρβαροι
5 οἰκοῦμεν.ʼ καὶ τὰ ἑξῆς. φύσει γὰρ ἐξακούεται τὰ πράγματα κομπωδέστερα ἀγεληδὸν οὕτως τῶν ὀνομάτων ἐπισυντιθεμένων. οὐ μέντοι δεῖ ποιεῖν αὐτὸ ἐπʼ ἄλλων, εἰ
μὴ ἐφʼ ὧν δέχεται τὰ ὑποκείμενα αὔξησιν ἢ πληθὺν ἢ
ὑπερβολὴν ἢ πάθος, ἕν τι τούτων ἢ τὰ πλείονα, ἐπεί τοι
10 τὸ πανταχοῦ κώδωνας ἐξῆφθαι λίαν σοφιστικόν.   194

XXIV

Ἀλλὰ μὴν καὶ τοὐναντίον τὰ ἐκ τῶν πληθυντικῶν εἰς
τὰ ἑνικὰ ἐπισυναγόμενα ἐνίοτε ὑψηλοφανέστατα. ʻἔπειθʼ
ἡ Πελοπόννησος ἅπασα διειστήκειʼ φησί. ʻκαὶ δὴ
Φρυνίχῳ δρᾶμα Μιλήτου ἅλωσιν διδάξαντι εἰς δάκρυα
15 ἔπεσε τὸ θέητρον.ʼ τὸ ἐκ τῶν διῃρημένων εἰς τὰ ἡνωμένα
ἐπισυστρέψαι τὸν ἀριθμὸν σωματοειδέστερον. 2. αἴτιον
δʼ ἐπʼ ἀμφοῖν τοῦ κόσμου ταὐτὸν οἶμαι· ὅπου τε γὰρ ἑνικὰ
ὑπάρχει τὰ ὀνόματα, τὸ πολλὰ ποιεῖν αὐτὰ παρὰ δόξαν
ἐμπαθοῦς· ὅπου τε πληθυντικά, τὸ εἰς ἕν τι εὔηχον συγ-
20 κορυφοῦν τὰ πλείονα διὰ τὴν εἰς τοὐναντίον μεταμόρφωσιν
τῶν πραγμάτων ἐν τῷ παραλόγῳ.

XXV

Ὅταν γε μὴν τὰ παρεληλυθότα τοῖς χρόνοις εἰσάγῃς
ὡς γινόμενα καὶ παρόντα, οὐ διήγησιν ἔτι τὸν λόγον, ἀλλʼ

---

3 αἴγυπτ*οί P.   8 ὑποκείμενα] Petra, ὑπερκείμενα P.   αὔξησιν] El. Robortellus, αὔχησιν P.   Vide Append. A.   12 ἔπειθʼ ἡ codd. Demosthenis,
Manutius : ἐπειδὴ P.   15 ἔπεσε τὸ θέητρον] codd. Herodoti Tollius
Iahnius Spengelius Hammerus : ἔπεσον οἱ θεώμενοι P Vahlenus qui lacunam
indicat et supplendum censet δάκρυα < ἔπεσε τὸ θέητρον ἀντὶ τοῦ > ἔπεσον οἱ
θεώμενοι.   18 τὸ] Robortellus, τὰ P.   19 ἐμπαθοῦς] Faber, εὐπαθοῦσ P.
ὅπου τε] Manutius, ὅπουτε ὁπότε P.

and in that passage of Plato concerning the Athenians which we have quoted elsewhere.   4.   'For no Pelopes, nor Cadmi, nor Aegypti and Danai, nor the rest of the crowd of born foreigners dwell with us, but ours is the land of pure Greeks, free from foreign admixture,' etc.[1]   For naturally a theme seems more imposing to the ear when proper names are thus added, one upon the other, in troops.   But this must only be done in cases in which the subject admits of amplification or redundancy or exaggeration or passion—one or more of these—since we all know that a richly caparisoned style is extremely pretentious.

XXIV

Further (to take the converse case) particulars which are combined from the plural into the singular are sometimes most elevated in appearance.   'Thereafter,' says Demosthenes, 'all Peloponnesus was at variance[2].'   'And when Phrynichus had brought out a play entitled the *Capture of Miletus*, the whole theatre burst into tears[3].'   For the compression of the number from multiplicity into unity gives more fully the feeling of a single body.   2.   In both cases the explanation of the elegance of expression is, I think, the same.   Where the words are singular, to make them plural is the mark of unlooked-for passion ; and where they are plural, the rounding of a number of things into a fine-sounding singular is surprising owing to the converse change.

XXV

If you introduce things which are past as present and now taking place, you will make your story no longer a narration

---

[1] Plat. *Menex.* 245 D.   [2] Dem. *de Cor.* 18.   [3] Herod. VI. 21.

ἐναγώνιον πρᾶγμα ποιήσεις. ʿπεπτωκὼς δέ τιςʾ φησὶν
ὁ Ξενοφῶν ʿὑπὸ τῷ Κύρου ἵππῳ καὶ πατούμενος παίει
τῇ μαχαίρᾳ εἰς τὴν γαστέρα τὸν ἵππον· ὁ δὲ σφαδάζων
ἀποσείεται τὸν Κῦρον, ὁ δὲ πίπτει.ʾ τοιοῦτος ἐν τοῖς
5 πλείστοις ὁ Θουκυδίδης.

XXVI

Ἐναγώνιος δ᾽ ὁμοίως καὶ ἡ τῶν προσώπων ἀντιμετάθεσις καὶ πολλάκις ἐν μέσοις τοῖς κινδύνοις ποιοῦσα τὸν
ἀκροατὴν δοκεῖν στρέφεσθαι·

φαίης κ᾽ ἀκμῆτας καὶ ἀτειρέας
10   ἄντεσθ᾽ ἐν πολέμῳ· ὡς ἐσσυμένως ἐμάχοντο.

καὶ ὁ Ἄρατος

μὴ κείνῳ ἐνὶ μηνὶ περικλύζοιο θαλάσσῃ.

2. ὧδέ που καὶ ὁ Ἡρόδοτος· ʿἀπὸ δὲ Ἐλεφαντίνης
πόλεως ἄνω πλεύσεαι, καὶ | ἔπειτα ἀφίξῃ ἐς πεδίον λεῖον· 195
15 διεξελθὼν δὲ τοῦτο τὸ χωρίον αὖθις εἰς ἕτερον πλοῖον
ἐμβὰς πλεύσεαι δύ᾽ ἡμέρας, ἔπειτα ἥξεις ἐς πόλιν μεγάλην,
ἧ ὄνομα Μερόη.ʾ ὁρᾷς, ὦ ἑταῖρε, ὡς παραλαβών σου τὴν
ψυχὴν διὰ τῶν τόπων ἄγει τὴν ἀκοὴν ὄψιν ποιῶν; πάντα
δὲ τὰ τοιαῦτα πρὸς αὐτὰ ἀπερειδόμενα τὰ πρόσωπα ἐπ᾽
20 αὐτῶν ἵστησι τὸν ἀκροατὴν τῶν ἐνεργουμένων. 3. καὶ
ὅταν ὡς οὐ πρὸς ἅπαντας, ἀλλ᾽ ὡς πρὸς μόνον τινὰ λαλῇς,

Τυδείδην δ᾽ οὐκ ἂν γνοίης, ποτέροισι μετείη,

ἐμπαθέστερόν τε αὐτὸν ἅμα καὶ προσεκτικώτερον καὶ
ἀγῶνος ἔμπλεων ἀποτελέσεις, ταῖς εἰς ἑαυτὸν προσφω-
25 νήσεσιν ἐξεγειρόμενον.

---

3 τὸ*ν P.   16 πλευσε*αι P.   18 ὄψιν ποιῶν; πάντα δὲ τὰ τοιαῦτα πρὸς
om. P, addidit in marg. eadem manus.   25 ἐξεγειρόμενοσ P, corr. Faber.

but an actuality. Xenophon furnishes an illustration. 'A man,' says he, 'has fallen under Cyrus' horse, and being trampled strikes the horse with his sword in the belly. He rears and unseats Cyrus, who falls[1].' This construction is specially characteristic of Thucydides.

XXVI

In like manner the interchange of persons produces a vivid impression, and often makes the hearer feel that he is moving in the midst of perils :—

Thou hadst said that with toil unspent, and all unwasted of limb,
They closed in the grapple of war, so fiercely they rushed to the
    fray[2];

and the line of Aratus :—

Never in that month launch thou forth amid lashing seas[3].

2. So also Herodotus : 'From the city of Elephantine thou shalt sail upwards, and then shalt come to a level plain ; and after crossing this tract, thou shalt embark upon another vessel and sail for two days, and then shalt thou come to a great city whose name is Meroe[4].' Do you observe, my friend, how he leads you in imagination through the region and makes you *see* what you hear? All such cases of direct personal address place the hearer on the very scene of action. 3. So it is when you seem to be speaking, not to all and sundry, but to a single individual :—

But Tydeides—thou wouldst not have known him, for whom that
    hero fought[5].

You will make your hearer more excited and more attentive, and full of active participation, if you keep him on the alert by words addressed to himself.

---

[1] Xen. *Cyrop.* VII. I. 37.   [2] *Il.* xv. 697, 8.
[3] Appendix C, *Aratus*.   [4] Herod. II. 29.   [5] *Il.* v. 85.

XXVII

Ἔτι γε μὴν ἔσθ᾽ ὅτε περὶ προσώπου διηγούμενος ὁ συγγραφεὺς ἐξαίφνης παρενεχθεὶς εἰς τὸ αὐτὸ πρόσωπον ἀντιμεθίσταται, καὶ ἔστι τὸ τοιοῦτον εἶδος ἐκβολή τις πάθους.

5　Ἕκτωρ δὲ Τρώεσσιν ἐκέκλετο μακρὸν ἀΰσας,
νηυσὶν ἐπισσεύεσθαι, ἐᾶν δ᾽ ἔναρα βροτόεντα.
ὃν δ᾽ ἂν ἐγὼν ἀπάνευθε νεῶν ἐθέλοντα νοήσω,
αὐτοῦ οἱ θάνατον μητίσομαι.

οὐκοῦν τὴν μὲν διήγησιν ἅτε πρέπουσαν ὁ ποιητὴς προσ-
10 ῆψεν ἑαυτῷ, τὴν δ᾽ ἀπότομον ἀπειλὴν τῷ θυμῷ τοῦ ἡγεμόνος ἐξαπίνης οὐδὲν προδηλώσας περιέθηκεν· ἐψύχετο γάρ, εἰ παρενετίθει· ᾽ἔλεγε δὲ τοῖά τινα καὶ τοῖα ὁ Ἕκτωρ·᾽ νυνὶ δ᾽ ἔφθακεν ἄφνω τὸν μεταβαίνοντα ἡ τοῦ λόγου μετάβασις. 2. διὸ καὶ ἡ πρόχρησις τοῦ σχήματος τότε,
15 ἡνίκα ὀξὺς ὁ καιρὸς ὢν διαμέλλειν τῷ γράφοντι μὴ διδῷ, ἀλλ᾽ εὐθὺς | ἐπαναγκάζῃ μεταβαίνειν ἐκ προσώπων εἰς 195ᵛ πρόσωπα, ὡς καὶ παρὰ τῷ Ἑκαταίῳ· ᾽Κῆϋξ δὲ ταῦτα δεινὰ ποιούμενος αὐτίκα ἐκέλευε τοὺς Ἡρακλείδας ἐπι-γόνους ἐκχωρεῖν· οὐ γὰρ ὑμῖν δυνατός εἰμι ἀρήγειν. ὡς
20 μὴ ὢν αὐτοί τε ἀπόλησθε κἀμὲ τρώσητε, ἐς ἄλλον τινὰ δῆμον ἀποίχεσθαι.᾽ 3. ὁ μὲν γὰρ Δημοσθένης κατ᾽ ἄλλον τινὰ τρόπον ἐπὶ τοῦ Ἀριστογείτονος ἐμπαθὲς τὸ πολυπρόσωπον καὶ ἀγχίστροφον παρέστακεν. ᾽καὶ οὐδεὶς ὑμῶν χολὴν᾽ φησὶν ᾽οὐδ᾽ ὀργὴν ἔχων εὑρεθήσεται, ἐφ᾽ οἷς
25 ὁ βδελυρὸς οὗτος καὶ ἀναιδὴς βιάζεται ; ὅς, ὦ μιαρώτατε ἁπάντων, κεκλειμένης σοι τῆς παρρησίας οὐ κιγκλίσιν οὐδὲ θύραις, ἃ καὶ παρανοίξειεν ἄν τις᾽ ἐν ἀτελεῖ τῷ νῷ

---

1 διηγούμενου|μένον P.　　6 ἐπισεύεσθαι P.　　8 μητίσομαι P.
9 πρέπουσαν El. Robortellus, τρέπουσαν P.　　19 ἡμῖν P, corr. Stephanus.
εἰ μὴ ἀρήγειν P.　　20 ὢν P.　　ἀπόλησθε—τρώσητε] Robortellus,
ἀπόλεσθε—τρώσετε P, ἀπολέεσθε—τρώσετε Cobetus.　　24 χολὴν] libri Demosthenis, σχολὴν P.　　26 κεκλει*μένησ P.　　οὐ κιγκλίσιν] libri Demosthenis
Manutius, κιγκλίοιν P.

XXVII

There is further the case in which a writer, when relating something about a person, suddenly breaks off and converts himself into that selfsame person. This species of figure is a kind of outburst of passion :—

Then with a far-ringing shout to the Trojans Hector cried,
Bidding them rush on the ships, bidding leave the spoils blood-
    dyed—
And whomso I mark from the galleys aloof on the farther side,
I will surely devise his death[1].

The poet assigns the task of narration, as is fit, to himself, but the abrupt threat he suddenly, with no note of warning, attributes to the angered chief. It would have been frigid had he inserted the words, ' Hector said so and so.' As it is, the swift transition of the narrative has outstripped the swift transitions of the narrator. 2. Accordingly this figure should be used by preference when a sharp crisis does not suffer the writer to tarry, but constrains him to pass at once from one person to another. An example will be found in Hecataeus : ' Ceyx treated the matter gravely, and straightway bade the descendants of Heracles depart ; for I am not able to succour you. In order, therefore, that ye may not perish yourselves and injure me, get you gone to some other country[2].' 3. Demosthenes in dealing with Aristogeiton has, somewhat differently, employed this variation of person to betoken the quick play of emotion. ' And will none of you,' he asks, ' be found to be stirred by loathing or even by anger at the violent deeds of this vile and shameless fellow, who—you whose licence of speech, most abandoned of men, is not confined by barriers nor by doors, which might perchance be opened[3]!' With the sense thus incomplete, he suddenly

---

[1] *Il.* xv. 346.   [2] Appendix C, *Hecataeus.*
[3] Demosth. *c. Aristog.* I. 27.

R.   8

ταχὺ διαλλάξας καὶ μόνον οὐ μίαν λέξιν διὰ τὸν θυμὸν εἰς
δύο διασπάσας πρόσωπα ' ὅς, ὦ μιαρώτατε,' εἶτα πρὸς
τὸν Ἀριστογείτονα τὸν λόγον ἀποστρέψας καὶ ἀπολιπεῖν
δοκῶν, ὅμως διὰ τοῦ πάθους πολὺ πλέον ἐπέστρεψεν.

5 4.　οὐκ ἄλλως ἢ Πηνελόπη,

κῆρυξ, τίπτε δέ σε πρόεσαν μνηστῆρες ἀγαυοί;
εἰπέμεναι δμωῇσιν Ὀδυσσῆος θείοιο
ἔργων παύσασθαι, σφίσι δ' αὐτοῖς δαῖτα πένεσθαι;
μὴ μνηστεύσαντες, μηδ' ἄλλοθ' ὁμιλήσαντες,
10　　　ὕστατα καὶ πύματα νῦν ἐνθάδε δειπνήσειαν,
οἳ θάμ' ἀγειρόμενοι βίοτον κατακείρετε πολλόν,
κτῆσιν Τηλεμάχοιο δαΐφρονος· οὐδέ τι πατρῶν
ὑμετέρων τῶν πρόσθεν ἀκούετε παῖδες ἐόντες,
οἷος Ὀδυσσεὺς ἔσκε.

XXVIII

15　Καὶ μέντοι περίφρασις ὡς οὐχ ὑψηλοποιόν, οὐδεὶς ἂν
οἶμαι διστάσειεν. ὡς γὰρ ἐν μουσικῇ διὰ τῶν παρα|φώνων 19
καλουμένων ὁ κύριος φθόγγος ἡδίων ἀποτελεῖται, οὕτως ἡ
περίφρασις πολλάκις συμφθέγγεται τῇ κυριολογίᾳ καὶ εἰς
κόσμον ἐπὶ πολὺ συνηχεῖ, καὶ μάλιστ' ἂν μὴ ἔχῃ φυσῶδές
20 τι καὶ ἄμουσον ἀλλ' ἡδέως κεκραμένον. 2. ἱκανὸς δὲ
τοῦτο τεκμηριῶσαι καὶ Πλάτων κατὰ τὴν εἰσβολὴν τοῦ
Ἐπιταφίου· ' ἔργῳ μὲν ἡμῖν οἵδ' ἔχουσι τὰ προσήκοντα
σφίσιν αὐτοῖς, ὧν τυχόντες πορεύονται τὴν εἱμαρμένην
πορείαν, προπεμφθέντες κοινῇ μὲν ὑπὸ τῆς πόλεως, ἰδίᾳ δὲ
25 ἕκαστος ὑπὸ τῶν προσηκόντων.' οὐκοῦν τὸν θάνατον εἶπεν
εἱμαρμένην πορείαν, τὸ δὲ τετυχηκέναι τῶν νομιζομένων

2　τὸν πρὸσ τὸν Ἀριστογείτονα λόγον P, corr. Manutius.　　5　ἢ Πηνελόπη]
Spengelius, ἢ Πηνελόπην P, ἡ Πηνελόπη Faber Vahlenus.　　7　δμωιῆσιν P.
8　σφήσι P.　　11　θά*|μ' P.　　κατακείρ*τε P.　　12　κτῆσιν Τηλε-
μάχοιο δαΐφρονος· οὐδέ τι πατρῶν] libri Homeri Spengelius, κτῆσιν Τηλεμάχοιο
δαΐφρονος om. P quem sequitur Vahlenus coll. p. 110. 9, ubi ad versum supplendum desideratur ἀλλήλοισιν.　　13　ἡ ὑμετέρων P.　　ὄντες P.　　14　οἷο*σ P.
15　περίφρασισ in marg. P.　　20　ἡδέως] Manutius, ἀδεῶς P.

breaks off and in his anger almost tears asunder a single expression into two persons,—'he who, O thou most abandoned!' Thus, although he has turned aside his address and seems to have left Aristogeiton, yet through passion he directs it upon him with far greater force. 4. Similarly with the words of Penelope :—

Herald, with what behest art thou come from the suitor-band?
To give to the maids of Odysseus the godlike their command
To forsake their labours, and yonder for them the banquet to lay?
I would that of all their wooing this were the latest day,
That this were the end of your banquets, your uttermost revelling-
    hour,
Ye that assemble together and all our substance devour,
The wise Telemachus' store, as though ye never had heard,
In the days overpast of your childhood, your fathers' praising word,
How good Odysseus was[1].

XXVIII

As to whether or no Periphrasis contributes to the sublime, no one, I think, will hesitate. For just as in music the so-called accompaniments bring out the charm of the melody, so also periphrasis often harmonises with the normal expression and adds greatly to its beauty, especially if it has a quality which is not inflated and dissonant but pleasantly tempered. 2. Plato will furnish an instance in proof at the opening of his Funeral Oration. 'In truth they have gained from us their rightful tribute, in the enjoyment of which they proceed along their destined path, escorted by their country publicly, and privately each by his kinsmen[2].' Death he calls 'their destined path,' and the tribute of ac-

---

[1] *Odyss.* IV. 681—689.   [2] Plato, *Menex.* 236 D.

προπομπήν τινα δημοσίαν ὑπὸ τῆς πατρίδος. ἆρα δὴ
τούτοις μετρίως ὤγκωσε τὴν νόησιν, ἢ ψιλὴν λαβὼν τὴν
λέξιν ἐμελοποίησε, καθάπερ ἁρμονίαν τινὰ τὴν ἐκ τῆς
περιφράσεως περιχεάμενος εὐμέλειαν; 3. καὶ Ξενοφῶν·
5 'πόνον δὲ τοῦ ζῆν ἡδέως ἡγεμόνα νομίζετε· κάλλιστον δὲ
πάντων καὶ πολεμικώτατον κτῆμα εἰς τὰς ψυχὰς συγκε-
κόμισθε· ἐπαινούμενοι γὰρ μᾶλλον ἢ τοῖς ἄλλοις πᾶσι
χαίρετε.' ἀντὶ τοῦ 'πονεῖν θέλετε' 'πόνον ἡγεμόνα τοῦ
ζῆν ἡδέως ποιεῖσθε' εἰπὼν καὶ τἆλλ' ὁμοίως ἐπεκτείνας
10 μεγάλην τινὰ ἔννοιαν τῷ ἐπαίνῳ προσπεριώρισατο. 4. καὶ
τὸ ἀμίμητον ἐκεῖνο τοῦ Ἡροδότου· 'τῶν δὲ Σκυθέων τοῖς
συλήσασι τὸ ἱερὸν ἐνέβαλεν ἡ θεὸς θήλειαν νοῦσον.'

XXIX

Ἐπίκηρον μέντοι τὸ πρᾶγμα, ἡ περίφρασις, τῶν
ἄλλων πλέον, εἰ μὴ συμμέτρως τινὶ λαμβάνοιτο· εὐθὺς
15 γὰρ ἀβλεμὲς προσπίπτει, κουφολογίας τε ὄζον καὶ παχύ-
τατον· | ὅθεν καὶ τὸν Πλάτωνα (δεινὸς γὰρ ἀεὶ περὶ
σχῆμα κἄν τισιν ἀκαίρως) ἐν τοῖς νόμοις λέγοντα 'ὡς
οὔτε ἀργυροῦν δεῖ πλοῦτον οὔτε χρυσοῦν ἐν πόλει ἱδρυ-
μένον ἐᾶν οἰκεῖν' διαχλευάζουσιν, ὡς εἰ πρόβατα, φησίν,
20 ἐκώλυε κεκτῆσθαι, δῆλον ὅτι προβάτειον ἂν καὶ βόειον
πλοῦτον ἔλεγεν.
2. Ἀλλὰ γὰρ ἅλις ὑπὲρ τῆς εἰς τὰ ὑψηλὰ τῶν σχημάτων χρήσεως ἐκ παρενθήκης τοσαῦτα πεφιλολογῆσθαι,
Τερεντιανὲ φίλτατε· πάντα γὰρ ταῦτα παθητικωτέρους
25 καὶ συγκεκινημένους ἀποτελεῖ τοὺς λόγους· πάθος δὲ
ὕψους μετέχει τοσοῦτον, ὁπόσον ἦθος ἡδονῆς.

---

1 ἆρα] Manutius, ἄρα P.   3 τινὰ|τῇ τὴν P.   6 συγκεκόμισθε* P.
9 ποι**σθε P ποιεῖσθε P.   14 πλέο*ν P.   15 ἀβλεμέσ in marg. P.
16 τὸν supra versum add. P.

customed rites he calls 'being escorted publicly by their
fatherland.' Is it in a slight degree only that he has magnified
the conception by the use of these words? Has he not rather,
starting with unadorned diction, made it musical, and shed
over it like a harmony the melodious rhythm which comes
from periphrasis? 3. And Xenophon says, 'You regard toil
as the guide to a joyous life. You have garnered in your souls
the goodliest of all possessions and the fittest for warriors.
For you rejoice in praise more than in all else[1].' In using,
instead of 'you are willing to toil,' the words 'you deem
toil the guide to a joyous life,' and in expanding the rest of
the sentence in like manner, he has annexed to his eulogy
a lofty idea. 4. And so with that inimitable phrase of
Herodotus: 'The goddess afflicted with an unsexing malady
those Scythians who had pillaged the temple[2].'

XXIX

A hazardous business, however, eminently hazardous is
periphrasis, unless it be handled with discrimination; otherwise it speedily falls flat, with its odour of empty talk and
its swelling amplitude. This is the reason why Plato (who is
always strong in figurative language, and at times unseasonably
so) is taunted because in his *Laws* he says that 'neither gold
nor silver treasure should be allowed to establish itself and
abide in the city[3].' The critic says that, if he had been
forbidding the possession of cattle, he would obviously have
spoken of ovine and bovine treasure. 2. But our parenthetical
disquisition with regard to the use of figures as bearing upon
the sublime has run to sufficient length, my dear Terentianus;
for all these things lend additional passion and animation to
style, and passion is as intimately allied with sublimity as
sketches of character with entertainment.

[1] Xen. *Cyrop.* I. 5. 12.　　　[2] Herod. I. 105.　　　[3] Plato, *Leges*, 801 B.

XXX

Ἐπειδὴ μέντοι ἡ τοῦ λόγου νόησις ἥ τε φράσις τὰ
πλείω δι᾽ ἑκατέρου διέπτυκται, ἴθι δή, ἂν τοῦ φραστικοῦ
μέρους ᾖ τινα λοιπὰ ἔτι, προσεπιθεασώμεθα. ὅτι μὲν
τοίνυν ἡ τῶν κυρίων καὶ μεγαλοπρεπῶν ὀνομάτων ἐκλογὴ
5 θαυμαστῶς ἄγει καὶ κατακηλεῖ τοὺς ἀκούοντας, καὶ ὡς
πᾶσι τοῖς ῥήτορσι καὶ συγγραφεῦσι κατ᾽ ἄκρον ἐπιτήδευμα, μέγεθος ἅμα κάλλος εὐπίνειαν βάρος ἰσχὺν κράτος,
ἔτι δὲ τἆλλα ἂν ὦσί τινα, τοῖς λόγοις ὥσπερ ἀγάλμασι
καλλίστοις δι᾽ αὐτῆς ἐπανθεῖν παρασκευάζουσα, καὶ οἱονεὶ
10 ψυχήν τινα τοῖς πράγμασι φωνητικὴν ἐντιθεῖσα, μὴ καὶ
περιττὸν ᾖ πρὸς εἰδότας διεξιέναι. φῶς γὰρ τῷ ὄντι
ἴδιον τοῦ νοῦ τὰ καλὰ ὀνόματα. 2. ὁ μέντοι γε ὄγκος
αὐτῶν οὐ πάντη χρειώδης, ἐπεὶ τοῖς μικροῖς πραγματίοις
περιτιθέναι μεγάλα καὶ σεμνὰ ὀνόματα ταὐτὸν ἂν φαί-
15 νοιτο, ὡς εἴ τις τραγικὸν προσωπεῖον μέγα παιδὶ περι-
θείη νηπίῳ, πλὴν ἐν μὲν ποιήσει καὶ ἱ . . . .

DESVNT QVATVOR FOLIA

XXXI

. . . . | θρεπτικώτατον καὶ γόνιμον, τὸ δ᾽ Ἀνακρέοντος· 19
‘οὐκέτι Θρηικίης ἐπιστρέφομαι.’ ταύτῃ καὶ τὸ τοῦ
Θεοπόμπου καινὸν ἐπαινετόν· διὰ τὸ ἀνάλογον ἔμοιγε
20 σημαντικώτατα ἔχειν δοκεῖ· ὅπερ ὁ Κεκίλιος οὐκ οἶδ᾽
ὅπως καταμέμφεται. ‘δεινὸς ὢν’ φησὶν ‘ὁ Φίλιππος
ἀναγκοφαγῆσαι πράγματα.’ ἔστιν ἄρ᾽ ὁ ἰδιωτισμὸς

2 δι᾽] Manutius Vahlenus, δὲ P Spengelius. *ἢ P δὴ P. 3 ᾖ] Spengelius, εἴ P. 8 τἆλλα Manutius, τ᾽ P. 11 ᾖ P. 16 καὶ ἱ] P,
καὶ ἱστορίᾳ Tollius ; desinit hic secundum folium quaternionis ΚΗ, desunt folia III.
IV. V. VI.; incipit septimum a litteris πτικώτατον, quibus praeposuit m. rec. θρε.
17 τὸ δ᾽* (τὸ in ras. corr.) P. 18 θρηκίησ P. ἐπιστρέφο*μαι P.
19 καινὸν ἐπαινετόν] Vahlenus, καὶ τὸν ἐπήνετον P Spengelius, ἐκεῖνο τὸ ἐπαινετόν
Manutius, ἐκεῖνο ἐπαινετόν Hammerus. τὸ* P.

XXX

Since, however, it is the case that, in discourse, thought
and diction are for the most part developed one through the
other, come let us proceed to consider any branches of the
subject of diction which have so far been neglected. Now
it is, no doubt, superfluous to dilate to those who know it
well upon the fact that the choice of proper and striking
words wonderfully attracts and enthralls the hearer, and
that such a choice is the leading ambition of all orators
and writers, since it is the direct agency which ensures
the presence in writings, as upon the fairest statues, of
the perfection of grandeur, beauty, mellowness, dignity, force,
power, and any other high qualities there may be, and
breathes into dead things a kind of living voice. All this it
is, I say, needless to mention, for beautiful words are in very
truth the peculiar light of thought.   2.   It may, however, be
pointed out that stately language is not to be used everywhere,
since to invest petty affairs with great and high-sounding
names would seem just like putting a full-sized tragic mask
upon an infant boy.   But in poetry and......

XXXI

......full of vigour and racy ; and so is Anacreon's line,
' That Thracian mare no longer do I heed[1].'   In this way, too,
that original expression of Theopompus merits praise.   Owing
to the correspondence between word and thing it seems to
me to be highly expressive ; and yet Caecilius for some
unexplained reason finds fault with it.   ' Philip,' says
Theopompus, ' had a genius for *stomaching* things[2].'   Now

---

[1] Appendix C, *Anacreon*.   [2] Appendix C, *Theopompus*.

ἐνίοτε τοῦ κόσμου παρὰ πολὺ ἐμφανιστικώτερον· ἐπιγινώσκεται γὰρ αὐτόθεν ἐκ τοῦ κοινοῦ βίου, τὸ δὲ
σύνηθες ἤδη πιστότερον. οὐκοῦν ἐπὶ τοῦ τὰ αἰσχρὰ
καὶ ῥυπαρὰ τλημόνως καὶ μεθ᾽ ἡδονῆς ἕνεκα πλεονεξίας
5 καρτεροῦντος τὸ ἀναγκοφαγεῖν τὰ πράγματα ἐναργέστατα
παρείληπται. 2. ὧδέ πως ἔχει καὶ τὰ Ἡροδότεια· ᾽ὁ
Κλεομένης᾽ φησὶ ᾽μανεὶς τὰς ἑαυτοῦ σάρκας ξιφιδίῳ
κατέτεμεν εἰς λεπτά, ἕως ὅλον καταχορδεύων ἑαυτὸν διέ-
φθειρεν.᾽ καὶ ᾽ὁ Πύθης ἕως τοῦδε ἐπὶ τῆς νεὼς ἐμάχετο,
10 ἕως ἅπας κατεκρεουργήθη.᾽ ταῦτα γὰρ ἐγγὺς παραξύει
τὸν ἰδιώτην, ἀλλ᾽ οὐκ ἰδιωτεύει τῷ σημαντικῶς.

XXXII

Περὶ δὲ πλήθους μεταφορῶν ὁ μὲν Κεκίλιος ἔοικε
συγκατατίθεσθαι τοῖς δύο ἢ τὸ πλεῖστον τρεῖς ἐπὶ ταὐτοῦ
νομοθετοῦσι τάττεσθαι. ὁ γὰρ Δημοσθένης ὅρος καὶ τῶν
15 τοιούτων. ὁ τῆς χρείας δὲ καιρός, ἔνθα τὰ πάθη χειμάρρου
δίκην ἐλαύνεται, καὶ τὴν πολυπλήθειαν αὐτῶν ὡς ἀναγ-
καίαν ἐνταῦθα συνεφέλκεται. 2. ᾽ἄνθρωποι᾽ φησὶ
᾽μιαροὶ καὶ κόλακες, ἠκρωτηριασμένοι τὰς ἑαυτῶν ἕκα-
στοι πατρίδας, τὴν ἐλευθερίαν προπεπωκότες πρότερον
20 Φιλίππῳ, νυνὶ δὲ Ἀλεξάνδρῳ, τῇ γαστρὶ μετροῦντες καὶ
τοῖς αἰσχίστοις τὴν εὐδαιμονίαν, τὴν δ᾽ ἐλευθερίαν καὶ 197
τὸ μηδένα ἔχειν δεσπότην, ἃ τοῖς πρότερον Ἕλλησιν ὅροι
τῶν ἀγαθῶν ἦσαν καὶ κανόνες, ἀνατετροφότες.᾽ ἐνταῦθα
τῷ πλήθει τῶν τροπικῶν ὁ κατὰ τῶν προδοτῶν ἐπιπροσθεῖ
25 τοῦ ῥήτορος θυμός. 3. διόπερ ὁ μὲν Ἀριστοτέλης καὶ ὁ
Θεόφραστος μειλίγματά φασί τινα τῶν θρασειῶν εἶναι
ταῦτα μεταφορῶν, τὸ ᾽ὡσπερεὶ᾽ φάναι καὶ ᾽οἱονεὶ᾽ καὶ
᾽εἰ χρὴ τοῦτον εἰπεῖν τὸν τρόπον᾽ καὶ ᾽εἰ δεῖ παρακινδυ-

---

5 ἀναγκο*φαγεῖν P.   7 ξιφειδίῳ P.   8 κ*|τέτεμεν P κα|τέτεμεν P.
12 μεταφορῶν] Robortellus, καὶ μεταφορῶν P.   13 τοῖς δύο] Robortellus, τοὺς
δύο P.   24 ἐπιπροσθεῖ] Robortellus, ἐπίπροσθε P.   26 θρασέων P, corr.
Robortellus.   27 τὸ] Spengelius, τὰ P.

a homely expression of this kind is sometimes much more telling than elegant language, for it is understood at once since it is drawn from common life, and the fact that it is familiar makes it only the more convincing. So the words 'stomaching things' are used most strikingly of a man who, for the sake of attaining his own ends, patiently and with cheerfulness endures things shameful and vile. 2. So with the words of Herodotus. 'Cleomenes,' he says, 'went mad, and with a small sword cut the flesh of his own body into strips, until he slew himself by making mincemeat of his entire person[1].' And, 'Pythes fought on shipboard, until he was utterly hacked to pieces[2].' These phrases graze the very edge of vulgarity, but they are saved from vulgarity by their expressiveness.

XXXII

Further, with regard to the number of metaphors to be employed, Caecilius seems to assent to the view of those who lay it down that not more than two, or at the most three, should be ranged together in the same passage. Demosthenes is, in fact, the standard in this as in other matters. The proper time for using metaphors is when the passions roll like a torrent and sweep a multitude of them down their resistless flood. 2. 'Men,' says he, 'who are vile flatterers, who have maimed their own fatherlands each one of them, who have toasted away their liberty first to Philip and now to Alexander, who measure happiness by their belly and their lowest desires, and who have overthrown that liberty and that freedom from despotic mastery which to the Greeks of an earlier time were the rules and standards of good[3].' Here the orator's wrath against the traitors throws a veil over the number of the tropes. 3. In the same spirit, Aristotle and Theophrastus point out that the following phrases serve to soften bold metaphors—'as if,' and 'as it were,' and 'if one may so say,' and 'if one may venture such an expression'; for the

---

[1] Herod. VI. 75.   [2] Herod. VII. 181.
[3] Dem. *de Cor.* 296.

νευτικώτερον λέξαι.' ἡ γὰρ ὑποτίμησις, φασίν, ἶαται τὰ
τολμηρά. 4. ἐγὼ δὲ καὶ ταῦτα μὲν ἀποδέχομαι, ὅμως
δὲ πλήθους καὶ τόλμης μεταφορῶν, ὅπερ ἔφην κἀπὶ τῶν
σχημάτων, τὰ εὔκαιρα καὶ σφοδρὰ πάθη καὶ τὸ γενναῖον
5 ὕψος εἶναί φημι ἴδιά τινα ἀλεξιφάρμακα, ὅτι τῷ ῥοθίῳ
τῆς φορᾶς ταυτὶ πέφυκεν ἅπαντα τἆλλα παρασύρειν καὶ
προωθεῖν, μᾶλλον δὲ καὶ ὡς ἀναγκαῖα πάντως εἰσπράττεσθαι τὰ παράβολα, καὶ οὐκ ἐᾷ τὸν ἀκροατὴν σχολάζειν
περὶ τὸν τοῦ πλήθους ἔλεγχον διὰ τὸ συνενθουσιᾶν τῷ
10 λέγοντι. 5. ἀλλὰ μὴν ἔν γε ταῖς τοπηγορίαις καὶ δια-
γραφαῖς οὐκ ἄλλο τι οὕτως κατασημαντικὸν ὡς οἱ συν-
εχεῖς καὶ ἐπάλληλοι τρόποι. δι' ὧν καὶ παρὰ Ξενοφῶντι
ἡ τἀνθρωπίνου σκήνους ἀνατομὴ πομπικῶς καὶ ἔτι μᾶλλον
ἀναζωγραφεῖται θείως παρὰ τῷ Πλάτωνι. τὴν μὲν κεφα-
15 λὴν αὐτοῦ φησιν ἀκρόπολιν, ἰσθμὸν δὲ μέσον διῳκοδο-
μῆσθαι μεταξὺ τοῦ στήθους τὸν αὐχένα, σφονδύλους τε
ὑπεστηρίχθαί φησιν οἷον στρόφιγγας, καὶ τὴν μὲν ἡδονὴν
ἀνθρώποις εἶναι κακοῦ | δέλεαρ, γλῶσσαν δὲ γεύσεως 198ʳ
δοκίμιον· ἄναμμα δὲ τῶν φλεβῶν τὴν καρδίαν καὶ πηγὴν
20 τοῦ περιφερομένου σφοδρῶς αἵματος, εἰς τὴν δορυφορικὴν
οἴκησιν κατατεταγμένην· τὰς δὲ διαδρομὰς τῶν πόρων
ὀνομάζει στενωπούς· 'τῇ δὲ πηδήσει τῆς καρδίας, ἐν τῇ
τῶν δεινῶν προσδοκίᾳ καὶ τῇ τοῦ θυμοῦ ἐπεγέρσει, ἐπειδὴ
διάπυρος ἦν, ἐπικουρίαν μηχανώμενοι' φησὶ 'τὴν τοῦ
25 πλεύμονος ἰδέαν ἐνεφύτευσαν, μαλακὴν καὶ ἄναιμον καὶ σή-
ραγγας ἐντὸς ἔχουσαν οἷον μάλαγμα, ἵν' ὁ θυμὸς ὁπότ' ἐν
αὐτῇ ζέσῃ, πηδῶσα εἰς ὑπεῖκον μὴ λυμαίνηται.' καὶ τὴν
μὲν τῶν ἐπιθυμιῶν οἴκησιν προσεῖπεν ὡς γυναικωνῖτιν,

---

3 κἀπὶ] Pearcius, κάπειτα P.   5 ἀλεξιφάρκακα P.   7 ***προωθεῖν P.
ἀναγκα** P ἀναγκαῖα P.   10 ταὶ***πηγορίαισ P ταῖσ τοπηγορίαισ P.

                                                                                    ναι
11 κατασημαντ***ὴν P κατασημαντικὸν P.   18 εἰκακὸν P superscripto ναι a
m. rec., correxit Vahlenus ex Platonis Timaeo 69 D.   24 φασί P, corr. Tollius.
25 ἐνεφύτευσε P, corr. Manutius.   26 ὁποῖον P.   ὁπό*|τ' P.

        * *
28 προσεῖπεν P.

qualifying words mitigate, they say, the audacity of expression[1].
4. I accept that view, but still for number and boldness of
metaphors I maintain, as I said in dealing with figures, that
strong and timely passion and noble sublimity are the appropriate palliatives. For it is the nature of the passions, in their
vehement rush, to sweep and thrust everything before them,
or rather to demand hazardous turns as altogether indispensable. They do not allow the hearer leisure to criticise
the number of the metaphors because he is carried away by
the fervour of the speaker. 5. Moreover, in the treatment
of commonplaces and in descriptions there is nothing so
impressive as a number of tropes following close one upon
the other. It is by this means that in Xenophon the
anatomy of the human tabernacle is magnificently depicted,
and still more divinely in Plato. Plato says that its head is a
citadel; in the midst, between the head and the breast, is
built the neck like some isthmus. The vertebrae, he says,
are fixed beneath like pivots. Pleasure is a bait which tempts
men to ill, the tongue the test of taste; the heart is the knot
of the veins and the wellspring of the blood that courses
round impetuously, and it is stationed in the guard-house of
the body. The passages by which the blood races this way
and that he names alleys. He says that the gods, contriving
succour for the beating of the heart (which takes place when
dangers are expected, and when wrath excites it, since it
then reaches a fiery heat), have implanted the lungs, which
are soft and bloodless and have pores within, to serve as a
buffer, in order that the heart may, when its inward wrath
boils over, beat against a yielding substance and so escape
injury. The seat of the desires he compared to the women's

---

[1] Appendix C, *Aristotle.*

τὴν τοῦ θυμοῦ δὲ ὥσπερ ἀνδρωνῖτιν· τόν γε μὴν σπλῆνα
τῶν ἐντὸς μαγεῖον, ὅθεν πληρούμενος τῶν ἀποκαθαι-
ρομένων μέγας καὶ ὕπουλος αὔξεται. ' μετὰ δὲ ταῦτα
σαρξὶ πάντα' φησί ' κατεσκίασαν, προβολὴν τῶν ἔξωθεν
5 τὴν σάρκα, οἷον τὰ πιλήματα, προθέμενοι·' νομὴν δὲ
σαρκῶν ἔφη τὸ αἷμα· τῆς δὲ τροφῆς ἕνεκα, φησί, διω-
χέτευσαν τὸ σῶμα, τέμνοντες ὥσπερ ἐν κήποις ὀχετούς,
ὡς ἔκ τινος νάματος ἐπιόντος, ἀραιοῦ ὄντος αὐλῶνος τοῦ
σώματος, τὰ τῶν φλεβῶν ῥέοι νάματα. ἡνίκα δὲ ἡ
10 τελευτὴ παραστῇ, λύεσθαί φησι τὰ τῆς ψυχῆς οἱονεὶ
νεὼς πείσματα, μεθεῖσθαί τε αὐτὴν ἐλευθέραν. 6. ταῦτα
καὶ τὰ παραπλήσια μυρί' ἄττα ἐστὶν ἑξῆς· ἀπόχρη δὲ
τὰ δεδηλωμένα, ὡς μεγάλαι τε φύσιν εἰσὶν αἱ τροπικαί,
καὶ | ὡς ὑψηλοποιὸν αἱ μεταφοραί, καὶ ὅτι οἱ παθητικοὶ 198ᵛ
15 καὶ φραστικοὶ κατὰ τὸ πλεῖστον αὐταῖς χαίρουσι τόποι.
7. ὅτι μέντοι καὶ ἡ χρῆσις τῶν τρόπων, ὥσπερ τἆλλα
πάντα καλὰ ἐν λόγοις, προαγωγὸν ἀεὶ πρὸς τὸ ἄμετρον,
δῆλον ἤδη, κἂν ἐγὼ μὴ λέγω. ἐπὶ γὰρ τούτοις καὶ τὸν
Πλάτωνα οὐχ ἥκιστα διασύρουσι, πολλάκις ὥσπερ ὑπὸ
20 βακχείας τινὸς τῶν λόγων εἰς ἀκράτους καὶ ἀπηνεῖς μετα-
φορὰς καὶ εἰς ἀλληγορικὸν στόμφον ἐκφερόμενον. ' οὐ
γὰρ ῥᾴδιον ἐπινοεῖν' φησὶν ' ὅτι πόλιν εἶναι δεῖ δίκην
κρατῆρος κεκερασμένην, οὗ μαινόμενος μὲν οἶνος ἐγκεχυμένος ζεῖ, κολαζόμενος δ' ὑπὸ νήφοντος ἑτέρου θεοῦ,
25 καλὴν κοινωνίαν λαβὼν ἀγαθὸν πόμα καὶ μέτριον ἀπερ-
γάζεται.' νήφοντα γάρ, φασί, θεὸν τὸ ὕδωρ λέγειν,
κόλασιν δὲ τὴν κρᾶσιν, ποιητοῦ τινος τῷ ὄντι οὐχὶ

2 μάγειον P superscripto ῥεῖ a m. rec., corr. Is. Vossius. πληρούμενοσ* P.
4 φησί] Robortellus, φύσιν P. 5 πηδήματα P, corr. Toupius. 6 διοχέ-
τευσαν P. 12 ἀπόχρη δεδηλωμένα P, δὲ τὰ extra lineam addidit m. rec.
17 αἰεὶ P. 22 δεῖ om. P, add. ex Platone Manutius. 23 κεκερα*|σμένην P.
οὗ] ἀντὶ τοῦ ὅπου in marg. P. ἐγκεχυμένος codd. Platonis, Manutius. ἐκκεχυ-
μένοσ P. 24 ζῇ P, ζεῖ m. rec. P. 26 τὸ* ὕδωρ P.

apartments in a house, that of anger to the men's. The
spleen he called the napkin of the inward parts, whence it is
filled with secretions and grows to a great and festering bulk.
After this, the gods canopied the whole with flesh, putting
forward the flesh as a defence against injuries from without,
as though it were a hair-cushion. The blood he called the
fodder of the flesh. 'In order to promote nutrition,' he continues, 'they irrigated the body, cutting conduits as in gardens,
in order that, with the body forming a set of tiny channels,
the streams of the veins might flow as from a never-failing
source.' When the end comes, he says that the cables of the
soul are loosed like those of a ship, and she is allowed to go
free[1]. 6. Examples of a similar nature are to be found in
a never-ending series. But those indicated are enough to
show that figurative language possesses great natural power,
and that metaphors contribute to the sublime ; and at the
same time that it is impassioned and descriptive passages
which rejoice in them to the greatest extent. 7. It is obvious,
however, even though I do not dwell upon it, that the use of
tropes, like all other beauties of expression, is apt to lead to
excess. On this score Plato himself is much criticised, since
he is often carried away by a sort of frenzy of words into
strong and harsh metaphors and into inflated allegory. 'For
it is not readily observed,' he says, 'that a city ought to be
mixed like a bowl, in which the mad wine seethes when it has
been poured in, though when chastened by another god who
is sober, falling thus into noble company, it makes a good
and temperate drink[2].' For to call water 'a sober god,' and
mixing 'chastening,' is—the critics say—the language of a

---

[1] Plato, *Tim.* 65 C—85 E.
[2] Plato, *Leges*, 773 C.

νήφοντός ἐστι. 8. τοῖς τοιούτοις ἐλαττώμασιν ἐπιχειρῶν
ὅμως αὐτὸ καὶ ὁ Κεκίλιος ἐν τοῖς ὑπὲρ Λυσίου συγγράμμασιν ἀπεθάρρησε τῷ παντὶ Λυσίαν ἀμείνω Πλάτωνος
ἀποφήνασθαι, δυσὶ πάθεσι χρησάμενος ἀκρίτοις· φιλῶν
5 γὰρ τὸν Λυσίαν ὡς οὐδ᾽ αὐτὸς αὑτόν, ὅμως μᾶλλον μισεῖ
τῷ παντὶ Πλάτωνα ἢ Λυσίαν φιλεῖ. πλὴν οὗτος μὲν ὑπὸ
φιλονεικίας, οὐδὲ τὰ θέματα ὁμολογούμενα, καθάπερ
ᾠήθη. ὡς γὰρ ἀναμάρτητον καὶ καθαρὸν τὸν ῥήτορα
προφέρει πολλαχῇ διημαρτημένου τοῦ Πλάτωνος, τὸ δ᾽
10 ἦν ἄρα οὐχὶ τοιοῦτον, οὐδὲ ὀλίγου δεῖ.

XXXIII

Φέρε δή, λάβωμεν τῷ ὄντι καθαρόν τινα συγ|γραφέα 199ʳ
καὶ ἀνέγκλητον. ἆρ᾽ οὐκ ἄξιόν ἐστι διαπορῆσαι περὶ
αὐτοῦ τούτου καθολικῶς, πότερόν ποτε κρεῖττον ἐν ποιήμασι καὶ λόγοις, μέγεθος ἐν ἐνίοις διημαρτημένοις, ἢ τὸ
15 σύμμετρον μὲν ἐν τοῖς κατορθώμασιν, ὑγιὲς δὲ πάντη
καὶ ἀδιάπτωτον; καὶ ἔτι νὴ Δία, πότερόν ποτε αἱ πλείους
ἀρεταὶ τὸ πρωτεῖον ἐν λόγοις ἢ αἱ μείζους δικαίως ἂν
φέροιντο; ἔστι γὰρ ταῦτ᾽ οἰκεῖα τοῖς περὶ ὕψους σκέμ-
ματα καὶ ἐπικρίσεως ἐξ ἅπαντος δεόμενα. 2. ἐγὼ δ᾽
20 οἶδα μέν, ὡς αἱ ὑπερμεγέθεις φύσεις ἥκιστα καθαραί· τὸ
γὰρ ἐν παντὶ ἀκριβὲς κίνδυνος μικρότητος, ἐν δὲ τοῖς
μεγέθεσιν, ὥσπερ ἐν τοῖς ἄγαν πλούτοις, εἶναί τι χρὴ καὶ
παρολιγωρούμενον· μήποτε δὲ τοῦτο καὶ ἀναγκαῖον ᾖ, τὸ
τὰς μὲν ταπεινὰς καὶ μέσας φύσεις διὰ τὸ μηδαμῇ παρα-
25 κινδυνεύειν μηδὲ ἐφίεσθαι τῶν ἄκρων ἀναμαρτήτους ὡς
ἐπὶ τὸ πολὺ καὶ ἀσφαλεστέρας διαμένειν, τὰ δὲ μεγάλα

---

1 ἐλαττώμασι P, ν add. m. rec. P.   2 ὅμωσ αὐτὸ καἰκιλιοσ (αι in ras.
corr., ὁ κε superscr. a m. rec.) P.   10 δεῖ* P.   16 πότερόνποτε P.
19 δεόμενα P.   20 ** γὰρ (τὸ add. m. rec.) P.   22 κίνδυνος σμικρότητος]
Manutius, κίνδυνοισμικρότητοσ P.   23 τοῦτο] Manutius, τούτου P.   ἢ P, ῇ m.
rec. P.   26 τὰ] Robortellus, τὸ P.

poet, and one who is in truth far from sober.   8.   Fastening
upon such defects, however, Caecilius ventured, in his writings
in praise of Lysias, to make the assertion that Lysias was
altogether superior to Plato.   In so doing he gave way to two
blind impulses of passion.   Loving Lysias better even than
himself, he nevertheless hates Plato more perfectly than he
loves Lysias.   In fact, he is carried away by the spirit of
contention, and even his premisses are not, as he thought,
admitted.   For he prefers the orator as faultless and
immaculate to Plato as one who has often made mistakes.
But the truth is not of this nature, nor anything like it.

XXXIII

Come, now, let us take some writer who is really
immaculate and beyond reproach.   Is it not worth while,
on this very point, to raise the general question whether we
ought to give the preference, in poems and prose writings, to
grandeur with some attendant faults, or to success which
is moderate but altogether sound and free from error?
Aye, and further, whether a greater number of excellences,
or excellences higher in quality, would in literature rightly
bear away the palm?   For these are inquiries appropriate to
a treatise on the sublime, and they imperatively demand a
settlement.   2.   For my part, I am well aware that lofty
genius is far removed from flawlessness; for invariable
accuracy incurs the risk of pettiness, and in the sublime, as
in great fortunes, there must be something which is overlooked.   It may be necessarily the case that low and average
natures remain as a rule free from failing and in greater
safety because they never run a risk or seek to scale the
heights, while great endowments prove insecure because of

ἐπισφαλῆ δι᾿ αὐτὸ γίνεσθαι τὸ μέγεθος. 3. ἀλλὰ μὴν
οὐδὲ ἐκεῖνο ἀγνοῶ τὸ δεύτερον, ὅτι φύσει πάντα τὰ ἀνθρώπεια ἀπὸ τοῦ χείρονος ἀεὶ μᾶλλον ἐπιγινώσκεται καὶ τῶν
μὲν ἁμαρτημάτων ἀνεξάλειπτος ἡ μνήμη παραμένει, τῶν
5 καλῶν δὲ ταχέως ἀπορρεῖ. 4. παρατεθειμένος δ᾿ οὐκ
ὀλίγα καὶ αὐτὸς ἁμαρτήματα καὶ Ὁμήρου καὶ τῶν ἄλλων,
ὅσοι μέγιστοι, καὶ ἥκιστα τοῖς πταίσμασιν ἀρεσκόμενος,
ὅμως δὲ οὐχ ἁμαρτήματα μᾶλλον αὐτὰ ἑκούσια καλῶν ἢ
παροράματα δι᾿ ἀμέλειαν εἰκῆ που καὶ ὡς ἔτυχεν ὑπὸ
10 μεγαλοφυΐας ἀνεπιστάτως παρενηνεγμένα, οὐδὲν | ἧττον 199
οἶμαι τὰς μείζονας ἀρετάς, εἰ καὶ μὴ ἐν πᾶσι διομαλίζοιεν,
τὴν τοῦ πρωτείου ψῆφον μᾶλλον ἀεὶ φέρεσθαι, κἂν εἰ
μὴ δι᾿ ἑνὸς ἑτέρου, τῆς μεγαλοφροσύνης αὐτῆς ἕνεκα·
ἐπείτοιγε καὶ ἄπτωτος ὁ Ἀπολλώνιος ἐν τοῖς Ἀργοναύταις
15 ποιητὴς κἂν τοῖς βουκολικοῖς πλὴν ὀλίγων τῶν ἔξωθεν
ὁ Θεόκριτος ἐπιτυχέστατος, ἆρ᾿ οὖν Ὅμηρος ἂν μᾶλλον
ἢ Ἀπολλώνιος ἐθέλοις γενέσθαι; 5. τί δέ; Ἐρατοσθένης
ἐν τῇ Ἠριγόνῃ (διὰ πάντων γὰρ ἀμώμητον τὸ ποιημάτιον)
Ἀρχιλόχου πολλὰ καὶ ἀνοικονόμητα παρασύροντος, κἀκεί-
20 νης τῆς ἐκβολῆς τοῦ δαιμονίου πνεύματος, ἣν ὑπὸ νόμον
τάξαι δύσκολον, ἆρα δὴ μείζων ποιητής; τί δ᾿; ἐν μέλεσι
μᾶλλον ἂν εἶναι Βακχυλίδης ἕλοιο ἢ Πίνδαρος καὶ ἐν
τραγῳδίᾳ Ἴων ὁ Χῖος ἢ νὴ Δία Σοφοκλῆς; ἐπειδὴ οἱ μὲν
ἀδιάπτωτοι καὶ ἐν τῷ γλαφυρῷ πάντη κεκαλλιγραφημένοι·
25 ὁ δὲ Πίνδαρος καὶ ὁ Σοφοκλῆς ὁτὲ μὲν οἷον πάντα ἐπιφλέγουσι τῇ φορᾷ, σβέννυνται δ᾿ ἀλόγως πολλάκις,
καὶ πίπτουσιν ἀτυχέστατα. ἢ οὐδεὶς ἂν εὖ φρονῶν ἑνὸς

---

2 ἐκεῖνο] Manutius, ἐκείνου P.   3 αἰεὶ P.   6 ἁμαρτήματα P.
11 ἀρετάς] Petra, αἰτίασ P.   12 αἰεὶ P.   14 ἐπείτοίγε P.   Ἀπολλώνιος
ἐν τοῖς] Spengelius, ἀπόλλων τοῖσ P, ἀπολλώνιτοισ (h. e. ἀπολλώνοις τοῖς) m. rec. P.
ἀργοναῦτ" P.   15 βουκολιοῖσ P.   19 Ἀρχιλόχου] Manutius, ἀρχίλοχον P.
παρασύροντος] Manutius, παρασύροντασ P.   21 μεῖζον P.   μέλεσσι P.
24 κεκαλληγραφημένοι P κεκαλλιγραφημένοι P.

their very greatness. 3. In the second place, I am not ignorant that it naturally happens that the worse side of human character is always the more easily recognised, and that the memory of errors remains indelible, while that of excellences quickly dies away. 4. I have myself noted not a few errors on the part of Homer and other writers of the greatest distinction, and the slips they have made afford me anything but pleasure. Still I do not term them wilful errors, but rather oversights of a random and casual kind, due to neglect and introduced with all the heedlessness of genius. Consequently I do not waver in my view that excellences higher in quality, even if not sustained throughout, should always on a comparison be voted the first place, because of their sheer elevation of spirit if for no other reason. Granted that Apollonius in his *Argonautica* shows himself a poet who does not trip, and that in his pastorals Theocritus is, except in a few externals, most happy, would you not, for all that, choose to be Homer rather than Apollonius? 5. Again: does Eratosthenes in the *Erigone* (a little poem which is altogether free from flaw) show himself a greater poet than Archilochus with the rich and disorderly abundance which follows in his train and with that outburst of the divine spirit within him which it is difficult to bring under the rules of law? Once more: in lyric poetry would you prefer to be Bacchylides rather than Pindar? And in tragedy to be Ion of Chios rather than—Sophocles? It is true that Bacchylides and Ion are faultless and entirely elegant writers of the polished school, while Pindar and Sophocles, although at times they burn everything before them as it were in their swift career, are often extinguished unaccountably and fail most lamentably. But would anyone in his senses regard

R.

9

δράματος, τοῦ Οἰδίποδος, εἰς ταὐτὸ συνθεὶς τὰ Ἴωνος
ἀντιτιμήσαιτο ἑξῆς;

XXXIV

Εἰ δ᾽ ὄρῳ μὴ τῷ ἀληθεῖ κρίνοιτο τὰ κατορθώματα,
οὕτως ἂν καὶ Ὑπερίδης τῷ παντὶ προέχοι Δημοσθένους.
5 ἔστι γὰρ αὐτοῦ πολυφωνότερος καὶ πλείους ἀρετὰς ἔχων,
καὶ σχεδὸν ὕπακρος ἐν πᾶσιν ὡς ὁ πένταθλος, ὥστε τῶν
μὲν πρωτείων ἐν ἅπασι τῶν ἄλλων ἀγωνιστῶν λείπεσθαι,
πρωτεύειν δὲ τῶν ἰδιωτῶν. 2. ὁ μέν γε Ὑπερίδης πρὸς
τῷ πάντα ἔξω γε τῆς συνθέσεως | μιμεῖσθαι τὰ Δημο- 20
10 σθένεια κατορθώματα καὶ τὰς Λυσιακὰς ἐκ περιττοῦ
περιείληφεν ἀρετάς τε καὶ χάριτας. καὶ γὰρ λαλεῖ μετὰ
ἀφελείας ἔνθα χρή, καὶ οὐ πάντα ἑξῆς καὶ μονοτόνως ὡς
ὁ Δημοσθένης λέγει· τό τε ἠθικὸν ἔχει μετὰ γλυκύτητος
ἡδὺ λιτῶς ἐφηδυνόμενον· ἄφατοί τε περὶ αὐτόν εἰσιν
15 ἀστεϊσμοί, μυκτὴρ πολιτικώτατος, εὐγένεια, τὸ κατὰ τὰς
εἰρωνείας εὐπάλαιστρον, σκώμματα οὐκ ἄμουσα οὐδ᾽
ἀνάγωγα κατὰ τοὺς Ἀττικοὺς ἐκείνους, ἀλλ᾽ ἐπικείμενα,
διασυρμός τε ἐπιδέξιος καὶ πολὺ τὸ κωμικὸν καὶ μετὰ
παιδιᾶς εὐστόχου κέντρον, ἀμίμητον δὲ εἰπεῖν τὸ ἐν πᾶσι
20 τούτοις ἐπαφρόδιτον· οἰκτίσασθαί τε προσφυέστατος, ἔτι
δὲ μυθολογῆσαι κεχυμένος καὶ ἐν ὑγρῷ πνεύματι διεξο-
δεῦσαι ἔτι εὐκαμπὴς ἄκρως, ὥσπερ ἀμέλει τὰ μὲν περὶ
τὴν Λητὼ ποιητικώτερα, τὸν δ᾽ ἐπιτάφιον ἐπιδεικτικῶς,
ὡς οὐκ οἶδ᾽ εἴ τις ἄλλος, διέθετο. 3. ὁ δὲ Δημοσθένης
25 ἀνηθοποίητος, ἀδιάχυτος, ἥκιστα ὑγρὸς ἢ ἐπιδεικτικός,
ἁπάντων ἑξῆς τῶν προειρημένων κατὰ τὸ πλέον ἄμοιρος.
ἔνθα μέντοι γελοῖος εἶναι βιάζεται καὶ ἀστεῖος, οὐ γέλωτα

---

3 ὄρῳ] Iohannes P. Postgate, ἀριθμῷ P.   4 περὶ ὑπερίδου Ση in marg. P.
6 ὕπακρωσ (o superscripto a m. rec.) P.   11 λαλεῖ μετὰ] Pearcius, λαλεύματα P.
13 λέγει] Manutius, λέγεται P.   15 αστ*ισμοὶ P ἀστεισμοί P.   16 εὐπά-
λαιστον ρ eraso P.   σκώμματα ex σκόμματα P.   19 παιδείας (ι superscripto
a m. rec.) P.   22 ἄκρως] Manutius, ἄκροσ P Spengelius.   25 ὑγρὸ*σ P.

all the compositions of Ion put together as an equivalent for the single play of the *Oedipus*?

XXXIV

If successful writing were to be estimated by number of merits and not by the true criterion, thus judged Hyperides would be altogether superior to Demosthenes. For he has a greater variety of accents than Demosthenes and a greater number of excellences, and like the pentathlete he falls just below the top in every branch. In all the contests he has to resign the first place to his rivals, while he maintains that place as against all ordinary persons. 2. Now Hyperides not only imitates all the strong points of Demosthenes with the exception of his composition, but he has embraced in a singular degree the excellences and graces of Lysias as well. For he talks with simplicity, where it is required, and does not adopt like Demosthenes one unvarying tone in all his utterances. He possesses the gift of characterisation in a sweet and pleasant form and with a touch of piquancy. There are innumerable signs of wit in him—the most polished raillery, high-bred ease, supple skill in the contests of irony, jests not tasteless or rude after the well-known Attic manner but naturally suggested by the subject, clever ridicule, much comic power, biting satire with well-directed fun, and what may be termed an inimitable charm investing the whole. He is excellently fitted by nature to excite pity; in narrating a fable he is facile, and with his pliant spirit he is also most easily turned towards a digression (as for instance in his rather poetical presentation of the story of Leto), while he has treated his Funeral Oration in the epideictic vein with probably unequalled success. 3. Demosthenes, on the other hand, is not an apt delineator of character, he is not facile, he is anything but pliant or epideictic, he is comparatively lacking in the entire list of excellences just given. Where he forces himself to be jocular and pleasant, he does not excite laughter but rather becomes

κινεῖ μᾶλλον ἢ καταγελᾶται, ὅταν δὲ ἐγγίζειν θέλῃ τῷ
ἐπίχαρις εἶναι, τότε πλέον ἀφίσταται. τό γέ τοι περὶ
Φρύνης ἢ Ἀθηνογένους λογίδιον ἐπιχειρήσας γράφειν ἔτι
μᾶλλον ἂν Ὑπερίδην συνέστησεν. 4. ἀλλ᾽ ἐπειδήπερ,
5 οἶμαι, τὰ μὲν θατέρου καλά, καὶ εἰ πολλά, ὅμως ἀμεγέθη
καρδίῃ νήφοντος ἀργὰ καὶ τὸν ἀκροατὴν ἠρεμεῖν ἐῶντα
(οὐδεὶς γοῦν Ὑπερίδην ἀναγινώσκων φοβεῖται), ὁ δὲ ἔνθεν
ἑλὼν τοῦ μεγαλοφυεστάτου καὶ ἐπ᾽ ἄκρον ἀρετὰς συντε- 20
τελεσμένας, ὑψηγορίας τόνον, ἔμψυχα πάθη, περιουσίαν,
10 ἀγχίνοιαν, τάχος, ἔνθα δὴ κύριον, τὴν ἅπασιν ἀπρόσιτον
δεινότητα καὶ δύναμιν, ἐπειδὴ ταῦτα, φημί, ὡς θεόπεμπτα
δεινὰ δωρήματα (οὐ γὰρ εἰπεῖν θεμιτὸν ἀνθρώπινα) ἀθρόα
ἐς ἑαυτὸν ἔσπασεν, διὰ τοῦτο οἷς ἔχει καλοῖς ἅπαντας
ἀεὶ νικᾷ καὶ ὑπὲρ ὧν οὐκ ἔχει, καὶ ὡσπερεὶ καταβροντᾷ
15 καὶ καταφέγγει τοὺς ἀπ᾽ αἰῶνος ῥήτορας· καὶ θᾶττον ἄν
τις κεραυνοῖς φερομένοις ἀντανοῖξαι τὰ ὄμματα δύναιτο, ἢ
ἀντοφθαλμῆσαι τοῖς ἐπαλλήλοις ἐκείνου πάθεσιν.

XXXV

Ἐπὶ μέντοι τοῦ Πλάτωνος καὶ ἄλλη τίς ἐστιν, ὡς
ἔφην, διαφορά· οὐ γὰρ μεγέθει τῶν ἀρετῶν ἀλλὰ καὶ τῷ
20 πλήθει πολὺ λειπόμενος αὐτοῦ Λυσίας ὅμως πλεῖον ἔτι
τοῖς ἁμαρτήμασι περιττεύει ἢ ταῖς ἀρεταῖς λείπεται.
2. τί ποτ᾽ οὖν εἶδον οἱ ἰσόθεοι ἐκεῖνοι καὶ τῶν μεγίστων
ἐπορεξάμενοι τῆς συγγραφῆς, τῆς δ᾽ ἐν ἅπασιν ἀκριβείας
ὑπερφρονήσαντες; πρὸς πολλοῖς ἄλλοις ἐκεῖνο, ὅτι ἡ
25 φύσις οὐ ταπεινὸν ἡμᾶς ζῷον οὐδ᾽ ἀγεννὲς ἔκρινε τὸν
ἄνθρωπον, ἀλλ᾽ ὡς εἰς μεγάλην τινὰ πανήγυριν εἰς τὸν

2 ἐπίχαρις] Portus, ἐπιχαρησ P.   3 Φρύνης] Schurzfleischius, φρυγίησ P.
6 καρδίη P.   7 ὑπερἁδην P, ὑπερίδην m. rec. P.   ἀναγιν⋇σκων P.
13 αὐτὸν (ἑ superscripto a m. rec.) P.   κα⋇λοῖσ (λ ut videtur eraso) P.
                   * λ
15 καταφέγγει] Manutius : καταφέγγη P, λ superscr. a m. rec., unde καταφλέγει
Tollius Iahnius.   20 αὐτοῦ Λυσίας] Pearcius, ἀπουσίασ P.   ὅμως] Toupius,
ὁ* μὲν P.   23 ἐν|⋇ἅπασιν P.   25 ἔ⋇κρινε P.

the subject of it, and when he wishes to approach the region of charm, he is all the farther removed from it. If he had attempted to write the short speech about Phryne or about Athenogenes, he would have all the more commended Hyperides to our regard.   4. The good points of the latter, however, many though they be, are wanting in elevation; they are the staid utterances of a sober-hearted man and leave the hearer unmoved, no one feeling terror when he reads Hyperides.   But Demosthenes draws—as from a store—excellences allied to the highest sublimity and perfected to the utmost, the tone of lofty speech, living passions, copiousness, readiness, speed (where it is legitimate), and that power and vehemence of his which forbid approach.   Having, I say, absorbed bodily within himself these mighty gifts which we may deem heaven-sent (for it would not be right to term them *human*), he thus with the noble qualities which are his own routs all comers even where the qualities he does not possess are concerned, and overpowers with thunder and with lightning the orators of every age.   One could sooner face with unflinching eyes a descending thunderbolt than meet with steady gaze his bursts of passion in their swift succession.

XXXV

But in the case of Plato and Lysias there is, as I said, a further point of difference.   For not only in the degree of his excellences, but also in their number, Lysias is much inferior to Plato; and at the same time he surpasses him in his faults still more than he falls below him in his excellences. 2.   What fact, then, was before the eyes of those superhuman writers who, aiming at everything that was highest in composition, contemned an all-pervading accuracy?   This besides many other things, that Nature has appointed us men to be no base or ignoble animals; but when she ushers us into

βίον καὶ εἰς τὸν σύμπαντα κόσμον ἐπάγουσα, θεατάς
τινας τῶν ὅλων αὐτῆς ἐσομένους καὶ φιλοτιμοτάτους ἀγω-
νιστάς, εὐθὺς ἄμαχον ἔρωτα ἐνέφυσεν ἡμῶν ταῖς ψυχαῖς
παντὸς ἀεὶ τοῦ μεγάλου καὶ ὡς πρὸς ἡμᾶς δαιμονιωτέρου.
5 3. διόπερ τῇ θεωρίᾳ καὶ διανοίᾳ τῆς ἀνθρωπίνης ἐπι-
βολῆς οὐδ᾽ ὁ σύμπας κόσμος ἀρκεῖ, ἀλλὰ καὶ τοὺς τοῦ
περιέχοντος πολλάκις ὅρους ἐκβαίνουσιν αἱ | ἐπίνοιαι, καὶ 20
εἴ τις περιβλέψαιτο ἐν κύκλῳ τὸν βίον, ὅσῳ πλέον ἔχει
τὸ περιττὸν ἐν πᾶσι καὶ μέγα καὶ καλόν, ταχέως εἴσεται,
10 πρὸς ἃ γεγόναμεν.   4. ἔνθεν φυσικῶς πως ἀγόμενοι μὰ
Δί᾽ οὐ τὰ μικρὰ ῥεῖθρα θαυμάζομεν, εἰ καὶ διαυγῆ καὶ
χρήσιμα, ἀλλὰ τὸν Νεῖλον καὶ Ἴστρον ἢ Ῥῆνον, πολὺ
δ᾽ ἔτι μᾶλλον τὸν Ὠκεανόν· οὐδέ γε τὸ ὑφ᾽ ἡμῶν τουτὶ
φλογίον ἀνακαιόμενον, ἐπεὶ καθαρὸν σῴζει τὸ φέγγος,
15 ἐκπληττόμεθα τῶν οὐρανίων μᾶλλον, καίτοι πολλάκις
ἐπισκοτουμένων, οὐδὲ τῶν τῆς Αἴτνης κρατήρων ἀξιοθαυμαστότερον νομίζομεν, ἧς αἱ ἀναχοαὶ πέτρους τε ἐκ
βυθοῦ καὶ ὅλους ὄχθους ἀναφέρουσι καὶ ποταμοὺς ἐνίοτε
τοῦ γηγενοῦς ἐκείνου καὶ αὐτοῦ μόνου προχέουσιν πυρός.
20 5. ἀλλ᾽ ἐπὶ τῶν τοιούτων ἁπάντων ἐκεῖν᾽ ἂν εἴποιμεν, ὡς
εὐπόριστον μὲν ἀνθρώποις τὸ χρειῶδες ἢ καὶ ἀναγκαῖον,
θαυμαστὸν δ᾽ ὅμως ἀεὶ τὸ παράδοξον.

XXXVI

Οὐκοῦν ἐπί γε τῶν ἐν λόγοις μεγαλοφυῶν, ἐφ᾽ ὧν
οὐκέτ᾽ ἔξω τῆς χρείας καὶ ὠφελείας πίπτει τὸ μέγεθος,
25 προσήκει συνθεωρεῖν αὐτόθεν, ὅτι τοῦ ἀναμαρτήτου πολὺ
ἀφεστῶτες οἱ τηλικοῦτοι ὅμως πάντες εἰσὶν ἐπάνω τοῦ
θνητοῦ· καὶ τὰ μὲν ἄλλα τοὺς χρωμένους ἀνθρώπους
ἐλέγχει, τὸ δ᾽ ὕψος ἐγγὺς αἴρει μεγαλοφροσύνης θεοῦ·

---

7 ἐκβαίνουσι*ν P.   10 γεγόν*μεν P γεγόναμεν P.   11 εἰ] Faber, ἢ P.
14 σώζει P.   19 γηγενοῦς] Marklandus, γένους P.   22 αἰεὶ P.
23 ἐπί (ι corr. in ras.) P.   25 προσή*κει P.

life and into the vast universe as into some great assembly, to
be as it were spectators of the mighty whole and the keenest
aspirants for honour, forthwith she implants in our souls the
unconquerable love of whatever is elevated and more divine
than we.   3. Wherefore not even the entire universe suffices
for the thought and contemplation within the reach of the
human mind, but our imaginations often pass beyond the
bounds of space, and if we survey our life on every side and
see how much more it everywhere abounds in what is striking,
and great, and beautiful, we shall soon discern the purpose of
our birth.   4. This is why, by a sort of natural impulse, we
admire not the small streams, useful and pellucid though they
be, but the Nile, the Danube or the Rhine, and still more
the Ocean. Nor do we view the tiny flame of our own
kindling (guarded in lasting purity as its light ever is) with
greater awe than the celestial fires though they are often
shrouded in darkness; nor do we deem it a greater marvel
than the craters of Etna, whose eruptions throw up stones
from its depths and great masses of rock, and at times
pour forth rivers of that pure and unmixed subterranean fire.
5. In all such matters we may say that what is useful or
necessary men regard as commonplace, while they reserve
their admiration for that which is astounding.

XXXVI

Now as regards the manifestations of the sublime in
literature, in which grandeur is never, as it sometimes is in
nature, found apart from utility and advantage, it is fitting to
observe at once that, though writers of this magnitude are
far removed from faultlessness, they none the less all rise
above what is mortal; that all other qualities prove their
possessors to be men, but sublimity raises them near the
majesty of God; and that, while immunity from errors

καὶ τὸ μὲν ἄπταιστον οὐ ψέγεται, τὸ μέγα δὲ καὶ θαυμάζεται. 2. τί χρὴ πρὸς τούτοις ἔτι λέγειν, ὡς ἐκείνων
τῶν ἀνδρῶν ἕκαστος ἅπαντα τὰ σφάλματα ἑνὶ ἐξωνεῖται
πολλάκις ὕψει καὶ κατορθώματι, καὶ τὸ κυριώτατον, ὡς, εἴ
5 γε ἐκλέξας | τὰ Ὁμήρου, τὰ Δημοσθένους, τὰ Πλάτωνος, 201
τῶν ἄλλων, ὅσοι δὴ μέγιστοι, παραπτώματα πάντα ὁμόσε
συναθροίσειεν, ἐλάχιστον ἄν τι, μᾶλλον δ᾽ οὐδὲ πολλοστημόριον ἂν εὑρεθείη τῶν ἐκείνοις τοῖς ἥρωσι πάντη
κατορθουμένων; διὰ ταῦθ᾽ ὁ πᾶς αὐτοῖς αἰὼν καὶ βίος,
10 οὐ δυνάμενος ὑπὸ τοῦ φθόνου παρανοίας ἁλῶναι, φέρων
ἀπέδωκε τὰ νικητήρια καὶ ἄχρι νῦν ἀναφαίρετα φυλάττει
καὶ ἔοικε τηρήσειν,

ἔστ᾽ ἂν ὕδωρ τε ῥέῃ, καὶ δένδρεα μακρὰ τεθήλῃ.

3. πρὸς μέντοι γε τὸν γράφοντα, ὡς ὁ Κολοσσὸς ὁ ἡμαρ-
15 τημένος οὐ κρείττων ἢ ὁ Πολυκλείτου Δορυφόρος, παράκειται πρὸς πολλοῖς εἰπεῖν, ὅτι ἐπὶ μὲν τέχνης θαυμάζεται
τὸ ἀκριβέστατον, ἐπὶ δὲ τῶν φυσικῶν ἔργων τὸ μέγεθος,
φύσει δὲ λογικὸν ὁ ἄνθρωπος· κἀπὶ μὲν ἀνδριάντων
ζητεῖται τὸ ὅμοιον ἀνθρώπῳ, ἐπὶ δὲ τοῦ λόγου τὸ ὑπέρ-
20 αἶρον, ὡς ἔφην, τὰ ἀνθρώπινα. 4. προσήκει δ᾽ ὅμως
(ἀνακάμπτει γὰρ ἐπὶ τὴν ἀρχὴν ἡμῖν τοῦ ὑπομνήματος ἡ
παραίνεσις), ἐπειδὴ τὸ μὲν ἀδιάπτωτον ὡς ἐπὶ τὸ πολὺ
τέχνης ἐστὶ κατόρθωμα, τὸ δ᾽ ἐν ὑπεροχῇ πλὴν οὐχ
ὁμότονον μεγολοφυΐας, βοήθημα τῇ φύσει πάντη πορί-
25 ζεσθαι τὴν τέχνην· ἡ γὰρ ἀλληλουχία τούτων ἴσως
γένοιτ᾽ ἂν τὸ τέλειον.

Τοσαῦτα ἦν ἀναγκαῖον ὑπὲρ τῶν προτεθέντων ἐπι-
κρῖναι σκεμμάτων· χαιρέτω δ᾽ ἕκαστος οἷς ἥδεται.

relieves from censure, it is grandeur that excites admiration.
2.   What need to add thereto that each of these supreme
authors often redeems all his failures by a single sublime and
happy touch, and (most important of all) that if one were to
pick out and mass together the blunders of Homer, Demosthenes, Plato, and all the rest of the greatest writers, they
would be found to be a very small part, nay an infinitesimal
fraction, of the triumphs which those heroes achieve on every
hand?   This is the reason why the judgment of all posterity
—a verdict which envy itself cannot convict of perversity—
has brought and offered those meeds of victory which up
to this day it guards intact and seems likely still to
preserve,

Long as earth's waters shall flow, and her tall trees burgeon and
bloom[1].

3.   In reply, however, to the writer who maintains that the
faulty Colossus is not superior to the Spearman of Polycleitus, it is obvious to remark among many other things that
in art the utmost exactitude is admired, grandeur in the works
of nature; and that it is by nature that man is a being
gifted with speech.   In statues likeness to man is the quality
required; in discourse we demand, as I said, that which
transcends the human.   4.   Nevertheless—and the counsel
about to be given reverts to the beginning of our memoir—
since freedom from failings is for the most part the successful
result of art, and excellence (though it may be unevenly
sustained) the result of sublimity, the employment of art is
in every way a fitting aid to nature; for it is the conjunction
of the two which tends to ensure perfection.

Such are the decisions to which we have felt bound to
come with regard to the questions proposed; but let every
man cherish the view which pleases him best.

[1] Appendix C, *Scr. Inc.* (6).

XXXVII

Ταῖς δὲ μεταφοραῖς γειτνιῶσιν (ἐπανιτέον γὰρ) αἱ
παραβολαὶ καὶ εἰκόνες, ἐκείνῃ μόνον παραλλάττουσαι...

DESVNT DVO FOLIA

XXXVIII

... |στοι καὶ αἱ τοιαῦται· 'εἰ μὴ τὸν ἐγκέφαλον ἐν ταῖς 202ʳ
πτέρναις καταπεπατημένον φορεῖτε.' διόπερ εἰδέναι χρὴ
5 τὸ μέχρι ποῦ παροριστέον ἕκαστον· τὸ γὰρ ἐνίοτε περαι-
τέρω προεκπίπτειν ἀναιρεῖ τὴν ὑπερβολὴν καὶ τὰ τοιαῦτα
ὑπερτεινόμενα χαλᾶται, ἔσθ' ὅτε δὲ καὶ εἰς ὑπεναντιώσεις
ἀντιπεριΐσταται. 2. ὁ γοῦν Ἰσοκράτης οὐκ οἶδ' ὅπως
παιδὸς πρᾶγμα ἔπαθεν διὰ τὴν τοῦ πάντα αὐξητικῶς
10 ἐθέλειν λέγειν φιλοτιμίαν. ἔστι μὲν γὰρ ὑπόθεσις αὐτῷ
τοῦ Πανηγυρικοῦ λόγου, ὡς ἡ Ἀθηναίων πόλις ταῖς εἰς
τοὺς Ἕλληνας εὐεργεσίαις ὑπερβάλλει τὴν Λακεδαιμονίων,
ὁ δ' εὐθὺς ἐν τῇ εἰσβολῇ ταῦτα τίθησιν· 'ἔπειθ' οἱ λόγοι
τοσαύτην ἔχουσι δύναμιν, ὥσθ' οἷόν τ' εἶναι καὶ τὰ
15 μεγάλα ταπεινὰ ποιῆσαι καὶ τοῖς μικροῖς περιθεῖναι μέγεθος, καὶ τὰ παλαιὰ καινῶς εἰπεῖν καὶ περὶ τῶν νεωστὶ
γεγενημένων ἀρχαίως διελθεῖν.' οὐκοῦν, φησί τις, Ἰσό-
κρατες, οὕτως μέλλεις καὶ τὰ περὶ Λακεδαιμονίων καὶ
Ἀθηναίων ἐναλλάττειν; σχεδὸν γὰρ τὸ τῶν λόγων ἐγκώ-
20 μιον ἀπιστίας τῆς καθ' αὑτοῦ τοῖς ἀκούουσι παράγγελμα
καὶ προοίμιον ἐξέθηκε. 3. μήποτ' οὖν ἄρισται τῶν
ὑπερβολῶν, ὡς καὶ ἐπὶ τῶν σχημάτων προείπομεν, αἱ
αὐτὸ τοῦτο διαλανθάνουσαι ὅτι εἰσὶν ὑπερβολαί. γίνεται
δὲ τὸ τοιόνδε, ἐπειδὰν ὑπὸ ἐκπαθείας μεγέθει τινὶ

---

2 ἐκείνηι (ι addito a m. rec.) P. desunt folia IV et V quaternionis ΚΘ, sexti
folii vocabulum primum καταγέλαστοι esse conicit Dobraeus. 12 Λακε-
δαιμονίων] Robortellus, λακεδαιμονίαν P. 19 ἐναλλάττειν (λ superscripto a m.
rec.) P.

XXXVII

Closely related to Metaphors (for we must return to our point) are comparisons and similes, differing only in this respect...

XXXVIII

...such Hyperboles as: 'unless you carry your brains trodden down in your heels[1].' It is necessary, therefore, to know where to fix the limit in each case; for an occasional overshooting of the mark ruins the hyperbole, and such expressions, when strained too much, lose their tension, and sometimes swing round and produce the contrary effect. 2. Isocrates, for example, fell into unaccountable puerility owing to the ambition which made him desire to describe everything with a touch of amplification. The theme of his *Panegyric* is that Athens surpasses Lacedaemon in benefits conferred upon Greece, and yet at the very outset of his speech he uses these words: 'Further, language has such capacity that it is possible thereby to debase things lofty and invest things small with grandeur, and to express old things in a new way, and to discourse in ancient fashion about what has newly happened[2].' 'Do you then, Isocrates,' it may be asked, 'mean in that way to interchange the facts of Lacedaemonian and Athenian history?' For in his eulogy of language he has, we may say, published to his hearers a preamble warning them to distrust himself. 3. Perhaps, then, as we said in dealing with figures generally, those hyperboles are best in which the very fact that they are hyperboles escapes attention. This happens when, through stress of strong emotion, they are uttered in connexion with some great crisis, as is

---

[1] [Demosth.] *de Halonneso* 45.—App. C, *Demosthenes*.　　[2] Isocr. *Paneg.* 8.

συνεκφωνῶνται περιστάσεως, ὅπερ ὁ Θουκυδίδης ἐπὶ τῶν
ἐν Σικελίᾳ φθειρομένων ποιεῖ. ' οἵ τε γὰρ Συρακούσιοι '
φησὶν ' ἐπικαταβάντες τοὺς | ἐν τῷ ποταμῷ μάλιστα 202ᵛ
ἔσφαζον, καὶ τὸ ὕδωρ εὐθὺς διέφθαρτο· ἀλλ' οὐδὲν ἧσσον
5 ἐπίνετο ὁμοῦ τῷ πηλῷ ᾑματωμένον καὶ τοῖς πολλοῖς ἔτι
ἦν περιμάχητον.' αἷμα καὶ πηλὸν πινόμενα ὅμως εἶναι
περιμάχητα ἔτι ποιεῖ πιστὸν ἡ τοῦ πάθους ὑπεροχὴ καὶ
περίστασις. 4. καὶ τὸ Ἡροδότειον ἐπὶ τῶν ἐν Θερμο-
πύλαις ὅμοιον. ' ἐν τούτῳ ' φησὶν ' ἀλεξομένους μαχαί-
10 ρῃσιν, ὅσοις αὐτῶν ἔτι ἐτύγχανον περιοῦσαι, καὶ χερσὶ
καὶ στόμασι, κατέχωσαν οἱ βάρβαροι.' ἐνταῦθ', οἷόν
ἐστι τὸ καὶ στόμασι μάχεσθαι πρὸς ὡπλισμένους καὶ
ὁποῖόν τι τὸ κατακεχῶσθαι βέλεσιν, ἐρεῖς, πλὴν ὁμοίως
ἔχει πίστιν· οὐ γὰρ τὸ πρᾶγμα ἕνεκα τῆς ὑπερβολῆς
15 παραλαμβάνεσθαι δοκεῖ, ἡ ὑπερβολὴ δ' εὐλόγως γεννᾶσθαι πρὸς τοῦ πράγματος. 5. ἔστι γάρ, ὡς οὐ δια-
λείπω λέγων, παντὸς τολμήματος λεκτικοῦ λύσις καὶ
πανάκειά τις τὰ ἐγγὺς ἐκστάσεως ἔργα καὶ πάθη· ὅθεν
καὶ τὰ κωμικὰ καίτοιγ' εἰς ἀπιστίαν ἐκπίπτοντα πιθανὰ
20 διὰ τὸ γελοῖον·

ἀγρὸν ἔσχ' ἐλάττω γῆν ἔχοντ' ἐπιστολῆς.

καὶ γὰρ ὁ γέλως πάθος ἐν ἡδονῇ. 6. αἱ δ' ὑπερβολαὶ
καθάπερ ἐπὶ τὸ μεῖζον, οὕτως καὶ ἐπὶ τοὔλαττον, ἐπειδὴ
κοινὸν ἀμφοῖν ἡ ἐπίτασις· καί πως ὁ διασυρμὸς ταπει-
25 νότητός ἐστιν αὔξησις.

XXXIX

Ἡ πέμπτη μοῖρα τῶν συντελουσῶν εἰς τὸ ὕψος, ὧν
γε ἐν ἀρχῇ προὐθέμεθα, ἔθ' ἡμῖν λείπεται, κράτιστε,

8 ἡροδότειο*ν P.   11 κατέχωσαν] codd. Herodoti, Manutius: κατίσχυσαν P.
12 ὡπλι*|σμένουσ P.   14 πράγμα P.   15 εὐλόγως] Robortellus,
εὐλόγουσ P.   18 πανάκια P, πανάκειά m. rec. P.   ἐκστάσεως] Portus,
ἐξετάσεωσ P.   20 γέλοιον P.   21 ἔσχα P.   ἔχοντ' ἐπιστολῆς] Valcke-
narius, ἔχον γὰρ στολῆσ P.   27 κράτιστε* P.

done by Thucydides in the case of those who perished in Sicily. 'The Syracusans,' he says, 'came down to the water's edge and began the slaughter of those chiefly who were in the river, and the water at once became polluted, but none the less it was swallowed although muddy and mixed with blood, and to most it was still worth fighting for[1].' That a draught of blood and mud should still be worth fighting for, is rendered credible by the intensity of the emotion at a great crisis. 4. So with the passage in which Herodotus tells of those who fell at Thermopylae. 'On this spot,' he says, 'the barbarians buried them as they defended themselves with daggers—those of them who had daggers still left—and with hands and mouths[2].' Here you may be inclined to protest against the expressions 'fight with their very mouths' against men in armour, and 'being buried' with darts. At the same time the narrative carries conviction; for the event does not seem to be introduced for the sake of the hyperbole, but the hyperbole to spring naturally from the event. 5. For (as I never cease to say) the deeds and passions which verge on transport are a sufficient lenitive and remedy for every audacity of speech. This is the reason why the quips of comedy, although they may be carried to the extreme of absurdity, are plausible because they are so amusing. For instance,

Smaller his field was than a Spartan letter[3].

For mirth, too, is an emotion, an emotion which has its root in pleasure. 6. Hyperboles are employed in describing things small as well as great, since exaggeration is the common element in both cases. And, in a sense, ridicule is an amplification of the paltriness of things.

XXXIX

The fifth of those elements contributing to the sublime which we mentioned, my excellent friend, at the beginning, still

---

[1] Thucyd. VII. 84.   [2] Herod. VII. 225.
[3] Appendix C, *Scr. Inc.* (2).

ἡ διὰ τῶν λόγων αὐτὴ ποιὰ σύνθεσις. ὑπὲρ ἧς ἐν δυσὶν
ἀποχρώντως ἀποδεδωκότες συντάγμασιν, ὅσα γε τῆς
θεωρίας | ἦν ἡμῖν ἐφικτά, τοσοῦτον ἐξ ἀνάγκης προσ- 203
θείημεν ἂν εἰς τὴν παροῦσαν ὑπόθεσιν, ὡς οὐ μόνον ἐστὶ
5 πειθοῦς καὶ ἡδονῆς ἡ ἁρμονία φυσικὸν ἀνθρώποις, ἀλλὰ
καὶ μεγαληγορίας καὶ πάθους θαυμαστόν τι ὄργανον.
2. οὐ γὰρ αὐλὸς μὲν ἐντίθησίν τινα πάθη τοῖς ἀκροω-
μένοις καὶ οἷον ἔκφρονας καὶ κορυβαντιασμοῦ πλήρεις
ἀποτελεῖ, καὶ βάσιν ἐνδούς τινα ῥυθμοῦ πρὸς ταύτην
10 ἀναγκάζει βαίνειν ἐν ῥυθμῷ καὶ συνεξομοιοῦσθαι τῷ
μέλει τὸν ἀκροατήν, κἂν ἄμουσος ᾖ παντάπασι, καὶ νὴ
Δία φθόγγοι κιθάρας, οὐδὲν ἁπλῶς σημαίνοντες, ταῖς τῶν
ἤχων μεταβολαῖς καὶ τῇ πρὸς ἀλλήλους κρούσει καὶ
μίξει τῆς συμφωνίας θαυμαστὸν ἐπάγουσι πολλάκις, ὡς
15 ἐπίστασαι, θέλγητρον 3. (καίτοι ταῦτα εἴδωλα καὶ μιμή-
ματα νόθα ἐστὶ πειθοῦς, οὐχὶ τῆς ἀνθρωπείας φύσεως, ὡς
ἔφην, ἐνεργήματα γνήσια), οὐκ οἰόμεθα δ' ἄρα τὴν σύν-
θεσιν, ἁρμονίαν τινὰ οὖσαν λόγων ἀνθρώποις ἐμφύτων
καὶ τῆς ψυχῆς αὐτῆς, οὐχὶ τῆς ἀκοῆς μόνης ἐφαπτομένων,
20 ποικίλας κινοῦσαν ἰδέας ὀνομάτων νοήσεων πραγμάτων
κάλλους εὐμελείας, πάντων ἡμῖν ἐντρόφων καὶ συγγενῶν,
καὶ ἅμα τῇ μίξει καὶ πολυμορφίᾳ τῶν ἑαυτῆς φθόγγων τὸ
παρεστὼς τῷ λέγοντι πάθος εἰς τὰς ψυχὰς τῶν πέλας
παρεισάγουσαν καὶ εἰς μετουσίαν αὐτοῦ τοὺς ἀκούοντας
25 ἀεὶ καθιστᾶσαν, τῇ τε τῶν λέξεων ἐποικοδομήσει τὰ
μεγέθη συναρμόζουσαν, δι' αὐτῶν τούτων κηλεῖν τε ὁμοῦ,
καὶ πρὸς ὄγκον τε καὶ ἀξίωμα καὶ ὕψος καὶ πᾶν ὃ ἐν

---

1 αὐτὴ] Spengelius, αὕτη P.   *ἧσ P.   2 Σημ περὶ συνθέσεωσ ἔγραψε
Διονύσιοσ in marg. P.   6 μεγαληγορίας] Tollius, μετ' ἐλευθερίασ P.
7 ἐντίθησιν] Faber, ἐπιτίθησιν P.   ἀκροομένοισ P ἀκροωμένοισ P.   10 ἀναγ-
κάζει] Manutius, ἀναγκάσει P.   11 ἄμουσοσ ᾖ] Boivinus, ἄλλουσ ὅση P.
12 σημαίνονταῖσ (αῖ in ras. corr.: τεσ superscr. a m. rec.) P.   15 ἐπίστασαι]
Faber, ἐπίστασιν P.   ταῦτα] Morus, ταῦτα τὰ P.   18 ἐμφύτων]
Manutius, ἐμφύτωσ (ex ἐμφύτοισ ut videtur) m. rec. P.   25 αἰεὶ P.
26 κηλεῖν] Robortellus, καλεῖν P.

remains to be dealt with, namely the arrangement of the words
in a certain order.   In regard to this, having already in two
treatises sufficiently stated such results as our inquiry could
compass, we will add, for the purpose of our present undertaking, only what is absolutely essential, namely the fact that
harmonious arrangement is not only a natural source of
persuasion and pleasure among men but also a wonderful in-
strument of lofty utterance and of passion.   2. For does
not the flute instil certain emotions into its hearers and as it
were make them beside themselves and full of frenzy, and
supplying a rhythmical movement constrain the listener to
move rhythmically in accordance therewith and to conform
himself to the melody, although he may be utterly ignorant of
music?   Yes, and the tones of the harp, although in themselves
they signify nothing at all, often cast a wonderful spell, as you
know, over an audience by means of the variations of sounds,
by their pulsation against one another, and by their mingling
in concert.   3. And yet these are mere semblances and
spurious copies of persuasion, not (as I have said) genuine
activities of human nature.   Are we not, then, to hold that
composition (being a harmony of that language which is
implanted by nature in man and which appeals not to the
hearing only but to the soul itself), since it calls forth manifold
shapes of words, thoughts, deeds, beauty, melody, all of them
born at our birth and growing with our growth, and since by
means of the blending and variation of its own tones it seeks to
introduce into the minds of those who are present the emotion
which affects the speaker and since it always brings the
audience to share in it and by the building of phrase upon
phrase raises a sublime and harmonious structure: are we not,
I say, to hold that harmony by these selfsame means allures
us and invariably disposes us to stateliness and dignity and

αὐτῇ περιλαμβάνει καὶ ἡμᾶς ἑκάσ|τοτε συνδιατιθέναι, 203
παντοίως ἡμῶν τῆς διανοίας ἐπικρατοῦσαν; ἀλλ᾽ εἰ καὶ
μανία τὸ περὶ τῶν οὕτως ὁμολογουμένων διαπορεῖν, ἀποχρῶσα γὰρ ἡ πεῖρα πίστις, 4. ὑψηλόν γέ που δοκεῖ νόημα
5 καὶ ἔστι τῷ ὄντι θαυμάσιον, ὃ τῷ ψηφίσματι ὁ Δημοσθένης ἐπιφέρει· ʽτοῦτο τὸ ψήφισμα τὸν τότε τῇ πόλει
περιστάντα κίνδυνον παρελθεῖν ἐποίησεν, ὥσπερ νέφος·᾽
ἀλλ᾽ αὐτῆς τῆς διανοίας οὐκ ἔλαττον τῇ ἁρμονίᾳ πεφώ-
νηται· ὅλον τε γὰρ ἐπὶ τῶν δακτυλικῶν εἴρηται ῥυθμῶν·
10 εὐγενέστατοι δ᾽ οὗτοι καὶ μεγεθοποιοί, διὸ καὶ τὸ ἡρῷον,
ὧν ἴσμεν κάλλιστον, μέτρον συνιστᾶσι· τό τε* ἐπείτοιγε
ἐκ τῆς ἰδίας αὐτὸ χώρας μετάθες, ὅποι δὴ ἐθέλεις, ʽτοῦτο
τὸ ψήφισμα, ὥσπερ νέφος, ἐποίησε τὸν τότε κίνδυνον
παρελθεῖν,᾽ ἢ νὴ Δία μίαν ἀπόκοψον συλλαβὴν μόνον
15 ʽἐποίησε παρελθεῖν ὡς νέφος,᾽ καὶ εἴσῃ πόσον ἡ ἁρμονία
τῷ ὕψει συνηχεῖ. αὐτὸ γὰρ τὸ ʽὥσπερ νέφος᾽ ἐπὶ
μακροῦ τοῦ πρώτου ῥυθμοῦ βέβηκε, τέτρασι καταμετρουμένου χρόνοις· ἐξαιρεθείσης δὲ τῆς μιᾶς συλλαβῆς
ʽὡς νέφος᾽ εὐθὺς ἀκρωτηριάζει τῇ συγκοπῇ τὸ μέγεθος,
20 ὡς ἔμπαλιν, ἐὰν ἐπεκτείνῃς ʽπαρελθεῖν ἐποίησεν ὡσπερεὶ
νέφος,᾽ τὸ αὐτὸ σημαίνει, οὐ τὸ αὐτὸ δὲ ἔτι προσπίπτει,
ὅτι τῷ μήκει τῶν ἄκρων χρόνων συνεκλύεται καὶ διαχα-
λᾶται τὸ ὕψος τὸ ἀπότομον.

XL

Ἐν δὲ τοῖς μάλιστα μεγεθοποιεῖ τὰ λεγόμενα, καθά-
25 περ τὰ σώματα, ἡ τῶν μελῶν ἐπισύνθεσις, ὧν ἓν μὲν
οὐδὲν τμηθὲν ἀφ᾽ ἑτέρου καθ᾽ ἑαυτὸ ἀξιόλογον ἔχει, πάντα

---

1 αὐτῇ] Tollius, αὐτῆ P.   4 που δοκεῖ] Reiskius, τοῦ δοκεῖν P.   6 τότε]
codd. Demosthenis, Manutius : τότ᾽ ἐν P.   11 Vide App. A.   17 κατα-
μετρουμένου] Tollius, καταμετρούμενον P.   19 τῇ συγκοπῇ] Robortellus, τῆ
συγκοπῆ P.   20 ὡσπερεὶ] Tollius, ὥσπερ P.   21 οὐ τὸ* P.

elevation and every emotion which it contains within itself, gaining absolute mastery over our minds? But it is folly to dispute concerning matters which are generally admitted, since experience is proof sufficient.   4. An example of a conception which is usually thought sublime and is really admirable is that which Demosthenes associates with the decree: 'This decree caused the danger which then beset the city to pass by just-as a cloud[1].' But it owes its happy sound no less to the harmony than to the thought itself.   For the thought is expressed throughout in dactylic rhythms, and these are most noble and productive of sublimity ; and therefore it is that they constitute the heroic, the finest metre that we know.   [And the order of the expression ὥσπερ νέφος is exactly right.]   For if you derange the words of the sentence and transpose them in whatever way you will, as for example 'This decree just-as a cloud caused the danger of the time to pass by'; nay, if you cut off a single syllable only and say 'caused to pass by as a cloud,' you will perceive to what an extent harmony is in unison with sublimity.   For the very words 'just-as a cloud' begin with a long rhythm, which consists of four metrical beats ; but if one syllable is cut off and we read 'as a cloud,' we immediately maim the sublimity by the abbreviation.   Conversely, if you elongate the word and write 'caused to pass by just-as-if a cloud,' it means the same thing, but no longer falls with the same effect upon the ear, inasmuch as the abrupt grandeur of the passage loses its energy and tension through the lengthening of the concluding syllables.

XL

Among the chief causes of the sublime in speech, as in the structure of the human body, is the collocation of members, a single one of which if severed from another

---

[1] Demosth. *de Cor.* 188.

δὲ μετ' ἀλλήλων ἐκπληροῖ τέλειον σύστημα, οὕτως τὰ
μεγά|λα, σκεδασθέντα μὲν ἀπ' ἀλλήλων, ἄλλοσ' ἄλλῃ ἅμα 20
ἑαυτοῖς συνδιαφορεῖ καὶ τὸ ὕψος, σωματοποιούμενα δὲ τῇ
κοινωνίᾳ καὶ ἔτι δεσμῷ τῆς ἁρμονίας περικλειόμενα αὐτῷ
5 τῷ κύκλῳ φωνήεντα γίνεται· καὶ σχεδὸν ἐν ταῖς περιόδοις
ἔρανός ἐστι πλήθους τὰ μεγέθη.   2. ἀλλὰ μὴν ὅτι γε
πολλοὶ καὶ συγγραφέων καὶ ποιητῶν οὐκ ὄντες ὑψηλοὶ
φύσει, μήποτε δὲ καὶ ἀμεγέθεις, ὅμως κοινοῖς καὶ δημώδεσι τοῖς ὀνόμασι καὶ οὐδὲν ἐπαγομένοις περιττὸν ὡς τὰ
10 πολλὰ συγχρώμενοι, διὰ μόνου τοῦ συνθεῖναι καὶ ἁρμόσαι
ταῦτα δ' ὅμως ὄγκον καὶ διάστημα καὶ τὸ μὴ ταπεινοὶ
δοκεῖν εἶναι περιεβάλοντο, καθάπερ ἄλλοι τε πολλοὶ καὶ
Φίλιστος, Ἀριστοφάνης ἔν τισιν, ἐν τοῖς πλείστοις Εὐριπίδης, ἱκανῶς ἡμῖν δεδήλωται.   3. μετά γέ τοι τὴν
15 τεκνοκτονίαν Ἡρακλῆς φησι,

γέμω κακῶν δὴ κοὐκέτ' ἔσθ' ὅποι τεθῇ.

σφόδρα δημῶδες τὸ λεγόμενον, ἀλλὰ γέγονεν ὑψηλὸν τῇ
πλάσει ἀναλογοῦν, εἰ δ' ἄλλως αὐτὸ συναρμόσεις, φανή-
σεταί σοι, διότι τῆς συνθέσεως ποιητὴς ὁ Εὐριπίδης
20 μᾶλλόν ἐστιν ἢ τοῦ νοῦ.   4. ἐπὶ δὲ τῆς συρομένης ὑπὸ
τοῦ ταύρου Δίρκης,

εἰ δέ που τύχοι
πέριξ ἑλίξας, * * εἶλχ' ὁμοῦ λαβὼν
γυναῖκα πέτραν δρῦν μεταλλάσσων ἀεί,

25 ἔστι μὲν γενναῖον καὶ τὸ λῆμμα, ἁδρότερον δὲ γέγονε τῷ
τὴν ἁρμονίαν μὴ κατεσπεῦσθαι μηδ' οἷον ἐν ἀποκυλί-
σματι φέρεσθαι, ἀλλὰ στηριγμούς τε ἔχειν πρὸς ἄλληλα
τὰ ὀνόματα καὶ ἐξερείσματα τῶν χρόνων πρὸς ἑδραῖον
διαβεβηκό|τα μέγεθος.   20

---

2 τὰ μά|λα sed in marg. τὰ μεγάλα P.   ἄλλοσ' (superscripto a m. rec. ἄλληι)
P.   6 γε] Tollius, τε P.   16 καὶ οὐκ ἔτ' P.   18 συναρμόσ**σ P συναρ-
μόσεισ P.   20 ἐπὶ] Manutius, ἐπεὶ P.   23 ἑλίξας εἷλκε ὁμοῦ P, εἷλκεν
εἶλχ' conicit Adam.   25 λῆμμα] Robortellus, λῆ|μα P.   26 ἐν] Toupius,
μὲν P.

possesses in itself nothing remarkable, but all united together
make a full and perfect organism. So the constituents of
grandeur, when separated from one another, carry with them
sublimity in distraction this way and that, but when formed
into a body by association and when further encircled in
a chain of harmony they become sonorous by their very
rotundity; and in periods sublimity is, as it were, a contribution made by a multitude. 2. We have, however, sufficiently
shown that many writers and poets who possess no natural
sublimity and are perhaps even wanting in elevation have
nevertheless, although employing for the most part common
and popular words with no striking associations of their own,
by merely joining and fitting these together, secured dignity
and distinction and the appearance of freedom from meanness.
Instances will be furnished by Philistus among many others,
by Aristophanes in certain passages, by Euripides in most.
3. In the last-mentioned author, Heracles, after the scene in
which he slays his children, uses the words :—

> Full-fraught am I with woes—no space for more[1].

The expression is a most ordinary one, but it has gained
elevation through the aptness of the structure of the line.
If you shape the sentence in a different way, you will see
this plainly, the fact being that Euripides is a poet in virtue
of his power of composition rather than of his invention.
4. In the passage which describes Dirce torn away by the
bull :—

> Whitherso'er he turned
> Swift wheeling round, he haled and hurled withal
> Dame, rock, oak, intershifted ceaselessly[2],

the conception itself is a fine one, but it has been rendered
more forcible by the fact that the harmony is not hurried or
carried as it were on rollers, but the words act as buttresses
for one another and find support in the pauses, and issue
finally in a well-grounded sublimity.

---

[1] Eurip. *Herc. Fur.* 1245.   [2] Appendix C, *Euripides*.

XLI

Μικροποιοῦν δ᾽ οὐδὲν οὕτως ἐν τοῖς ὑψηλοῖς, ὡς ῥυθμὸς
κεκλασμένος λόγων καὶ σεσοβημένος, οἷον δὴ πυρρίχιοι
καὶ τροχαῖοι καὶ διχόρειοι, τέλεον εἰς ὀρχηστικὸν συνεκ-
πίπτοντες· εὐθὺς γὰρ πάντα φαίνεται τὰ κατάρυθμα
5 κομψὰ καὶ μικροχαρῆ καὶ ἀπαθέστατα διὰ τῆς ὁμοειδίας
ἐπιπολάζοντα· 2. καὶ ἔτι τούτων τὸ χείριστον ὅτι, ὥσπερ
τὰ ᾠδάρια τοὺς ἀκροατὰς ἀπὸ τοῦ πράγματος ἀφέλκει καὶ
ἐφ᾽ αὑτὰ βιάζεται, οὕτως καὶ τὰ κατερρυθμισμένα τῶν
λεγομένων οὐ τὸ τοῦ λόγου πάθος ἐνδίδωσι τοῖς ἀκούουσι,
10 τὸ δὲ τοῦ ῥυθμοῦ, ὡς ἐνίοτε προειδότας τὰς ὀφειλομένας
καταλήξεις αὐτοὺς ὑποκρούειν τοῖς λέγουσι καὶ φθάνοντας
ὡς ἐν χορῷ τινι προαποδιδόναι τὴν βάσιν. 3. ὁμοίως δὲ
ἀμεγέθη καὶ τὰ λίαν συγκείμενα καὶ εἰς μικρὰ καὶ βραχυσύλλαβα συγκεκομμένα καὶ ὡσανεὶ γόμφοις τισὶν ἐπαλ-
15 λήλοις κατ᾽ ἐγκοπὰς καὶ σκληρότητας ἐπισυνδεδεμένα.

XLII

Ἔτι γε μὴν ὕψους μειωτικὸν καὶ ἡ ἄγαν τῆς φράσεως
συγκοπή· πηροῖ γὰρ τὸ μέγεθος, ὅταν εἰς λίαν συνάγηται
βραχύ· ἀκουέσθω δὲ νῦν μὴ τὰ δεόντως συνεστραμμένα,
ἀλλ᾽ ὅσα ἄντικρυς μικρὰ καὶ κατακεκερματισμένα· συγ-
20 κοπὴ μὲν γὰρ κολούει τὸν νοῦν, συντομία δ᾽ ἐπ᾽ εὐθύ,
δῆλον δ᾽ ὡς ἔμπαλιν τὰ ἐκτάδην ἀπόψυχα· τὰ γὰρ
ἄκαιρον μῆκος ἀνακαλούμενα.

---

1 μι*κροποιοῦν P.   2 λόγων] Faber, λόγω P. Cp. p. 46. 27 supra.
3 διχόρειο*ι (o et ι in ras.) P.   ὀρ|χηστι*κὸν (χ in ras.) P.   5 ὁμοειδ*ίασ P.
6 ὅτι ὥσπερ] Manutius, ὅπωσ ὥσπερ P.   8 ἐπ᾽ αὑτὰ P.   10 ῥυ*|θμοῦ
(θ a m. rec.) P.   12 χο*ρῷ P.   15 σκληρότητοσ P σκληρότητασ P.
17 πηροῖ] Manutius, πληροῖ P.   18 μὴ τὰ δεόντως] Manutius, μὴ τὰ οὐ
δεόντωσ P.   20 κολούει] Faber, κωλούει P, κωλύει Robortellus.

XLI

There is nothing in the sphere of the sublime, that is so lowering as broken and agitated movement of language, such as is characteristic of pyrrhics and trochees and dichorees, which fall altogether to the level of dance-music. For all over-rhythmical writing is at once felt to be affected and finical and wholly lacking in passion owing to the monotony of its superficial polish. 2. And the worst of it all is that, just as petty lays draw their hearer away from the point and compel his attention to themselves, so also over-rhythmical style does not communicate the feeling of the words but simply the feeling of the rhythm. Sometimes, indeed, the listeners knowing beforehand the due terminations stamp their feet in time with the speaker, and as in a dance give the right step in anticipation. 3. In like manner those words are destitute of sublimity which lie too close together, and are cut up into short and tiny syllables, and are held together as if with wooden bolts by sheer inequality and ruggedness.

XLII

Further, excessive concision of expression tends to lower the sublime, since grandeur is marred when the thought is brought into too narrow a compass. Let this be understood not of proper compression, but of what is absolutely petty and cut into segments. For concision curtails the sense, but brevity goes straight to the mark. It is plain that, *vice versa*, prolixities are frigid, for so is everything that resorts to unseasonable length.

XLIII

Δεινὴ δ' αἰσχῦναι τὰ μεγέθη καὶ ἡ μικρότης τῶν
ὀνομάτων. παρὰ γοῦν τῷ Ἡροδότῳ κατὰ μὲν τὰ λήμ-
ματα δαι|μονίως ὁ χειμὼν πέφρασται, τινὰ δὲ νὴ Δία 20
περιέχει τῆς ὕλης ἀδοξότερα, καὶ τοῦτο μὲν ἴσως 'ζεσάσης
5 δὲ τῆς θαλάσσης,' ὡς τὸ 'ζεσάσης' πολὺ τὸ ὕψος περισπᾷ
διὰ τὸ κακόστομον· ἀλλ' 'ὁ ἄνεμος' φησὶν 'ἐκοπίασεν,'
καὶ τοὺς περὶ τὸ ναυάγιον δρασσομένους ἐξεδέχετο 'τέλος
ἀχάριστον.' ἄσεμνον γὰρ τὸ κοπιάσαι ἰδιωτικόν, τὸ δ'
ἀχάριστον τηλικούτου πάθους ἀνοίκειον. 2. ὁμοίως καὶ
10 ὁ Θεόπομπος ὑπερφυῶς σκευάσας τὴν τοῦ Πέρσου κατά-
βασιν ἐπ' Αἴγυπτον ὀνοματίοις τισὶ τὰ ὅλα διέβαλεν.
'ποία γὰρ πόλις ἢ ποῖον ἔθνος τῶν κατὰ τὴν Ἀσίαν οὐκ
ἐπρεσβεύετο πρὸς βασιλέα; τί δὲ τῶν ἐκ τῆς γῆς γεννωμένων ἢ τῶν κατὰ τέχνην ἐπιτελουμένων καλῶν ἢ τιμίων
15 οὐκ ἐκομίσθη δῶρον ὡς αὐτόν; οὐ πολλαὶ μὲν καὶ πολυτελεῖς στρωμναὶ καὶ χλανίδες τὰ μὲν ἁλουργῆ, τὰ δὲ
ποικιλτά, τὰ δὲ λευκά, πολλαὶ δὲ σκηναὶ χρυσαῖ κατε-
σκευασμέναι πᾶσι τοῖς χρησίμοις, πολλαὶ δὲ καὶ ξυστίδες
καὶ κλῖναι πολυτελεῖς; ἔτι δὲ καὶ κοῖλος ἄργυρος καὶ
20 χρυσὸς ἀπειργασμένος καὶ ἐκπώματα καὶ κρατῆρες, ὧν
τοὺς μὲν λιθοκολλήτους, τοὺς δ' ἄλλους ἀκριβῶς καὶ
πολυτελῶς εἶδες ἂν ἐκπεπονημένους. πρὸς δὲ τούτοις
ἀναρίθμητοι μὲν ὅπλων μυριάδες τῶν μὲν Ἑλληνικῶν,
τῶν δὲ βαρβαρικῶν, ὑπερβάλλοντα δὲ τὸ πλῆθος ὑποζύγια
25 καὶ πρὸς κατακοπὴν ἱερεῖα σιτευτά· καὶ πολλοὶ μὲν ἀρτυ-
μάτων μέδιμνοι, πολλοὶ δ' οἱ θύλακοι καὶ σάκκοι καὶ
χάρται βυβλίων καὶ τῶν ἄλλων ἁπάντων χρησίμων· |

---

1 αἰσχύν∗αι P.   3 νὴ Δία] Manutius, γήδια P.   7 τέλος ἀχάριστον]
Robortellus, τέλοσ ἀχαριστί P, τέλος...ἀχαρι codd. Herodoti.   13 γενομένων P
γεννωμένων P.   14 τιμίων] Manutius, τιμῶν P.   15 ἐκομί∗σθη (σ a m. rec.) P.
16 στρομναὶ P στρωμναὶ P.   17 κατασκευασμέναι P, corr. Manutius.
21 λιθο∗∗λλίτουσ P λιθοκολλήτουσ P.   25 σιτευτά] Canterus, εἰσ ταῦτα P εἰς
ταὐτὰ Spengelius.   26 σάκοι P.

XLIII

Triviality of expression is also apt to disfigure sublimity. In Herodotus, for example, the tempest is described with marvellous effect in all its details, but the passage surely contains some words below the dignity of the subject. The following may serve as an instance—'when the sea seethed[1].' The word 'seethed' detracts greatly from the sublimity because it is an ill-sounding one. Further, 'the wind,' he says, 'grew fagged,' and those who clung to the spars met 'an unpleasant end[2].' The expression 'grew fagged' is lacking in dignity, being vulgar; and the word 'unpleasant' is inappropriate to so great a disaster. 2. Similarly, when Theopompus had dressed out in marvellous fashion the descent of the Persian king upon Egypt, he spoilt the whole by some petty words. 'For which of the cities (he says) or which of the tribes in Asia did not send envoys to the Great King? Which of the products of the earth or of the achievements of art was not, in all its beauty or preciousness, brought as an offering to his presence? Consider the multitude of costly coverlets and mantles, in purple or white or embroidery; the multitude of pavilions of gold furnished with all things useful; the multitude, too, of tapestries and costly couches. Further, gold and silver plate richly wrought, and goblets and mixing-bowls, some of which you might have seen set with precious stones, and others finished with care and at great price. In addition to all this, countless myriads of Greek and barbaric weapons, and beasts of burden beyond all reckoning and victims fattened for slaughter, and many bushels of condiments, and many bags and sacks and sheets of papyrus and all other useful things, and an equal number

---

[1] Herod. VII. 188.   [2] Herod. VII. 191 and VIII. 13.

τοσαῦτα δὲ κρέα τεταριχευμένα παντοδαπῶν ἱερείων, ὡς 20ε
σωροὺς αὐτῶν γενέσθαι τηλικούτους, ὥστε τοὺς προσ-
ιόντας πόρρωθεν ὑπολαμβάνειν ὄχθους εἶναι καὶ λόφους
ἀντωθουμένους.' 3. ἐκ τῶν ὑψηλοτέρων εἰς τὰ ταπει-
5 νότερα ἀποδιδράσκει, δέον ποιήσασθαι τὴν αὔξησιν
ἔμπαλιν· ἀλλὰ τῇ θαυμαστῇ τῆς ὅλης παρασκευῆς ἀγγε-
λίᾳ παραμίξας τοὺς θυλάκους καὶ τὰ ἀρτύματα καὶ τὰ
σακκία μαγειρείου τινὰ φαντασίαν ἐποίησεν. ὥσπερ γὰρ
εἴ τις ἐπ' αὐτῶν ἐκείνων τῶν προκοσμημάτων μεταξὺ τῶν
10 χρυσίων καὶ λιθοκολλήτων κρατήρων καὶ ἀργύρου κοίλου
σκηνῶν τε ὁλοχρύσων καὶ ἐκπωμάτων, φέρων μέσα
ἔθηκεν θυλάκια καὶ σακκία, ἀπρεπὲς ἂν ἦν τῇ προσόψει
τὸ ἔργον· οὕτω καὶ τῆς ἑρμηνείας τὰ τοιαῦτα ὀνόματα
αἴσχη καὶ οἱονεὶ στίγματα καθίσταται παρὰ καιρὸν
15 ἐγκατατατττόμενα. 4. παρέκειτο δ' ὡς ὁλοσχερῶς ἐπελ-
θεῖν καὶ ὡς ὄχθους λέγει συμβεβλῆσθαι, καὶ περὶ τῆς
ἄλλης παρασκευῆς οὕτως ἁμάξας εἰπεῖν καὶ καμήλους καὶ
πλῆθος ὑποζυγίων φορταγωγούντων πάντα τὰ πρὸς τρυφὴν
καὶ ἀπόλαυσιν τραπεζῶν χορηγήματα, ἢ σωροὺς ὀνο-
20 μάσαι παντοίων σπερμάτων καὶ τῶν ἅπερ διαφέρει πρὸς
ὀψοποιΐας καὶ ἡδυπαθείας, ἢ εἴπερ πάντως ἐβούλετο αὐ-
τάρκη οὕτως θεῖναι, καὶ ὅσα τραπεζοκόμων εἰπεῖν καὶ
ὀψοποιῶν ἡδύσματα. 5. οὐ γὰρ δεῖ καταντᾶν ἐν τοῖς
ὕψεσιν εἰς τὰ ῥυπαρὰ καὶ ἐξυβρισμένα, | ἂν μὴ σφόδρα 20ε
25 ὑπό τινος ἀνάγκης συνδιωκώμεθα, ἀλλὰ τῶν πραγμάτων
πρέποι ἂν καὶ τὰς φωνὰς ἔχειν ἀξίας καὶ μιμεῖσθαι τὴν
δημιουργήσασαν φύσιν τὸν ἄνθρωπον ἥτις ἐν ἡμῖν τὰ
μέρη τὰ ἀπόρρητα οὐκ ἔθηκεν ἐν προσώπῳ, οὐδὲ τὰ τοῦ

---

1 τοσαῦτα] Robortellus, τοιαῦτα P.   2 γένεσθαι P.   13 ἐρ******ασ P
ἑρμηνείας P.   16 ὡς] Spengelius, οὖσ P.   17 ἁμάξας] Toupius, ἀλλάξασ P.
καὶ (ante καμήλους) add. Toupius, om. P.   21 πάντως] Spengelius, πάντα ὡσ P.
24 εἰς τὰ ῥυπαρὰ] Pearcius, ******παρὰ sex fere litteris propemodum deletis P.
26 ἀξίαν P, ἀξίασ m. rec. P.   27 διμιουργήσασαν P δημιουργήσασαν P.   28 ἐμ
(ante προσ.) sed corr. ἐν P.

of pieces of salted flesh from all manner of victims, so that the
piles of them were so great that those who were approaching
from a distance took them to be hills and eminences
confronting them[1].'   3. He runs off from the more elevated
to the more lowly, whereas he should, on the contrary, have
risen higher and higher. With his wonderful description of
the whole outfit he mixes bags and condiments and sacks,
and conveys the impression of a confectioner's shop! For
just as if, in the case of those very adornments, between the
golden vessels and the jewelled mixing-bowls and the silver
plate and the pavilions of pure gold and the goblets, a man
were to bring and set in the midst paltry bags and sacks, the
proceeding would have been offensive to the eye, so do such
words when introduced out of season constitute deformities
and as it were blots on the diction.   4. He might have
described the scene in broad outline just as he says that
hills blocked their way, and with regard to the preparations
generally have spoken of 'waggons and camels and the
multitude of beasts of burden carrying everything that
ministers to the luxury and enjoyment of the table,' or have
used some such expression as 'piles of all manner of grain
and things which conduce preeminently to good cookery and
comfort of body,' or if he must necessarily put it in so un-
compromising a way, he might have said that 'all the dainties
of cooks and caterers were there.'   5. In lofty passages we
ought not to descend to sordid and contemptible language
unless constrained by some overpowering necessity, but it is
fitting that we should use words worthy of the subject and
imitate nature the artificer of man, for she has not placed in
full view our grosser parts or the means of purging our

---

[1] Appendix C, *Theopompus.*

παντὸς ὄγκου περιηθήματα, ἀπεκρύψατο δὲ ὡς ἐνῆν καὶ
κατὰ τὸν Ξενοφῶντα τοὺς τούτων ὅτι πορρωτάτω ὀχετοὺς
ἀπέστρεψεν, οὐδαμῇ καταισχύνασα τὸ τοῦ ὅλου ζῴου
κάλλος.

5   6. Ἀλλὰ γὰρ οὐκ ἐπ᾽ εἴδους ἐπείγει τὰ μικροποιὰ
διαριθμεῖν· προϋποδεδειγμένων γὰρ τῶν ὅσα εὐγενεῖς καὶ
ὑψηλοὺς ἐργάζεται τοὺς λόγους, δῆλον ὡς τὰ ἐναντία
τούτων ταπεινοὺς ποιήσει κατὰ τὸ πλεῖστον καὶ ἀσχή-
μονας.

XLIV

10   Ἐκεῖνο μέντοι λοιπὸν (ἕνεκα τῆς σῆς χρηστομαθείας
οὐκ ὀκνήσομεν ἐπιπροσθεῖναι) διασαφῆσαι, Τερεντιανὲ
φίλτατε, ὅπερ ἐζήτησέ τις τῶν φιλοσόφων προσέναγχος,
'θαῦμά μ᾽ ἔχει,' λέγων, 'ὡς ἀμέλει καὶ ἑτέρους πολλούς,
πῶς ποτε κατὰ τὸν ἡμέτερον αἰῶνα πιθαναὶ μὲν ἐπ᾽ ἄκρον
15 καὶ πολιτικαί, δριμεῖαί τε καὶ ἐντρεχεῖς, καὶ μάλιστα πρὸς
ἡδονὰς λόγων εὔφοροι, ὑψηλαὶ δὲ λίαν καὶ ὑπερμεγέθεις,
πλὴν εἰ μή τι σπάνιον, οὐκέτι γίνονται φύσεις. τοσαύτη
λόγων κοσμική τις ἐπέχει τὸν βίον ἀφορία. 2. ἢ νὴ
Δί᾽ ἔφη 'πιστευτέον ἐκείνῳ τῷ θρυλουμένῳ, ὡς ἡ δημο-
20 κρατία τῶν μεγάλων ἀγαθὴ τιθηνός, ᾗ μόνῃ σχεδὸν καὶ
συνήκμασαν οἱ περὶ λόγους δεινοὶ καὶ συναπέθανον;
θρέψαι τε γάρ φησιν ἱκανὴ τὰ φρονήματα τῶν μεγαλο-
φρόνων ἡ ἐλευθερία καὶ | ἐπελπίσαι καὶ ἅμα διελθεῖν τὸ 206
πρόθυμον τῆς πρὸς ἀλλήλους ἔριδος καὶ τῆς περὶ τὰ
25 πρωτεῖα φιλοτιμίας. 3. ἔτι γε μὴν διὰ τὰ προκείμενα ἐν
ταῖς πολιτείαις ἔπαθλα ἑκάστοτε τὰ ψυχικὰ προτερήματα
τῶν ῥητόρων μελετώμενα ἀκονᾶται καὶ οἷον ἐκτρίβεται
καὶ τοῖς πράγμασι κατὰ τὸ εἰκὸς ἐλεύθερα συνεκλάμπει.

---

1 περιηθήματα] Pearcius, περιθήματα P.   2 τούτων] codd. Xenophontis,
Manutius : τῶν P.   3 καται*|σχύνασα (prius σ a m. rec.) P.   5 ἐπ᾽ εἴδους]
Toupius, ἐπιδοῦσ P.   11 ὀκνήσο*μεν P.   ἐπιπροσθεῖναι Manutius, ἐπιπροσ-
θῆναι P.   16 δὲ] Manutius, τε P.   26 ἑκάστοτε] Robortellus, ἑκα-
στόστε P.   28 πρά*|γμασι (γ a m. rec.) P.

frame, but has hidden them away as far as was possible, and as Xenophon says has put their channels in the remotest background, so as not to sully the beauty of the entire creature. 6. But enough; there is no need to enumerate, one by one, the things which produce triviality. For since we have previously indicated those qualities which render style noble and lofty, it is evident that their opposites will for the most part make it low and base.

XLIV

It remains however (as I will not hesitate to add, in recognition of your love of knowledge) to clear up, my dear Terentianus, a question which a certain philosopher has recently mooted. ' I wonder,' he says, ' as no doubt do many others, how it happens that in our time there are men who have the gift of persuasion to the utmost extent, and are well fitted for public life, and are keen and ready, and particularly rich in all the charms of language, yet there no longer arise really lofty and transcendent natures unless quite exceptionally. So great and world-wide a dearth of high utterance attends our age.' 2. ' Can it be,' he continued, ' that we are to accept the trite explanation that democracy is the kind nursing-mother of genius, and that literary power may be said to share its rise and fall with democracy and democracy alone? For freedom, it is said, has power to feed the imaginations of the lofty-minded and to inspire hope, and where it prevails there spreads abroad the eagerness of mutual rivalry and the emulous pursuit of the foremost place. 3. Moreover, owing to the prizes which are open to all under popular government, the mental excellences of the orator are continually exercised and sharpened, and as it were rubbed bright, and shine forth (as it is natural they should) with all the freedom which inspires the doings of the state. To-day,'

οἱ δὲ νῦν ἐοίκαμεν᾽ ἔφη ᾽παιδομαθεῖς εἶναι δουλείας
δικαίας, τοῖς αὐτῆς ἔθεσι καὶ ἐπιτηδεύμασιν ἐξ ἁπαλῶν
ἔτι φρονημάτων μόνον οὐκ ἐνεσπαργανωμένοι καὶ ἄγευ-
στοι καλλίστου καὶ γονιμωτάτου λόγων νάματος, τὴν
5 ἐλευθερίαν᾽ ἔφη ᾽λέγω, διόπερ οὐδὲν ὅτι μὴ κόλακες ἐκ-
βαίνομεν μεγαλοφυεῖς.᾽   4. διὰ τοῦτο τὰς μὲν ἄλλας ἕξεις
καὶ εἰς οἰκέτας πίπτειν ἔφασκεν, δοῦλον δὲ μηδένα γίνεσθαι ῥήτορα· εὐθὺς γὰρ ἀναζεῖ τὸ ἀπαρρησίαστον καὶ
οἷον ἔμφρουρον ὑπὸ συνηθείας ἀεὶ κεκονδυλισμένον·
10 5. ᾽ἥμισυ γάρ τ᾽ ἀρετῆς᾽ κατὰ τὸν Ὅμηρον ᾽ἀποαίνυται
δούλιον ἦμαρ.᾽   ᾽ὥσπερ οὖν, εἴ γε᾽ φησὶ ᾽τοῦτο πιστὸν
ἀκούω, τὰ γλωττόκομα, ἐν οἷς οἱ Πυγμαῖοι καλούμενοι δὲ
νᾶνοι τρέφονται, οὐ μόνον κωλύει τῶν ἐγκεκλεισμένων τὰς
αὐξήσεις, ἀλλὰ καὶ συναραιοῖ διὰ τὸν περικείμενον τοῖς
15 σώμασι δεσμόν· οὕτως ἅπασαν δουλείαν, κἂν ᾖ δικαιοτάτη, ψυχῆς γλωττόκομον καὶ κοινὸν δή τις ἀπεφήνατο
δεσμωτήριον.᾽   6. ἐγὼ μέντοι γε ὑπολαμβάνων ᾽ῥᾴδιον,᾽
ἔφην, ᾽ὦ βέλτιστε, καὶ ἴδιον ἀνθρώπου τὸ καταμέμφεσθαι
τὰ ἀεὶ παρόντα· ὅρα δέ, μή ποτε οὐχ ἡ τῆς οἰκουμένης
20 εἰρήνη διαφθείρει τὰς μεγά|λας φύσεις, πολὺ δὲ μᾶλλον ὁ   207ʳ
κατέχων ἡμῶν τὰς ἐπιθυμίας ἀπεριόριστος οὑτοσὶ πόλεμος καὶ νὴ Δία πρὸς τούτῳ τὰ φρουροῦντα τὸν νῦν βίον
καὶ κατ᾽ ἄκρας ἄγοντα καὶ φέροντα ταυτὶ πάθη.   ἡ γὰρ
φιλοχρηματία, πρὸς ἣν ἅπαντες ἀπλήστως ἤδη νοσοῦμεν,
25 καὶ ἡ φιληδονία δουλαγωγοῦσι, μᾶλλον δέ, ὡς ἂν εἴποι τις,
καταβυθίζουσιν αὐτάνδρους ἤδη τοὺς βίους, φιλαργυρία

---

2 αὐτοῖσ, P αὐτῆσ m. rec. P.   4 γο∗νιμωτάτου P.   11 δούλιον P, ει
superscripto a m. rec.   πιστόν ἐστιν P, ἐστιν del. Pearcius, δ add. Pearcius.
12 ἐν|∗οῖσ (ν a m. rec.) P.   13 νᾶνοι] Manutius, νάοι P.   14 συναραιοῖ]
Schmidius, συνάροι P.   15 σώμασι] Scaliger, στόμασι P.   16 ἀποφήνετο
(αι superscr. a m. rec.) P.   17 ὑπολαμβάνων] Tollius, ὑπολαμβάνω P.
18 ἔφην] Portus, ἔφη P.   ἴδιο P : inter compingendum librum ut videtur
evanuit littera postrema.   καταμέμφε|σθαι (deletas litteras αταμέμφ restituit m.
rec.) P.   19 μή ποτε οὐχ ἡ τῆς] Spengelius, μή|πο∗∗∗∗χ η∗∗∗ (τῆσ addito in
ras. a m. rec.) P.   25 δουλαγωγ∗ῦσι P δουλαγωγοῦσι P.

he went on, 'we seem in our boyhood to learn the lessons of a righteous servitude, being all but enswathed in its customs and observances, when our thoughts are yet young and tender, and never tasting the fairest and most productive source of eloquence (by which,' he added, 'I mean freedom), so that we emerge in no other guise than that of sublime flatterers.' 4. This is the reason, he maintained, why no slave ever becomes an orator, although all other faculties may belong to menials. In the slave there immediately burst out signs of fettered liberty of speech, of the dungeon as it were, of a man habituated to buffetings. 5. 'For the day of slavery,' as Homer has it, 'takes away half our manhood[1].' 'Just as,' he proceeded, 'the cages (if what I hear is true) in which are kept the Pygmies, commonly called *nani*, not only hinder the growth of the creatures confined within them, but actually attenuate them through the bonds which beset their bodies, so one has aptly termed all servitude (though it be most righteous) the cage of the soul and a public prison-house.' 6. I answered him thus : 'It is easy, my good sir, and characteristic of human nature, to find fault with the age in which one lives. But consider whether it may not be true that it is not the world's peace that ruins great natures, but far rather this war illimitable which holds our desires in its grasp, aye, and further still those passions which occupy as with troops our present age and utterly harry and plunder it. For the love of money (a disease from which we all now suffer sorely) and the love of pleasure make us their thralls, or rather, as one may say, drown us body and soul in the depths, the love of riches being a malady which makes men petty,

---

[1] *Odyss.* XVII. 322.

μὲν νόσημα μικροποιόν, φιληδονία δ᾽ ἀγεννέστατον.
7. οὐ δὴ ἔχω λογιζόμενος εὑρεῖν, ὡς οἷόν τε πλοῦτον
ἀόριστον ἐκτιμήσαντας, τὸ δ᾽ ἀληθέστερον εἰπεῖν, ἐκθειά-
σαντας, τὰ συμφυῆ τούτῳ κακὰ εἰς τὰς ψυχὰς ἡμῶν
5 ἐπεισιόντα μὴ παραδέχεσθαι. ἀκολουθεῖ γὰρ τῷ ἀμέτρῳ
πλούτῳ καὶ ἀκολάστῳ συνημμένη καὶ ἴσα, φασί, βαίνουσα πολυτέλεια, καὶ ἅμα ἀνοίγοντος ἐκείνου τῶν πόλεων
καὶ οἴκων τὰς εἰσόδους εὐθὺς ἐμβαίνει καὶ συνοικίζεται.
χρονίσαντα δὲ ταῦτα ἐν τοῖς βίοις νεοττοποιεῖται, κατὰ
10 τοὺς σοφούς, καὶ ταχέως γενόμενα περὶ τεκνοποιΐαν ἀλαζονείαν τε γεννῶσι καὶ τῦφον καὶ τρυφὴν οὐ νόθα ἑαυτῶν
γεννήματα ἀλλὰ καὶ πάνυ γνήσια. ἐὰν δὲ καὶ τούτους
τις τοῦ πλούτου τοὺς ἐκγόνους εἰς ἡλικίαν ἐλθεῖν ἐάσῃ,
ταχέως δεσπότας ταῖς ψυχαῖς ἐντίκτουσιν ἀπαραιτήτους,
15 ὕβριν καὶ παρανομίαν καὶ ἀναισχυντίαν. 8. ταῦτα γὰρ
οὕτως ἀνάγκη γίνεσθαι καὶ μηκέτι τοὺς ἀνθρώπους ἀναβλέπειν μηδ᾽ ἕτερα φήμης εἶναί τινα λόγον, ἀλλὰ τοιούτων
ἐν κύκλῳ τελεσιουργεῖσθαι κατ᾽ ὀλίγον τὴν τῶν βίων |
διαφθοράν, φθίνειν δὲ καὶ καταμαραίνεσθαι τὰ ψυχικὰ 207ᵛ
20 μεγέθη, καὶ ἄζηλα γίνεσθαι, ἡνίκα τὰ θνητὰ ἑαυτῶν μέρη
ἐκθαυμάζοιεν, παρέντες αὔξειν τἀθάνατα. 9. οὐ γὰρ ἐπὶ
κρίσει μέν τις δεκασθεὶς οὐκ ἂν ἐπὶ τῶν δικαίων καὶ
καλῶν ἐλεύθερος καὶ ὑγιὴς ἂν κριτὴς γένοιτο· ἀνάγκη
γὰρ τῷ δωροδόκῳ τὰ οἰκεῖα μὲν φαίνεσθαι καλὰ καὶ
25 δίκαια· ὅπου δὲ ἡμῶν ἑκάστου τοὺς ὅλους ἤδη βίους
δεκασμοὶ βραβεύουσι καὶ ἀλλοτρίων θῆραι θανάτων καὶ

---

1 ἀγενέστατον P. 3 ἀλιθέστερον P ἀληθέστερον P. 4 εἰ|∗ὰσ P, εἰσ|τὰσ
m. rec. P. 6 βαίνουσα (β corr. ex μ) P. 7 καὶ ἅμα] Pearcius, καὶ ἄλλα P.
8 οἶκον P οἴκων P. εὐθὺς] Mathewsius, εἰς ἃς P. post εἰς ἃς supplet
ἐκεῖνος οἰκίας Vahlenus. 10 ἀλαζονείαν τε] Is. Vossius : ἀνάλεξον εν αντι
(ἔντι a m. rec.; in marg. γρ ἔν αντι) P. 11 γεννῶσα (σι superscr. a m. rec.) P.
12 τούτους] Tollius, τούτου P. 15 ὕβρ∗ν P. π∗∗∗νομίαν P. 20 καπανητά
post μέρη praebet P quod ut ex proximis ἠνί|κατὰθνητὰ perperam repetitum Vahlenus
delendum esse censet. 21 τἀθάνατα] Pearcius, τὰς|άνατα P. ἐπικρί∗σει P.
22 δεκασθεὶς] Manutius, δικασθεῖσ P. 24 τὸ (in τω a m. rec. corr.) P.

and the love of pleasure one which makes them most ignoble.
7. On reflexion I cannot discover how it is possible for us, if
we value boundless wealth so highly, or (to speak more truly)
deify it, to avoid allowing the entrance into our souls of the
evils which are inseparable from it. For vast and unchecked
wealth is accompanied, in close conjunction and step for step
as they say, by extravagance, and as soon as the former
opens the gates of cities and houses, the latter immediately
enters and abides. And when time has passed the pair
build nests in the lives of men, as the wise say, and quickly
give themselves to the rearing of offspring, and breed
ostentation, and vanity, and luxury, no spurious progeny of
theirs, but only too legitimate. If these children of wealth
are permitted to come to maturity, straightway they beget in
the soul inexorable masters—insolence, and lawlessness, and
shamelessness. 8. This must necessarily happen, and men
will no longer lift up their eyes or have any further regard
for fame, but the ruin of such lives will gradually reach its
complete consummation and sublimities of soul fade and
wither away and become contemptible, when men are lost in
admiration of their own mortal parts and omit to exalt that
which is immortal. 9. For a man who has once accepted a
bribe for a judicial decision cannot be an unbiassed and
upright judge of what is just and honourable (since to the
man who is venal his own interests must seem honourable
and just), and the same is true where the entire life of each
of us is ordered by bribes, and huntings after the death of

ἐνέδραι διαθηκῶν, τὸ δ᾽ ἐκ τοῦ παντὸς κερδαίνειν ὠνού-
μεθα τῆς ψυχῆς ἕκαστος πρὸς τῆς * ἠνδραποδισμένοι, ἆρα
δὴ ἐν τῇ τοσαύτῃ λοιμικῇ τοῦ βίου διαφθορᾷ δοκοῦμεν
ἔτι ἐλεύθερόν τινα κριτὴν τῶν μεγάλων ἢ διηκόντων
5 πρὸς τὸν αἰῶνα κἀδέκαστον ἀπολελεῖφθαι καὶ μὴ καταρχαιρεσιάζεσθαι πρὸς τῆς τοῦ πλεονεκτεῖν ἐπιθυμίας;
10. ἀλλὰ μήποτε τοιούτοις οἷοί περ ἐσμὲν ἡμεῖς, ἄμεινον
ἄρχεσθαι ἢ ἐλευθέροις εἶναι· ἐπείτοιγε ἀφεθεῖσαι τὸ
σύνολον, ὡς ἐξ εἱρκτῆς ἄφετοι, κατὰ τῶν πλησίον αἱ
10 πλεονεξίαι κἂν ἐπικαύσειαν τοῖς κακοῖς τὴν οἰκουμένην.
11. ὅλως δὲ δαπανῶν ἔφην εἶναι τῶν νῦν γεννωμένων
φύσεων τὴν ῥᾳθυμίαν, ᾗ πλὴν ὀλίγων πάντες ἐγκατα-
βιοῦμεν, οὐκ ἄλλως πονοῦντες ἢ ἀναλαμβάνοντες εἰ μὴ
ἐπαίνου καὶ ἡδονῆς ἕνεκα, ἀλλὰ μὴ τῆς ζήλου καὶ τιμῆς
15 ἀξίας ποτὲ ὠφελείας. 12. κράτιστον εἰκῆ ταῦτ᾽ ἐᾶν, ἐπὶ
δὲ τὰ συνεχῆ χωρεῖν· ἦν δὲ ταῦτα τὰ πάθη, περὶ ὧν ἐν
ἰδίῳ προηγουμένως ὑπεσχόμεθα γράψειν ὑπομνήματι,
τήν τε τοῦ ἄλλου λόγου καὶ αὐτοῦ τοῦ ὕψους μοῖραν
ἐπεχόντων, ὡς ἡμῖν δοκεῖ...

---

1 ἔνεδραι P. 2 πρὸσ τῆσ P, πρὸς τῆς* Robortellus. Vide Append. A.
ἆρα P. 4 μεγάλων ἢ] Robortellus, μεγάλων ἢ μεγάλων ἢ P. 5 αἰῶνα
Portus, ἀγῶνα P. κἀδέκαστον] unus ex libris Vaticanis, καθέκαστον P. μὴ]
Manutius, μοι P. 9 πλησίων P πλησίον P. 12 ᾗ] Manutius, οἱ P, οἱ
Robortellus. 16 ἐν ἰδίῳ—19 ἡμῖν addidit m. rec. in P, consentientibus
libris deterioribus. 19 δοκεῖ add. Robortellus.

others, and the laying of ambushes for legacies, while gain from any and every source we purchase—each one of us—at the price of life itself, being the slaves of pleasure. In an age which is ravaged by plagues so sore, is it possible for us to imagine that there is still left an unbiassed and incorruptible judge of works that are great and likely to reach posterity, or is it not rather the case that all are influenced in their decisions by the passion for gain? 10. Nay, it is perhaps better for men like ourselves to be ruled than to be free, since our appetites, if let loose without restraint upon our neighbours like beasts from a cage, would set the world on fire with deeds of evil. 11. Summing up, I maintained that among the banes of the natures which our age produces must be reckoned that half-heartedness in which the life of all of us with few exceptions is passed, for we do not labour or exert ourselves except for the sake of praise and pleasure, never for those solid benefits which are a worthy object of our own efforts and the respect of others. 12. But ''tis best to leave these riddles unresolved[1],' and to proceed to what next presents itself, namely the subject of the Passions, about which I previously undertook to write in a separate treatise. These form, as it seems to me, a material part of discourse generally and of the Sublime itself.

[1] Eurip. *Electra* 379.

APPENDICES.

APPENDIX A.

TEXTUAL. WITH CRITICAL NOTES.

In the Appendices and Indices reference is sometimes made to pages (e.g. 17) or to pages and lines (e.g. 96. 12), at other times to chapters (e.g. ii.) or to chapters and sections (e.g. xii. 2).

The known manuscripts of the *De Sublimitate* are eleven in number, of which four are preserved at Paris, three at Rome, one at Milan, one at Venice, one at Florence, and one at Cambridge. Their designations are as follows :

1. **Codex Parisinus s. Parisiensis 2036.** Tenth Century. By far the oldest and the best. Detailed particulars with regard to it, in itself and in its relation to the rest, will be given later. Here it need only be said that, in the textual criticism of the *De Sublimitate*, this codex deserves even a higher position than that occupied in their respective spheres by three other remarkable Paris manuscripts, that of the *Poetics* of Aristotle (A^c), that of the *Republic* of Plato (A), and that of Demosthenes (S).

2. **Codex Parisinus 985.** Fifteenth Century. Only extends as far as the word θεωρίαν in c. ii. 3. The opening sections of the περὶ ὕψους are interpolated, as it were, in the text of the *Problems* of Aristotle, to which work a large part of this miscellaneous codex is devoted. As this case is only one of several in which the περὶ ὕψους is grouped with the *Problems*, there is just a possibility that fragments of the former may yet be discovered in manuscripts of the latter.

3. **Codex Parisinus 2960.** Fifteenth Century. Contains (in addition to the περὶ ὕψους) some orations of Dion Chrysostom and of Themistius, together with the *Ars Rhetorica* of Hermogenes and some *Problemata Rhetorica.* Part at least of this manuscript was written in the year 1491, the date being given.

4. **Codex Parisinus 2974.** Sixteenth Century. Consists of the περὶ ὕψους alone.—Manuscripts 3 and 4, as well as 1 and 2, are preserved in the Bibliothèque Nationale. The present editor has examined all the Paris manuscripts and has carefully re-collated P 2036.

5. **Codex Vaticanus 285.** Fifteenth Century. A fragment, agreeing with Parisinus 985, from which it is supposed to have been transcribed.

6. **Codex Vaticanus 194.** Fifteenth or Sixteenth Century.

7. **Codex Vaticanus 1417.** Fifteenth or Sixteenth Century. 6 and 7 are carelessly written manuscripts, copied probably from dictation.

8. **Codex Mediolanensis s. Ambrosianus.** Fifteenth or Sixteenth Century. In the Biblioteca Ambrosiana at Milan.

9. **Codex Venetus s. Marcianus.** Fifteenth Century. In the Biblioteca Nazionale di San Marco at Venice.

10. **Codex Florentinus s. Laurentianus.** Fifteenth or Sixteenth Century. In the Biblioteca Mediceo-Laurenziana at Florence.—These three manuscripts (8, 9, and 10) possess no distinctive features of importance. It is probable that the Venetus was used by Manutius in the preparation of his edition.

11. **Codex Eliensis s. Cantabrigiensis.** Sixteenth Century. In the University Library at Cambridge. Continental scholars have often expressed curiosity and some expectancy with regard to this manuscript. Upon examination, however, it is found to have no independent value. Its worth and character are discussed in the *Classical Review* xii. pp. 299—301. Its chief interest lies in two facts : (*a*) it stands in close relation to the two first editions of the treatise, viz. those of Robortello and Manutius ; (*b*) in the margin it has some interesting Italian notes. There are four of these : (1) *tutto questo è confusamente preso da Platone* (xxxii. 5) ; (2) *tutto questo dubito che sia stato trasportato dal margine nel testo, et che sia giudicio di qualch' uno che biasima Longino, perchè da tante lodi a Hyperide*

(xxxiv. 3); (3) *in Herodoto non si leggono cosi continuate queste parole* (xliii. 1); (4) *qui manca perauentura qualche voce significante altro uitio che seguita le gran ricchezze, et poi uien dietro* καὶ ἄλλα (xliv. 7).

Mr H. J. Edwards (of Trinity and Selwyn Colleges, Cambridge) some years ago made a complete collation of this manuscript,—a collation which he has with great kindness permitted the present editor to consult. For critical purposes the manuscript, when it comes into comparison with P 2036, occupies (like the rest of the later manuscripts) a strictly subordinate position. It has, however, been cited in the critical footnotes once or twice when it gives a reading attributed hitherto to Robortello. Mr Edwards believes that the date of the Cod. El. lies somewhere between 1525 and 1560 A.D., and that the evidence (especially that furnished by the water-mark) is rather in favour of the earlier portion of these 35 years.

To the eleven manuscripts just enumerated a twelfth is sometimes added :—

12. **Codex Dudithianus s. Junianus.** But it is possible that this manuscript, whose place of preservation is unknown, is identical with the Codex Eliensis. Cp. *Classical Review* xii. 301.

While the other manuscripts may be dismissed with a bare mention, P 2036 claims minute attention as the paramount authority in the constitution of the text.

P 2036 is a minuscule manuscript; and among minuscule manuscripts it may, in virtue of its early date, be classed as one of the *codices vetustissimi.* M. Henri Omont, who assigns it to the tenth century, has given the following description of it : ' MS. grec 2036 (*Regius* 3083). Parchemin. 207 feuillets. 195 sur 152 millimètres. Reliure aux armes et chiffre de Henri IV. Provient de J. Lascaris, du cardinal Nicolas Ridolfi, puis de Catherine de Médicis[1].' It was, thus, preserved at Florence, before it came to Paris in the year 1599.

---

[1] Henri Omont, *Facsimilés des plus anciens manuscrits grecs en onciale et en minuscule de la Bibliothèque Nationale du iv⁰ au xii⁰ siècle.* Planche xxxi. Paris, 1892.—It may be added here that in P 2036 the scribe writes *below* the guiding-line, a practice which was introduced in the tenth century. In minuscule manuscripts of the ninth century the writing is found above the line.

The first and larger part (fol. 1—178^v) of the manuscript is occupied by Ἀριστοτέλους φυσικὰ προβλήματα, which work is followed by the περὶ ὕψους. The portion which contains the περὶ ὕψους consisted of seven quaternions, which are signed (by a later hand) ΚΔ. [ΚΕ is wanting.] ΚϚ. ΚΖ. ΚΗ. ΚΘ. Λ. The gaps in the treatise have been noted in the text as they occur. The portions missing in the various quaternions are as follows: fol. iv. and v. in ΚΔ, the whole of ΚΕ (though fol. i. and fol. viii. are preserved elsewhere), fol. iv. and v. in ΚϚ, fol. iv. and v. in ΚΖ, fol. iii., iv., v. and vi. in ΚΗ, fol. iv. and v. in ΚΘ. Of Λ (the last quaternion) the three first folia are preserved.

The total loss suffered by P may be estimated (without taking the conclusion of the treatise into account) as follows :—

First	lacuna	(c. ii.)	= 2	folia, viz. about	100	lines.
Second	„	(c. viii.)	= 8	„	„	400	„
Third	„	(c. xii.)	= 2	„	„	100	„
Fourth	„	(c. xviii.)	= 2	„	„	100	„
Fifth	„	(c. xxx.)	= 4	„	„	200	„
Sixth	„	(c. xxxvii.)	= 2	„	„	100	„

20 folia.   1000 lines.

Thus P has lost some 20 folia, or about 1000 lines. As the number of folia actually preserved may be given as 30, it follows that more than one-third of the treatise has disappeared from P.

The fact that these lacunae exist not only in P but in all the later manuscripts first suggested the conclusion, now generally adopted, that P is the original from which the rest have been derived[1]. It is true that for a few supplementary words or pages (already noted in the critical apparatus) we are indebted to the later manuscripts. But there is every reason to believe that these portions were derived, directly or indirectly, from P at a date anterior to the year 1568, by which time it is known to have reached its present state. The cause of loss has probably been careless preservation of the leaves before they were bound, and then equally careless binding. At the end of the treatise, for instance, it is likely that the binder

---

[1] It is noteworthy that M. Raoul Pessonneaux (*Annales de la Faculté des Lettres de Bordeaux*, v. 3 p. 303) declares against the contrary view maintained many years ago by Émile Egger.

sacrificed a mutilated leaf, but before so doing transcribed, at the bottom of the previous leaf, the three top lines which he found to be still legible. Some lines at the end of chapter ii. have also been sacrificed in the binding, but not before they had been copied in other manuscripts. Something similar has happened in the case of the two outer leaves now represented by parts of chapters viii. and ix. These parts would seem to have been transcribed from P, before the two outer leaves became detached and disappeared in the same way as the six inner leaves.

It is in the filling up of the gaps just mentioned that the secondary manuscripts are of most service. Over and above this, they occasionally—very occasionally—furnish a better reading in the parts common to them and P. But there is no reason to suppose that such readings (examples of which will be found on pp. 48. 2, 100. 21, 108. 8, 160. 5) are other than more or less obvious conjectures on the part of the copyists who transcribed the manuscripts or of the scholars who used them. On the other side, the inferior manuscripts are disfigured by errors, sometimes of a gross description; but of these it would serve no useful purpose to accumulate instances. The readings selected from them by Weiske and Vaucher, and by still earlier editors, are enough to show their true character.

The antiquity of P was recognised several centuries ago by the distinguished scholar Petrus Victorius; and this fact makes it only the more remarkable that the long line of editors since his time should not have paid more systematic deference to it. Petrus Victorius (Pietro Vettori, 1499—1584 A.D.) refers to the manuscript as 'liber antiquissimus[1].' It was by using Victorius' collation (made while the manuscript was still at Florence, and now preserved in a copy of Robortello's edition to be found in the Munich Library) that Spengel nearly three centuries later first gave something like its due weight to the authority of P in the constitution of the text (Spengel, *Rhetores Graeci*, vol. 1; Leipzig, 1853). A fresh collation of P, made by Vahlen in 1861, was used by Jahn in his edition of 1867. The present editor has examined the manuscript at Paris in two successive years (1897 and 1898), and has endeavoured to add to the completeness and correctness of previous collations.

---

[1] *Variarum Lectionum Libri xxxviii.* p. 331. (In the edition of 1582; the first edition of this portion of his work appeared at Florence in 1569.)

While due credit is given to the Italian scholar Vettori for discerning the antiquity of P and to the German scholar Spengel for making full use of it in an edition, it should also be remembered that the French scholar Boivin (1663—1726) was the first to show, from an examination of the gaps in it, that it was not only the oldest codex, but in all probability also the archetype of all existing manuscripts of the treatise. It now only remains in a new presentation of the text to bring more clearly into relief than previous editors have done the general character and excellence of P,—to treat it, in fact, as the premier manuscript of any author should be treated. In the present edition, therefore, all deviations—however minute—from P have been entered in the critical footnotes, where even the erasures are indicated (according to Vahlen's notation) by means of asterisks. It appears to the editor that the vast array of conjectural emendations found beneath Jahn-Vahlen's text (1887) creates an utterly false impression of general unsoundness and uncertainty. A few *loci desperati* there no doubt are ; but, taken as a whole, the text offered by P is good and trustworthy. For a critical examination of some conjectural emendations by distinguished scholars reference may be made to the following pages. Here it is enough to record all the readings of P and to estimate the value of the manuscript. To the unpractised eye the rejected readings may, like the conjectural emendations already mentioned, give rise to a feeling of uncertainty ; but at this stage in the history of the printed text it is, nevertheless, best to record them in full. A later and more fortunate editor may find it in his power to keep his list both of unaccepted conjectures and of unaccepted manuscript readings within a very narrow compass. The task of the moment is to sustain, and if possible enhance, the credit of P by the only true method, namely, the full disclosure of its weaknesses as well as of its strength.

The patent errors of P are, as a glance at the critical footnotes will show, of the mechanical order. They are the offspring of carelessness or mental slowness, rather than of that vexatious cleverness which is not content to transcribe but must improve. The bad blunders are few relatively to the difficulty of the subject-matter. The scribe's spelling (that excellent criterion of the value of manuscripts) is, on the whole, good. He does not indeed present such refinements as the ι subscr. in $\theta\nu\dot{\eta}\sigma\kappa\epsilon\iota\nu$ and $\sigma\dot{\omega}\zeta\epsilon\iota\nu$, but it is not safe to assume that these minutiae, though attested by Attic inscriptions and found in the Laurentian manuscript of Sophocles, were observed by the text from which he copied. Most of the mistakes which beset the honest but frail transcriber can be illustrated from this manuscript. *Dittography*: λέγεις λέγεις for λέγεις (94. 3), ὅπουτε ὁπότε for ὅπου τε (108. 19). *Haplography* or *lipography*: παραλάττει for παραλλάττει (76. 2), πολοστημόριον for πολλοστημόριον (136. 7), ἐμπαθὲς for ἐμπαθὲς ἐς (58. 20). *Itacism*: μέθει for μέθῃ (52. 14), ἐμπρισμὸς for ἐμπρησμὸς (78. 4), δίεισι for διήσει (84. 26), ξιφειδίῳ for ξιφιδίῳ (120. 7), ἐπιχαρὴς for ἐπίχαρις (132. 2), ἢ for εἰ (134. 11), παντὶ for πάντῃ (136. 24). *Transposition of letters*: διμηουργήσασαν for δημιουργήσασαν (152. 27). *Confusion of similar words*: ἀδεῶς for ἡδέως (114. 20), εὐπαθοὺς for ἐμπαθοὺς (108. 19). *Wrong division of words* (together with consequent variation of letters): ἀψίδας ἦν for ἀψῖδα σὴν (84. 25), ὄπισθεν ὦτα for ὄπισθε νῶτα (86. 5), πράγμασιν ὁρίων for πράγμασι μορίων (76. 14), ἀπουσίας for αὐτοῦ Λυσίας (132. 20), ἄλλους ὅση for ἄμουσος ὅση (142. 11), ἐπιδοὺς for ἐπ' εἴδους (154. 5). *Interpolation of words*: either ἰταμὸν or τὴν ἀναίδειαν (50. 29). *Mistakes in proper names and alien words*: Φλωρεντιανὲ (40. 3), Φρυγίης for Φρύνης (132. 3), νάοι for νᾶνοι (156. 13).

The above may seem a serious list of errors dully made or dully reproduced, but two things are to be remembered: (1) the list is fairly comprehensive, and (2) it shows no sign of a desire gratuitously to improve the text. The general carefulness of the scribe may perhaps be inferred from the marginal notes in his hand. These notes sometimes explain words, e.g. ἀντὶ τοῦ εἰπὼν (42. 3), ἀντὶ τοῦ διόλου (48. 6), ἀντὶ τοῦ ὅπου (124. 23), the respective words explained being εἶπας, ἐξ ὅλου, οὗ. Or they call attention to an unusual word: περιαυγῶ (96. 8), δοξοκοπῶ (106. 15), ἀβλεμὲς (116. 15). Or they refer to authors: τοῦτο Ξενοφῶντος (50. 22), περὶ Πλάτωνος (52. 7). Or they indicate the nature of the subject-matter under discussion: ὅρος αὐξήσεως (76. 4), τίνι παραλάτει (sic) Κικέρων Δημοσθένους (76. 25), περὶ σχημάτων (90. 19), συνδ. (100. 26: the reference is to τοὺς συνδέσμους), περὶ ὑπερβατῶν ὅρος ὑπερβατοῦ (102. 11), περίφρασις (114. 15), περὶ ὑπερίδου Ση (130. 4)[1]. Or again they make a correction in the text: ὑπ' ἀγωνίας (104. 27: in place of ὑπογωνία); or they make an addition: ὅταν αὐτὸ τοῦτο διαλανθάνῃ ὅτι σχῆμα (94. 28), ὄψιν ποιῶν; πάντα δὲ τὰ τοιαῦτα πρὸς (110. 18). In these two last cases the accidental omission, or 'skipping,' of a line is in this way rectified. Another feature of the margin is the occurrence of (Ƕ (= N.B.) and

---

[1] It may be well to explain that there are no chapter-marks or section-marks in the original hand of P.

of $\overset{\frown}{\underset{\wedge}{\text{P}}}$ (= ὡραῖον)[1].   In the margin of the present edition the folia of the manuscript (*folium rectum* and *folium versum*) are duly noted for convenience of reference, and in other respects pains have been taken to secure the close correspondence of codex and printed text. The appended critical notes have been kept down as much as possible both in number and in bulk.   But many passages of the treatise present serious difficulties which should be fully stated, and there are some typical instances of conjectural emendations which should be briefly noticed even when not accepted.

CRITICAL NOTES.

p. 40

The TITLE which the treatise bears in the manuscripts is discussed in the Introduction, pp. 3, 4.

l. 3.   φλωρεντιανὲ.   This is the reading of P 2036, and it seems better (as pointed out in the Introduction pp. 19, 20) to retain it until some emendation more satisfactory palaeographically than Manutius' Τερεντιανὲ has found acceptance.   At the same time it is as well not to lay any special stress on the mere presence of the dot.   A close examination of the manuscript shows that the dot is added in a later hand, and in any case its signification is not absolutely certain.

l. 7.   εἴγ'.   Spengel's emendation may be adopted as palaeographically easy, and as in keeping with the author's usage (cp. i. 4). εἴτ' is, however, neither impossible nor altogether unlikely: for the accent in P, cp. 88. 28.

ll. 13 and 20.   Cp. p. 74, lines 10, 15, 18: and p. 78, lines 5, 8.   The erasures in P 2036 are numerous.   Often they are due simply to the desire of the original scribe, or a later corrector, to give a better division of a word at the end of a line[2].   Probably the change of arrangement in 40. 13 is from the original hand; in 74. 10 (and in several other instances on that page and on the next) the changes are probably from another hand.

---

[1] The symbol $\overset{\widetilde{\text{P}}}{\underset{\wedge}{}}$ occurs opposite ix. 10 (end of section).   The abbreviation $\overset{\overline{\text{H}}}{\underset{\text{T}}{}}$ occurs opposite xxx. 1 (end of section).   The last sentence in xiii. 2 has *both* symbols entered opposite to it.—On fol. 200ʳ P has the abbreviation π̄μ̄ι for πνεύματι.   Similar contractions occur elsewhere for such words as ἄνθρωπος.

[2] The end of lines is marked in the collation, wherever it seems important to do so, by a vertical stroke.

p. 42

l. 7. οὐκ ἄλλοθέν ποθεν ἢ ἐνθένδε, Weiske. So Cobet (*Mnemosyne* *N.S.* x. 319), 'Transpone : οὐκ ἄλλοθέν ποθεν ἢ ἐνθένδε ἐπρώτευσαν.' Changes of this class seem extremely doubtful.

l. 14. Tanaquil Faber (an excellent scholar in his day) proposed πάντως for παντός. But though πάντως would be quite characteristic of our author, the order παντὸς ἐπάνω τοῦ ἀκροωμένου is no less characteristic of him.

l. 19. Erwin Rohde (*Rheinisches Museum N.F.* xxxv. 309) suggests διεφώτισεν. διεφόρησεν, however, seems more in keeping with ἐξενεχθὲν and with σκηπτοῦ.

l. 24. ἢ βάθους. Jahn (in his edition of 1867) regarded these words as an interpolation, and W. Schmid (*Rhein. Mus.* lii. 446) conjectures βάρους, while H. Diels (*Hermes* xiii. 5) has suggested μεγέθους—palaeographically an easier change, he maintains, than it might seem. Others still have favoured πάθους, which word however does not cover the same ground as ὕψος (cp. viii. 2). In defence of the manuscript reading, see M. Rothstein in *Hermes* xxii. 538. Reference may also be made to the Linguistic Appendix under βάθος.—The manuscript tradition is probably right in the converse case on p. 92. 12, where πάθος as given by P should be adopted rather than βάθος, the emendation proposed by Ruhnken and Spengel.

l. 26. φασί Manutius and most subsequent editors. So in Cod. El. φησί has been altered into φασί. But a comparison with xxix. 1 makes it probable that Κεκίλιος should be supplied as subject : cp. L. Martens, *De Libello* Περὶ Ὕψους, p. 10. Or φησί may be used quite generally for 'says one,' 'it is said' : cp. *inquit.*

p. 48

l. 2. μήποτε seems right : cp. xl. 2. Manutius gave δήποτε, Reiske ἤδη ποτε, Cobet ἐνίοτε.—In the same sentence Wilamowitz (*Hermes* x. 334—346) would insert ἐπὶ before λόγων.

l. 14. ἄκαιρον καὶ κενόν. Wilamowitz, l.c., proposes ἄκαιρον κείμενον.

p. 50

l. 2. It has been usual to insert ἔτεσι after ἐλάττοσι, and it must be admitted that after -τοσι or -τοσιν the word might very easily fall out. In defence of the reading of P it may, however, be urged that the author occasionally allows himself such omissions where (as here) they create no real ambiguity : cp. the omission of ἔχειν in xxxi. 2. See Starkie's *Wasps of Aristophanes* pp. 131, 132.

l. 29. It seems impossible to translate the text of P as it stands. Either ἰταμὸν or ἀναίδειαν should probably be regarded as a gloss. For a fuller discussion of the passage, see *Classical Review*, Vol. XIII. No. 1.

p. 52

l. 2. ὡς φὼρ ἰοῦ τινος, Rohde in *Rhein. Mus.* XXXV. 310. Approved by Bury in *Classical Review* I. 302, and by Martens in *Philologische Rundschau* I. 338. But the emendation is ingenious rather than convincing : cp. the explanation given, 'Wie ein Dieb, der (aus Unkunde oder Versehen) eines Giftes (statt gesunder Speise) sich bemächtigt, so stiehlt Timaeus dem Xen. jenes ψυχρόν.'

p. 54

l. 3. The reading ὦ φίλος seems right and is retained by all editors. The author, here as elsewhere, has chosen a less usual form in order to avoid hiatus.

p. 58

l. 20. It is possible that συντελεῖν (without ἐς) might be rendered *contribuere* or *conficere.*

p. 64

l. 6. In place of ἐχώρησε the following emendations have been offered : ἐγνώρισε (Manutius), ἐχορήγησε (Rohde), ἐθεώρησε (Robinson Ellis).

p. 68

l. 3. συοφορβουμένους. For this, the reading of P, συνομορφου-μένους was substituted by Valckenaer, who is followed by Vahlen.

p. 70

ll. 1—17. The corrections (comparatively few, here as elsewhere) necessary in the text of P are due to Robortello, Ahrens, Bergk, and others: see Bergk (ut infra). The several contributions of these scholars have not been specified in the critical footnotes, as it seemed more important to reproduce in full the exact text (continuously written) found in P. Elsewhere the fusion of words has usually been disregarded in reporting the text of P.—In line 13 Ahrens' emendation καδ δέ has been adopted. Mr G. B. Mathews (to whom it occurred independently) remarks that it is confirmed by (1) the reading of P, and (2) the words κὰμ μὲν in line 9, where κὰμ has clearly puzzled the scribes; while Bergk's ἀ δέ involves the strange gender ἀ ἱδρώς, which is hardly sufficiently established by the statement (Cram. *Anecd. Oxon.* I. 208), ἱδρώς· τοῦτο παρ' Αἰολεῦσι θηλυκῶς λέγεται· ἀναδέχεται κλίσιν ἀκόλουθον θηλυκῷ γένει 'ἄδεμ' ἱδρὼς κακὸς (cp. ψυχρός in P) χέεται.'—As to the final words of the ode, Bergk (*Poetae Lyrici Graeci*[4] III. 90) says: 'Quae sequuntur—ἐπεὶ καὶ πένητα—uncis inclusi, nam videntur haec ad Longini orationem pertinere, fort. ἀλλὰ πᾶν τολματόν, ἐπεῖπεν· εἶτα (vel κᾶτα) οὐ θαυμάζοις, κ.τ.λ.' In Otto Crusius' *Anthologia Lyrica* (edited after Bergk and Hiller, in 1897), the ode is (p. 195) made to end thus:—

τεθνάκην δ' ὀλίγω 'πιδεύ(ης)
φαίνομαι ἄλλα.

For another view, see Robinson Ellis, in *Hermathena*, XXII. 385.

p. 72

ll. 18—21. Various efforts have been made by edd. to introduce uniformity into the words ἄϊδ' ἐρύκει.........ἄϊδ' ἀπείργει.........οὐκοῦν ἀπείργει. But the variety is due simply to the author's desire to replace a more poetical by a less poetical word, 'ward off' or 'fend off' by 'keep off.'—The interpretation of οὐκοῦν ἀπείργει was also once a source of difficulty, and led to the omission of the words. Rightly understood, they are distinctly happy and seem to show (cp. 50. 4, 88. 17, 124. 27, 128. 23, 130. 27, 152. 8) that the author was not without a sense of humour.

p. 74

ll. 8—10. In this vexed passage, with the present editor's proposed insertion of ἐς, ἐμποιοῦντα should be retained and should be taken to agree with ταῦτα and to govern ψύγματα ἢ ἀραιώματα. The passage requires illustration from the language of architecture at all periods and from the usage of later writers generally:—

(1) **ψύγματα.** Manutius' emendation ψήγματα has been strangely followed by most of the best editors, including Spengel and C. Hammer. But ψήγματα, *chips*, is not so appropriate here as ψύγματα, *chinks*. The latter term is used by Dionys. Hal. *de Comp. Verb.* xx. of the gap, or hiatus, between words which do not run smoothly together. As applied to a building, it bears no doubt the same meaning of ' breathing-space,' ' air-hole,' ' gap' which we find in the Latin *spiramentum* : cp. Vitruv. *de Architectura* (ed. V. Rose et H. Müller-Strübing) iv. 7 : ' cum enim inter se tangunt (trabes) et non spiramentum et perflatum venti recipiunt, concalefaciuntur et celeriter putrescunt'; and Plin. *Hist. Nat.* xxxiv. 49 : ' hoc videtur facere laxatis spiramentis ad satietatem infusus aer.'

(2) **ἀραιώματα,** *openings, fissures, orifices.* For the use here cp. Strab. *Geograph.* iv. 4 p. 195 : διόπερ οὐ συνάγουσι τὰς ἁρμονίας τῶν σανίδων, ἀλλ᾽ ἀραιώματα καταλείπουσι.

(3) **ἐμποιέω.** This word is primarily used of buildings, as in *Iliad* vii. 438 :

ἐν δ᾽ αὐτοῖσι πύλας ἐνεποίεον εὖ ἀραρυίας,

where αὐτοῖσι = πύργοις. It is also used in the metaphorical sense *to foist in*, as by Herodotus vii. 6 ἐμποιέων ἐς τὰ Μουσαίου χρησμόν, and by Dionys. Hal. *Antiqq. Rom.* iv. 62 (χρησμοὶ) ἐμπεποιημένοι τοῖς Σιβυλλείοις.

(4) **συνοικονομούμενα.** This word is not applied specially to build_ings. The nearest parallel to the present passage will perhaps be found in Lucian *Quomodo historia conscribenda sit* 51, where the un-compounded word is used of the due ordering, or management, of his material by an artist (ἐς δέον οἰκονομήσασθαι τὴν ὕλην). It is possible that we should, with Manutius, read συνοικοδομούμενα, thus changing a single letter. It must, however, be confessed that both συνοικονομούμενα and συνοικοδομούμενα seem somewhat superfluous and disconnected, and we may either suspect a gloss or regard this as an instance of that redundancy to which the author is prone.

(5) **μεγέθη** = *magnitudines.* Cp. Vitruv. *de Arch.* vi. 11, 'itaque si angulares pilae erunt spatiosis magnitudinibus, continendo cuneos firmitatem operibus praestabunt.' The metaphor occurs again in *De Sublim.* xxxix. 3, τῇ τε τῶν λέξεων ἐποικοδομήσει τὰ μεγέθη συναρμόζουσαν.

It may be added that Robinson Ellis (*Hermathena* xxii. 386)

thinks that the last word in the sentence may have been: συνεστοι-
χισμένα or συνεστιχισμένα, ' set in a row side by side.'

p. 76

l. 10. διὸ κεῖνο is the reading of P here. The former was
changed by Manutius to διόπερ, and the latter by Robortello to
ἐκεῖνο. Spengel and Hammer agree in both cases. But it is better,
with Vahlen, to reproduce the manuscript reading: for κεῖνος cp.
80. 16, and for διὸ cp. 90. 9 and 112. 14. Granted the διό, the κεῖνο
seems to follow: cp. H. v. Rohden, *Quas rationes in hiatu vitando
scriptor de Sublimitate et Onesander secuti sint*, p. 70.

l. 22. ἐπέστραπται. Bentley's conjecture ἀπαστράπτει ('does not
show the lightning's flash in equal measure') seems, at first sight,
itself a flash of inspiration. In its metaphor it is in harmony with
what precedes and with what follows, and the word might well have
been written by the author had he thought of it. But ἐπέστραπται
(' is not so direct, earnest, vehement'), though less striking, is a
thoroughly appropriate word, and it is, together with its cognates, a
favourite term in rhetoric. In fact the perfect of this very verb is
elsewhere applied to the style of Demosthenes, as it here is to the
orator himself: Philostr. *Vitae Sophist.* p. 504, σεμνότης δὲ ἡ μὲν
Δημοσθένους ἐπεστραμμένη μᾶλλον, ἡ δὲ Ἰσοκράτους ἀβροτέρα τε καὶ
ἡδίων: cp. Herod. viii. 62, σημαίνων δὲ ταῦτα τῷ λόγῳ διέβαινε
(Θεμιστοκλῆς) ἐς Εὐρυβιάδεα, λέγων μᾶλλον ἐπεστραμμένα. Cp. also
the adj. ἐπιστρεφής (= *intentus*) in Xen. *Hellen.* vi. 3, 7, μάλα δοκῶν
ἐπιστρεφὴς εἶναι ῥήτωρ: in Aesch. *c. Timarch.* § 71, ἐπιστρεφῶς καὶ
ῥητορικῶς......φήσουσι: and in Dionys. Hal. *Antiqq. Rom.* vii. 34,
ἐπιστρεφῶς πάνυ καὶ θρασέως ἁπάντων αὐτῶν καθήπτετο. Finally, our
author himself supplies an illustration in a much misunderstood
passage (xxviii. 3), where ἐπέστρεψεν (which governs the preceding
τὸν λόγον) is contrasted with ἀποστρέψας. Similarly, in xxii. 2
ἀπέστρεψε (given by P) should be retained in the sense of ' turn
aside,' ' divert.'

p. 80

l. 20. ἠθῶν, the reading of P, may possibly be translated 'like
taking, as from noble characters, an impression of (i.e. consisting in)
images or (other) pieces of workmanship.' Cp. τὸ τῆς φύσεως τοῦτο
πλάσμα καὶ δημιούργημα, ὁ τοῦ Πολυκλείτου (Lucian, *de Morte Peregrini*,
viii.), ' this image fashioned by Nature's own hands, this paragon of

Polycleitus'), with which in turn may be compared τὴν δημιουργήσασαν φύσιν τὸν ἄνθρωπον (*de Sublim.* xliii. 5).

But the substitution of εἰδῶν for ἠθῶν diminishes the harshness of the construction, the meaning being 'the imitation of pictures or statues or other works of art.' The stages of corruption may have been : εἰδῶν, εἰ δ' ὦν, ἠθῶν (for the confusion of θ and δ, cp. p. 160. 5 supra). Diels (*Hermes* xiii. 6) has suggested λίθων. Bury (*Classical Review* i. 301) would prefer ἢ θεῶν ('sights,' 'spectacles'), though he doubts whether any alteration is needed.

p. 82

l. 13. It seems just possible that πεπαῖχθαι may stand, in the sense of 'fingere' or 'sibi fingere,' with ὑπέχειν dependent upon it. This perfect is found in an active sense in Kaibel's *Epigrammata Graeca ex lapidibus conlecta*, p. 409, οἷα πέπαιγμαι | οὐ κενά. It occurs also in the sentence πεπαῖχθαί τις ἂν οἰηθείη τὴν λέξιν (Timarch. ap. Athen. 501 E) ; and the word is, it may be added, frequently used by Plutarch, e.g. τοῦτο τὸ παιζόμενον, 'said in proverbial jest,' *Non posse suaviter vivi*, vi. 4 ; τὸ Μενεδήμῳ πεπαιγμένον, 'iocus Menedemi,' *De profectibus in virt.* x.

But there has been an erasure, and it is not certain what the original reading of P may have been at the point where the letters αι now stand. If we are driven to conjecture, it might seem best to adopt προσῆχθαι, with Weiske fil. προσάγειν would keep up the forensic metaphor, since it is used by Plutarch (*de Stoicorum repugnantiis* xxxii. 2) of 'bringing into court.'—But with either reading the dependence of the preceding infinitive is harsh. Vahlen supposes that several words have fallen out ; Wilamowitz regards πεπαῖχθαι as a gloss. Others suggest τετάχθαι or πεπεῖσθαι.

ll. 16, 17. The meaning is that a writer should not be deterred by any regard for the conventions of the hour from giving utterance to eternal truths. Cp. Lucian, *Hermotimus*, lxvii. ὑπερήμερον γίγνεσθαι τἀληθὲς τοῦ ἑκάστου βίου.

If Pearce's conjecture οὐ φθέγξαιτο be adopted, the rendering will be 'if one fears at the time that he will not utter anything to outlast his own life and age.' The οὐ may easily have been lost after χρόνον, but probably the text is right as it is. A writer is not to shrink from expressing the truth that is in him through a nervous dread lest he be considered an *exalté*, to use a word which seems naturally suggested by ὕψος. He should avoid the fate of Thomas Gray in later times who, according to the contemporary judgment quoted by Matthew Arnold, *never spoke out.*

l. 22. Schurzfleisch's substitution of Τερεντιανὲ for νεανία is followed even by Vahlen and C. Hammer. For a defence of the reading of P, see the Introduction p. 19 supra.

l. 23. Robinson Ellis (*Hermathena* XXII. 386) suggests τὰς αὐτάς, 'such at least is the name given by some to what is also called imagery.'

p. 84

l. 5. P seems to separate the τό τε, thus suggesting that some such word as ἐνθουσιαστικόν, or παθητικόν, has disappeared. The former view is that of Rothstein, who would also read ὁμοίως in place of ὅμως.

p. 86

l. 5. The editors commonly adopt the conjecture σειραίου in place of σειρίου as given by P. But Mr A. S. Way prefers the manuscript reading, on which he comments as follows in a letter to the editor : 'If the sun be imagined as a chariot of horses, there is nothing improbable in Sirius (or a fiery star) being represented as a single horse. In *Ion* 1150, Night is represented as drawn by two horses. So in *Orestes* 1005, Dawn (which may be taken as the morning-star) is spoken of as having *a single steed*, which seems a pretty close analogy to that of the dog-star (or any fiery-blazing star) being a single horse.' σειραίου is (Mr Way thinks) tamer and hard to reconcile with ὄπισθε.

p. 88

l. 15. Robinson Ellis' proposal τοῦ ἀλόγου ('the absurd' or 'irrational') avoids the dependence of τοῦ λόγου on τὸ πλάσμα,—a dependence which is unlikely even in a book so free in the order of its words and in its treatment of the article as the περὶ ὕψους.

p. 90

l. 17. Probably ἢ should be added before μιμήσεως or omitted before φαντασίας. As it stands, the sentence is awkward and ambiguous.

l. 27. The addition of ἄνδρες Ἀθηναῖοι, as proposed by Manutius and adopted by Vahlen, seems hardly necessary if we remember that the author commonly quotes from memory and with some freedom (cp. Hersel *Qua in citandis scriptorum et poetarum locis auctor libelli περὶ ὕψους usus sit ratione*, p. 26). Exact citation was in antiquity neither an easy matter nor one to which much importance was attached, and we see in this passage how a late writer half unconsciously introduces small changes (τῆς τῶν Ἑλλήνων ἐλευθερίας for τῆς ἁπάντων ἐλευθερίας, and ἐν Μαραθῶνι προκινδυνεύσαντας for Μαραθῶνι προκινδυνεύσαντας[1]) which make the language more immediately intelligible in his own age.

p. 92

l. 11. Manutius changed μεθεστακὼς into μεθιστάς,—unnecessarily, as the use of παρέστακεν (112. 23) shows.

p. 94

l. 13. The omission by P (as here in δημοσία) of any recognition of the ι *subscr.* has not, as a rule, been noted in the present collation. An instance of the insertion (or adscription) of the ι will be found on p. 96. 7 (fol. 191ʳ), τῶι φωτὶ αὐτῶι. The capriciousness of P in this matter is shown in the next line (96. 8) where it gives τῶι ἡλίω.

p. 96

l. 2. The meaning given to παραληφθεῖσα......τοῖς κάλλεσι καὶ μεγέθεσι in the translation is somewhat strained, and 'introduced by' (cp. xxxviii. 4) might be a better rendering. It might be better still to accept Bury's suggestion περιλαμφθεῖσα, in support of which he quotes ᾧ τὸ πραγματικὸν ἐγκρύπτεται περιλαμπόμενον from c. xv. 11 (cp. also τίνι γὰρ ἐνταῦθ' ὁ ῥήτωρ......τὸ μέγεθος, xvii. 2).—On the other hand, the change of κάλλεσι to πάθεσι (made by Toll, Spengel and Hammer) seems hardly justified by the consideration that πάθος is often found in association with ὕψος or μέγεθος.

l. 18. κατακαλύψει is in accord with the preceding metaphor, but οἷον (unless it refers specially to τηρεῖ) would almost seem to suggest that a new metaphor is about to be introduced. Possibly, therefore, καταλήψει—as found in the inferior MSS. and adopted by Spengel and Hammer—should be admitted into the text.

---

[1] Forced by the verse, he gives Μαραθῶνι in xvi. 3 and (by association) in xvi. 4, but in xvii. 2 he reverts to the preposition.

p. 98

l. 9. It is perhaps hardly likely that παροξύνοντες (the reading of P) can be used in a neuter sense, as ἐθίζει is best taken on p. 64. 12 (cp. ἀκρωτηριάζει, p. 144. 19).

l. 23. It seems better to adhere to the ἧσσον of P than to substitute the ἧττον of Robortello and subsequent edd. No doubt ττ is more common than σσ in P, in which ἧττον itself is found. But in such matters it is hardly safe to demand uniformity from Augustan Greek any more than from Elizabethan English; the author himself may well have used both forms. For σσ, cp. νεοσσὸν on p. 68. 4 and γλῶσσαν on p. 122. 18, though it should be added that in both these cases the word may be regarded as a quotation or reminiscence, as is the case also with ἧσσον on p. 140. 4.

p. 102

l. 10. It is not easy to decide between ἀπολύει, *looses*, and ἀπολλύει, *loses, perdit.* But on the whole, it seems better to depart from the reading of P. Perhaps it is an objection rather than otherwise to ἀπολύει that it continues the preceding metaphors, and certainly the active voice is unnatural unless some such general notion as 'the hindrance' is to be taken as the subject.

p. 104

l. 9. ἐφεστώς. Spengel and Hammer would change to ἐφεστὸς, and they make a similar change on p. 142. 23 where P gives παρεστώς. But it is probably the grammatical form they introduce, not the one they eject, that most requires defence. 'ἐστώς, the organically correct form of the neuter of the Strong Perf. Part. of ἵστημι, is the only form recognised by recent German authorities (Hartel, Kaegi, etc.): ἐστός appears in some MSS. (e.g. in *Oed. Tyr.* 633, τὸ νῦν παρεστὸς νεῖκος, Jebb).' E. A. Sonnenschein, *Greek Accidence*[2], p. 141.

p. 108

l. 8. Robortello's reading αὔξησιν, 'amplification,' has been generally accepted. Rothstein has, however, pointed out (*Hermes* XXII. 537) that αὔχησιν is no less appropriate, and seems to fit in well with the preceding words, φύσει γὰρ ἐξακούεται τὰ πράγματα κομπωδέστερα ἀγεληδὸν οὕτως τῶν ὀνομάτων ἐπισυντιθεμένων. He thinks that αὔχησις, like ἐπίδειξις, may have been a term used in the rhetorical

schools; and he quotes from Hesychius, 'αὔχησις (editur αὐχῆτις)·
σεμνότης.'

Rothstein, it may be mentioned, describes αὔξησιν as 'Robortelli
coniectura.' As a matter of fact, the reading is found (as a correction,
but one proceeding probably from the copyist himself) in Cod. El.,
which manuscript also gives πρέπουσαν (112. 9) and θεσμοδείτης
(64. 5).

p. 112

l. 9. Rothstein (*Hermes* XXII. 544) finds the reading πρέπουσαν
unsatisfactory: 'hoc moneo, minime certam videri Robortelli emen-
dationem neque multo magis placere quam traditum ἅτε τρέπουσαν;
nimis enim exiliter dictum est quod restituit quam ut hunc scriptorem
deceat, ut omittam ne formam quidem orationis aptam esse, cum
ἑαυτῷ ad πρέπουσαν cogitari vix possit. sententiae satisfaceret fortasse
aut ἅτε ἠρεμοῦσαν aut ἅτε περὶ προσώπου οὖσαν.'

l. 14. πρόχρησις has not made its way into Liddell and Scott's
lexicon. But there can be little doubt that the word, though ἅπαξ
εἰρημένον, is genuine, being one of those prepositional compounds to
which our author is so much addicted, and meaning 'first use,' 'use
by preference,' 'proper use.' χρῆσις, πρόσχρησις, and ἡ κυρία χρῆσις
have been suggested. But no change is required. In fact, as it
stands, the text might be interpreted by means of the last of these
suggestions, ἡ κυρία χρῆσις.

l. 15. ἡνίκα......διδῷ should be compared with ὁπότε......ζέσῃ
and ἡνίκα......παραστῇ on p. 122. 27 and p. 124. 10. The absence
of the ἄν can of course be illustrated from earlier as well as later
Greek, and our author may have thought (cp. Goodwin, *Syntax of
Greek Verb*, p. 208) that he was following good Platonic precedent.

p. 116

l. 19. Manutius and subsequent editors read φασίν in place of
φησίν as given by P. But the latter should probably be adopted,
Κεκίλιος being supplied as subject. Cp. p. 171 supra.

p. 118

l. 8. Some such word as φάνωσιν may possibly underlie the τ' ἂν
ὦσι of P.

p. 120

l. 11. Vahlen has defended the reading of P, viz. τῷ σημαντικῶς. He supplies ἔχειν, comparing σημαντικώτατα ἔχειν (xxxi. 1). τῷ σημαντικῷ and similar suggestions seem unnecessary.

p. 122

l. 1. Vahlen, following Stephanus, would read ἐπιτίμησις in place of ὑποτίμησις. As Robinson Ellis (*Hermathena* ix. 387) says, ὑποτίμησις should not be altered, but should be understood to be nearly = 'correction,' or 'speaking under correction.'

p. 126

l. 2. Apparently αὐτό (if this and ὅμως and καί are genuine) is more or less of a Latinism, and must be taken with ἀπεθάρρησε and regarded as preparing the way for τῷ παντὶ...ἀποφήνασθαι. To the various emendations offered must now be added Tucker's conjecture ὁ Μῶμος αὐτοῦ (*Classical Review*, February 1898, p. 24), in which (ingenious as the suggestion is) the αὐτοῦ raises a couple of difficulties. Is αὐτοῦ (= Πλάτωνος) altogether likely when Πλάτωνος occurs later in the same clause, and is ὁ Μῶμος αὐτοῦ a possible phrase for 'his bitter censor'? However, Blass (*Griech. Bereds.* p. 192) gives ὁμοίως αὐτοῦ, though he does not construe the words.

ll. 6—8. To translate this passage at all, it appears necessary to place a comma after φιλονεικίας, and to understand 'he (is carried away) by contentiousness, and even his premisses (are) not, as he thought, admitted.' Kayser would, in the latter half of the sentence, add παρίστησι. But the author is occasionally elliptical (as well as redundant), and may be so here.

p. 128

l. 3. It will be seen that P gives αἰεὶ here and on pp. 124. 17, 128. 12, 134. 22, 142. 25. It is possible that the author read αἰεὶ in his text of Plato (the form is often found in our own MSS.) and deliberately adopted the archaism. For an archaism it must have been in his day: cp. Meisterhans, *Grammatik der attischen Inschriften*, p. 25, 'In den Staatspsephismen findet man bis zum Jahre 361 v. Chr. abwechselnd αἰεί und ἀεί; von da an nur noch die letztere Form. Nur in den Dekreten religiöser Genossenschaften (Thiasoten) begegnet αἰεί noch im ii Jahrhundert v. Chr.'

l. 11.   Rothstein (*Hermes* XXII. 539) thinks it possible that αἰτίας may be right.

p. 130

l. 3.   Pearce, and most subsequent editors, read τῷ μεγέθει for τῷ ἀληθεῖ, but see Rothstein (*Hermes* XXII. 539).—'For ἀριθμῷ we should read ὅρῳ, retaining P's ἀληθεῖ.   The corruption is due to an abbreviated writing of ἀριθμός: see Dr Jackson's note in the *Journal of Philology* XXVI. p. 157, where the converse corruption is removed from the Eudemian Ethics 1243 b,' J. P. Postgate (communicated).

l. 14.   For ἡδὺ λιτῶς Tucker (*Classical Review* XII. 24) would read εἰδυλλικῶς.   Perhaps the emendation may derive some support from the fact that between the υ and the λ a slight erasure (not noted by the editors) has taken place in P.

ll. 17, 18.   A difficult passage, which has been very variously emended: κατὰ τοὺς Ἀττικοὺς κώμους, κατὰ τοὺς ἀστικοὺς ἐκείνους, ἀλλ' ἐπιεικῆ, ἀλλ' ἐπιχαριτώμενα, ἀλλ' εὐσχήμονα, κατὰ τοὺς Ἀττικοὺς ἐκείνους ἅλας ἐπικείμενα.   The last is Tucker's suggestion, and the rendering he gives is, 'seasoned with wit after the manner of the classic Athenians.'   He argues that 'Longinus would certainly not have said of the classic Athenians that their jests were ἄμουσα or ἀνάγωγα.'   But the reference in κατὰ τοὺς Ἀττικοὺς ἐκείνους may possibly be not to 'the classic Athenians' but to the teachers of Attic diction in and before the author's time.   There is more force in Tucker's observation that the sense of ἐπικείμενα is obscure. Rothstein (who thinks that the Athenian comic poets are in question) would understand ἐπικείμενα 'de salibus leviter et eleganter orationi adspersis, ubi alii ἐπιτρέχειν vel ἐπανθεῖν potius dixissent.'   Robinson Ellis suggests the meaning 'urgent, giving no quarter,' the reference being to the directness and unsparing character of the repartee.

p. 132

l. 6.   Robinson Ellis (*Hermathena* IX. 387) defends καρδίῃ νήφοντος, quoting Plut. *de Garrul.* p. 503 F, τὸ γὰρ ἐν τῇ καρδίᾳ νήφοντος ἐπὶ τῆς γλώττης ἐστὶ τοῦ μεθύοντος, ὡς οἱ παροιμιαζόμενοί φασιν.   He adds that the Ionic dative seems to prove that the proverb was known in a poetical form.

l. 25.   Robinson Ellis (l.c.) remarks that the ἔ**κρινε of Jahn-Vahlen seems to point to ἐπέκρινε as the true reading.   But the space is small—too small for πε as usually written in this MS.

p. 134

l. 2. τῶν ἄθλων αὐτῆς, 'her triumphs,' is commonly read in place of τῶν ὅλων αὐτῆς, 'her mighty fabric.' But the expression τὰ ὅλα is frequent in later Greek, and it is better not to anticipate φιλοτιμοτά-τους ἀγωνιστὰς by reading ἄθλων. The addition of φιλοτιμ. ἀγων. is in the spirit of Bacon's comment upon the saying of Pythagoras that he was a *spectator* of life : ' Men ought to know that in the theatre of human life it is only for God and angels to be *spectators.*'

l. 19. In place of αὐτοῦ μόνου the following emendations have been proposed : αὐτόχθονος (Ruhnken), αὐτονόμου (Wyttenbach), αὐτομάτου (Haupt), ὑπονόμου (M. Schmidt). See further in the Literary Appendix under *Pindar.*

p. 142

l. 6. Ernesti (*Lexicon Technologiae Graecorum Rhetoricae,* p. 101) defended μετ' ἐλευθερίας, and offered the following translation of the passage : 'harmonia non solum natura adiumentum est blande ducendi et oblectandi, sed etiam, si modo anxium artis studium et putidam concinnitatis diligentiam vites, adfectui mirifice inservit.' He thus took ἐλευθερία to refer to freedom of arrangement, and the καί before πάθους to mean 'also,' like the καί after ἀλλά.

p. 144

l. 2. Manutius conjectured ἔοικε μανίᾳ, Spengel εἴη ἂν μανία.

l. 11. The best discussion of the whole of this passage will be found in a little known but excellent paper by G. Amsel, published under the title 'De vi atque indole Rhythmorum quid Veteres iudicaverint' in the *Breslauer Philologische Abhandlungen* (Vratisl., 1887), vol. I. pt 3, pp. 1—112. After τό τε in l. 11 Amsel supposes that a number of words have been lost, the first of them perhaps being τέλος. Further down he explains τέτρασι καταμετρουμένου χρόνοις thus : 'efficiuntur igitur secundum Pseudo-Longinum verbis ὥσπερ νέφος duo rhythmi, id est pedes : – –, ⏑ ⏑̆, quorum prior – – est τετράσημος.'

It is obvious that by δακτυλικοὶ ῥυθμοί something more is meant than we should understand by dactylic rhythms. It is not unlikely that the author would have divided the sentence for rhythmical purposes thus, τοῦτο τὸ ψήφ|ισμα τὸν τότ|ε τῇ πόλει | περιστάντα | κίνδυν|ον παρελθεῖν | ἐποίησεν | ὥσπερ νέφος; and that he would have regarded each of these divisions as forming a ῥυθμὸς δακτυλικός (cp. Amsel, l.c., p. 87).   But even upon this and other suppositions, the passage is full of difficulties, which our imperfect knowledge of Greek rhythms is unable to remove. See, however, the description of the 'iambic-dactyl' in the newly-discovered metrical fragment (probably of Aristoxenus) in Grenfell and Hunt's *Oxyrhynchus Papyri*, Part I. pp. 15—19.

l. 19. ἀκρωτηριάζεται is also read, but the verb is probably intransitive here. Cp. note on p. 179 supra.

p. 148

l. 15. In this difficult and suspected passage Mr Mathews is no doubt right in suggesting that the words ἐγκοπὰς and σκληρότητας refer to 'notches' or 'incisions' and 'roughnesses,'—to dovetailing and friction as used in carpentry.

ll. 19—22. The following emendations have been suggested in this much disputed and probably corrupt passage. In the earlier part: δ᾿∗ἐπ᾿ εὐθύ Manutius, δ᾿ ἄγει ἐπ᾿ εὐθύ H. Stephanus, δ᾿ ἐπευθύνει Petra, δὲ σπεύδει Rohde. In the latter part : ἀπόψυχα γὰρ τὰ μῆκος ἄκαιρον ἀνακαλούμενα Manutius, ἄψυχα γὰρ διὰ μῆκος ἄκαιρον (ἄπειρον) ἀναχαλώμενα Faber, ἀπόψυχα τὰ παρ᾿ ἄκαιρον μῆκος ἀνακαλούμενα Pearce, ἀπόψυχα ἄτε παρὰ μῆκος ἄκαιρον ἀναχαλώμενα Toup, ἀποψύχεται εἰς (πρὸς Wilamowitz) ἄκαιρον μῆκος ἀναχαλώμενα Ruhnken, ἀπόψυχα γὰρ τὰ ἄκαιρον μῆκος ἀνακαλινδούμενα Spengel.—In the earlier part (to revert to it) Meinel would read συντομία δὲ τείνει ἐπ᾿ εὐθύ, comparing xiii. 2 καὶ ἄλλη τις παρὰ τὰ εἰρημένα ὁδὸς ἐπὶ τὰ ὑψηλὰ τείνει and Plut. *Demosth. Vit.* xxvi. 5, τὴν εὐθὺ τοῦ θανάτου τείνουσαν (ὁδόν).

The words δῆλον—ἀνακαλούμενα seem like the addition of a transcriber who thought he detected an omission in the treatment of the subject ; or they may be rough notes of the author himself.

p. 152

l. 17. ἀλλάξας, the reading of P, may possibly be explained in the sense of 'changing the sentence thus,' the nominative being employed as though ἐδύνατο or the like had preceded.

p. 154

l. 12. Cobet (*Novae Lectiones*, p. 645) would read πρὸς ἐμὲ ἔναγχος in place of προσέναγχοσ as given by P, and the alteration is a tempting one. But προσέναγχος has in its favour not only the manuscript tradition but the known partiality of our author for compounds and double compounds beginning with πρός.

p. 156

l. 14. The recent conjecture (συναραιοῖ) of W. Schmid has been adopted here: see *Rheinisches Museum* LIII. (1897) p. 446. Among other conjectures may be mentioned: συνάγει, συναιρεῖ, συναμαυροῖ. Meinel has suggested σιναροῖ, a verb formed from the adjective σιναρός.

p. 158

l. 17. For μηδ᾽ ἕτερα (which reading perhaps will just stand, and is, in fact, retained by the most recent editors) the following substitutions have been suggested: μηδὲ πέρα, μηδὲ παρά, μηδὲ περί. More likely than any of these is Ruhnken's μηδ᾽ ὑστεροφημίας (in place of μηδ᾽ ἕτερα φήμης): cp. p. 82. 19 supra.

l. 20. ʽθνητά is a gloss on δαπανητά, of which καπανητά is a corruption. Accordingly δαπανητά should be restored to its place before ἑαυτῶν. The use of δαπανᾶν in this sense has been established by M. Rothstein in *Hermes* XXII. p. 546 from Dion. Hal. 4. 81 and Plutarch *Galba* 17. He proposes (besides καὶ γεννητά) καὶ δαπανητά, which is tautological if θνητά is retained,' J. P. Postgate (communicated).

p. 160

l. 2. The gap assumed by Robortello has been filled by later scholars in various ways. πρὸς τῆς ἑαυτοῦ Manutius, πρὸς τῆς τοῦ πλεονεκτεῖν ἐπιθυμίας Ruhnken (these words being taken from l. 6), πρὸς τῆς ἑαυτοῦ φιλοχρηματίας Toll.

l. 10. The emendation ἐπικλύσειαν has been accepted by some of the best editors. But is there not more confusion of metaphor in speaking of escaped prisoners as 'flooding' the world with calamity than as 'firing' it? In the latter case they have turned incendiaries and ignite the world with evil deeds.

l. 11. δαπανῶν is difficult and probably corrupt.

l. 16. As already indicated, P ends a page (fol. 207ᵛ) with the words περὶ ὧν, the remaining leaves having been lost.

APPENDIX B.

LINGUISTIC. WITH A SELECT GLOSSARY, CHIEFLY OF RHETORICAL TERMS.

In his 'Historical Greek Grammar,' Dr Jannaris has followed the growth of the Greek language in five successive stages, the last of which brings us down to our own time :—

1. Attic or Classical Period, 500—300 B.C.
2. Hellenistic or Alexandrian Period, 300—150 B.C.
3. Graeco-Roman Period, 150 B.C.—300 A.D.
4. Transitional Period, 300—600 A.D.
5. Neohellenic Period, 600—1900 A.D.

The *De Sublimitate* belongs to the Graeco-Roman period, but in that period it stands somewhat apart. It cannot be assigned to the strict 'Atticist' school, the diction of which (as seen in Dionysius of Halicarnassus, Dion Chrysostom, Lucian, Aristeides, and others) has lately been so exhaustively studied by W. Schmid[1]. Rather, it is conceived in the spirit of protest against the position assumed by Caecilius, one of the leaders of the Atticist movement, who had presumed to exalt Lysias at the expense of Plato, of whom our author is a perfervid admirer and a diligent imitator. At the same time, though the author does not 'Atticise' in the narrower sense, he is a true follower of such Attic writers as Plato himself, and he has a genuine distaste for the vices of the Asiatic style[2].

The general features of his own style are fairly obvious. A single short chapter, such as c. vii., might serve as a sample of the whole treatise. In this chapter, or elsewhere, we find superabundance of

---

[1] W. Schmid, *Der Atticismus in seinen Hauptvertretern von Dionysius von Halikarnass bis auf den zweiten Philostratus*, Stuttgart, 1887—1897, 5 vols. Reference may also be made to E. Norden, *Die antike Kunstprosa: vom vi. Jahrhundert v. Christ bis in die Zeit der Renaissance*, Leipzig, 1898.

[2] With regard to the author's relation to Caecilius, more will be said in the Literary Index under that writer's name.—For the Asiatic rhetoric, see (besides F. Blass, *Die griechische Beredsamkeit in dem Zeitraum von Alexander bis auf Augustus*, Berlin, 1865) Erwin Rohde's article 'Die asianische Rhetorik und die zweite Sophistik' in *Rheinisches Museum*, vol. XLI. (year 1886), pp. 170—190.

words and of metaphors; we find compound words in the same excessive plenty; we find poetical expressions, and expressions of doubtful currency. But we feel at the same time the warm imaginative glow which pervades the book and redeems all its minor shortcomings. *Décadent* though the writer may sometimes seem in his language, he breathes nevertheless the spirit of the best classic or heroic age. And even in his phraseology, where it may seem most poetical, it is always well to inquire whether there may not be Platonic authority for the words chosen. For example, δίκην (= 'like,' i. 4; xxxii. 1) is found in Plato, and that in a passage which happens to be quoted in the περὶ ὕψους itself (c. xiii.). δειλός (ii. 1) is another poetical word common to Plato and the *De Sublimitate*; and many other cases of coincidence will appear in the succeeding lists. It is quite open to anyone to urge, as Caecilius of Calacte would no doubt have done, that the prose of Plato, with its strong *color poeticus*, is a dangerous model for ordinary uninspired mortals to follow; but the fact that such a model was followed should always be kept in mind.

Another marked characteristic of the *De Sublimitate* is its long and rhythmical sentences[1]. The opening sentence of all might, if the exercise were not curious rather than profitable, be arranged, clause by clause, with a parallelism as elaborate as would become any excerpt from the Hebrew Bible. But it would be unjust to the author to imply that he thought first of the form, and only secondly of the matter. He has himself (xli. 2) recognised the dangers of what we may term over-rhythm. It must, however, be admitted that late rhetoricians (Dionysius of Halicarnassus, for example) sometimes lay themselves open to misconception when they describe the style of the great literary models. They are too apt to speak as if something like their own process of analysis had preceded and governed the original act of construction. They remind us of those who, in an analytical age like our own, find hexameter lines in the Authorised Version of the Scriptures : *He poureth contempt upon princes and weakeneth the strength of the mighty,* and *God is gone up with a shout, the Lord with the sound of a trumpet.* Only, in Greek the recognised varieties of metre and metrical feet are so much more numerous than

---

[1] In this respect the treatise should be compared, in English, with the prose not of the nineteenth but of the seventeenth century, that of Milton for example. Modern Italian can also reproduce effectively the fine roll and cadence of its sonorous sentences.

in English that the most ingenious writer could hardly hope to avoid the toils of the enthusiastic and leisured analyst of a later day. With regard to the *De Sublimitate* in particular it will be enough here to add that its rhythms seem sometimes (e.g. vii. 4, xiv. 3, xxxv. 3) to be Latin rhythms rather than Greek. Possibly the writer was not conscious of this himself (he makes no pretensions to Latin scholarship, cp. xii. 4), but the fact remains. At the time when he wrote, Rome had begun to make herself felt in the domain of Greek style as well as in other fields. In his own treatise probable examples of Latin influence upon Greek construction and phrasing are: καὶ ὑπ ὄψιν τιθῇς τοῖς ἀκούουσιν (xv. 1, = Lat. *et auditoribus ob oculos ponas*), εἰς καταφρόνησιν ἑαυτοῦ λαμβάνων τὸν παραλογισμόν (xvii. 1, = Lat. *fraudem in contemptum sui trahit, interpretatur ut in contemptum sui dictum*), εἰς ἦθος ἐκλύεται (ix. 15, = Lat. *laxatum in moratam orationem desinit*), and (according to the reading of some MSS.) καὶ οἷον ἐν καταλήψει τηρεῖ (xvii. 3, = Lat. *et quasi in custodia servat, vel retinet*).

Before the question of the vocabulary of the treatise is entered upon, a few grammatical points (chiefly characteristic of post-classical Greek) deserve mention. Such are the uses of the prepositions in : συμπλήρωσις ἀπό (xii. 2), ἡ ἐν ἀξιώματι καὶ διάρσει σύνθεσις (viii. 1), ἐν ὕψει (xii. 4), ἐν τῷ παραλόγῳ (xxiv. 2), ἐν τῷ γλαφυρῷ πάντη κεκαλλιγραφημένοι (xxxiii. 5), ὑπέρ (xxxix. 1 : hardly distinguishable here from περί, whereas in iv. 2 and xxxii. 8 it seems to have its full meaning), διά (ix. 12 [bis], xxxiii. 5, xxxix. 1), ἐπὶ τοῦ Πλάτωνος (xxxv. 1). The following adverbial expressions with ἐξ are found : ἐξ ἅπαντος (viii. 3), 'on every side,' 'throughout,' 'as an indispensable ingredient'; ἐξ ἅπαντος (xxxiii. 1), 'from every source,' 'imperatively'; ἐξ ὅλου (viii. 4), 'altogether,' 'entirely'; ἐκ περιττοῦ (xxxiv. 2), 'in a singular degree'; ἐκ παντός (ii. 2), 'utterly.' Noteworthy too are : κατ' ἄκρον (xxx. 1), ἐπ' ἄκρον (xxxiv. 4), κατ' ἄκρας (xliv. 6). Again, καίτοι (xxxv. 4) and καίτοιγε (iv. 4, xxxviii. 5) occur in the sense of καίπερ and with the same participial construction. There are also some uses of the article which are worthy of note: ἐκ τοῦ κατ' ἀκολουθίαν (xxii. 1), τὸ κατὰ τάξιν (xxii. 2), τὸ δ' ἐν ὑπεροχῇ (xxxvi. 4), τῶν κατὰ τοὺς ἀριθμούς (xxiii. 2), κατὰ τὸ ἑξῆς (xxi. 1). The insertion and omission of the article, its position in relation to the noun, and its general use in the *De Sublimitate* are decidedly erratic if judged by strict Attic standards.

The first point to be remarked in the vocabulary itself is that, though the treatise is a short one, many words occur in it which are not elsewhere found in extant Greek literature. The following list of some forty words will, it is hoped, be found fairly accurate and complete :

ἀδιανέμητος (xxii. 3)
ἀδρεπήβολος (viii. 1)
ἀναχοή (xxxv. 4)
ἀνθυπαντᾶν (xviii. 1, 2)
ἀντανοίγω (xxxiv. 4)
ἀντισυμμαχέω (xvii. 1)
ἀπακμή (ix. 15)
ἀπαύξησις (vii. 3)
ἀποκύλισμα (xl. 4)
ἀπόψυχος (xv. 8)
βιολογέω (ix. 15)
διακληρονομέω (xii. 4)
διαριστεύομαι (xiii. 4)
δυσδαιμονέω (xii. 4)
ἐκπάθεια (xxxviii. 3)
ἐναλήθης (xv. 8)
ἐξέρεισμα (xl. 4)
ἐποικονομία (xi. 2)
εὐπάλαιστρος (xxxiv. 2)
εὐπίνεια (xxx. 1)

καινόσπουδος (v.)
κατάρυθμος (xli. 1)
κατασημαντικός (xxxii. 5)
καταφέγγω (xxxiv. 4)
μεγεθοποιός (xxxix. 4)
μικροποιέω (xli. 1)
μικροποιός (xliii. 6)
ὀνυμάτιον (xliii. 2)
ποκοειδής (xv. 5)
προεμφανίζομαι (xvii. 3)
προσέναγχος (xliv. 1)
προσεπιθεάομαι (xxx. 1)
προσπεριορίζομαι (xxviii. 3)
πρόχρησις (xxvii. 2)
συνεμπνέω (ix. 11)
συοφορβέω (ix. 14)
τοπηγορία (xi. 2)
ὑψηλοποιός (xxviii. 1)
ὑψηλοφανής (xxiv. 1)
φορταγωγέω (xliii. 4)

This list has been framed with care because it seems to have an important bearing upon the question of the authorship. The fact that some 40 separate words (or *forms*, if exception be taken to 'words') can be enumerated which occur in this short treatise but occur in no other known writing or body of writings, appears to suggest that the author is not represented by any other surviving work. The argument may not tell quite conclusively against his identification with the historical Longinus, whose fragments are not very considerable, but the negative presumption is great where authors so voluminous as Plutarch or Dionysius of Halicarnassus are concerned. To countervail this marked independence, surely a large number of special coincidences should be required. Can these be produced ?

To begin with the historical Longinus. Although the fragments of Longinus cannot be said to be very considerable when compared with the collected works of Dionysius and Plutarch, yet Vaucher is able to muster 1335 words from those fragments for comparison with

2220 words drawn from the περὶ ὕψους. And as the result of a minute and exhaustive analysis (*Études*, pp. 68—79) he concludes that the vocabulary in the two cases is marked by divergence rather than by agreement. With regard to the style generally he is of the same opinion[1]. The arguments on which he relies seem cogent enough. But it is only right to remember that all evidence of this kind must be received with great reserve. In comparisons founded upon style and vocabulary there are many uncertainties. There is the fact that critics disagree so widely in their judgments upon such matters. There is also the fact that an author's manner of expressing himself may, during one period of his life or when he is writing upon one subject, differ altogether from that which characterises him during another period of his life or when writing upon another subject[2]. There is, further, the danger of incomplete investigation. To illustrate this last point, it may be mentioned that it was once urged, as evidence of the traditional ascription, that the word ἀλληγορία, found in the treatise, did not occur before Plutarch's time. This often-repeated statement was a rash one in any case, in view of the fact that we possess only a few fragments of the writings of antiquity, but it did not even take full account of the materials we actually possess. As a matter of fact, the word occurs twice in Cicero, by whom it was probably derived from Stoic sources.

These and similar considerations apply to Vaucher's arguments from style when they lead to a positive no less than when they lead to a negative conclusion. If they are precarious in the one case, they are precarious in the other also. Many of the verbal coincidences (see Vaucher, op. cit. pp. 96 ff.) which strengthen Vaucher's belief

---

[1] Vaucher, op. cit. p. 50 : *la différence sensible que l'on remarque entre le style simple et égal des fragments de Longin, et le style animé, véhément, figuré du Traité* περὶ ὕψους, *dont le sujet, quoi qu'il en dise, ne prêtait pas plus à l'éloquence que ceux des Fragments*. Ruhnken, it is true, took another view, but he is not supported in it by his modern successor Cobet. See further in the Literary Appendix under *Longinus*.

[2] A signal instance of such variation in our own day is afforded by the style of Thomas Carlyle. Suppose that nearly two thousand years had passed since he wrote, and with what confidence we can imagine the position assumed and maintained that Carlyle the Edinburgh reviewer and Carlyle the philosopher of Chelsea could not possibly be identical. Treacherous always, such comparisons are doubly treacherous when they concern men of marked individuality who have been driven, more and more, into themselves by the circumstances of the times in which they live.

that Plutarch is the author of the περὶ ὕψους may be explained by the supposition that the two writers lived about the same time, and were, both of them, greatly influenced by Plato. As examples of words for the most part rare in other authors but found alike in Plato, Plutarch and the περὶ ὕψους, the following may be given:—

αἰσχυντηλός (iv. 4)
ἀποσκιάζειν (xvii. 3)
ἀποχετεύειν (xiii. 3)
ἀσχημονεῖν (iii. 5)
βακχεία (xxxii. 7)
δείνωσις (xi. 2)
δημώδης (xl. 2, 3)
διακριβοῦν (xvi. 1)
διαλανθάνειν (xvii. 1)
διαπτύσσειν (xxx. 1)
διήκειν (xliv. 9)
διστάζειν (xxviii. 1)
δουλοπρεπής (ix. 3)
ἐγκύμων (ix. 1)
ἑδραῖος (xl. 4)
εἰδωλοποιεῖν (xv. 7)
ἐκπληροῦν (xl. 1)
ἔκφρων (xxxix. 2)
ἐμπίπτειν (ix. 4)
ἐνάργεια (xv. 2)
ἐνθουσιᾶν (iii. 2)
ἐξυβρίζειν (xliii. 5)
ἐπίκηρος (xxix. 1)
ἐπικίνδυνος (ii. 2)
ἐπικρατεῖν (xvii. 1)
ἐπικρίνειν (xii. 4)
ἐπισφαλής (xxxiii. 2)
ἐπίχαρις (xxxiv. 3)
ἔρανος (xl. 1)
εὐβουλία (ii. 3)
ἐφικτός (xxxix. 1)
ζωγραφία (xvii. 3)
ἥδυσμα (xliii. 4)
ἠρεμεῖν (xx. 2)
θρεπτικός (xxxi. 1)

ἰδιωτεύειν (xxxi. 2)
καταισχύνειν (xliii. 5)
κηλεῖν (xxxix. 5)
λείψανον (ix. 12)
λῆψις (x. 3)
μεγαλαυχία (vii. 2)
μεγαλοπρεπής (xii. 3)
μεγαλοφροσύνη (vii. 3)
μεγαλόφρων (ix. 2)
μεγαλοψυχία (vii. 1)
μυθολογεῖν (xxxiv. 2)
μυθώδης (ix. 13)
νικητήρια (xxxvi. 2)
νόημα (xii. 1)
νόησις (iii. 4)
ξηρότης (iii. 3)
οἰδεῖν (iii. 1)
ὀξύρροπος (xviii. 1)
ὀρχηστικός (xli. 1)
ὀχληρός (ix. 10)
ὀψοποιΐα (xliii. 4)
παιδαριώδης (iv. 1)
παντελής (xxii. 4)
πάντη (i. 4)
πάντως (i. 2)
παραβολή (xxvii. 1)
παραλλάττειν (xi. 3)
παρεικάζειν (ix. 13)
παρολιγωρεῖν (xxiii. 2)
πέλαγος (xii. 2)
περιμάχητος (xxxviii. 3)
περιουσία (xxxiv. 4)
περιττεύειν (xxxv. 1)
περιφρονεῖν (vii. 1)
πηροῦν (xlii. 1)

πρωτεῖα (xiii. 4)

συγκινδυνεύειν (ix. 6)

συνεκπίπτειν (xli. 1)

συνεπικρίνειν (i. 2)

συνεπισπᾶσθαι (xxii. 3)

σωματοειδής (xxiv. 1)

τεχνίτης (xvii. 1)

ὑπεναντίος (iii. 4)

ὑπεραίρειν (iii. 4)

ὑπεροχή (xxxvi. 4)

ὑπερφυῶς (xliii. 2)

ὑπόγυος (xviii. 2)

φιλόνεικος (xiii. 4)

φιλοχρηματία (xliv. 6)

χαῦνος (vii. 1)

χειμάρρους (xxxii. 1)

χρησμῳδεῖν (xiii. 2)

Such a list seems to show that it was from Plato that the author of the περὶ ὕψους derived his love of compound and semi-poetical words and his desire (as indicated in his ἅπαξ εἰρημένα) to fashion words of the same kind himself. But it does not show, or even create a presumption, that Plutarch wrote the treatise. For there are comparatively few verbal correspondences between the περὶ ὕψους and Plutarch which cannot be proved to have their origin in Plato, while there are many words in the περὶ ὕψους, short as it is, which are not found in Plutarch's writings, extensive as those are.

The *Sprachstatistik* of the περὶ ὕψους, as of so many other works, is of interest for its bearing on the affinities, rather than on the paternity, of the treatise. The distant descent of the book from Plato is abundantly clear[1]. Clear also are the traces it exhibits of Polybian diction in such words as ἀνεπιστάτως (xxxiii. 4), παράπτωμα (xxxvi. 2), ῥωπικός (iii. 4), ἰσχυροποιέω (xii. 2), παιδομαθής (xliv. 3). But this is no more than to say that it is in the current of that non-classical speech which sets in so markedly with Polybius. Its affinities with Philo, a much later writer than Polybius and possibly a contemporary of our author, are also noteworthy, though Plato (as in the case of Plutarch and the περὶ ὕψους) can often be shown to be the common fount. Examples will be found not only in the passage quoted in the Introduction (p. 13 supra), but in single words such as :—

ἀγεληδόν (xxiii. 4)

ἀνερμάτιστος (ii. 2 : cp. Plat.)

ἀντισπᾶσθαι (xxii. 1)

διαπτύσσειν (xxx. 1)

εἰδοποιΐα (xviii. 1)

εἰκονογραφεῖν (x. 6)

εἱρμός (xxii. 1)

ἐκτιμᾶν (xliv. 7)

[1] To the words already given might be added such expressions as: ἀνερμάτιστος (ii. 2; *Theaet.* 144 A), καταντλεῖν (xii. 5; *Rep.* I. 344 D), ἀψοφητὶ ῥέων (xiii. 1; *Theaet.* 144 B), ὕπακρος (xxxiv. 1; *Erast.* 136 A,—if this dialogue is Platonic).

ἐπάλληλος (ix. 13) πάμφυρτος (ix. 7)
ἐπιπροσθεῖν (xxxii. 2) παράστημα (ix. 1) .
ἠρεμεῖν (xx. 2) περιλάμπεσθαι (xv. 11)
κατασκελετεύειν (ii. 1) προκόσμημα (xliii. 3)
κονδυλίζειν (xliv. 4) προσυπογράφειν (xiv. 2)
μαγειρεῖον (xliii. 3) προϋποκεῖσθαι (viii. 1)
νεοττοποιεῖσθαι (xliv. 7) τεκμηριοῦν (xxviii. 2)

The verbal coincidences between Dionysius of Halicarnassus and the περὶ ὕψους are less marked where general vocabulary is in question, Dionysius belonging to a different school of writing. But where the technical terms of rhetoric are concerned, there are (as will appear in the Select Glossary) many links between the treatise and Latin writers such as Cicero and Quintilian, and between it and Greek writers such as Dionysius and (probably) Caecilius. Henry Nettleship (*Lectures and Essays*, Second Series, p. 56) rightly noticed in Graeco-Roman literary criticism the growth of a number of new aesthetic terms such as : τραχύς, αὐστηρός, αὐθάδης, αὐχμηρός, εὐπινής, στρυφνός, συνεσπασμένος, ἀντίτυπος, ἀρχαϊκός, πυκνός, δεινός, συστρέφειν, ἀξιωματικός, τραγικός, σεμνός, δαιμόνιος, πνεῦμα, χάρις, Ἀφροδίτη, γλαφυρός, ἀνθηρός, στρογγύλος, κτενίζω, βοστρυχίζω, ἡδονή, πειθώ, ῥώμη, ἰσχύς, ἀφελής, μεγαλοφυής, μεγαλοπρεπής, περιττός. Of such terms not a few are found in the περὶ ὕψους.—It should be added here that, in the absence of special lexicons to some of the authors just mentioned, it has not been found possible to present an exhaustive statement of all the linguistic questions that arise. But some help has been derived from the following special studies : B. Weissenberger, *Die Sprache Plutarchs von Chaeronea und die pseudo-plutarchischen Schriften* (2 parts : Straubing, 1895 and 1896); C. Siegfried, *Philo von Alexandria* (Jena, 1875); L. Goetzeler, *De Polybii Elocutione* (Wirceburgi, 1887).

It is hoped that the Select Glossary may serve as a supplement to the translation, and in order to further this object a few miscellaneous words have been included in it. In the main, however, it will be found to be confined to rhetorical terms.

SELECT GLOSSARY CHIEFLY OF RHETORICAL TERMS.

ἀγχίστροφος. ix. 13, xxvii. 3, xxii. 1 (ἀγχιστρόφως). Often used by the rhetoricians to signify rapidity of transition in thought or expression. Its general meaning of 'suddenly changing' may be illustrated by ἀγχίστροφος μεταβολή Thucyd. II. 53, and by ἀστάθμητόν ἐστιν εὐτυχία πρᾶγμα καὶ ἀγχίστροφον Dionys. Hal. *Antiqq. Rom.* IV. 23.

ἀγών. xv. 1, xxvi. 3. A *contest* in the assembly or the law-court, and the lively qualities appropriate to such a contest. In xxvi. 3, ἀγῶνος ἔμπλεως is said of a hearer who is, as it were, made to participate in what is being described. Similarly, the adjective ἀγωνιστικός (xxii. 3, xxiii. 1) refers to the vehemence of public debate. Cp. ἐναγώνιος (ix. 13, xv. 9, xxv., xxvi. 1), ἐναγωνίως (xviii. 2). Aristotle (*Rhet.* III. 1) distinguishes between γραφικὴ λέξις and ἀγωνιστικὴ λέξις.

ἀδρεπήβολος. τὸ περὶ τὰς νοήσεις ἀδρεπήβολον, viii. 1. *The power of forming great conceptions* : cp. τὸ μεγαλοφυές, ix. 1, ἀδρότερον, xl. 4.—ἀδρός, 'noble,' is an alternative for δεινός, 'vehement,' in the triple classification of varieties of style which some of the Greek rhetoricians (other than Dionysius of Halicarnassus) adopt, viz. (1) ἀδρὸν ἢ δεινόν, (2) ἰσχνὸν ἢ λιτόν, (3) μέσον ἢ ἀνθηρόν (cp. Cic. *Orator*, v. 20 ff., *grandiloqui, tenues et acuti, temperati* ; Quintil. *Inst. Or.* XII. 10, 57—65, *grande atque robustum, subtile, medium.* Sandys' notes on the former passage should be consulted).

ἀθροισμός. xxiii. 1. = συναθροισμός, *congeries*, συναγωγὴ τῶν πεπραγμένων ἢ πραχθῆναι δυναμένων εἰς ἓν κεφάλαιον : Alexand. περὶ σχημάτων (Spengel, *Rhetores Graeci*, III. 17), where an illustrative extract is given from Demosth. *de Cor.* p. 248. Cp. Quintil. viii. 4, 27.

ἀλληγορία. ix. 7. The word is to be understood, like ὑπόνοια, of the inner meaning of a fable. Cp. Plut. *De audiendis poetis* p. 19 E, where it is stated that ἀλληγορία had supplanted ὑπόνοια in this sense. [ὑπόνοια occurs in π. ὕψ. xvii. 1, 2 with the meaning *secret feeling*.] The use here of ἀλληγορία has, as already noted (p. 190 supra), been wrongly thought to indicate late authorship. The passages of Cicero in which it is found are *Orat.* xxvii. 94 ;

ad Att. ii. 20, 3. F. A. Wolf (*Litterarische Analekten*, IV. 526) pointed out the error.

With the passage in *De Sublim.* ix. 7, cp. Heraclitus, *All. Hom.* I πάντως γὰρ ἠσέβησεν (sc. Ὅμηρος) εἰ μηδὲν ἠλληγόρησεν.

ἀμέλει. xii. 1, xliv. 1. *No doubt, surely, you know.* In two passages the meaning seems to approximate to 'for instance,' viii. 1 (ὡς καὶ τὸ πάθος ἀμέλει), xxxiv. 2 (ὥσπερ ἀμέλει τὰ μὲν περὶ τὴν Λητὼ ποιητικώτερα).

ἀναλαμβάνειν. xliv. 11. The meaning is 'to recover oneself.' Cp. Thucyd. vi. 26, ἄρτι δ᾽ ἀνειλήφει ἡ πόλις ἑαυτὴν ἀπὸ τῆς νόσου. Medical writers use the word absolutely, and so does Plato, *Rep.* v. 467 B.

ἀναφορά xx. 1. The *repetition* of a word, clause after clause. Lat. *repetitio* (Quintil. *Inst. Or.* ix. 3, 29). Ἐπαναφορά in the same sense, xx. 2.

ἀποστροφή. xvi. 2. The figure *apostrophe.* The term is applied by the author to Demosthenes' adjuration, μὰ τοὺς Μαραθῶνι προκινδυνεύσαντας. Cp. Quintil. ix. 2, 38; aversus quoque a iudice sermo, qui dicitur ἀποστροφή, mire movet, sive adversarios invadimus, sive ad invocationem aliquam convertimur, sive ad invidiosam implorationem.

ἀστεϊσμοί. xxxiv. 2. *ioci urbani.*

ἀσύνδετα, τά. xx. 1. *Asyndeta; broken sentences, sentences without copulatives.* Illustrated in xx. 1 from the *Meidias* of Demosthenes. The author has previously (vii. 4) supplied a good example of his own.

αὔξησις. xi. 1, 2, xii. 1. *Amplification.* Cp. Arist. *Rhet.* iii. 12, 4.

αὐτίκα. xxiii. 2. Sometimes interpreted here in the 'Attic' sense 'for example.' Such an imitation of Plato would be in keeping with the predilections of our author.

αὐτόθεν. xiii. 2, xiv. 3, xxxi. 1, xxxvi. 1. A favourite word of the author in the sense *at the time, at once.* Cp. Shilleto's note on Thucyd. i. 141, 1.

ἀφέλεια. xxxiv. 2. *Plain, simple style.* Of this style Lysias was accounted the chief exemplar.

βάθος. ii. 1, εἰ ἔστιν ὕψους τις ἢ βάθους τέχνη. These words seem capable of bearing either of two meanings: (1) 'whether there is such a thing as an art of the sublime or its opposite.' Cp. 'Martinus Scriblerus περὶ βάθους: or, Or of the Art of Sinking in

Poetry' (Elwin and Courthope's edition of Pope's *Works*, x. pp. 344—409), which skit may be regarded as a kind of parody of the Treatise on the Sublime. (2) 'whether there is an art of the lofty or profound,' the two words indicating the same thing from different points of view. Cp. Coleridge, *Table Talk*, p. 79 (H. Morley's edition): 'Think of the sublimity, I should rather say the profundity, of that passage in Ezekiel (xxxvii. 3), "Son of man, can these bones live? And I answered, O Lord God, thou knowest."'

γλαφυρός. x. 6, xxxiii. 5. *Elegant, polished.* Cp. Plut. *Mar. Vit.* iii. τὸν δὲ ἄλλον χρόνον ἐν κώμῃ Κιρραιάτωνι τῆς Ἀρπίνης δίαιταν εἶχε, πρὸς μὲν ἀστεῖον καὶ γλαφυρὸν βίον ἀγροικότερον, σώφρονα δὲ καὶ ταῖς πάλαι Ῥωμαίων τροφαῖς ἐοικυῖαν. Dionys. Hal. (*de Comp. Verb.* xxi.) distinguishes three styles, viz. (1) αὐστηρόν, (2) γλαφυρὸν ἢ ἀνθηρόν, (3) κοινόν.

γλωττόκομον. xliv. 5. *Case, cage.* The word is very rare in Attic Greek, and is only found in its literal meaning, viz. the 'tongue-case' of a clarinet. In Old Testament Greek it is used for 'ark'; in the New Testament (*Gospel of St John*, xii. 6, xiii. 29) it is applied to the 'bag,' or rather 'chest,' which Judas had. In still later Greek it meant a 'coffin'; in Modern Greek it is used of a 'purse.' Cp. Edwin Hatch, *Essays in Biblical Greek*, p. 42.—A comparatively early instance of its use in the sense of 'coffer' will be found in Grenfell's *Greek Papyri chiefly Ptolemaic*, p. 33.

γοῦν. xv. 4, xxxviii. 2, xliii. 1. This particle shades off into the meaning *to give an instance, for example.*—The author is also, it may here be noted, somewhat inclined to the epideictic collocation γε μήν (xxiii. 1, xxvii. 1), when introducing a fresh point in his exposition.

δεινότης. xii. 4. *Oratorical power or intensity.* A quality attributed to Demosthenes above all others. Cp. τὴν ἅπασιν ἀπρόσιτον δεινότητα καὶ δύναμιν (xxxiv. 4), δείνωσιν (xi. 2), ταῖς δεινώσεσι (xii. 5), δεδείωται (iii. 1).

δημώδης. xl. 2, κοινοῖς καὶ δημώδεσι τοῖς ὀνόμασι, *verbis vulgaribus et tritis.*—References to the use of this word in Plato will be found upon consulting the Index (p. 544) to Lutoslawski's *Origin and Growth of Plato's Logic.* A glance at Lutoslawski's Index generally will show how much the language of the περὶ ὕψους owes to that of the Platonic dialogues.

διαίρειν. ii. 2, vii. 1. τὰ διῃρμένα = τὰ ὑψηλά. So δίαρμα (κεῖται τὸ μὲν ὕψος ἐν διάρματι, xii. 1). So also διάρσις (ἡ ἐν ἀξιώματι καὶ διάρσει σύνθεσις, viii. 1). This sense of δίαρσις, and this passage, are not noticed in Liddell and Scott's *Greek-English Lexicon* (eighth edition). διάστημα (xl. 2) has the same meaning of *distinction, elevation, sublimity.*

διασυρμός. xxxiv. 2, xxxviii. 6. *Elevatio, irrisiv.* καί πως ὁ διασυρμὸς ταπεινότητός ἐστιν αὔξησις, xxxiv. 6. Cp. Coblentz, *De libelli περὶ ὕψους auctore*, pp. 21, 22.

διατύπωσις. xx. 1. *Vivid representation.* Classed as a rhetorical figure, together with Asyndeton and Anaphora. Cp. Coblentz, op. cit., pp. 19, 20.

δοξοκοπεῖν. xxiii. 2. *To crave popularity.* Cp. Plut. *Pericl. Vit.* v. 4, τοὺς δὲ τοῦ Περικλέους τὴν σεμνότητα δοξοκοπίαν τε καὶ τῦφον ἀποκαλοῦντας ὁ Ζήνων παρεκάλει καὶ αὐτούς τι τοιοῦτο δοξοκοπεῖν. Can the word convey any notion of 'striking the popular imagination,' 'hitting the fancy'?

εἶδος. xxvii. 1. *Species (of figure)*: cp. εἰδοποιίαι (xviii. 1). εἴδη (xiii. 4), *beautiful forms.* τὰ ἐπ᾽ εἴδους (xiii. 3), *the particulars* : cp. ἐπ᾽ εἴδους (xliii. 6). In a similar sense τὰ ἐπὶ μέρους, *the several details* (i. 2).

εἰδωλοποιεῖν. xv. 7. *To form an image, to represent by an image.* So εἰδωλοποιίαι (xv. 1), *images formed in the mind.* In xiv. 1 by ἀνειδωλοποιούμενα μέτρα are meant *standards conceived in the mind.* Cp. Hermogenes, *Progymn.* (Walz, *Rhetores Graeci*, 1. 45) εἰδωλοποιίαν δέ φασιν ἐκεῖνο, ὅταν τοῖς τεθνεῶσι λόγους περιάπτωμεν.

εἰκόνες. xxxvii. *Images, similes.* In the same fragmentary chapter cp. μεταφοραί = *metaphors*, and παραβολαὶ = *comparisons.*

ἔμπρακτος. xi. 2, xv. 8, xviii. 1. *Lively, effective, vehement.* Cp. ἀγών, p. 194 supra.

ἐμφερόμενα. x. 1 (e coniect. Toll.), xii. 2. The *constituent parts* of a thing. The use is noted in Stephanus (Hase—G. et L. Dindorf), but not in Liddell and Scott's *Lexicon.*

ἐνάργεια. xv. 2. *Clearness, vividness.* Cp. Dionys. Hal. *de Lysia*, vii. : ἔχει δὲ καὶ τὴν ἐνάργειαν πολλὴν ἡ Λυσίου λέξις· αὕτη δ᾽ ἐστὶ δύναμίς τις ὑπὸ τὰς αἰσθήσεις ἄγουσα τὰ λεγόμενα, γίνεται δ᾽ ἐκ τῆς τῶν παρακολουθούντων λήψεως. See also Quintil. *Inst. Or.* VIII. 3, 62. [The meaning of the passage from Dionysius is well given by one of the French translators : *Le style de Lysias est aussi très vivant ;*

cette qualité, c'est le talent de rendre sensible ce que l'on dit, et elle vient de l'emploi des détails accessoires.]

ἐνέργημα. xxxix. 3, ἐνεργήματα γνήσια, *genuine activities.* Cp. Polyb. iv. 8, 7.

ἔνθεν ἑλών. xxxiv. 4. This rhapsodical formula is echoed from Homer : cp. *Odyssey*, viii. 500, where the meaning is 'taking up the story at the point where.' Here the meaning seems to be quite general, 'drew as from a store'; if there is a particular reference in the ἔνθεν, it will be to Thucydides rather than to Hyperides. The passage in which the phrase occurs is a notoriously difficult one, and has led to many conjectural restorations.

ἐνσπαργανόω. xliv. 3. *To enwrap as in swaddling-clothes.* Cp. p. 13 supra.

ἐντάφιον. ix. 10. *Shroud, winding-sheet :* as in Simonides' epigram, ἐντάφιον δὲ τοιοῦτον οὔτ᾽ εὐρὼς | οὔθ᾽ ὁ πανδαμάτωρ ἀμαυρώσει χρόνος.

ἐπείγει. xliii. 6, οὐκ...ἐπείγει. Intransitive : *there is no hurry, no urgent need.* Cp. Plut. *Sert. Vit.* iii. 2, τὰ ἐπείγοντα, *pressing matters or business.* Examples of the use might be added from Arrian, Josephus, and Diodorus Siculus.

ἐπέχειν. ix. 10, xliv. 1. *To cover, overspread.* ix. 1, xliv. 12, μοῖραν ἐπέχειν, *to cover a large part, hold a foremost rank.* In Dionys. Hal. *Antiqq. Rom.* v. 67, προσθήκης μοῖραν ἐπέχειν means 'to act as auxiliaries,' 'to fill the rôle of supernumeraries.' The imperfect account which Liddell and Scott take of the language of the περὶ ὕψους is illustrated again in their article on this word.

ἐπιγέννημα. vi. καίτοι τὸ πρᾶγμα δύσληπτον· ἡ γὰρ τῶν λόγων κρίσις πολλῆς ἐστι πείρας τελευταῖον ἐπιγέννημα : or as Canna gives the sentence, *Ardua cosa veramente : perocchè il giudizio degli scritti è di molta esperienza l' ultimo frutto.* Perhaps here, as elsewhere in the περὶ ὕψους, we have an echo of Stoic phraseology. Examples of such coincidence are given by F. Striller in his *De Stoicorum studiis rhetoricis* ; and instances of similar agreement in tone and sentiment might be added from Epictetus and Marcus Aurelius in illustration of such chapters as xxxv. and xliv.

ἐπιδεικτικός. xii. 5. *Declamatory.* The ἐπιδεικτικὸν γένος is well known as one of the three Aristotelian divisions of rhetoric (Arist. *Rhet.* i. 3).

ἐπίλογος. xii. 5. *Peroration.* Cp. Arist. *Rhet.* iii. 13, 3, 4; iii. 19, 1.

ἐπιμονή. xii. 2. The word is defined in the *Rhetoric* of Alexander (Spengel, *Rhet. Gr.* iii. 17, 28) as follows : ἐπιμονὴ δέ ἐστιν, ὡς καὶ αὐτὸ τὸ ὄνομα δηλοῖ, ἐπὶ πλεῖον ἐπὶ τοῦ αὐτοῦ νοήματος ἐπιμονὴ μετὰ αὐξήσεως. Cp. M. Rothstein, *Hermes,* XXIII. 17.

ἐπιχείρησις. xv. 9. *Dialectical reasoning.* Cp. Dionys. Hal. *ad Amm. Ep.* 1. viii. The word came down to the rhetorical schools from Aristotle.

ἔρανος. xl. 2, καὶ σχεδὸν ἐν ταῖς περιόδοις ἔρανός ἐστι πλήθους τὰ μεγέθη. The sense is that given by Meinel, 'Darum kann man sagen, dass in den Perioden die Grösse ein Erträgnis der Vielheit ist'; or by Canna, 'Onde si può dire che nei periodi la nobilità viene da molte cose contribuita.' The verb ἐρανίζειν is found in xx. 1.

ἐρώτησις. xviii. 1, τὰς πεύσεις τε καὶ ἐρωτήσεις, *interrogations and questions.* The distinction intended by the writers on rhetoric apparently is that of a series of questions as contrasted with an isolated one. Cp. Quintil. *Inst. Or.* ix. 6—8, and Cic. *Orator,* xl. 137 (with Sandys' notes).

εὐπίνεια. xxx. 1. *A fine old style.* The metaphor is that of a statue mellowed—with all its harshnesses toned down—by age. Liddell and Scott compare *nitor obsoletus* (Auct. ad Herenn. iv. 34, 46).

ἐφηδύνειν. xv. 6, xxxiv. 2. A word used more than once by Plutarch in the sense *to impart a relish, to season.* The uncompounded verb occurs in one of the best known passages of the *Poetics,* vi. 2, ἡδυσμένῳ λόγῳ χωρὶς ἑκάστῳ τῶν εἰδῶν ἐν τοῖς μορίοις. In the περὶ ὕψους xxxiv. 2, λιτῶς ἐφηδυνόμενον may be translated *with a slight, unobtrusive relish,* the reference being to the ἀφέλεια which Hyperides could command at need. [λιτὸς is Aristotelian and post-Attic.] In xv. 6 the line of Euripides is regarded as less harsh or crude (ἐφηδύνας ἐξεφώνησεν) than that of Aeschylus. So Mr A. S. Way: 'The metaphor of Aeschylus which made hall and roof not only living things, but living things possessed, probably seemed too violent, too crude a personification of the inanimate. Euripides, on the other hand, does not give an independent personality to the mountain; the soul, the passion, is infused into it by the presence of possessed humanity, and passes from it with their passing.'

ἦθος. ix. 15. *Delineation of character: oratio morata, qua vitam communem imitamur.* Similarly, in the same chapter and section, ἠθικῶς βιολογούμενα and κωμῳδία ἠθολογουμένη. So also τὸ ἠθικόν in c. xxxiv. 2, and ἀνηθοποίητος in c. xxxiv. 3. Cp. Butcher, *Aristotle's Theory*[2] *etc.,* 327 ff.

In ἠθοποιία, or power of characterisation, Lysias was eminent among the Attic orators, as we are often reminded by Dionysius of Halicarnassus. In πάθος, on the other hand, Lysias was deficient. ἦθος, as contrasted with πάθος (cp. π. ὕψ., xxix. 2), was considered a special mark of comedy as distinguished from tragedy. Hence ἐν ἤθει [sc. τοῦτο ἔφη] = 'in character' or 'humorously' (Rutherford, *Schol. Aristophan.* ii. 442 : cp. Plut. *De audiendis poetis,* iv. 20). Cp. Quintil. *Inst. Or.* vi. 2, 8 sq. ; Cic. *Orator,* 37, 128. In the passage of Cicero the distinction between the two words is clearly marked : 'quorum alterum est, quod Graeci ἠθικὸν vocant, ad naturas et ad mores et ad omnem vitae consuetudinem accommodatum ; alterum, quod iidem παθητικὸν nominant, quo perturbantur animi et conci-tantur, in quo uno regnat oratio.'

ἥρως. iv. 4, xxxvi. 2. *A hero, or demi-god, of literature.* In the first passage Xenophon and Plato are thus described ; in the second, Homer, Plato and Demosthenes.

θεοφορεῖσθαι. xiii. 2, xv. 6. A rare word used twice by our author with the meaning *to be possessed.* The word is found in Philo.

ἰδιώτης. xxxi. 2, ταῦτα γὰρ ἐγγὺς παραξύει τὸν ἰδιώτην, ἀλλ᾽ οὐκ ἰδιωτεύει τῷ σημαντικῶς. It is perhaps best to supply λόγον with τὸν ἰδιώτην, but it is not absolutely necessary to do so, since by 'the plain man' may be understood the plain man's speech : cp. Dionys. Hal. *de Lys.* iii. p. 457. With ἰδιώτης and ἰδιωτεύειν, as used of ordinary or common speech, cp. ἰδιωτισμός (π. ὕψ., xxxi. 1) and ἰδιωτικός (xliii. 1). ἰδιώτης λόγος will be found conjoined in Dionys. Hal. *De admir. vi dicendi in Demosth.* c. ii.

καινόσπουδος. v., τὸ περὶ τὰς νοήσεις καινόσπουδον. *Die Jagd nach neuen Gedanken* (Meinel), *la sollecitudine di trovare concetti nuovi* (Canna). The word is ἅπαξ εἰρημένον. Vaucher (*Études,* pp. 152 and 410) suggests κενόσπουδον, an adjective found more than once in Plutarch. Cobet (*Mnemosyne, N. S.* x. p. 320), without Vaucher's bias in favour of a Plutarchic word, would also read κενόσπουδον. But the expressive and original καινόσπουδον seems to bear the stamp of its own genuineness upon it.

κακόζηλος. iii. 4, τὸ κακόζηλον, *affectation, preciosity.* The first writer, as far as we know, to use this term was Neanthes Cyzicenus (B.C. 240 circ.). It is somewhat remarkable that it does not occur in Dionysius of Halicarnassus. Quintilian, on the contrary, has it and defines it[1]. It is found, too, in other Latin writers of the first century A.D., and in Greek writers of the second and third. It sometimes approaches the meaning of *bad style* generally. Cp. Vaucher, *Études,* p. 87, Reuter, *De Quintiliani libro qui fuit de causis corruptae eloquentiae,* pp. 5 et seqq.—For ζῆλος, as applied to *style,* see *American Journal of Philology,* XVIII. p. 305.

κανονίζειν. xvi. 4. *To apply a rule, to measure.* Cp. Arist. *Eth. Nic.* ii. 3, 8 : κανονίζομεν δὲ καὶ τὰς πράξεις, οἱ μὲν μᾶλλον οἱ δ᾽ ἧττον, ἡδονῇ καὶ λύπῃ, i.e. we make pleasure and pain the standard of our actions.

κατακερματίζειν. xlii. 1. *To divide a narrative into small sections :* εἰς μικρὰς κατακερματιζομένη τομὰς ἡ διήγησις, Dionys. Hal. *de Thucyd.* ix. p. 828. The word properly means *to change into small coin,* and is one of the many expressions which our author copies from Plato. Cp. Pl. *Rep.* III. p. 395 B, φαίνεταί μοι εἰς σμικρότερα κατακεκερματίσθαι ἡ τοῦ ἀνθρώπου φύσις. Demetrius (*de Eloc.* c. iv. ; Spengel, *Rhetores Graeci,* III. 260) has : κατακεκομμένη γὰρ ἔοικεν ἡ σύνθεσις καὶ κεκερματισμένη, καὶ εὐκαταφρόνητος διὰ τὸ μικρὰ σύμπαντα ἔχειν.

κατακορής. xxii. 3, ἐν τῷ γένει τούτῳ κατακορέστατος, *most insatiable.* Again a favourite Platonic word : cp. παρρησίᾳ κατακορεῖ καὶ ἀναπεπταμένῃ, *Phaedr.* 240 E.—ὑπερκορής in the same sense in Herondas, *Mimiambi,* v. 1.

καταρχαιρεσιάζειν. xliv. 9, καὶ μὴ καταρχαιρεσιάζεσθαι πρὸς τῆς τοῦ πλεονεκτεῖν ἐπιθυμίας. *To corrupt in an election or other public action.* The word is used by Plutarch (*C. Gracch. Vit.* xi.) in the more natural sense of gaining an (unfair) electoral triumph over an opponent.

κατασκελετεύειν. ii. 1, ταῖς τεχνολογίαις κατασκελετευόμενα, *reduced to skeletons, robbed of flesh and blood, by technical precepts.* One of those bold metaphors which our author affects. The word is used in its literal sense by Plutarch.

---

[1] Quint. *Inst. Or.* viii. 3, 56. ' Κακόζηλον, id est mala adfectatio, per omne dicendi genus peccat : nam et tumida et pusilla et praedulcia et abundantia et arcessita et exultantia sub idem nomen cadunt.'

κατόρθωμα. xxxiii. 1. xxxiv. 1. xxxvi. 2 : cp. συνταγμάτων κατόρθωσις, c. v. The word is applied by the rhetorical writers (cp. Dionys. Hal. *de Thucyd.* xlviii. p. 932) to a style which hits the mark not by chance but by due observance of rule. The term is, in fact, borrowed from the realm of morals (cp. Arist. *Magna Mor.* ii. 3, 2), and transferred to literature in the same sense of a success following on right judgment.

κλῖμαξ. xxiii. 1. *Climax;* Lat. *gradatio.* A good illustration of climax (and of asyndeton) is Cicero's *abiit, excessit, evasit, erupit.* Cp. Quintil. *Inst. Or.* ix. 3, 55.

κλοπή. xiii. 4. *Literary theft, plagiarism.* The expression (ἐστὶ δ' οὐ κλοπὴ τὸ πρᾶγμα, xiii. 4) is used of the relation of Plato to Homer, the whole subject being handled in a singularly liberal and discriminating spirit : cp. the remarks in ch. xvi. as to the oath of Eupolis and that of Demosthenes.

κυριολογία. xxviii. 1. *Authorised language, normal diction;* the equivalent given in xxviii. 2 is ψιλὴ λέξις, *unadorned language.* Cp. Dionys. Hal. *de Lysia*, iii. κύρια καὶ κοινὰ καὶ ἐν μέσῳ κείμενα ὀνόματα. The contrast intended is that between an ordinary lucid style and one that is metaphorical and elaborate. The distinction derives from Aristotle: cp. *Poetics*, xxii. 8, διὰ γὰρ τὸ μὴ εἶναι ἐν τοῖς κυρίοις ποιεῖ τὸ μὴ ἰδιωτικὸν ἐν τῇ λέξει ἅπαντα τὰ τοιαῦτα.

κώδων. xxiii. 4, ἐπεί τοι τὸ πανταχοῦ κώδωνας ἐξῆφθαι λίαν σοφιστικόν, 'for to have bells suspended at every point is the height of affectation.' The reference is to excessive ornamentation of style ; the metaphor is that of the tinkling bells which formed part of the head-gear of a charger in a festal procession.

The expression seems to be as old as [Demosthenes] : καὶ ἃ τῶν ἄλλων τῶν ἠτυχηκότων ἕκαστος ἀψοφητὶ ποιεῖ, ταῦθ' οὗτος μόνον οὐ κώδωνας ἐξαψάμενος διαπράττεται (*c. Aristog.* A, 797. 12). For another coincidence with Demosthenes, cp. *De Subl.* ix. 3 with *Olynth.* iii. 32.

λῆμμα. x. 1, xi. 3, xv. 10, xl. 4, xliii. 1. In all these passages, although the meaning may sometimes perhaps be best expressed by the rendering 'details' or 'particulars,' the root idea seems to be that of the 'assumption' or 'idea' or 'matter' of a sentence as opposed to their expression in language. Cp. Dionys. Hal. *De admir. vi dicendi in Demosth.* xx. p. 1013, ἐν τούτοις οὐ μέμφομαι τὸν ἄνδρα τοῦ λήμματος· γενναία γὰρ ἡ διάνοια καὶ δυναμένη κινῆσαι πάθος· τὸ δὲ τῆς λέξεως λεῖον καὶ μαλακὸν αἰτιῶμαι.

λόγοι. ii. 3, iii. 1, v., vi., vii. 1, 3, 4, xv. 2, 9, xvii. 3, xxxiii. 1 (*bis*), xxxvi. 1, xliv. 1 (*bis*). In these passages λόγοι may be rendered by such equivalents as *diction, style, discourse, language, composition.* It is probably the nearest Greek equivalent for *literature,* though more especially applied to *prose writings* (cp. ἐν ποιήμασι καὶ λόγοις, vii. 1, xv. 2); sometimes the word oscillates in one and the same passage between the broader and the more restricted sense (cp. vii. 1, 3 and xxxiii. 1). In xliv. 1 λόγων ἀφορία denotes the dearth of high utterance, of 'eloquence' in the best sense. In iii. 1 λόγοι ἀληθινοί = *the narration of fact.*

μεγαλοφροσύνη. vii. 3, ix. 2, xiv. 1, xv. 12. *Greatness of soul, elevated conception.*

μεγεθοποιεῖν. xl. 1. *To invest with sublimity* (cp. ὑψοῦν). The converse expression is μικροποιεῖν, xli. 1.

μέλος. iii. 1, τὸ παρὰ μέλος οἰδεῖν, *tasteless tumidity.* Cp. εἰ πὰρ μέλος ἔρχομαι, Pind. *Nem.* vii. 101; παρὰ μέλος φθέγγεσθαι, Plat. *Phileb.* 28 B. The same metaphor occurs in πλημμελεῖν.

μέρος. xii. 5, καὶ οὐκ ὀλίγοις ἄλλοις μέρεσιν ἁρμόδιος. *Kinds of style, departments of literature.* Cp. Latin *genus.*

μεταβολή. v., xxiii. 1. *Variety of style:* cp. Dionys. Hal. *Ep. ad Cn. Pomp.* iii. p. 772, ὡς ἡδὺ χρῆμα ἐν ἱστορίαις γραφῆς μεταβολὴ καὶ ποικίλον. The same idea repeated in an altered form would constitute a μεταβολή. Cp. Quintil. *Inst. Or.* ix. 3, 38: 'hanc rerum coniunctam diversitatem Caecilius μεταβολὴν vocat.' In his *History of Greece* (III. 443, Engl. Trans.) Adolf Holm has an interesting note upon the μεταβολαί, or rapid emotional transitions, of Demosthenes.

μήποτε. iii. 4, xxxviii. 3, xl. 2, xliv. 10. *Perhaps.* The expression has a less abbreviated form in xxxiii. 2, μήποτε δὲ τοῦτο καὶ ἀναγκαῖον ᾖ, where the ellipse is obvious: cp. μὴ καὶ περιττὸν ᾖ (xxx. 1). This use of μήποτε in the sense of *nescio an* is found as early as Aristotle (*Eth. Nic.* x. 1, 3).

μυκτήρ. xxxiv. 2. *Irony.* Cp. Quintil. *Inst. Or.* viii. 6, 59: 'μυκτηρισμός, dissimulatus quidam, sed non latens derisus.'

νᾶνοι. xliv. 5. *Dwarfs.* The reference to these νᾶνοι, or Πυγμαῖοι, has sometimes been supposed to bear upon the question of the date of the treatise. In the same way, it may be remembered, the

presence of a *nain* (to use the French term) is often interpreted as an
indication of the date of the so-called Bayeux tapestry, but only
because the addition of the dwarf's name *Turold* may be taken to
imply some contemporary knowledge of the events and persons
portrayed. *Souvent, dans une discussion de ce genre, ce sont les
moindres détails qui fournissent les meilleures inductions*, as M. l'Abbé
J. Laffetay well remarks. But in our treatise, unfortunately, there
are few if any significant details to contribute to a solution of the
problem of authorship.—Much recondite information with regard to
the Pygmies, both in ancient and in modern times, will be found in
B. A. Windle's edition of Edward Tyson's ʻ Philological Essay concerning the Pygmies of the Ancients,ʼ one of the volumes included in
Nutt's *Bibliothèque de Carabas*.

νόησις. iii. 4, xxx. 1. *Thought, way of thinking.* Ἔννοια is not
uncommonly used by our author in a similar sense, as in ix. 2, ψιλὴ
καθ᾽ ἑαυτὴν ἡ ἔννοια, *the bare idea, the mere notion.* In xxvii. 3 νοῦς
(another word which may conveniently be grouped here) means the
sense of a sentence, in the phrase ἐν ἀτελεῖ τῷ νῷ.

ὄγκος. viii. 3, xv. 1, xxxix. 4. *Dignity.* So ὀγκηρός, *stately*, iii. 1.

πάθος. viii. 1, 2, 4, xii. 1, xxxix. 1. The word is not easily
rendered into English. *Pathos*, or *emotion*, will sometimes give it ;
but more often *passion*, in the sense of strong feeling, will be the
nearest equivalent. Cp. τὰ παθητικά in ii. 2, = ʻ the pathetic.ʼ

It has been said (Dowden, *History of French Literature*, p. 282)
of Vauvenargues that, in an age tending towards an exaggerated
homage to reason, he honoured the passions : ʻ Great thoughts come
from the heartʼ; ʻ We owe, perhaps, to the passions the greatest
gains of the intellectʼ; ʻ The passions have taught men reason.ʼ
A similar feeling may underlie the attitude of the περὶ ὕψους (cp.
viii. 4).

πάντη. i. 4, viii. 2, xii. 4, xv. 8, xvi. 4, xx. 3, xxii. 1, xxx. 2,
xxxiii. 5, xxxvi. 4. *On every side, in every way, altogether.* The
adverb is so evidently a favourite with our author that it may be well
to give a reference to all the passages in which it occurs. In the use
of this word also he is probably imitating Plato.

πάντως. i. 2, ii. 3, ix. 3, xii. 1, xvii. 1, xxii. 3. Another favourite
adverb, meaning *by all means, absolutely, inevitably, come what may.*

παράβασις. xii. 5, xv. 8. A rhetorical term for a *digression*. Cp.
ʻ egressioʼ and ʻ excessus ʼ in Latin (Quintil. *Inst. Or.* iii. 9, 4).

παράγγελμα. ii. 1, τεχνικὰ παραγγέλματα, *technical rules or precepts.* So ὡς εἰπεῖν ἐν παραγγέλματι (c. vi.) = 'if I must speak in the way of precept.'

παράστημα. ix. 1, ἐγκύμονας ἀεὶ......γενναίου παραστήματος, *gravidi sempre di generosi sensi* (Canna). The word may best be translated *inspiration* : cp. Dionys. Hal. *Antiqq. Rom.* viii. 39, θείῳ τινὶ παραστήματι κινηθεῖσα.

παρατράγῳδος. iii. 1. *Pseudo-tragic, bombastic.* The word is applied to burlesque by Plutarch as well as by our author. In vii. 1, προστραγῳδούμενον is found in a somewhat different sense, with which cp. Strab. *Geograph.* xvii. 1, 43.

παρένθυρσος. iii. 5. *Misplaced or exaggerated passion.* The term was used by Theodorus : τρίτον τι κακίας εἶδος ἐν τοῖς παθητικοῖς, ὅπερ ὁ Θεόδωρος παρένθυρσον ἐκάλει. ἔστι δὲ πάθος ἄκαιρον καὶ κενὸν ἔνθα μὴ δεῖ πάθους, ἢ ἄμετρον ἔνθα μετρίου δεῖ (iii. 5). It looks as if Theodorus had formed the word himself in order to suggest a *faux enthousiasme* (Vaucher) beyond that of the Bacchic devotee. Rothstein (*Hermes*, XXIII. 2) thinks that the form used by Theodorus was probably τὸ παρένθυρσον rather than ὁ παρένθυρσος.

περιέχων. xxxv. 3, ἀλλὰ καὶ τοὺς τοῦ περιέχοντος πολλάκις ὅρους ἐκβαίνουσιν αἱ ἐπίνοιαι. With ὁ περιέχων = *atmosphere,* ἀὴρ or αἰθὴρ is to be supplied : cp. ὁ περὶ χθόν' ἔχων φαεινὸς αἰθήρ Eurip. *Fragm.* 911. The meaning here (c. xxxv. 3) is *the physical horizon, the bounds of space* (Canna, *i limiti del mondo* ; Meinel, *die Grenzen der Umgebung*). Cp. Lucret. *de Rer. Nat.* i. 74 :—

> 'Ergo vivida vis animi pervicit, et extra
> Processit longe flammantia moenia mundi.'

The passage of the *De Sublimitate* has in it much of the loftiness of Sir Thomas Browne : 'Men that look upon my outside, perusing only my condition and fortunes, do err in my altitude, for I am above Atlas's shoulders......That mass of flesh that circumscribes me limits not my mind......There is surely a piece of divinity in us—something that was before the elements, and owes no homage unto the sun. He that understands not thus much hath not his introduction or first lesson, and is yet to begin the alphabet of man.'

περίοδος. The virtues of the *period* are described with some elaboration in c. xl. But for a short definition we must turn to Arist. *Rhet.* iii. 9, 3 : λέγω δὲ περίοδον λέξιν ἔχουσαν ἀρχὴν καὶ τελευτὴν αὐτὴν καθ᾽ αὐτὴν καὶ μέγεθος εὐσύνοπτον. Dionysius of Halicarnassus ⟨*de Comp. Verb.* c. ii.) briefly describes the formation of a period thus: ἡ τούτων (sc. τῶν κώλων) ἁρμονία τὰς καλουμένας συμπληροῖ περιόδους.

περίστασις. xxxviii. 3 (*bis*). *Danger, crisis.* A favourite Polybian word, e.g. εἰς πᾶν ἦλθον περιστάσεως (Polyb. iv. 45, 10).

περίφρασις. xxviii. 1. Quintilian (*Inst. Or.* viii. 6, 61) gives a definition, together with a Latin equivalent to which he takes exception : 'quidquid significari brevius potest, et cum ornatu latius ostenditur, περίφρασις est, cui nomen latine datum est non sane aptum orationis virtuti *circumlocutio*' : cp. viii. 6, 59. See Coblentz, op. cit. pp. 32—34.

πίπτειν. xxxvi. 1. *Occurs, is found:* cp. πίπτειν εἰς, *cadere in,* xliv. 4. Compare also the compound προσπίπτειν as used in xxi. 1, xxiii. 2, xxix. 1 (ἀβλεμὲς προσπίπτει=*falls flat*), xxxix. 4.

πολιτικός. i. 2, ix. 13, xxxiv. 2, xliv. 1. *Political, public;* especially used of *public speech* (*oratio civilis*). Meinel and Canna see a reference to oratory even in i. 2 and xliv. 1. ('Etwas Brauchbares für den Redner,' M. ; 'alcuna cosa utile agli oratori,' C. : i. 2. 'Eine Sache öffentlich zu vertreten,' M. ; 'periti nelle cause forensi,' C. : xliv. 1.) A good account of the word is given by Coblentz, *De libelli* περὶ ὕψους *auctore,* pp. 46—50. Cp. also p. 3 of C. Hammer's *Bericht über die auf die griechischen Rhetoren und späteren Sophisten bezüglichen von Anfang* 1890 *bis Ende* 1893 *erschienenen Schriften,* in which he reviews C. Brandstaetter's *De notionum* πολιτικὸς *et* σοφιστὴς *usu rhetorico.*

πολύπτωτος. xxiii. 1. πολύπτωτα, rhetorical figures in which many cases (πτώσεις) are employed. Cp. Quintil. *Inst. Or.* ix. 3, 37, where an illustration is offered from the *Pro Cluentio,* lx. 167.

πολύφωνος. xxxiv. 1. *With many tones.* Contrast μονοτόνως in the next section of c. xxxiv.—In xxviii. 1 οἱ παράφωνοι is used as a noun, in some such sense as 'accompaniments.'

πραγματικός. xv. 9, 10, 11. Used with reference to the *matter* or *argument* of a speech, as distinguished from the mere expression. Cp. Baudat, *Étude sur Denys d'Halicarnasse,* p 28 n. 2.

προηγουμένως. xl. 12. Either *previously* or *expressly;* both senses are appropriate here, and both can be paralleled from Plutarch.

προσπίπτειν. xxi. 1, xxiii. 2, xxix. 1, xxxix. 4, xiv. 1 (conjecturally). *To fall on the ear, to strike one.* A favourite word of the author.

ῥήτωρ. ix. 3, xi. 2, xxxii. 8. *Orator.* In xii. 3 ὁ ῥήτωρ (*par excellence*) = Demosthenes. In xxx. 1 we have the collocation πᾶσι τοῖς ῥήτορσι καὶ συγγραφεῦσι, 'all orators and writers.'

ῥωπικός. iii. 4, ἐποκέλλοντες εἰς τὸ ῥωπικὸν καὶ κακόζηλον. *Trumpery ornamentation.* An adjective used by Polybius and Plutarch as well as by our author.

σοφιστής. iv. 2. The reference is to Isocrates; *rhetorician* would here seem a nearer English equivalent than *sophist.*—In xxiii. 4 the adjective σοφιστικός denotes *affectation, idle ostentation.*

στόμφος. iii. 1, xxxii. 7. *Mouthing; high-sounding words; bombast.* Cp. Latin *ampullae.*

συγγραμμάτιον. i. 1. *Treatise* had best be retained as being the usual English rendering. But such equivalents as *tractate, tract, pamphlet, memoir, essay, dissertation, disquisition,* have something to be said for them, in so far as they may imply less extent and less system than does the word *treatise.* Canna's *trattatello* seems to be near the mark. See also under the word ὑπόμνημα infra.

συγγραφεύς. i. 3, ix. 15, xiii. 2, xl. 2. In these passages the word denotes a *prose-writer* as distinguished from a *poet.* In xxx. 1 the contrast is between it and ῥήτωρ. In xxii. 1 and xxxiii. 1 the word is used, quite generally, for *writer.* It does not seem, in the περὶ ὕψους, to be used in the limited sense of *historian.*

συγκατάθεσις. vii. 4. *Assent:* cp. the Stoic use and Cicero's translation of the word in the Academics (*Ac. Pr.* ii. 12, 37). In xxxii. 1 συγκατατίθεσθαι = 'to assent,' the author probably having in mind Plat. *Gorg.* 501 C, σὺ δὲ δὴ πότερον συγκατατίθεσαι ἡμῖν περὶ τούτων τὴν αὐτὴν δόξαν, ἢ ἀντίφης;

συγκοπή. xlii. *Concision,* or *truncation,* of expression. The word is contrasted with συντομία, which signifies a proper brevity or compression.—It is worth remark that the use of ἄγαν with a substantive (ἡ ἄγαν συγκοπή in this chapter, and τοῖς ἄγαν πλούτοις in c. xxxiii. 2) is a reminiscence of Platonic usage (cp. ἡ ἄγαν ἐλευθερία, Pl. *Rep.* viii. 564 A).

συμμορία. xx. 1. *Partnership.* In this metaphorical use of the word, the author agrees with Josephus who has δειπνοῦντες κατὰ συμμορίας (*Antiqq. Iud.* v. 7, 3).

σύνολον. xii. 5, xvii. 1, xliv. 10 τὸ σύνολον = *entirely, altogether.* So perhaps τὸ ὅλον in the corrupt passage at the end of c. x. Similarly τέλεον in c. xli. ad init.

σύστασις. viii. 1. The word plays an important part in the *Poetics.* 'The recurring phrase of the *Poetics,* σύστασις (or σύνθεσις) τῶν πραγμάτων, does not denote a mechanical piecing together of incidents, but a vital union of the parts,' S. H. Butcher, *Aristotle's Theory of Poetry and Fine Art*[2], p. 278.—σύνθεσις occurs in viii. 1, xxxiv. 2, etc.; ἐπισύνθεσις in x. 1. These terms naturally vary in dignity with the objects which they are supposed to 'combine' or 'compose.'

σχολαστικός. iii. 4. *Trivial, pedantic.* Vaucher (*Études Critiques,* pp. 87, 88) regards this use as indicating a comparatively early date for the treatise.

σχολικός. iii. 5, x. 7. *Tedious;* like the discussions of the schools. *Bookish, pedantic, affected.*

τεχνολογία. i. 1, ii. 1. *Systematic treatment* of a subject, especially of the subject of rhetoric. The word is used by Cicero, *ad Att.* iv. 16 : 'reliqui libri τεχνολογίαν habent, ut scis.' In c. xii. 1 οἱ τεχνογράφοι are *writers on rhetoric.*

τοπηγορία. xi. 2, xii. 5, xxxii. 5. *Treatment of* τόποι *or commonplaces.*

τρόποι. xii. 1, xxxii. 5. *Turns of language, tropes, figures.* Cicero (*Brut.* xvii. 6) gives *verborum immutationes* as a Latin rendering. Cp. ἡ τροπική (viii. 1), τῶν τροπικῶν (xxxii. 2), αἱ τροπικαί (xxxii. 6).

τύπος. xiii. 1, ἀνεγνωκὼς τὰ ἐν τῇ Πολιτείᾳ τὸν τύπον οὐκ ἀγνοεῖς. The meaning is perhaps rather 'his manner' than 'this typical passage.' τύπος also occurs in xii. 2 in the phrase ὡς τύπῳ περιλαβεῖν, 'to sum up the matter in a general way,' with which cp. Pl. *Rep.* iii. 414 A, ὡς ἐν τύπῳ, μὴ δι' ἀκριβείας, εἰρῆσθαι.

ὑπόμνημα. xxxvi. 4, xliv. 12. *Memoir, tract.* Similarly ὑπομνηματισμός in the title of Dionysius' work περὶ τῶν ἀρχαίων ῥητόρων ὑπομνηματισμοί. Similarly also the verb ὑπομνηματίζεσθαι in the *De Subl.* i. 2. Cp. F. Blass, *De Dionysii Halicarnassensis Scriptis Rhetoricis,* p. 7 : 'ὑπομνηματισμοί opponuntur scholicis praelectionibus, quae longius explicant brevius illic praeposita τοῦ ὑπομνῆσαι gratia : cf. Dionys. Hal. *de Dem.* 46, μήποτε ἡ σύνταξις εἰς τοὺς σχολικοὺς ἐκβῇ χαρακτῆρας ἐκ τῶν ὑπομνηματισμῶν.' The passage in

xxxvi. 4 is interesting as showing that the author describes his own book as a ὑπόμνημα, or *commentarius*.

ὑποφέρειν. xvi. 4. In the Translation τὸν ἀκροατήν is regarded as object after ὑποφέρει. But the words may be governed by φθάνων, and ὑποφέρειν may be taken as = 'to add by way of reply,' for which sense cp. Plut., *De audiendis poetis*, p. 73: οὐ χεῖρόν ἐστιν ὑπενεγκεῖν τό·
εἰ θεοί τι δρῶσι φαῦλον, οὐκ εἰσὶν θεοί.

ὕψος. This important word, the key-word of the whole treatise, requires a note of some length.

It is difficult to trace the history of ὕψος as a stylistic term. But it was in use among the Atticist writers of the first century B.C. Caecilius had written (being possibly the first to do so) a treatise with the word as a subject and probably as a title (τὸ μὲν τοῦ Κεκιλίου συγγραμμάτιον ὃ περὶ ὕψους συνετάξατο, *De Sublim.*, i. 1). The corresponding adjective is used by Dionysius Hal. in a context which makes its meaning perfectly clear: ὑψηλὴ δὲ καὶ μεγαλοπρεπὴς οὐκ ἔστιν ἡ Λυσίου λέξις, *De Lys. Iud.* xiii.[1] With the employment here of the alternative adjective μεγαλοπρεπὴς may be compared the fact that the so-called 'Demetrius περὶ ἑρμηνείας' (a work sometimes assigned to the first century A.D.) distinguishes the four following styles: χαρακτὴρ ἰσχνός, μεγαλοπρεπής, γλαφυρός, δεινός. The word ὕψος does not, it may be added, occur in the *Rhetoric* of the historical Longinus.

The author of the περὶ ὕψους rather describes than defines the quality about which he discourses. But some words in his first chapter (i. 3) make the meaning clear: ἀκρότης καὶ ἐξοχή τις λόγων ἐστὶ τὰ ὕψη[2]. It has been well said that anything which raises composition above the usual level, or infuses into it uncommon strength, beauty, or vivacity, comes fairly within the scope of his design[3]. The

---

[1] Cp. *Ep. ad Cn. Pompeium* ii. 9: παράδειγμα δὲ ποιοῦμαι τῆς γε ὑψηλῆς λέξεως ἐξ ἑνὸς βιβλίου τῶν πάνυ περιβοήτων. The reference is to Plato, and the γε (if this is the right reading, the manuscript variants being considerable) is ironical.

[2] See also xii. 1.

[3] Cp. Lowth, *De Sacra Poesi Hebraeorum*, p. 167: 'sublimitatem autem hic intelligo sensu latissimam sumptam : non eam modo quae res grandes magnifico imaginum et verborum apparatu effert ; sed illam, quaecumque sit, orationis vim, quae mentem ferit et percellit, quae movet affectus, quae rerum imagines clare et eminenter exprimit ; nihil pensi habens, simplici an ornata, exquisita an vulgari dictione utatur : in quo Longinum sequor, gravissimum in hoc argumento et intelligendi et dicendi auctorem.'

use of the corresponding verb (ὑψόω, ' to heighten ') should be noted
in this connexion : πῶς δ᾽ ἂν Πλάτων ἢ Δημοσθένης ὕψωσαν ἢ ἐν
ἱστορίᾳ Θουκυδίδης (xiv. 1). *Elevation, dignity, grandeur, eloquence*,
and other words of the kind will at various times best convey our
author's meaning.

Other expressions of a similar but not always an identical signification are used by him : τὰ ὑπερφυᾶ, τὰ μεγάλα, τὰ μεγέθη, τὸ
μεγαλοφυές, ἡ ὑψηγορία, τὸ θαυμάσιον, τὸ ὑπερτεταμένον. The plural
number is often used where specific instances or individual manifestations of the quality are meant (cp. i. 3, 4; xvii. 3; ix. 1, 4, 10).

The Latin words usually employed to translate περὶ ὕψους have
been such as *de grandi sive sublimi orationis genere, de sublimi genere
dicendi, de sublimitate*, etc.; and for this use of *sublimis* and *sublimitas*
there is warrant enough in Quintilian, who frequently thus uses the
words. *Elevatio* is, of course, out of court, being a term of deprecia-
tion similar to διασυρμός in Greek[1].

In the Romance languages the Latin title is naturally followed :
French, *du Sublime*; Italian, *del Sublime* or *della Sublimità*; Spanish,
de la Sublimidad. In the Teutonic tongues vernacular equivalents
are given : e.g. German, *Ueber das Erhabene* (which is also the title
of a short treatise by Schiller) ; and Dutch, *Over de Verheventheit en
Deftigheit des Styls*. In a recent Swedish translation the title *Om
det Sublima* is adopted.

In English a native rendering was originally attempted : *Of the
Height of Eloquence* (John Hall's Translation, 1662) ; *Of the Loftiness
or Elegancy of Speech* (John Pulteney's Translation, 1680). It is
a matter for some regret that these English titles, in some slightly
modified form, have not held their ground. They have given place,
under the influence of the Latin translators and of Boileau, to what
Dr Johnson called a *Gallicism* ; and misconception has been the
result, a misconception which the existence of Burke's homonymous
treatise *On the Sublime and Beautiful* has done much to increase.

φαντασία. xv. 1. *Image.* The word is treated fully by Coblentz,
De libello περὶ ὕψους *auctore*, pp. 42—46, with especial reference to
points in which the treatise is in harmony with Stoic doctrine. For
visiones as a Latin equivalent and for a definition, see Quintil., *Inst.
Or.*, vi. 2, 29.—With the wording of the definition in xv. 1, we may

---

[1] *Gravis*, as well as *sublimis*, might convey the general sense of ὑψηλός. Cp.
also such expressions as *magnifica et caelestia composuit* (Plin. *Ep.* ix. 26).

compare Aristot. *Poetics* xix. 1, ἔστι δὲ κατὰ τὴν διάνοιαν ταῦτα, ὅσα ὑπὸ τοῦ λόγου δεῖ παρασκευασθῆναι.

φλοιώδης. iii. 2, x. 7. *Empty, frivolous.* This word is common to Plutarch and the περὶ ὕψους.

χρηστομαθεῖν. ii. 3. *To desire to learn:* cp. the noun χρηστομάθεια in xliv. 1. This is the traditional interpretation, but it may be doubted whether the meaning is not rather *bonis (artibus s. litteris) studere.*

APPENDIX C.

LITERARY. WITH A LIST OF AUTHORS AND QUOTATIONS.

It will be convenient to open this Appendix with a concise summary, chapter by chapter, of the treatise. Only the briefest possible headings will be given, and (wherever possible) Greek words furnished by the author himself will be used as well as English.

Headings of Chapters.

i. Κεκιλίου περὶ ὕψους. The treatise of Caecilius and its short-comings.

ii. ὕψους τέχνη. Is there an art of the sublime? Can the sublime be taught?

iii. τὸ οἰδοῦν.—τὸ μειρακιῶδες.—ὁ παρένθυρσος.—Defects that are opposed to sublimity.

iv. τὸ ψυχρόν.—Frigidity.

v. τὸ περὶ τὰς νοήσεις καινόσπουδον. This the real cause and origin of the above defects.

vi. ἡ γὰρ τῶν λόγων κρίσις πολλῆς ἐστι πείρας τελευταῖον ἐπιγέννημα. Literary criticism is the late-born child of long experience.

vii. τὸ ἀληθὲς ὕψος. The true sublime.

viii. πέντε πηγαί τινες αἱ τῆς ὑψηγορίας. Five sources of sublimity.

ix. ἡ μεγαλοφροσύνη. Nobility of soul.

x. ἡ τῶν ἐμφερομένων σύνθεσις. Grouping of details.

xi. περὶ αὐξήσεως. Concerning amplification.

xii. ὁ τῆς αὐξήσεως ὅρος. Definition of amplification.

xiii. ὅτι ὁ Πλάτων μεγεθύνεται, καὶ περὶ τῆς μιμήσεως. Plato as an exemplar of the sublime: and concerning imitation.

xiv. τοιοῦτον ὑποτίθεσθαι τῶν ἰδίων λόγων δικαστήριον καὶ θέατρον. Some practical injunctions : aim high, match yourself with the great, imagine that you are appearing before a tribunal of the finest writers of the past, take heed that you do not act an unseemly part before the bar of the future.

xv. περὶ φαντασίας. Concerning imagery or imagination.

xvi. περὶ σχημάτων.—τὸ ὁμοτικὸν σχῆμα. Concerning figures.— The oath-figure, or figure of adjuration.

xvii. ὅτι φύσει πως συμμαχεῖ τε τῷ ὕψει τὰ σχήματα καὶ πάλιν ἀντισυμμαχεῖται θαυμαστῶς ὑπ' αὐτοῦ. Figures and the sublime are leagued together in mutual alliance.

xviii. περὶ πεύσεως καὶ ἀποκρίσεως. Concerning rhetorical question and answer.

xix. περὶ ἀσυνδέτων. Concerning asyndeton or the absence of conjunctions.

xx. ἡ τῶν σχημάτων σύνοδος. Accumulation of figures.

xxi. πρόσθες τοὺς συνδέσμους. The effect of adding conjunctions.

xxii. περὶ ὑπερβατῶν. Concerning hyperbata or inversions.

xxiii. αἱ τῶν ἀριθμῶν ἐναλλάξεις. Interchange of singular and plural number.

xxiv. τὰ ἐκ τῶν πληθυντικῶν εἰς τὰ ἑνικὰ ἐπισυναγόμενα ἐνίοτε ὑψηλοφανέστατα. The conversion of plurals into singulars sometimes conduces in a marked degree to elevation.

xxv. αἱ τῶν χρόνων ἐναλλάξεις. Interchange of tenses.

xxvi. περὶ τῆς τῶν προσώπων ἀντιμεταθέσεως. Concerning the variation of persons.

xxvii. περὶ τῆς εἰς τὸ αὐτοπρόσωπον ἀντιμεταστάσεως. Concerning sudden transition to the first person.

xxviii. περὶ περιφράσεως. Concerning periphrasis.

xxix. ἐπίκηρον μέντοι τὸ πρᾶγμα, ἡ περίφρασις. Perils of periphrasis.

xxx. περὶ τῆς τῶν ὀνομάτων ἐκλογῆς. Concerning the choice of words.

xxxi. περὶ ἰδιωτισμοῦ. Concerning familiar language.

xxxii. περὶ μεταφορῶν. Concerning metaphors.

xxxiii. σύγκρισις ἀρετῶν. Comparison of excellences. Superiority of sublimity with some defects to an uninspired correctness—to a flawless mediocrity.

xxxiv. Δημοσθένους καὶ Ὑπερίδου σύγκρισις. Comparison of Demosthenes and Hyperides.

xxxv. περὶ Πλάτωνος καὶ Λυσίου. Concerning Plato and Lysias.

xxxvi. περὶ τῶν ἐν λόγοις μεγαλοφυῶν. Concerning sublimity in literature: the fame it brings. [Chapters xxxiii.—xxxvi. are in the nature of a digression.]

xxxvii. περὶ παραβολῶν καὶ εἰκόνων. Concerning comparisons and similes.

xxxviii. περὶ ὑπερβολῶν. Concerning hyperboles.

xxxix. περὶ συνθέσεως. Concerning composition or the arrangement of words.

xl. περὶ τῆς τῶν μελῶν ἐπισυνθέσεως. Concerning the collocation of members.

xli. τὰ μικροποιά. Things that lower the tone of style.

xlii. περὶ φράσεως συγκοπῆς. Concerning concision of expression.

xliii. περὶ μικρότητος ὀνομάτων καὶ αὐξήσεως. Concerning trivial expressions and amplification.

xliv. περὶ λόγων ἀφορίας. Concerning the decay of eloquence.

A tabular analysis will make still clearer the connexion of chapters viii.—xl. The remaining chapters may be omitted from this analysis since cc. i.—vii. are introductory and c. xliv. is an epilogue, while cc. xli.—xliii. deal (as do cc. iii.—v. from another point of view) with vices of style opposed to sublimity, viz. 1. ῥυθμὸς κεκλασμένος: broken and undignified rhythms; 2. ἡ ἄγαν τῆς φράσεως συγκοπή: excessive conciseness; 3. μικρότης ὀνομάτων: trivial expressions.

TABULAR ANALYSIS OF CC. VIII.—XL.

Chapter viii. names the five following πηγαὶ τῆς ὑψηγορίας or

SOURCES OF THE SUBLIME.

I. τὸ περὶ τὰς νοήσεις ἁδρεπήβολον. **Grandeur of conception.**
Details of treatment :—

(1) Grandeur of thought springs from nobility of soul.
Examples from Homer and from *Genesis* (c. ix.).

(2) Choice and grouping of the most striking circumstances.
Ode of Sappho (c. x.).

(3) Amplification (cc. xi. xii.).

(4) Imitation of great models (cc. xiii. xiv.).

(5) Imagery (c. xv.).

II. τὸ σφοδρὸν καὶ ἐνθουσιαστικὸν πάθος. **Vehement and inspired passion.** [This topic is reserved for a separate work.]

III. ἡ τῶν σχημάτων πλάσις. **The due employment of
figures.**

(1) Figure of adjuration (c. xvi.). The close alliance between
figures and sublimity (c. xvii.).

(2) Rhetorical question (c. xviii.).

(3) Asyndeton (cc. xix.—xxi.).

(4) Hyperbaton (c. xxii.).

(5) Changes of number, person, tense, etc. (cc. xxiii.—xxvii.).

(6) Periphrasis (cc. xxviii. xxix.).

IV. ἡ γενναία φράσις. **Nobility of expression.**

(1) Choice of proper and striking words (c. xxx.).

(2) The use of familiar words (c. xxxi.).

(3) Metaphors (c. xxxii.).

(4) Comparisons and Similes (c. xxxvii.; cc. xxxiii.—xxxvi. being a digression).

(5) Hyperbole (c. xxxviii.).

V. ἡ ἐν ἀξιώματι καὶ διάρσει σύνθεσις. Dignified and elevated composition.

(1) Arrangement of words (c. xxxix.).

(2) Collocation of members (c. xl.).

[*Note*. III. IV. and V. may be regarded as the more technical, I. and II. as the more natural, sources of the sublime : viii. 1.]

As for the *lacunae* in the treatise, their number and extent and the chapters in which they occur have already been indicated in the Textual Appendix (p. 167). A conjectural attempt to supply them was made, early in the present century, in an ingenious English Essay (see Bibliographical Appendix, p. 254 infra). Reference may also be made to Rothstein's articles in *Hermes* XXII. and XXIIII.; to Canna, *Della Sublimità*, pp. 77, 90, 103, 112, 118, 165; to Meinel, *Dionysios oder Longinos Ueber das Erhabene*, pp. 57, 58 ; and to Martens, *De libello* περὶ ὕψους, p. 16. Schück's *Commentarii* περὶ ὕψους *argumentum* (Breslau, 1855) will also be found useful. Like the *Ars Poetica* of Horace, the περὶ ὕψους has often been arraigned because of want of system, but for this apparent looseness of structure (which it is easy to exaggerate) the gaps in the treatise are partly responsible. And in the case neither of the *Ars Poetica* nor of the περὶ ὕψους is it right to take absolutely for granted that the title comes from the author himself. It should be added that in one of the *lacunae* (ix. 4) the general sense of the missing words may be supplied from Arrian *Anab.* ii. 25, 2 :

Παρμενίωνα μὲν λέγουσιν Ἀλεξάνδρῳ εἰπεῖν ὅτι αὐτὸς ἂν Ἀλέξανδρος ὢν ἐπὶ τούτοις ἠγάπησε καταλύσας τὸν πόλεμον μηκέτι πρόσω κινδυνεύειν, Ἀλέξανδρον δὲ Παρμενίωνι ἀποκρίνασθαι ὅτι καὶ αὐτὸς ἂν εἴπερ Παρμενίων ἦν οὕτως ἔπραξεν.

After this analysis of the general contents of the *De Sublimitate* it will be well to present, also in a tabular form, a complete list of the authors who are mentioned in it.

Chronological Table of Authors mentioned in the De Sublimitate.

Anterior to 700 B.C.	Homer. Hesiod. [Moses.]
700—600 B.C.	Archilochus. Stesichorus. Sappho.
600—500 B.C.	[Aristeas.] Anacreon. Hecataeus.
500—400 B.C.	Pindar. Simonides. Bacchylides. Herodotus. Thucydides. Gorgias. Aeschylus. Sophocles. Euripides. Ion of Chios. Eupolis. Aristophanes.
400—300 B.C.	Xenophon. Plato. Aristotle. Theophrastus. Lysias. Isocrates. Demosthenes. Hyperides. Philistus. Theopompus. Timaeus. Zoilus.
300—200 B.C.	Callisthenes. Cleitarchus. Eratosthenes. Hegesias. Aratus. Theocritus. Apollonius Rhodius.
200—100 B.C.	Ammonius. Matris.
100 B.C.—1 A.D.	Amphicrates. Cicero. Caecilius. Theodorus.

Such a table shows better than words could do the wide range of our author's interests, and his zeal and industry. From the earliest times to the beginning of our era—hardly beyond that—no century is unrepresented in his fragmentary work, and few authors of the first rank are absent. Poetry and prose, and almost all departments of prose and poetry, have come within his observation. He preserves passages (including an ode of Sappho) nowhere else preserved, and he reminds us of plays by Euripides or Eupolis, of poems by Archilochus or Simonides or Bacchylides, of speeches by Hyperides, which have either been lost entirely or have only recently been recovered. He reminds us, too, that many authors of the Greek world are entirely unknown to us except for a casual mention here and there.

Thus much as to the authors. As to the quotations themselves, they are (where we can test them) not exact but free; often they appear to be made from memory. Examples of such laxity will be found in cc. xiii. 1, xv. 9, xviii. 1, xxvi. 2, xxxi. 2. Sometimes part of a line will be omitted, as in xxvi. 1 and xxvii. 4 (as given by P) ; in the latter passage the quotation also stops suddenly short. More than once (as in ix. 6 and 8) lines drawn from different parts of a poem are fused together[1].

With these preliminary remarks, the authors (and the quotations from them) may now be given in alphabetical order together with some brief particulars as to the more obscure writers, and with references to the pertinent chapters and sections of the *De Sublimitate*.

Authors and Quotations.

Aeschylus b. 525, d. 456 B.C.

From Aeschylus are quoted examples (taken from the *Septem c. Thebas* 42—46 and the *Lycurgia*) of imaginative daring (xv. 5, 6), and of bombast or the pseudo-tragic (iii. 1). The lines in iii. 1 and the single line in iii. 2 are probably from the *Orithyia*, for which see Meinel's *Dionysios oder Longinos etc.* p. 46 ; see also *Rhein. Mus.* XXXIX. (F. Buecheler) and XLVIII. (O. Immisch), *Hermes* X. 334 (Wilamowitz) and Cic. *ad Att.* ii. 16, 2 (with Tyrrell's notes). On the whole it would seem most likely that both Aeschylus and Sophocles had written an *Orithyia*, and that the five lines are by Aeschylus, and the single line by Sophocles, to whom in fact it is here expressly assigned.

Ammonius flor. 140 B.C. Pupil and successor of Aristarchus at Alexandria. Pauly-Wissowa, *Real-Encycl.*, I. p. 1865 ; Susemihl, *Gesch. d. griech. Litt. in der Alexandrinerzeit*, II. pp. 153—5.

See c. xiii. 3 and pp. 8, 9 supra.—It is stated (*Athenæum*, Nov. 12, 1898) that some scholia, by Ammonius, on *Iliad* xxi. have been discovered by Grenfell and Hunt among the Oxyrhynchus Papyri.

Amphicrates flor. 90 B.C. Athenian rhetorician. Pauly-Wissowa I. 1903 ; Susemihl II. 372 ; Blass, *Griechische Beredsamkeit*, 67. Condemned for his bombast, iii. 2, iv. 4. See further under *Hegesias* p. 226 infra.

Anacreon flor. 540 B.C.

Quoted to exemplify homely but forcible expression (xxxi. 1).

---

[1] It has seemed convenient to indicate citations (from prose authors) by means of quotation-marks in the Greek text as well as in the English translation. It is for convenience also that the references for all quotations have been entered beneath the translation only.

The words cited will be found in Bergk, *Poetae Lyrici Graeci*[4], III. 280, οὐκέτι Θρηϊκίης (πώλου) ἐπιστρέφομαι, where the word πώλου is added by Bergk, who in his first edition suggested παιδός. The meaning is, of course, the same in either case; but the passage in the περὶ ὕψους suggests that the less refined word is right.

Apollonius 'of Rhodes': flor. 240 B.C.: the chief epic poet of Alexandria. Pauly-Wissowa II. 126; Susemihl I. 383.

Nothing is quoted from Apollonius in the περὶ ὕψους, but in c. xxxiii. 4 reference is made to the *Argonautica* as a model of 'correctness': ἐπείτοιγε καὶ ἄπτωτος ὁ Ἀπολλώνιος ἐν τοῖς Ἀργοναύταις ποιητής.

Aratus flor. 270 B.C.: the chief didactic poet of Alexandria. Pauly-Wissowa II. 391; Susemihl I. 284.

Quoted in illustration of ἡ τῶν προσώπων ἀντιμετάθεσις (xxvi. 1). In his description of the perils of a storm he is contrasted with Homer (x. 6). Both these passages are taken from the *Phaenomena* (vv. 287 and 299). It will be remembered that the words τοῦ γὰρ καὶ γένος ἐσμέν are quoted (*Acts* xvii. 28) from the *Phaenomena* of Aratus by St Paul, who was like him a Cilician; and that the poem was translated into Latin by Cicero in his early youth (cp. *De Nat. Deor.* ii. 41).

The best text of the *Phaenomena* is that of E. Maass (Berlin, 1893); the best English translation, that of E. Poste (London, 1880).

Archilochus flor. 650 B.C. Iambic poet, of Paros.

Imitation of Homer (xiii. 3). Rich and disorderly profusion (xxxiii. 5). Graphic description of a shipwreck (x. 7), for which see Bergk *Poetae Lyrici Graeci*[4] II. 386 and Wilamowitz *Hermes* X. 344.

Aristeas. Aristeas of Proconnesus: flor. 580 B.C. Wrote a poem on the Arimaspians (Herod. iv. 13—15, and Pausanias i. 24, 6 : cp. Frazer's *Pausanias* II. 319, and Pauly-Wissowa II. 877). Suidas : Ἀριστέας Δημοχάριδος ἢ Καυστροβίου, Προκοννήσιος, ἐποποιός, τὰ Ἀριμάσπεια καλούμενα ἔπη· ἔστι δὲ ἱστορία τῶν Ὑπερβορέων Ἀριμασπῶν, βιβλία γ'. Dionysius Hal. *de Thucyd. Iud.* 23 : οὔθ' αἱ διασῳζόμεναι (γραφαὶ) παρὰ πᾶσιν ὡς ἐκείνων οὖσαι τῶν ἀνδρῶν πιστεύονται· ἐν αἷς εἰσὶν αἵ τε Κάδμου τοῦ Μιλησίου καὶ Ἀριστέου τοῦ Προκοννησίου καὶ τῶν παραπλησίων τούτοις. As a point of coincidence with this passage of Dionys. Hal., it will be noticed that the περὶ ὕψους speaks vaguely of ὁ τὰ Ἀριμάσπεια ποιήσας. Possibly this was one of those questions of authenticity with which the Graeco-Roman rhetorical schools were, to their credit, much concerned. The curious passage quoted from Aristeas (x. 3) is a description of a storm from the point of view of an inland people, probably the Arimaspi themselves, whose country the adventurous Aristeas had visited and described in hexameter verse. In the last line seasickness may possibly be indicated : cp. ἐμοῦντος τοῦ ἑτέρου καὶ λέγοντος τὰ σπλάγχνα ἐκβάλλειν in Plutarch *De vitando aere alieno* viii. Our author—with his usual range and impartiality—chooses Aratus a late, and Aristeas a comparatively early epic writer, for contrast with Homer. The few surviving fragments of Aristeas are printed in G. Kinkel's *Epicorum Graecorum Fragmenta* (Lipsiae, 1877), pp. 243—247.

Aristophanes 450—385 B.C. (approximately).

Shows, as do Euripides and Philistus, what virtue resides in the skilful arrangement of ordinary words (xl. 2).

Aristotle 384—322 B.C.

The only passage of Aristotle to which reference is made (xxxii. 3) is one in which he had pointed out that such words as ὡσπερεί serve to mitigate the harshness of metaphorical expressions. It has been suggested that this precept of Aristotle may have had a place in the *Poetics*. For the precept, cp. Cic. *de Orat*. iii. 41, 165 and Quintilian *Inst. Or.* viii. 3, 37. The last passage runs thus : ' Et si quid periculosius finxisse videbimur, quibusdam remediis praemuniendum est : *Ut ita dicam, Si licet dicere, Quodam modo, Permitte mihi.*' (With *remediis*, cp. ἡ γὰρ ὑποτίμησις, φασίν, ἰᾶται τὰ τολμηρά, *De Subl.* xxxii. 3. Possibly Quintilian and the author are drawing on some common source.)

Bacchylides flor. 475 B.C.

In xxxiii. 5 Bacchylides is ranked below Pindar. This judgment, and the grounds upon which it rests, have recently been put to the test in an altogether unexpected way. The *editio princeps* of the Poems of Bacchylides (edited in 1897 by F. G. Kenyon from a papyrus in the British Museum) has supplied an adequate basis for a comparison between the two poets, and the general view has been that—if it is fair to subject any poet to so severe a comparison—the critic's judgment stands confirmed[1]. It seems to be implied in

---

[1] W. Christ, *Gesch. d. griech. Litt.*, p. 167 (third edition, 1898) sums up thus : 'Bakchylides reicht weder an Originalität noch an Grossartigkeit der Diktion oder Tiefe der Gedanken an Pindar heran.'

c. xxxiii. that this and similar preferences of the author ran counter to the popular views of his day, and it is therefore all the more interesting that a witness (long silent like himself) should have arisen to justify him before the bar of Time, to which elsewhere (xiv. 3) he makes his appeal.

Caecilius. The numerous references to Caecilius throughout the *De Sublimitate*, and especially in its first chapter, make a somewhat detailed account of that author essential to a comprehension of the treatise.

Suidas, our principal authority with regard to the life of Caecilius, tells us that he was a Sicilian rhetorician who practised at Rome in the time of Augustus Caesar, that he was according to some accounts of servile birth, that his original name was Archagathus, and that he was ' in faith a Jew[1].' Suidas, it will be seen from the extract given below, adds (if the words are to be regarded as genuine) the surprising statement that his life extended till the advent of Hadrian, whose reign began more than a century after the death of Augustus. This inexactitude has led Blass to assume that Caecilius, the rhetorician, has here been confused with Q. Caecilius Niger, the quaestor of Verres, about whom Plutarch makes statements similar to those of Suidas[2]. It has led an earlier writer to go further still, and to assume the identity of the rhetorician and the quaestor[3]. But however much or however little truth there may be in these hypotheses, or in C. Müller's conjecture (*F. H. G.* III. 331 *a*) that his ancestors had been brought as slaves from Syria to Sicily, it is not disputed that Caecilius Calactinus taught rhetoric at Rome, wherein he resembled Dionysius, of whom he was in fact an intimate friend[4].

---

[1] Suidas, s. v. Καικίλιος· Καικίλιος (κεκίλιος codd.) Σικελιώτης Καλαντιανός, Κάλαντις δὲ πόλις Σικελίας, ῥήτωρ, σοφιστεύσας ἐν Ῥώμῃ ἐπὶ τοῦ Σεβαστοῦ Καίσαρος καὶ ἕως Ἀδριανοῦ, καὶ ἀπὸ δούλων, ὥς τινες ἱστορήκασι, καὶ πρότερον μὲν καλούμενος Ἀρχάγαθος, τὴν δὲ δόξαν Ἰουδαῖος. There seems little doubt (cp. Athen. vi. 272 F; xi. 466 A) that Καλακτῖνος and Καλάκτη should be read for Καλαντιανός and Κάλαντις. *Archagathus*, it may be added, seems to have been a specially Sicilian name : see G. Kaibel, *Inscriptiones Graecae Siciliae*, 210, 211, 212, 330 (conjecturally), 376.

[2] Plut. *Cic.* VII. : ἀπελευθερικὸς ἄνθρωπος, ἔνοχος τῷ ἰουδαΐζειν, ὄνομα Κεκίλιος.— Friedrich Blass, *Die griechische Beredsamkeit in dem Zeitraum von Alexander bis auf Augustus*, p. 174. But cp. Th. Reinach, *Revue des Études Juives*, XXVI. 36.

[3] G. Buchenau, *De scriptore libri περὶ ὕψους*, pp. 41, 42.

[4] Dionys. Hal., *Epist. ad Cn. Pompeium*, p. 777 (ed. Reiske): ἐμοὶ μέντοι καὶ τῷ φιλτάτῳ Καικιλίῳ δοκεῖ τὰ ἐνθυμήματα αὐτοῦ (sc. Θουκυδίδου) μάλιστά γε καὶ ζηλῶσαι Δημοσθένης.

Of the works of Caecilius, which may be classified under the
two heads of *history* and *literary criticism*, the present editor has
endeavoured to give (largely by way of conjectural reconstruction)
some account in the *American Journal of Philology*, xviii. pp. 303 ff.
Among the works of literary criticism were those indicated in the
De Sublimitate, viz. συγγραμμάτιον περὶ ὕψους (*De Subl.* 1. 1) and
συγγράμματα ὑπὲρ Λυσίου (*De Subl.* xxxii. 8). In this last passage the
plural and the preposition are to be noted. Caecilius, it seems to be
implied, had more than once dealt with Lysias, and in the spirit of
an advocate rather than in that of a judge. In the same thirty-
second chapter it is also implied that Caecilius was just as extreme in
his animosity towards Plato as in his love of Lysias. But we should
in fairness remember that the *De Sublimitate* is not without its
polemical side. We know from another source that Caecilius was
no mere blind and uncritical admirer of Lysias. On the contrary,
he found fault with him on the ground that he was less skilful in the
arrangement of arguments than in invention[1].

The work of Caecilius on the Sublime has been lost entirely,
while that of his successor exists only in a mutilated form. It is
impossible therefore to speak with any certainty about the relation of
the one book to the other. We do not even know whether Caecilius
confined (as he might almost seem to have done) his observations to
prose-writers, and excluded the poets, who figure so largely in the
De Sublimitate, from his survey. The references to him in the
De Sublimitate are either direct or indirect. The direct references,
besides those already mentioned, are the following. In the eighth
chapter we are told that he had omitted some of the five sources
of sublimity, πάθος being particularised ; and at the end of the same
chapter the criticism is driven home in a vigorous way. In c. xxxi.
Caecilius is again taken to task for finding fault with the word
ἀναγκοφαγῆσαι as used by Theopompus. In the next chapter it is
mentioned, apparently in an approving rather than in a merely
critical spirit, that 'with regard to the number of metaphors to be
employed, Caecilius seems to assent to the view of those who lay it
down that two, or at the most three, should be ranged together in the
same passage.' Finally, when in c. iv the author is illustrating the
vice of *frigidity* from the writings of the historian Timaeus, he excuses
himself from a lengthy enumeration of examples on the ground that
'most of them have already been quoted by Caecilius.'

---

[1] Phot., Cod. 262, p. 489 B, 13.

Thus the direct references are, as usually happens when a new writer is treating a subject previously handled by some one else, of a rather controversial nature. But this is not all. The general contents of the treatise, and its sequence, or want of sequence, seem sometimes to be influenced by the fact that the author had the book of Caecilius before him, and assumed the same of his reader or readers. This is probably the explanation of the rather abrupt way in which some of the literary illustrations make their appearance. And we may possibly include among indirect allusions to Caecilius such expressions as τὸν γράφοντα in c. xxxvi. 3, and the words ὁ τοῖς χρηστομαθοῦσιν ἐπιτιμῶν in c. ii. 3. It has also been maintained that in c. ii. 1 the word φησί should be understood of Caecilius, but this does not seem altogether probable. There is a more likely instance in xxix. 1[1].

Callisthenes. Writer of history: flor. 300 B.C. Pupil and nephew of Aristotle. Wrote Ἑλληνικά (probably covering the years 387—357 B.C.) and Περσικά. Pape-Benseler, *Griechische Eigennamen*, 604. W. Christ, *Gesch. d. griech. Litt.*[3] 363.

Mentioned in the περὶ ὕψους iii. 2 together with Cleitarchus, and as an example of the same vices of style.

Cicero b. 106 B.C., d. 43 B.C.

Comparison between Cicero and Demosthenes (xii. 4), for the significance of which see p. 10 supra.—'The comparison instituted between Cicero and Demosthenes is really masterly in its way. Pointing out that the grandeur of the Greek orator has something "abrupt" about it, while the Roman excels in diffusiveness (χύσις), he compares the former to a lightning flash which carries all before it in a straight line, while Cicero resembles the spreading fire that advances more leisurely and consumes all things round about it on its way. This comparison most felicitously expresses the directness and impetus of Demosthenes, and the diffusiveness, the *Umsichgreifen* of Cicero.' J. B. Bury, in *Classical Review*, I. 301.—Section 5 in

---

[1] On the whole question see M. Rothstein in *Hermes*, XXIII. 1—20; L. Martens, *De Libello* Περὶ Ὕψους, Bonnae, 1877; Morawski, *Quaestiones Quintilianeae*, Posnaniae, 1874, and *De Dionysii et Caecilii Studiis Rhetoricis* in *Rheinisches Museum*, XXXIV., pp. 370 seqq.; Burckhardt, *Caecili Rhetoris Fragmenta*, Basileae, 1863; Weise, *Quaestiones Caecilianae*, Berolini, 1888; F. Caccialanza, *Cecilio da Calatte e l' Ellenismo a Roma nel secolo di Augusto* in *Rivista di Filologia*, XVIII. 1—73. Brzoska's admirable article on *Caecilius* in Pauly-Wissowa is the latest and most exhaustive contribution to the subject.

c. xii. is interesting as well as section 4. It seems to show that the author of the π. ὕψ. had, notwithstanding his modest disclaimer, some considerable knowledge of the contents of Cicero's works.

Cleitarchus. Like Callisthenes, a writer of history; flor. 300 B.C. One of the historians of Alexander the Great. Pape-Benseler, 671; W. Christ, 363.

Bombast is attributed to him in the π. ὕψ. iii. 2. The judgment is confirmed by Demetrius (περὶ ἑρμηνείας, ad f.) who mentions that Cleitarchus had described a wasp in words some of which were more appropriate to the Erymanthian boar: κατανέμεται μέν, φησί, τὴν ὀρεινήν, εἰσίπταται δὲ εἰς τὰς κοίλας δρῦς.—It seems hitherto to have escaped notice that the frigidity of Cleitarchus' style is similarly condemned in the *Rhetoric* of Philodemus the Epicurean: [ψυχρό]-τερον ὅ τι τοῦ Κλειταρχείου, *frigidius vel Clitarchico sermone*, Herculan. volum. XI. 37.

Demosthenes b. 383, d. 322 B.C. Compared with Cicero, xii. 4; with Hyperides xxxiv. 1—4. Ranked with Homer, Plato, and Thucydides, as one of the supreme models (xiv. 1, 2).

The citations are many:—

c. *Aristocr.* 113	—*De Subl.*	ii.	3.
c. *Aristog.* I. 27	—	„	xxvii. 3.
de *Corona* 18	—	„	xxiv. 1.
„ 169	—	„	x. 7.
„ 188	—	„	xxxix. 4.
„ 208	—	„	xvi. 2, 3; xvii. 2.
„ 296	—	„	xxxii. 2.
in *Midiam* 72	—	„	xx. 1, 2, 3.
Philipp. I. 10 and 44—		„	xviii. 1.
c. *Timocr.* 208	—	„	xv. 9.

The qualities illustrated are such as the orator's skill shown in various ways,—in the selection of particulars, in the use of questions and asyndeta, in rapid transitions, etc. We are told that Demosthenes abounds in hyperbata (xxii. 3). In xxxviii. 1 the following words are quoted as an example of tasteless hyperbole: εἰ μὴ τὸν ἐγκέφαλον ἐν ταῖς πτέρναις καταπεπατημένον φορεῖτε. The words occur in the *de Halonneso* 45 (εἴπερ ὑμεῖς τὸν ἐγκέφαλον ἐν τοῖς κροτάφοις καὶ μὴ ἐν ταῖς πτέρναις καταπεπατημένον φορεῖτε); and we should like much to know whether our author, who is interested in questions of authenticity (cp. ix. 5), ascribed the *de Hal.* to Demosthenes. More probably he was of the same opinion as Libanius after him : καὶ μὴν καὶ τὸ ἐπὶ τέλει ῥηθὲν οὐ μικρὸν μαρτύριον τοῦ νόθον εἶναι τὸν λόγον ' εἴπερ ὑμεῖς τὸν ἐγκέφαλον ἐν τοῖς κροτάφοις καὶ μὴ ἐν ταῖς πτέρναις καταπεπατημένον φορεῖτε.' ὁ μὲν γὰρ Δημοσθένης εἴωθε παρρησίᾳ χρῆσθαι, τοῦτο δὲ ὕβρις ἐστὶ καὶ λοιδορία μέτρον οὐκ ἔχουσα (Libanii Argumentum 2). Modern critics also are inclined to regard the speech as spurious, together with *c. Aristog.* i. and ii.

In xxxiv. 3 it is said of Demosthenes : ἔνθα μὲν γελοῖος εἶναι βιάζεται καὶ ἀστεῖος, οὐ γέλωτα κινεῖ μᾶλλον ἢ καταγελᾶται (and then follows a comparison with another orator which will be noticed under *Hyperides*). Burke and Demosthenes had much in common in this as in other respects : 'His (Burke's) banter is nearly always ungainly, his wit blunt, as Johnson said of it, and very often unseasonable. We feel that Johnson must have been right in declaring that, though Burke was always in search of pleasantries, he never made a good joke in his life.' John Morley, *Burke*, p. 212. Mr Morley adds : 'As is usual with a man who has not true humour, Burke is also without true pathos. The thought of wrong or misery moved him less to pity for the victim than to anger against the cause.' Cp. S. H. Butcher, *Demosthenes*, pp. 161, 2.

The minute discussion in xxxix. 4 upon the order of words in a sentence can be illustrated from Dionysius of Halicarnassus. An obvious modern parallel of a burlesque character is that supplied by the variations played upon the words *Belle marquise, vos beaux yeux me font mourir d'amour* in the *Bourgeois Gentilhomme*.

Eratosthenes b. 276, d. 194 B.C. Alexandrian geographer and polymath. Among his accomplishments he included poetry, and wrote an elegy *Erigone*, suggested by the story of Icarius, his daughter Erigone, and his faithful dog Maera. The best special studies of the poem are those of E. Hiller, *Eratosthenis carminum reliquiae* (Lipsiae, 1872), pp. 94—114; and of E. Maass, in Kiessling and Wilamowitz-Moellendorff's *Philologische Untersuchungen* VI. pp. 59—138.

The *Erigone* is described (xxxiii. 5) as ποιημάτιον ἀμώμητον.

Eupolis. Athenian comic poet : flor. 415 B.C.

From the *Demi* of Eupolis are quoted (in xvi. 3) the two lines :

οὐ γὰρ μὰ τὴν Μαραθῶνι τὴν ἐμὴν μάχην
χαίρων τις αὐτῶν τοὐμὸν ἀλγυνεῖ κέαρ.

Some of those critics who are never happier than when they detect a plagiarism seem to have suspected Demosthenes of having borrowed from this passage of Eupolis for his famous oath in the *Crown* (*de Cor.* 208). The insinuation is ably met by our author. The real coincidence is between the passage of Eupolis and another in Euripides :—

οὐ γὰρ μὰ τὴν δέσποιναν, ἣν ἐγὼ σέβω,

....

χαίρων τις αὐτῶν τοὐμὸν ἀλγυνεῖ κέαρ.

Eurip., *Med.*, vv. 394, 397.

It is probable that Miltiades is the speaker in the *Demi* and that, in the mock-heroic vein, he draws upon Euripides. Cp. Meineke, *Frag. Comic. Graec.*, 172; Kock, *Comic. Att. Fragm.*, I. 279; Raspe, *de Eupolidis* Δήμοις, 45.

Euripides b. 480, d. 406 B.C.

Most of the citations are to be found in chapter xv. :—

Orestes 255	—*De Subl.* xv. 2.		
Iph. in Tauris 291—	,,	xv.	2.
Phaethon	—	,,	xv. 4.
Alexander	—	,,	xv. 4.
Bacchae 726	—.	,,	xv. 6.
Orestes 264	—	,,	xv. 8.

There are two further quotations in c. xl. :—

Herc. Fur. 1245—*De Subl.* xl. 3.
Antiope — ,, xl. 4.

For the *Alexander*, *Antiope*, and *Phaethon*, reference may be made to Wagner's *Fragmenta Euripidis*, pp. 630—635, 661—670, 800—809; and for the *Antiope* alone to H. Weil, *Études sur le drame antique*, pp. 213—246. Mahaffy has in the 'Cunningham Memoirs' of the Royal Irish Academy, No. viii., 1891, described the very ancient Fragments discovered by Flinders Petrie at Gurob in the Fayyum. In giving some account of the probable plot of the *Antiope*, Mahaffy says (pp. 28, 29): 'The moment when Dirce was tied to the bull is perpetuated in the famous marble group at Naples, the work of Apollonius and Tauriscus, the sculptors of Tralles. Her hideous death was then narrated by an eye-witness, from whose speech Longinus (xl. 4) has quoted a sentence as an example of majestic conciseness.'

It is worth noting that the phrase εὐκλείας στέφανος in the *De Subl.* xiii. 4 seems to be a reminiscence of a line in the *Antiope*, καὶ ταῦτα δρῶν | κάλλιστον ἕξεις στέφανον εὐκλείας ἀεί (Fr. 46, Wagn.); just as the words κἂν ἄμουσος ᾖ παντάπασι (xxxix. 2) recall the verse of the *Sthenoboea*, Ἔρως διδάσκει κἂν ἄμουσος ᾖ τὸ πρίν, and as the metaphor ἐν βακχεύμασι νήφειν ἀναγκαῖον (xvi. 4) seems suggested by ἐν βακχεύμασιν οὖσ᾽ ᾖ γε σώφρων οὐ διαφθαρήσεται (*Bacchae* 317). In xliv. 12 the words κράτιστον εἰκῇ ταῦτ᾽ ἐᾶν are from the *Electra* 379, κράτιστον εἰκῇ ταῦτ᾽ ἐᾶν ἀφειμένα.

The estimate of the poetry of Euripides in cc. xv. and xl. is a good example of the author's critical method. He gives Euripides full credit for his strong points (such as his power of affecting the imagination and his skill in handling common words), while he does not conceal the limitations which he finds in him. There is no carping, and at the same time there is no fear of meeting that current of popular approval which had long set strongly in favour of Euripides. This same honest independence has led the author to choose his examples for censure, as well as for praise, from all times and all ranks; and it is one of his most striking merits to have done so.

For the effective use of ordinary words by Euripides, cp. Arist. *Rhet.* iii. 2 : κλέπτεται δ᾽ εὖ, ἐάν τις ἐκ τῆς εἰωθυίας διαλέκτου ἐκλέγων συντιθῇ· ὅπερ Εὐριπίδης ποιεῖ καὶ ὑπέδειξε πρῶτος. See also Dionys. Hal., *de Comp. Verb.*, xxiii.

Gorgias.   Rhetorician, of Leontini in Sicily.   Flor. 440 B.C.

Instances of bombast are quoted from Gorgias : ταύτῃ καὶ τὰ τοῦ Λεοντίνου Γοργίου γελᾶται γράφοντος ᾽Ξέρξης ὁ τῶν Περσῶν Ζεύς,᾽ καὶ ᾽γῦπες ἔμψυχοι τάφοι᾽ (iii. 2). Cp. Hermogenes (Spengel's *Rhetores Graeci*, II. 292) : παρὰ δὲ τοῖς ὑποξύλοις τούτοις σοφισταῖς πάμπολλα εὕροις ἄν· τάφους τε γὰρ ἐμψύχους τοὺς γῦπας λέγουσιν, ὧνπερ εἰσὶ μάλιστα ἄξιοι, καὶ ἄλλα τινὰ ψυχρεύονται πάμπολλα.

Hecataeus.   Hecataeus of Miletus, the early historian and geographer.   Flor. 520 B.C.   For a full account of him see Giacomo Tropea, *Ecateo da Mileto* (Messina, 1896).

Hecataeus furnishes (*De Subl.* xxvii. 2) an example of rapid change from (grammatical) person to person, from narrative to allocution.

Hegesias.   Hegesias of Magnesia.   Rhetorician: flor. 270 B.C. Susemihl II. 464; Blass, *Griech. Bereds.*, 4, 5; 9, 10; 27 ff.; Baudat, *Étude sur Denys d'Halicarnasse*, pp. 3, 45, 55.   Some instructive remarks on the relation of Atticism to Asianism, and of Hegesias to both, will be found in Holm's *History of Greece* iv. 481, 2, and in Jebb's *Attic Orators* ii. 440—442, 445, 451. The truth is, as Holm points out, that the terms *Atticism* and *Asianism* are used most vaguely, the former including imitators of Attic writers as different as Plato and Demosthenes, as Lysias and Isocrates.—The question of the influence of Hegesias upon the style of Pausanias forms the subject of an interesting section in the introduction to Frazer's *Pausanias* i. lxix., lxx.

In the *De Sublimitate* iii. 2 Hegesias is classed with Amphicrates and Matris, and charged with the same faults.

Herodotus flor. 440 B.C.

The citations from Herodotus are many :—

Herod i.	105—*De Subl.* xxviii. 4.
„ ii.	29— „ xxvi. 2.
„ v.	18— „ iv. 7.
„ vi.	11— „ xxii. 1.
„ vi.	75— „ xxxi. 2.
„ vii.	181— „ xxxi. 2.
„ vii.	188— „ xliii. 1.
„ vii.	191— „ xliii. 1.
„ vii.	225— „ xxxviii. 4.
„ viii.	13— „ xliii. 1.

If examined in detail, the quotations from Herodotus in the *De Sublimitate* will be found to be made for the purpose both of praise and of blame, chiefly the former. It would be a sure passport to the author's regard and respect that Herodotus, like Plato, was Ὁμηρικώτατος (xiii. 3).

With the Herodotean expression criticised in iv. 7 may be compared that of Pericles, ἡ τοῦ Πειραιέως λήμη (Arist. *Rhet.* iii. 10, 7 ; Plut. *Peric. Vit.* c. 8).

Hesiod. Date uncertain : eighth century approximately.

The words ἀγαθὴ κ.τ.λ. in *De Subl.* xiii. 4 are from Hesiod (ἀγαθὴ δ᾽ ἔρις ἥδε βροτοῦσι, *Works and Days*, 24). In ix. 5 the *Shield* is quoted (τῆς ἐκ μὲν ῥινῶν μύξαι ῥέον, *Scut.* 267), with an interesting expression of doubt as to its authorship: εἴγε Ἡσιόδου καὶ τὴν Ἀσπίδα θετέον.

Homer. Date uncertain.

No author is so often quoted in the *De Sublimitate* as Homer, the citations from whom seem to suggest a familiar knowledge both of the *Iliad* and the *Odyssey* :—

Iliad	I.	225	—*De Subl.*	iv. 4.	
,,	IV.	442	—	,,	ix. 4 (allusion).
,,	V.	85	—	,,	xxvi. 3.
,,	V.	770	—	,,	ix. 5.
,,	XIII.	18	—	,,	ix. 8.
,,	XV.	346	—	,,	xxvii. 1.
,,	XV.	605	—	,,	ix. 11.
,,	XV.	624	—	,,	x. 5.
,,	XV.	697	—	,,	xxvi. 1.
,,	XVII.	645	—	,,	ix. 10.
,,	XX.	60	—	,,	ix. 8.
,,	XX.	61	—	,,	ix. 6.
,,	XX.	170	—	,,	xv. 3.
,,	XXI.	388, 9	—	,,	ix. 6.
Odyssey	III.	109	—	,,	ix. 12.
,,	IV.	681	—	,,	xxvii. 4.
,,	IX.	182	—	,,	ix. 14 (allusion).
,,	X.	17	—	,,	ix. 14 ,,
,,	X.	237	—	,,	ix. 14 ,,
,,	X.	251	—	,,	xix. 2.
,,	XI.	315	—	,,	viii. 2.
,,	XI.	543	—	,,	ix. 2 (allusion).
,,	XII.	62	—	,,	ix. 14 ,,
,,	XII.	447	—	,,	ix. 14 ,,
,,	XVII.	322	—	,,	xliv. 5.
,,	XXII.	79	—	,,	ix. 14 (allusion).

It may be remarked that the author clearly (ix. 14) did not agree with the *Chorizontes* in assigning the *Iliad* and the *Odyssey* to different poets. It may also be remarked that, devoted as he is to Homer, he does not, even in his case, refrain from disapprobation where he thinks disapprobation is required (ix. 14, xxiii. 4, xxxvi. 2). On the other side, his admiration for the great poet has inspired some of his most eloquent passages, as was felt by Gibbon, a dispassionate judge who did not readily fall a victim to foolish enthusiasms. 'The ninth chapter (of the *De Sublimitate*) is one of the finest monuments of antiquity. Till now, I was acquainted only with two ways of criticising a beautiful passage : the one, to shew, by an exact anatomy of it, the distinct beauties of it, and whence they sprung ; the other, an idle exclamation, or a general encomium, which leaves nothing behind it. Longinus has shewn me that there is a third. He tells me his own feelings upon reading it; and tells them with such energy, that he communicates them. I almost doubt which is most sublime, Homer's Battle of the Gods, or Longinus's Apostrophe to Terentianus upon it.' (Edward Gibbon, *Journal*, Sept. 3, 1762.) The *Iliad* and the *Odyssey* appeal as strongly (if a modern parallel may be adduced) to the author of the *De Sublimitate* as do Milton and the Book of Job to the author of the *Sublime and Beautiful*.

Over and above those already quoted, other references to Homer will be found in ix. 7, 10—15; x. 3; xiii. 3, 4; xiv. 1, 2.—The passage from the *Odyssey* x. 251 is also eulogised (and for the same reason) by Eustathius, who no doubt reflects Alexandrian views : καλὸν δ' ἐν τούτοις καὶ ἡ ἀσύνδετος εἰσβολή. Coincidences of this kind recall the remark in c. ix. 8 : πολλοῖς δὲ πρὸ ἡμῶν ὁ τόπος ἐξείργασται.

Hyperides. Attic orator. Date of death, 322 B.C.

The first allusion to Hyperides in the *De Subl.* (xv. 10) is prompted by a well-known saying of his, one which is also found in Plut. *Moralia* 849 A : αἰτιωμένων δέ τινων αὐτὸν ὡς παριδόντα πολλοὺς νόμους ἐν τῷ ψηφίσματι, Ἐπεσκότει, ἔφη, μοι τὰ Μακεδόνων ὅπλα, καὶ οὐκ ἐγὼ τὸ ψήφισμα ἔγραψα, ἡ δ' ἐν Χαιρωνείᾳ μάχη. In c. xxxiv. Hyperides is compared at length with Demosthenes, and reference is made to three of his productions,—the *Athenogenes*, the *Phryne* (see Athen. 590 E and Quintil. x. 5, 2), and the *Deliacus* (cp. Hermog. ap. Speng. II. 288, ἐπεὶ καὶ τὰ ἐν Δηλιακῷ τοῦ Ὑπερίδου ποιητικῶς μᾶλλον καὶ μυθικῶς εἴρηται). With πένταθλος (xxxiv. 1), cp. [Plat.] *Erast.* 135 E.

The *Athenogenes* has recently reappeared in one of those papyrus rolls from Egypt which have helped to illustrate the περὶ ὕψους and to enhance our faith in its critical estimates. The speech was printed, for the first time, in the course of the years 1891 and 1892 from a papyrus acquired by the Museum of the Louvre in 1888 ; and although the text is incomplete, enough remains whereby to form a conception of the entire composition. ' The recovery of the speech against Athenogenes is especially welcome, because there is excellent reason to believe that in it we have a thoroughly characteristic specimen of that class of oratory in which Hyperides especially excelled. The author of the treatise *De Sublimitate* couples it with the defence of Phryne as an example of a manner in which Hyperides was superior even to Demosthenes. As an advocate in a social *cause célèbre*, or in any matter which required light and delicate handling, Hyperides was unequalled ; and we are now in a far better position than formerly to judge of the character of his genius ' (F. G. Kenyon, *Hyperides : Orations against Athenogenes and Philippides*, p. xv.).

Ion. Ion of Chios. Tragic poet : flor. 440 B.C. Besides tragedies, Ion wrote elegies, hymns, dithyrambs, and (in prose) a book of travels and a history.

Correct poet as he is, he cannot for a moment be compared to Sophocles (c. xxxiii. 5).

Isocrates b. 436, d. 338 B.C.

An instance of puerile hyperbole is adduced (xxxviii. 2) from the *Panegyric* § 8 of Isocrates. In xxi. 1 it is effectively shown how, by the addition of connecting particles, the followers of Isocrates (οἱ Ἰσοκράτειοι) would be likely to enfeeble a forcible passage of Demosthenes.—In iv. 2 the author cites, as an example of frigidity, a passage in which Timaeus had described Alexander as spending fewer years in the conquest of Asia than Isocrates spent in the composition of his *Panegyric*. θαυμαστή γε τοῦ Μακεδόνος ἡ πρὸς τὸν σοφιστὴν σύγκρισις is the caustic comment of our author, who cannot away with the bookish parallels which so readily offer themselves to the literary man.

Lysias flor. 400 B.C.

Lysias, the Attic orator, is an important figure in the περὶ ὕψους, inasmuch as the treatise hinges upon the author's preference for the style of Plato, as compared with that of Lysias preferred by Caecilius ἐν τοῖς ὑπὲρ Λυσίου συγγράμμασιν (xxxii. 8). Caecilius was, it is alleged, moved by an unreasoning animosity against Plato. Our author, while admitting (xxxiv. 2) that Lysias has ἀρετάς τε καὶ χάριτας of his own, decides the question by reference to his main principle that elevation is to be sought even at the price of occasional error. That principle, he clearly thought, called for special emphasis in his own age, when writers were more likely to fall into the extreme of lifelessness than to run into the opposite extreme of exuberance.

Matris. Matris of Thebes. A rhetorician; of uncertain date, say 200 B.C.; wrote an ἐγκώμιον Ἡρακλέους (*Athen.* x. 412 B); showed the faults of the Asiatic manner. Susemihl, II. 469. Of the same class as Amphicrates and Hegesias (*De Subl.*, iii. 2).

Moses. The allusion (ix. 9) to the Hebrew scriptures in a Greek classic is so interesting and remarkable that it demands a brief discussion with special reference to the doubts which scholars have at various times cast upon its authenticity. Among the doubters have been Franciscus Portus in the sixteenth century, Daniel Wyttenbach in the eighteenth, and Leonhard Spengel[1] and Louis Vaucher[2] in our own century. The views of the two last critics invite particular attention, and it will be convenient to consider those of Vaucher first.

Vaucher's judgment, upon this point as upon others, is somewhat warped by his prepossessions. His object, throughout his ingenious but unconvincing book, is to prove that Plutarch is the author of the *De Sublimitate.* And with this theory the quotation from *Genesis* but ill accords, in view of Plutarch's general attitude towards the Jews and of the absence of any direct reference to the Jewish scriptures in his accepted works. This preoccupation led Vaucher to emphasise unduly the fact that the passage is not found in P 2036, which at this point has lost eight leaves, of which however the first and the last are preserved in the remaining MSS. These two leaves (of which the latter embraces ix. 9) appear in all the editions of the *De Sublimitate.* This is true of that of Vaucher himself. He prints the words they contain in full. Section 9, however, he places in brackets. And yet, as far as manuscript authority goes, that section stands or falls with those other sections which rest upon the same evidence. And all these are so characteristic in themselves, and fit so perfectly into their context, that it is impossible to doubt their authenticity. They begin with an enumeration of the five sources of sublimity, and they end by giving the larger half of an extract from Homer, of which the concluding words (ἐν δὲ φάει καὶ ὄλεσσον) appear duly at the point where P resumes.

Spengel's attitude is more consistent. He too brackets the passage (*Rhetores Graeci*, I. pp. xvi. and 255). But it is to be noted

---

[1] *Specimen Emendationum in Cornelium Tacitum*, Monachii, 1852.

[2] *Études Critiques sur le Traité du Sublime et sur les Écrits de Longin*, Genève, 1854. Spengel's view has been reaffirmed lately by J. C. Vollgraff in *Mnemosyne N. S.*, 1898, XXVI. pp. 123, 4.

that he does not reject the words on the ground of insufficient documentary support. It is not the external, but the internal evidence, that causes him to regard the section as an interpolation. The words do not seem to him to be at home in their surroundings. He would no doubt have agreed with F. A. Wolf, whom however he does not quote, that they seem to have 'fallen from the skies[1].'

But a glance at the context will show that the degree of abruptness with which the passage is introduced has been greatly exaggerated, and certainly need awaken little surprise when found in a work which is by no means free from digression and parenthesis. And in truth the abruptness would in some respects be greater if the passage were away. The general subject of the ninth chapter is nobility of nature as a source of lofty diction. Quoting one of his own best things in a somewhat off-hand manner, like a true critic, the author says at the beginning of the chapter: 'In some other place I have written to this effect: "Sublimity is the echo of a great soul."' (γέγραφά που καὶ ἐτέρωθι τὸ τοιοῦτον· ὕψος μεγαλοφροσύνης ἀπήχημα, ix. 2.) This train of thought he illustrates chiefly, but not entirely, from Homer. Outside Homer, there is in the sections we possess (and it must be remembered that six leaves are missing) a reference to a celebrated saying of Alexander, and another to a poem attributed to Hesiod. It is important to call attention to these particulars because the critics have sometimes spoken as if the whole chapter were filled with Homer. And when the Homeric passages come, they have a certain unity; they all speak of manifestations of the divine power under various shapes; they end with a reference to the divine greatness and purity, and the divine control over the elements. Into this unity the passage from *Genesis* enters naturally, and after it there comes, by a similarly natural transition, a reference to deeds of heroic *men* as depicted in Homer (ix. 10). Now Spengel would have us believe that section 9 is but a marginal comment— the work of some Christian or Jew—on Ajax' call for light, as quoted in section 10. We cannot deny that such a gloss, singularly inept though it would be, might conceivably have been entered in the margin, and from thence have been transferred into the text at the wrong point. But to this doubly improbable possibility most impartial judges will prefer the likelihood that the passage stands where it was first placed. And it may be added that the hand of the

---

[1] F. A. Wolf, *Vorlesungen über die Alterthumswissenschaft*, I. 330: 'Diese Stelle fällt wie vom Himmel hinein.'

author of the treatise seems clearly revealed in minute points of wording, such as the ταύτῃ καί (cp. ix. 4) with which the passage is introduced[1].

Another objection raised, on internal grounds, to the quotation is that it is not only *unexpected* but *inexact*. The first portion of the divine fiat differs slightly, and the second differs altogether, from the original as we know it. The question, indeed, suggests itself whether the passage can—with reference to any original known to us—properly be described as 'a quotation' at all. It reproduces the substance rather than the precise form of three verses at the beginning of *Genesis*. The verses may be transcribed here from the most recent edition of the Septuagint version, though we ought not to take it for granted that the author had that version in his mind or before his eyes, nor yet that he is echoing a Hebrew text in every way identical with ours. I. 3 : καὶ εἶπεν ὁ θεός Γενηθήτω φῶς· καὶ ἐγένετο φῶς. 9: καὶ εἶπεν ὁ θεός Συναχθήτω τὸ ὕδωρ τὸ ὑποκάτω τοῦ οὐρανοῦ εἰς συναγωγὴν μίαν, καὶ ὀφθήτω ἡ ξηρά· καὶ ἐγένετο οὕτως. 10 : καὶ ἐκάλεσεν ὁ θεὸς τὴν ξηρὰν γῆν[2]. Such 'conflations' are not unnatural when words are quoted from memory, and they are specially common in our author. Two examples, in which lines from different books of the *Iliad* are combined, will be found in sections 6 and 8 of this very chapter. It has been further suggested that, here as elsewhere, the author has been influenced, unconsciously no doubt, by his love of rhythm and parallelism :—

γενέσθω φῶς, καὶ ἐγένετο.
γενέσθω γῆ, καὶ ἐγένετο[3].

But this and all similar suggestions, however interesting, must be subject to the reservation that we do not know the exact nature of the source upon which the author is drawing.

It is necessary, moreover, to bear in mind that the more inexact the quotation, the less reason will there be for regarding the passage

---

[1] The question of the *sublimity* of the passage need hardly now be raised since it may be regarded as having been settled in the once famous controversy in which Boileau routed Huet and Leclerc. (See Boileau, *Œuvres* (edition of 1748), III. pp. 384 ff.) Even a 'bare idea,' to use our author's phrase, may be sublime. Brevity and simplicity, he implies, so far from being inconsistent with sublimity, are of its very essence.

[2] Or should we see a reflexion of i. 3, 6, rather than of i. 3. 9, 10?

[3] J. Freytag, *De Anonymi περὶ ὕψους sublimi genere dicendi*. Hildesheim, 1897.
P. 77.

as an interpolation. Only a Jew, or a Christian, would have been likely to interpolate it, and a Jew or Christian would have done the work with care and accuracy. Besides, such an interpolator would hardly have been content with describing Moses as 'no ordinary man.' Altogether, the arguments in favour of the theory of interpolation seem weak and precarious. The manuscript attestation is adequate; the passage harmonises with the context; the freedom in quotation is like our author and unlike an interpolator.

It remains, however, to glance at certain difficulties, of an *à priori* nature, which have been thought to attend this reference to the Jewish lawgiver in the work of a Greek writer. It has already been mentioned that Portus (1511—1581 A.D.) was the first scholar to express misgivings with regard to the authenticity of the section. In his day, and for long afterwards, the traditional ascription of the treatise to the historical Longinus was undisputed. But Portus thought it unlikely that the Longinus of history would be acquainted with the Jewish scriptures. In this view he has not found many to follow him. For was not Longinus a pupil of the leading Neoplatonists at Alexandria, and has not he himself ranked 'Paul of Tarsus' high in the hierarchy of Greek oratorical genius[1]?

But this is not all, for the commentator Schurzfleisch of Wittenberg has furnished an independent suggestion, with the design of removing the difficulty, if difficulty there be. In view of the wider acceptance which Schurzfleisch's suggestion has gained since an earlier date has been claimed for the treatise, it is important to observe that it was made by him as far back as the year 1711, when no one had begun to doubt that Longinus was the author. His words are worth quoting: 'Longinus fortasse non tam septuaginta seniores legit, quam hoc exemplum a Caecilio rhetore, qui τὴν δόξαν Ἰουδαῖος σοφὸς τὰ Ἑλληνικὰ vocatur a Suida, mutuatus est[2].' He thus threw out the pregnant hint that the illustration may have been taken, not directly from the Septuagint, but from Caecilius. Caecilius is described, in Suidas' biographical notice of him, as 'in faith a Jew[3].' It is, therefore, quite possible, as Schurzfleisch saw, that the author, whose treatise takes a similar work by Caecilius as its starting-point,

---

[1] The reference of course is to the fragment (if it is to be regarded as genuine) given, e.g., by Vaucher, *Études*, p. 309.

[2] Schurzfleischius, *Animadversiones ad Dionysii Longini περὶ ὕψους commentationem.* Vitembergae, 1711. P. 23.

[3] τὴν δόξαν Ἰουδαῖος.

may have borrowed this Hebraic illustration of sublimity from him. Thus viewed, the extract may be regarded as a vague recollection, and reproduction, of Caecilius. The suggestion is now generally accepted. But while the theory may be regarded as highly probable, we ought at the same time to recognise that the author's general conception of Moses does not seem to be entirely based upon this fragment of his writings. The very words 'no ordinary man' seem to imply some independent knowledge extending beyond this isolated quotation. The writer possesses the general knowledge that he is dealing with 'the Jewish lawgiver,' whose actual name seemingly he does not think his readers will require. He possesses also the particular knowledge that the passage is to be found 'at the very beginning of his laws.' It may further be noted that he appears to direct special attention to the sublimity of the passage by his somewhat rhetorical use of the interrogative pronoun in introducing it.

Thus far the truth of the traditional belief that Longinus was the author has, for the sake of argument, been assumed. But the passage under review must, if its authenticity is to be placed beyond question, be shown to harmonise with the view now widely accepted that the treatise belongs not to the third century but to the first. At this point the likelihood of the author's obligation in this as in other matters to Caecilius comes again to our aid; and the likelihood is perhaps all the greater if the author followed him closely in time as well as in general treatment. But independently of this, it would not be difficult to show that the Graeco-Roman world of the first century was no stranger to the history and the antiquities of the Jews[1].

Wolf, in the course of the passage already cited, admitted this. He thought that the section was probably a gloss by a Christian, though he would not expel it from the text, especially as the text itself was so fragmentary. But he states expressly that he does not base his scepticism on the inherent improbability of any reference to Moses. The name of Moses, as he remarks, occurs even in Strabo's writings; and he might have added, in those of Diodorus Siculus and earlier writers still[2].

---

[1] This point was emphasised (*Philologus* I. pp. 630, 631 : year 1846) by G. Roeper.

[2] Cp. Th. Reinach, *Textes d'auteurs Grecs et Romains relatifs au Judaisme*, pp. 14 ff.; Pape-Benseler, *Griechische Eigennamen*, p. 969 ; J. Freudenthal, *Hellenistische Studien*, II. pp. 177 ff.

The question of early references to, or quotations from, the
Old Testament in Greek writers deserves more attention than it
seems hitherto to have received. Hatch's *Essay on Early Quotations from the Septuagint* does not profess to be more than its title
implies. Ryle's *Philo and Holy Scripture* is exhaustive within its
field; but the example it sets needs to be followed in other directions.
In his introduction Ryle states with truth that 'Philo's testimony
to the Septuagint text has the twofold value of being earlier, by
more than two centuries, than our earliest extant MS.; and of being
derived from a non-Christian, a Graeco-Judaic, source, separate in
time and character from the great mass of other evidence.' The
present section (especially in the light of the conjecture that
Caecilius is its parent) possesses a somewhat parallel interest, an
interest which is in some respects not less but greater because of the
want of exact correspondence between the passage and any original
known to us.

It is important, once more, to notice not only the words contained
in the section, but also the way in which they are introduced. They
are attributed to ὁ τῶν Ἰουδαίων θεσμοθέτης, a designation which
corresponds closely with the words (ὁ τῶν Ἰουδαίων νομοθέτης Μωϋσῆς)
with which Philo himself introduces a quotation from the opening of
Genesis. Further, they are said to be found 'at the very beginning
of the laws.' Similarly, Philo denotes the Pentateuch by the term
οἱ νόμοι, though he more commonly refers to it as ὁ νόμος or ἡ νομο-
θεσία[1].

But the resemblances which the treatise affords with the writings
of Philo do not end with this passage. They include the remarkable
coincidence noted in the Introduction (p. 13 supra). Similarly, but
not so convincingly, τῇδε κἀκεῖσε ἀγχιστρόφως ἀντισπώμενοι (*De Subl.*
xxii. 1) may be compared with ἀνθελκόμενος πρὸς ἑκατέρου μέρους ὧδε
κἀκεῖσε (Philo, *De Vita Mosis*, iii. p. 678). And the likeness is seen
in single words as well as in clauses. In the section just quoted
from the *De Sublimitate*, we note the Philonic word εἱρμός, and
others elsewhere such as ἐπάλληλος, κατασκελετεύω, προκόσμημα,
μαγειρεῖον, προσυπογράφειν. And the word τὸ γλωττόκομον, used of a

---

[1] Ryle, op. cit. pp. xix., xx.—Reference should also be made to passages quoted
by Th. Reinach, *Textes d'auteurs, etc.*, pp. 18, 82, 361. The first passage is of
special interest, particularly if the very early date claimed for it is correct. In it
the end of 'the laws' seems to mean the end of *Leviticus*: προσγέγραπται δὲ καὶ
τοῖς νόμοις ἐπὶ τελευτῆς ὅτι Μωσῆς ἀκούσας τοῦ θεοῦ τάδε λέγει τοῖς Ἰουδαίοις.

'cage' in *De Subl.* xliv. 5, has a distinct affinity with the Septuagint, and also (at a later date) with Aquila, additions to whose remains have lately been discovered and issued[1].

The points of contact between the author of the περὶ ὕψους and the Jews are not, however, confined even to Moses, Caecilius, and Philo. There is also Josephus, who has referred to Moses in terms (quoted in the Introduction p. 12 supra) almost identical with those used in *De Subl.* ix. 9. There is also Theodorus, mentioned in iii. 5, who had possibly been one of the author's teachers in rhetoric, and who himself sprang from Gadara in Syria. And it is hardly necessary to add that the subjugation of Judaea by Pompey, and the provision by Alexandria of a common meeting-ground for Jews, Greeks, and Romans, must have multiplied points of contact in ways altogether unknown to us.

Mommsen, indeed, goes so far as to suggest that the author may himself possibly have been a Jew. He speaks of the treatise as one of the finest works of literary criticism surviving from antiquity, as written in the early days of the empire by an unknown author, and as the production, if not of a Jew, yet of a man who revered Moses and Homer alike (Mommsen, *Römische Geschichte*, v. 494). But against this tentative suggestion of Jewish origin must be set the general tone and character of ix. 9, and the fact that in xii. 4, when about to compare Cicero and Demosthenes, the author uses the words, 'if we *as Greeks* are at liberty to form an opinion upon the point[2].' If a Jew, he must have been a most highly Hellenised Jew.

Philistus. Philistus of Syracuse, the historian. Began his Σικελικὰ about the year 386 B.C.; perished when supporting Dionysius II. against Dion in 357 B.C.; an imitator of Thucydides, whence termed *pusillus Thucydides* by Cicero (*ad Q. Fr.* ii. 13, 4).

According to the *De Subl.* (xl. 2), Philistus possessed, in common with Aristophanes and Euripides, the power of making ordinary words effective through the artistic skill with which they were bound together.—See further Freeman, *Sicily*, III. 597 ff.

---

[1] F. C. Burkitt's *Fragments of the Book of Kings according to the Translation of Aquila, from a MS. formerly in the Geniza at Cairo.* (Cambridge, 1898.)

[2] xii. 4: εἰ καὶ ἡμῖν ὡς Ἕλλησιν ἐφεῖταί τι γινώσκειν. Cp. in the same chapter and section the use of the words ὁ μὲν ἡμέτερος as denoting Demosthenes.

Pindar b. 522, d. 448 B.C.

In xxxiii. 5 Pindar is preferred to Bacchylides, in the same way as Sophocles to Ion of Chios. See further under *Bacchylides* and *Sophocles*.

It seems likely that, in a vexed passage of c. xxxv. (οὐδὲ τῶν τῆς Αἴτνης κρατήρων ἀξιοθαυμαστότερον νομίζομεν, ἧς αἱ ἀναχοαὶ πέτρους τε ἐκ βυθοῦ καὶ ὅλους ὄχθους ἀναφέρουσι καὶ ποταμοὺς ἐνίοτε τοῦ γηγενοῦς ἐκείνου καὶ αὐτοῦ μόνου προχέουσιν πυρός, xxxv. 4), we have a reminiscence of *Pyth.* i. 21—24 :—

τᾶς ἐρεύγονται μὲν ἀπλάτου πυρὸς ἁγνόταται
ἐκ μυχῶν παγαί· ποταμοὶ δ᾽ ἁμέραισιν μὲν προχέοντι ῥόον
καπνοῦ
αἴθων᾽· ἀλλ᾽ ἐν ὄρφναισιν πέτρας
φοίνισσα κυλινδομένα φλὸξ ἐς βαθεῖαν φέρει πόντου πλάκα
σὺν πατάγῳ.

Our author would appear to offer us a somewhat bald prose paraphrase of this passage, representing πυρὸς ἁγνόταται ἐκ μυχῶν παγαί by ποταμοὺς γηγενοῦς ἐκείνου καὶ αὐτοῦ μόνου πυρός. The awkward collocation αὐτοῦ μόνου finds, therefore, its explanation in ἁγνόταται, unless indeed we are to suppose that ἀπλάτου or some such word has been changed by the scribes into αὐτοῦ μόνου.

Plato b. 427, d. 347 B.C.

Plato is among the four authors (the other three being Homer, Herodotus, and Demosthenes) who are oftenest quoted in the *De Sublimitate*. These are the citations, the area from which they are selected being—it will be seen—somewhat limited :—

Timaeus	65 C—*De Subl.*	xxxii.	5.
,,	69 D—	,,	,,
,,	72 C—	,,	,,
,,	74 A—	,,	,,
,,	74 B—	,,	,,
,,	74 D—	,,	,,
,,	77 C—	,,	,,
,,	78 E—	,,	,,
,,	80 E—	,,	,,
,,	85 E—	,,	,,
Leges	741 C—	,,	iv. 6.
,,	773 C—	,,	xxxii. 7.
,,	778 D—	,,	iv. 6.

Leges	801 b—*De Subl.* xxix. 1.
Menex.	236 d— „ xxviii. 2.
„	245 d— „ xxiii. 4.
Phaedr.	264 c— „ xxxvi. 2.
Resp.	586 a— „ xiii. 1.
„	573 e— „ xliv. 7[1].

Plato sometimes is at fault (as one or two of these citations are intended to show), but what—asks the author—are his shortcomings when compared with his divine perfections[2]? With the passage of the *Leges* (801 b) should be compared Aristoph. *Plut.* 1191 and in both cases Πλοῦτον should be written with a capital letter. See also Verrall in *Classical Review*, xix. 203. Whatever the view of Caecilius may have been, his contemporary and friend Dionysius of Halicarnassus (*Ep. ad Pomp.* 760 and 765, *De admir. vi dicendi in Demosth.* 966) presents some points of agreement with our author.

Sappho flor. 600 b.c.

Not the least of the debts we owe to two distinguished literary critics of the Roman Empire—Dionysius Halicarnassensis and our author—is that they have transmitted to posterity the two most considerable extant fragments of Sappho's poetry, the one preserving the Ode to Aphrodite

Ποικιλόθρον᾽ ἀθάνατ᾽ Ἀφροδίτα,

the other the Ode to Anactoria as it is traditionally entitled

Φαίνεταί μοι κῆνος ἴσος θεοῖσιν.

The former is quoted (Dionys. Hal., *De Comp. Verb.*, xxiii.) in illustration of the musical structure (so to say) of a perfect poem, —of the subtle harmony in it of words with thoughts. The latter is given (*De Subl.* x. 1, 2) as an example of the choice and grouping of the most striking manifestations of a passion such as that of love. Thus both Dionysius and our author wish to exemplify σύνθεσις, but σύνθεσις in a different sense, in the former case the reference

---

[1] With νεοττοποιεῖται (κατὰ τοὺς σοφούς, i.e. *secundum Platonem*) cp. Pl. *Rep.* (l.c.) ἆρα οὐκ ἀνάγκη τὰς μὲν ἐπιθυμίας βοᾶν πυκνάς τε καὶ σφοδρὰς ἐννενεοττευμένας; ' The passage is imitated by Longinus *de Sublim.* xliv. 7, where a poetical image is converted into a rhetorical figure,' Jowett and Campbell, *Rep.* vol. III. p. 412.

[2] c. xxxvi. 2. Such passages as xiii. 2 and xiv. 1 show clearly the relation in which the author stands to Plato: he is under his spell, or rather under his inspiration.

being more particularly to ὀνόματα, in the latter to ἄκρα λήμματα. The περὶ ὕψους does indeed deal with σύνθεσις as understood by Dionysius, but not till cc. xxxix. ff.

The following passages of Plutarch refer to the same Ode: *Eroticus* 763 A ἀλλ᾽ εἰ μὴ διὰ Λυσάνδραν, ὦ Δαφναῖε, τῶν παλαιῶν ἐκλέλησαι παιδικῶν, ἀνάμνησον ἡμᾶς, ἐν οἷς ἡ καλὴ Σαπφὼ λέγει, τῆς ἐρωμένης ἐπιφανείσης, τήν τε φωνὴν ἴσχεσθαι καὶ φλέγεσθαι τὸ σῶμα, καὶ καταλαμβάνειν ὠχρότητα καὶ πλάνον αὐτὴν καὶ ἴλιγγον. *Vit. Demetr.*

907 B, τῆς δὲ Στρατονίκης καὶ καθ᾽ ἑαυτὴν καὶ μετὰ τοῦ Σελεύκου φοιτώσης πολλάκις ἐγίνετο τὰ τῆς Σαπφοῦς ἐκεῖνα περὶ αὐτὸν πάντα, φωνῆς ἐπίσχεσις, ἐρύθημα πυρῶδες, ὄψεων ὑπολείψεις, ἱδρῶτες ὀξεῖς, ἀταξία καὶ θόρυβος ἐν τοῖς σφυγμοῖς, τέλος δὲ τῆς ψυχῆς κατὰ κράτος ἡττωμένης ἀπορία καὶ θάμβος καὶ ὠχρίασις.

The Ode is imitated by Catullus, li., *Ad Lesbiam* :—

> ille mi par esse deo videtur,
> ille, si fas est, superare divos,
> qui sedens adversus identidem te
> 　　spectat et audit
>
> dulce ridentem, misero quod omnis
> eripit sensus mihi : nam simul te,
> Lesbia, adspexi, nihil est super mi
> 　*　　*　　*　　*　　*
>
> lingua sed torpet, tenuis sub artus
> flamma demanat, sonitu suopte
> tintinant aures, gemina teguntur
> 　　lumina nocte.

There are some reminiscences of the Ode in Lucretius *De Rer. Nat.* iii. 154:—

> sudoresque ita palloremque existere toto
> corpore et infringi linguam vocemque aboriri,
> caligare oculos, sonere auris, succidere artus ;

and in Tennyson's early poems *Eleänore* and *Fatima*. Various English versions will be found in H. T. Wharton's *Sappho* (third edition), pp. 67—69 ; and some interesting matter is presented in F. Meda's tract *L' Ode Sublime di Saffo nelle principali Traduzioni.*

The enthusiasm with which the Italian scholars of the Renaissance heard of the discovery of an Ode of Sappho imbedded in the text of the περὶ ὕψους has had its parallels in our own day. For example, Blass was able to describe (*Rheinisches Museum,* 1880, vol. xxxv.)

some fragments—of Sappho, as he thought—discovered in the Egyptian Museum at Berlin among a number of manuscripts coming probably from the Fayyum. The fragments are too inconsiderable to add much to our knowledge of Sappho and their ascription is so doubtful as to make it safer to class them, with Bergk (*Poetae Lyrici Graeci*[4], III. 704, 5), as 'Fragmenta Adespota.' But the ode recently published as Sappho's by Grenfell and Hunt after Blass's restoration (Grenfell and Hunt, *Oxyrhynchus Papyri*, Part I. 1898) is a discovery of the first importance.

Simonides. Simonides of Ceos : b. 556, d. 468 B.C.

Simonides had, in a poem now lost, depicted with unequalled vividness the apparition of Achilles above the tomb as the Greeks were putting out to sea (c. xv. 7). Cp. Bergk, *Poetae Lyrici Graeci*[4], III. 526.

Sophocles b. 496, d. 406.

Reference is made to the following plays :—

> *Oed. T.* 1403 —*De Subl.* xxiii. 3.
> *Oed. Col.* 1586— „ xv. 7.
> *Polyxena* — „ xv. 7.

For the last-named play, cp. Porphyr. (Stob. *Ecl.* i. c. 41 § 50) ὡς ὁ Σοφοκλῆς ἐν Πολυξένῃ τὴν τοῦ Ἀχιλλέως ψυχὴν εἰσάγει κ.τ.λ., and Dindorf *Aesch. et Soph. Trag. et Fragm.* p. 278 (Didot edition). As to the line quoted from Sophocles in *De Subl.* iii. 2, see under *Aeschylus*, p. 217 supra.

In xxxiii. 5 the *Oedipus* (*Rex*) is mentioned as an unapproachable work of art, a judgment which brings the *De Sublimitate* into line with the *Poetics*. In the same chapter and section it is said of Pindar and Sophocles that ὁτὲ μὲν οἷον πάντα ἐπιφλέγουσι τῇ φορᾷ, σβέννυνται δ' ἀλόγως πολλάκις καὶ πίπτουσιν ἀτυχέστατα. The eulogistic half of this sentence seems perhaps more obviously true of Pindar than of Sophocles. What instances would the author have adduced in support of the latter half? In Pindar he may have taken exception to the elaborate periphrases for somewhat homely things[1]. As regards Sophocles, would he have referred us to the *Antigone*

---

[1] Cp. Galen, *De pulsuum differentia* (as quoted by Weiske) : οὐδ' ἀπὸ τῶν κυρίων, ὡς ἔτυχε, μεταφέρειν ἔξεστιν, οὐδὲ τοῖς ποιηταῖς. ἀλλὰ κἂν Πίνδαρός τις εἴη, ὠκεανοῦ τὰ πέταλα τὰς κρήνας λέγων, οὐκ ἐπαινεῖται, καὶ πολὺ μᾶλλον, ἐπειδὰν ἀψευδεῖ δὲ πρὸς ἄκμονι χαλκεύειν γλῶσσαν.

vv. 904—920, or to some lost and possibly spurious plays? Cp. Plutarch's reference (*De Recta Audiendi Ratione*, 13) to the ἀνωμαλία of Sophocles, and Dionys. Hal. (*De Vett. Script. Cens.* ii. 11) καὶ πολλάκις ἐκ πολλοῦ τοῦ μεγέθους εἰς διάκενον κόμπον ἐκπίπτων, οἷον εἰς ἰδιωτικὴν παντάπασι ταπεινότητα κατέρχεται.

Stesichorus flor. 600 B.C.   Choric poet, of Himera.
Like Archilochus, an imitator of Homer (c. xiii. 3).

Theocritus.   Theocritus of Syracuse : flor. 280 B.C.
Theocritus is spoken of as ἐν τοῖς βουκολικοῖς πλὴν ὀλίγων τῶν ἔξωθεν ἐπιτυχέστατος (c. xxxiii. 4).   But like Apollonius he is not to be classed with Homer.

Theodorus.   Theodorus of Gadara ; rhetorician ; flor. 30 B.C.
Wrote not only on rhetoric, but περὶ ἱστορίας, περὶ πολιτείας, περὶ κοίλης Συρίας.   Susemihl, II. 507—511 ; Blass, 158 ; C. Hammer, *Bericht über die auf die griechischen Rhetoren und späteren Sophisten bezüglichen von Anfang* 1890 *bis Ende* 1893 *erschienenen Schriften,* ad init.
See p. 9 supra.

Theophrastus.   Theophrastus the successor of Aristotle as head of the Peripatetic School, over which he presided from 322 to 287 B.C.
Coupled with Aristotle in c. xxxii. 3 as giving a useful hint with regard to the qualification of metaphors.

Theopompus.   Theopompus the historian ; flor. 350 B.C.
Among his works were Ἑλληνικαὶ ἱστορίαι and Φιλιππικά.
Theopompus is mentioned twice in the course of the περὶ ὕψους. In c. xxxi. he is praised for his employment of a homely but effective expression (ἀναγκοφαγῆσαι), while in c. xliii. we find quoted 'his description of the entry of the Great King into Egypt, beginning with magnificent tents and chariots, ending with bundles of shoe-leather and pickled meats.   The critic [sc. the author of the π. ὕψ.] complains of bathos; but the passage reads like the intentional bathos of satire.' (Murray, *Ancient Greek Literature,* p. 390.)
It may be added that, according to Cicero and Suidas, Isocrates said of his two pupils Theopompus and Ephorus that the former needed the curb, the latter the spur: an antithesis which is echoed in the π. ὕψ. ii. 2.

Thucydides flor. 428 B.C.

An exemplar of the elevated style in history, as in other branches are Homer, Plato, and Demosthenes (c. xiv. 1). Among his characteristics are mentioned: his use of hyperbaton (xxii. 3), of the historic present (xxv.), and of hyperbole (xxxviii. 3). Of the last an illustration is quoted from his History vii. 84, where some slight verbal discrepancies between the text (as we have it) and the quotation should be noted. In the best editions of Thucydides the text runs thus: οἵ τε Πελοποννήσιοι ἐπικαταβάντες.........ἐπίνετό τε ὁμοῦ τῷ πηλῷ ᾑματωμένον καὶ περιμάχητον ἦν τοῖς πολλοῖς.

Timaeus. Timaeus of Tauromenium, the Sicilian historian; flor. 310 B.C. Holm, *History of Greece*, IV. 504 and 511; Susemihl, 563—583.

In c. iv. Timaeus is taxed with frigidity and bombast, and with that censoriousness which (as we know from Diod. Sic. v. 1 and Athen. vi. 103) procured him the sobriquet of Ἐπιτίμαιος. With *De Subl.* iv. 3 (τοῖς δὲ......Ἕρμωνος), cp. Plut. *Nic. Vit.* 1.

Xenophon flor. 400 B.C.

Passages quoted:—

Hellen. iv. 3, 19 (cp. *Ages.* 2, 12)—*De Subl.* xix. 1.		
De Rep. Laced. iii. 5	— ,,	iv. 4.
Cyrop. i. 5, 12	— ,,	xxviii. 3.
,, vii. 1, 37	— ,,	xxv.
Memorab. i. 4, 5	— ,,	xxxii. 5.
,, i. 4, 6	— ,,	xliii. 5.

Faults and excellences alike are illustrated by these citations. In the passage of the *De Rep. Laced.* our manuscripts give τῶν ἐν τοῖς θαλάμοις (not ὀφθαλμοῖς) παρθένων. The form in which the words are quoted in the περὶ ὕψους suggests, of course, a play upon the two senses of κόρη. With the passage of the *Hellenica* cp. Voltaire *Henriade* VI. :—

> François, Anglois, Lorrains, que la fureur assemble,
> Avançoient, combattoient, frappoient, mouroient ensemble.

Zoilus. Zoilus the grammarian; of uncertain date, say 330 B.C. Best known by the epithet Ὁμηρομάστιξ which his assaults on Homer earned him.

Zoilus described the men whom Circe turned into swine as χοιρίδια κλαίοντα (c. ix. 14).

Scriptor Incertus. Under this designation may conveniently be included :—

(1) The τῶν φιλοσόφων τις who in c. xliv. propounds the problem presented by λόγων κοσμική τις ἀφορία. Had this philosopher any existence in fact, was he a writer as well as a speculator, and how are we to account for the coincidence of some of his words with those of Philo? These are questions we would gladly answer if we could.

(2) The author of the line :

ἀγρὸν ἔσχ᾿ ἐλάττω γῆν ἔχοντ᾿ ἐπιστολῆς (c. xxxviii. 5).

Might we hazard the conjecture that this line comes from Menander's Γεωργός, in the recently recovered fragments of which allusion is made to μάλα μικρὸν γῄδιον?

(3) The author of a saying quoted in i. 2. Something similar to this saying is attributed both to Pythagoras and to Demosthenes : cp. Ael. *Var. Hist.* xii. 59, Πυθαγόρας ἔλεγε δύο ταῦτα ἐκ τῶν θεῶν τοῖς ἀνθρώποις δεδόσθαι κάλλιστα, τό τε ἀληθεύειν καὶ τὸ εὐεργετεῖν· καὶ προσετίθει ὅτι καὶ ἔοικε τοῖς θεῶν ἔργοις ἑκάτερον. Arsen. *Viol.* 189, Δημοσθένης ἐρωτηθεὶς τί ἄνθρωπος ἔχει ὅμοιον θεῷ, ἔφη 'τὸ εὐεργετεῖν καὶ ἀληθεύειν.'

(4) The anonymous τεχνογράφοι quoted at the beginning of c. xii., where with αὔξησίς ἐστι, φασί, λόγος μέγεθος περιτιθεὶς τοῖς ὑποκειμένοις should be compared αὔξησίς ἐστι λόγος μεῖζον ποιῶν φαίνεσθαι τὸ πρᾶγμα, μείωσις δὲ λόγος μεῖον ποῖων φαίνεσθαι τὸ πρᾶγμα (Spengel, *Rhetores Graeci*, I. 457).

(5) The author of the line

ἐξῆλθον Ἕκτορές τε καὶ Σαρπήδονες

which is quoted (c. xxiii. 3) in exemplification of ἐναλλάξεις ἀριθμῶν.

(6) The author of the line

ἔστ᾿ ἂν ὕδωρ τε ῥέῃ καὶ δένδρεα μακρὰ τεθήλῃ (c. xxxvi. 2).

Cp. Pl. *Phaedr.* 264 C, καὶ εὑρήσεις τοῦ ἐπιγράμματος οὐδὲν διαφέροντα ὃ Μίδᾳ τῷ Φρυγί φασί τινες ἐπιγεγράφθαι...

χαλκῆ παρθένος εἰμί, Μίδα δ᾿ ἐπὶ σήματι κεῖμαι.
ὄφρ᾿ ἂν ὕδωρ τε νάῃ καὶ δένδρεα μακρὰ τεθήλῃ,
αὐτοῦ τῇδε μένουσα πολυκλαύτου ἐπὶ τύμβου,
ἀγγελέω παριοῦσι Μίδας ὅτι τῇδε τέθαπται.

(7) The author of the words μεγάλων ἀπολισθαίνειν ὅμως εὐγενὲς ἁμάρτημα (c. iii. 3). Cp. Plut. *Crassi Vit.* xxvi. εἰ δεῖ τι καὶ παθεῖν μεγάλων ἐφιεμένους, and Ov. *Metam.* ii. 328, magnis tamen excidit ausis.

(8) The author of the lines

αὐτίκα...λαὸς ἀπείρων

θύννον ἐπ᾽ ἠιόνεσσι διϊστάμενοι κελάδησαν (xxiii. 2).

(9) The author of the words εὐπόριστον μὲν ἀνθρώποις τὸ χρειῶδες ἢ καὶ ἀναγκαῖον, θαυμαστὸν δ᾽ ὅμως ἀεὶ τὸ παράδοξον (xxxv. 5). Possibly, however, the words are original.

(10) The author of the words δεῖ γὰρ αὐτοῖς...χαλινοῦ in ii. 2. Cp. Diog. Laert. v. 39, λέγεται δὲ ἐπ᾽ αὐτοῦ (Θεοφράστου) τε καὶ Καλλισθένους τὸ ὅμοιον εἰπεῖν Ἀριστοτέλην ὅπερ Πλάτωνα...φασὶν εἰπεῖν ἐπί τε Ξενοκράτους καὶ αὐτοῦ τούτου...ὡς τῷ μὲν χαλινοῦ δέοι, τῷ δὲ κέντρου. Suidas, Ἔφορος...ὁ γοῦν Ἰσοκράτης τὸν μὲν (Θεόπομπον) ἔφη χαλινοῦ δεῖσθαι, τὸν δὲ Ἔφορον κέντρου. Cp. p. 242 supra.

(11) The identification of οἱ Ἀττικοὶ ἐκεῖνοι (xxxiv. 2). 'Ἀττικοὺς interpretor illos, qui aetate auctoris et paulo ante docebant Attice dicere; his probabantur praeter ceteros Lysias et Hyperides,' C. Hammer. Others have taken the reference to be to the writers of the Old Attic Comedy. Cp. p. 182 supra.

Auctor. Such particulars with regard to the author himself (and his friend Terentianus) as are supplied by the internal evidence of the treatise will be found on pp. 11—22 supra.

Longinus. As the name of the historical Longinus has for so long a time been traditionally connected with the treatise, a few notes with regard to him and his writings may usefully be appended even in an edition which questions the traditional view :—

I. Life. Born about the year 213 A.D.; died 273 A.D. Attended the classes of the leading Neoplatonists at Alexandria. Taught for some thirty years at Athens, where he seems to have written his books. Famous as 'a living library and a walking museum' (βιβλιοθήκη τις ἦν ἔμψυχος καὶ περιπατοῦν μουσεῖον, Eunapius *Porphyr.*). Summoned by Queen Zenobia to Palmyra, where he instructed her in Greek letters and became her trusted counsellor and friend. Encouraged her in her resistance to Aurelian, who put him to death. [Reference may be made to Pape-Benseler's Dictionary and to the recently published *Prosopographia Imperii Romanii Saec. I. II. III.*; and for fuller particulars, to Ruhnken's dissertation, published under the name of P. J. Schardam, as well as to Cobet's remarks in *Mnemosyne N.S.* VII. 421.]

II. Writings other than the De Sublimitate. These may most conveniently be studied in Vaucher's *Études Critiques.* In *Hermes*, xxx. (year 1895) pp. 300 ff. will be found some discussion of οἱ φιλόλογοι or αἱ φιλόλογοι ὁμιλίαι. In the φιλόλογοι ὁμιλίαι there were clearly points of coincidence with the περὶ ὕψους (cp. Scholia ad Hermog. *de Id.* vi. p. 225 and vii. p. 963), lending some colour to the supposition that here if anywhere in Longinus the περὶ ὕψους must be sought for.

III. De Sublimitate. The chief arguments in favour of the Longinian authorship of the treatise are (*a*) tradition; (*b*) the reputation of the Palmyrene Longinus as ὁ κριτικός, and the nobility of his life and death; (*c*) the pervading influence of Plato in the book. The most recent statement of the conservative position is that by E. Brighentius, *De libelli περὶ ὕψους auctore dissertatio* (Patavii, 1895); and the same position is assumed by J. R. Mozley in Smith's *Dictionary of Christian Biography*, and supported with due reserve by W. D. Geddes in the *Encyclopaedia Britannica.* Reference may also be made to Canna, *Della Sublimità*, pp. 35 ff. ; to Vaucher, *Études Critiques*, pp. 42, 48, 55 ; and to Pessonneaux, *Annales etc.*, pp. 292—4. Edward Gibbon, in his *Journal* (under date September 11th, 1762) has some interesting remarks on the treatise: 'When I reflect on the age in which Longinus lived, an age which produced scarcely any other writer worthy of the attention of posterity; when real learning was almost extinct, philosophy sunk down to the quibbles of grammarians and the tricks of mountebanks, and the empire desolated by every calamity, I am amazed that at such a period, in the heart of Syria, and at the court of an Eastern monarch, Longinus should produce a work worthy of the best and freest days of Athens.'

Though he thus sees one of the difficulties involved, Gibbon did not dispute the traditional ascription, which was as yet unchallenged. He simply gave himself earnestly to the study of the work. On Sept. 12th he writes : 'I finished the first chapter of Longinus, with Boileau's translation and all the notes. The Greek is, from the figurative style and bold metaphors, extremely difficult : I am afraid that it is rather too difficult for me; but now I have entered upon it, *jacta est alea;* and I have nothing to do but to redouble my application to understand him correctly.'

APPENDIX D.

BIBLIOGRAPHICAL. WITH A GLANCE AT THE INFLUENCE
OF THE TREATISE IN MODERN TIMES.

A full bibliography is a necessary adjunct of any modern edition
which aims at completeness, and this is more than ever true when
such a bibliography is likely to throw considerable light upon the
influence and currency of the book edited. The literature which has
gathered round the *De Sublimitate* may conveniently be presented,
in chronological order, under the two headings: I. Editions and
Translations, II. Occasional and Periodical Publications.

I. EDITIONS AND TRANSLATIONS.

XVIth Century.

It is natural that in the sixteenth century Italian scholars should
head the list : they were the best equipped, they had ready access to
Greek manuscripts in the libraries of Italy, and by printing the περὶ
ὕψους they were ministering to that interest in the literary style of the
ancients which had been fostered by the striking growth of their own
national literature, and by the example and precepts of their great
countrymen Dante, Petrarch, and Boccaccio. The *editio princeps*
of the περὶ ὕψους is, therefore, due to an Italian, **F. Robortello.**
It appeared at Basle in 1554. Its title-page is as follows: Διονυσίου
Λογγίνου ῥήτορος περὶ ὕψους βιβλίον. *Dionysii Longini rhetoris
praestantissimi liber de grandi sive sublimi orationis genere. Nunc
primum a Francisco Robortello Utinensi in lucem editus eiusdemque
annotationibus latinis in margine appositis, quae instar commentario-
rum sunt, illustratus. nam ex iis methodus tota libri, et ordo
quaestionum, de quibus agitur, omnisque ratio praeceptionum, et alia
multa cognosci possunt. Basileae, per Ioannem Oporinum.* In his
dedication Robortello again calls attention to the fact that the work
was previously unknown : *opus hoc redivivum, antea ignotum, opera
industriaque sua e tenebris in lucem eductum atque expolitum.*

The second issue followed closely on the first. It was that of
Paulus Manutius, Venice, 1555. Διονυσίου Λογγίνου περὶ
ὕψους λόγον. *Dionysii Longini de sublimi genere dicendi. In quo cum*

alia multa praeclare sunt emendata, tum veterum poetarum versus, qui, confusi commixtique cum oratione soluta, minus intelligentem lectorem fallere poterant, notati atque distincti. Apud Paulum Manutium, Aldi F., Venetiis, 1555. The reference to the inconvenience of printing poetry as prose seems to be suggested by what Robortello had done the year before. There is little doubt that Manutius printed from the Codex Venetus. About Robortello's source there is more uncertainty; most probably it was one of the inferior copies of P 2036, either the Mediolanensis or (possibly) the Cantabrigiensis. A feature in Robortello's edition is his marginal analysis (in Latin), which is designed to serve as a kind of running commentary, and does not preclude an occasional address to the Reader.

The next edition (Geneva, 1569) is that of **F. Portus**, a Cretan, who was Professor of Greek in the University of Geneva. Οἱ ἐν τῇ ῥητορικῇ τέχνῃ κορυφαῖοι Ἀφθώνιος, Ἑρμογένης, Δ. Λόγγινος. *Aphthonius, Hermogenes, et Dionysius Longinus, praestantissimi artis rhetorices magistri, Francisci Porti Cretensis opera industriaque illustrati atque expoliti. Anchora Ioannis Crispi, M.D.LXIX.* The separate title-page of the περὶ ὕψους agrees partly with that of Robortello and partly with that of Manutius.

To the sixteenth century also belongs a Latin translation: *Dionysii Longini De sublimi dicendi genere. Liber a* **P. Pagano** *latinitate donatus. Venetiis,* 1572.

XVIIth Century.

In the seventeenth century appeared the following editions and translations:—

Gabriel de Petra. Διονυσίου Λογγίνου περὶ ὕψους λόγου βιβλίον. *Dionysii Longini rhetoris praestantissimi De grandi sive sublimi genere orationis. Latine redditus, ὑποθέσεσι συνοπτικαῖς et ad oram notationibus aliquot illustratus a Gab. de Petra, Professore Graeco in Academia Lausannensi. Geneva,* 1612.

G. Langbaine. Διονυσίου Λογγίνου ῥήτορος περὶ ὕψους λόγου βιβλίον. *Dionysii Longini rhetoris praestantissimi liber De grandi loquentia sive sublimi dicendi genere Latine redditus......Edendum curavit, et notarum insuper auctarium adjunxit G. L. Oxonii,* 1636.

Anonymous. *Dionysii Longini rhetoris praestantissimi liber de grandi sive sublimi dicendi genere orationis.* A Latin translation forming part of : *Degli autori del ben parlare......opere diverse. Ven.*, 1643.

C. Manolesius. *Dionysii Longini Graeci Rhetoris de sublimi genere dicendi libellus, nunc ultimo accurata ac triplici in Latinum expositione* (*G. de Petra, D. Pizimentii, P. Pagani*) *emissus, et luculenta praelectione illustratus, cura ac diligentia Caroli Manolesii Bibliopolae. Bononiae,* 1644.

John Hall. Περὶ ὕψους, *or Dionysius Longinus of the Height of Eloquence rendred out of the originall by J. H. Esq.   London,* 1652. [The first sentence in Hall's translation runs thus : ' When you and I (my dear Posthumius Terentianus) had together perused (as you remember) Cecilius his book of Height, methought, besides that it was not carried on with a greatnesse proportionate to the subject, it blanched many unnecessary (? necessary) points, and requited not the Reader with that profit which every diligent Writer ought principally to endeavour.']

Tanaquil Faber. *Dionysii Longini philosophi et rhetoris* Περὶ Ὕψους *libellus, cum notis, emendationibus, et praefatione T. Fabri. Salmurii,* 1663.

Boileau. Διονυσίου Λογγίνου περὶ ὕψους βιβλίον. *Traité du sublime ou du merveilleux dans le discours. Traduit du grec de Longin. Paris,* 1674. In the eighteenth century alone this famous volume was reprinted more than a dozen times. The following are only some of the years in which issues of it have appeared : 1674, 1677, 1683, 1685, 1689, 1694, 1695, 1701, 1702, 1714, 1716, 1718, 1729, 1740, 1746, 1747, 1768, 1772, etc.

J. Pulteney. *A Treatise of the Loftiness or Elegancy of Speech. Written originally in Greek by Longin ; and now translated out of French by Mr J. P. London,* 1680.

J. Toll. Διονυσίου Λογγίνου Περὶ Ὕψους καὶ τἄλλα εὑρισκόμενα. *Dionysii Longini De Sublimitate commentarius, ceteraque quae reperiri potuere......Jacobus Tollius e quinque codicibus MSS. emendavit, et F. Robortelli, F. Porti, G. de Petra, G. Langbaenii et T. Fabri notis integris suas subjecit, novamque versionem suam Latinam, et Gallicam Boilavii, cum ejusdem, ac Dacierii, suisque notis Gallicis addidit. Trajecti ad Rhenum,* 1694.

Anonymous. *An Essay upon Sublime. Translated from the Greek of Dionysius Longinus Cassius the Rhetorician. Compared with the French of the Sieur Despréaux Boileau. Oxford,* 1698.

XVIIIth Century.

J. Hudson. Διονυσίου Λογγίνου Περὶ ῞Υψους Βιβλίον. *Dionysii Longini De Sublimitate libellus, cum praefatione de vita et scriptis Longini, notis, indicibus, et variis lectionibus.* Oxoniae, 1710.

Welsted. *The Works of Dionysius Longinus on the Sublime: or, a treatise concerning the sovereign perfection of writing. Translated from the Greek, with some remarks on the English Poets, by Mr Welsted.* London, 1712.

P. Le Clercq. *D. Longinus: Verhandeling over de Verheventheit en Deftigheit des Styls......In het Nederduitsch vertaalt door P. Le Clercq.* Te Amsteldam, 1719.

Z. Pearce. Διονυσίου Λογγίνου Περὶ ῞Υψους ῾Υπόμνημα. *Dionysii Longini De Sublimitate commentarius, quem nova versione donavit, perpetuis notis illustravit, plurimisque in locis......emendavit, additis etiam omnibus ejusdem auctoris fragmentis, Z. Pearce.* Londini, 1724. A beautiful Foulis edition of this work of Pearce was published, at Glasgow, in 1751: Τὸ τοῦ Διονυσίου Λογγίνου περὶ ὕψους ὑπόμνημα. *Ex editione tertia Zachariae Pearce, Episcopi Bangoriensis, expressum.*

Hudson. Gori. Boileau. Διονυσίου Λογγίνου περὶ ὕψους βιβλίον ῾Ελληνιστὶ συγγραφθὲν, εἰς ῾Ρωμαϊκὴν, ᾽Ιταλικὴν, καὶ Γαλλικὴν φωνὴν μεταφρασθὲν, σὺν σχολίοις. *Dionysii Longini de Sublimi libellus Graece conscriptus; Latino, Italico, et Gallico sermone redditus, additis adnotationibus.* Veronae, 1733. The Latin version is by Hudson, the Italian by Gori, the French by Boileau.

Portus. Wetstein. Διονυσίου Λογγίνου Περὶ ῞Υψους ῾Υπόμνημα. *Dionysii Longini De Sublimitate commentarius, quem nova versione donavit, perpetuis notis illustravit, et......emendavit...... Z. Pearce......Editio tertia. Accessit F. Porti Cretensis in Longinum commentarius integer, nunc primum editus [by H. Wetstein].* Amstelaedami, 1733.

A. F. Gori. *Trattato del Sublime di Dionisio Longino. Tradotto dal Greco in Toscano da A. F. Gori.* Firenze, 1737. [Other issues of Gori have been: *Terza edizione, di note accresciuta.* Bologna, 1748.—*L' Aureo Trattato di Dionisio Longino intorno al Sublime Modo di Parlare e di Scrivere. Tradotto dal Greco da A. F. Gori.* Venezia, 1782.—*Di Dionisio Longino Trattato del Sublime. Tradotto*

...*da A. F. Gori. Con note antiche e nuove. Bologna,* 1821.—This Italian translation, like the French version of Boileau, has in fact been reprinted again and again. The same is true of the English rendering which follows next on the list, that of W. Smith.]

W. Smith. *Dionysius Longinus On the Sublime. Translated from the Greek with notes and observations, and some account of the life, writings and character of the author, by W. Smith. London,* 1739.

S. F. N. Morus. *Dionysius Longinus De Sublimitate ex recensione Z. Pearcii. Animadversiones interpretum excerpsit, suas et novam versionem adjecit S. F. N. Morus. Lipsiae,* 1769.

Oliveira. *Dionysio Longino Tratado do Sublime. Traduzido da Lingua Grega na Portugueza por Custodio José de Oliveira. Lisboa,* 1771.

J. Toup. *Dionysii Longini quae supersunt, Graece et Latine. Recensuit, notasque suas atque animadversiones adjecit Johannes Toupius. Accedunt emendationes Davidis Ruhnkenii. Oxonii, e Typographeo Clarendoniano:* 1778. This volume contains also the *Dissertatio Philologica de Vita et Scriptis Longini* which was written by **Ruhnken,** but issued under the name of P. J. Schardam.

J. G. Schlosser. *Longin vom Erhabenen. Mit Anmerkungen und einem Anhang von J. G. Schlosser. Leipzig,* 1781. A German translation with some notes and an appendix.

Bodoni. Διοννσίου Λογγίνου περὶ Ὕψους. *Parmae in aedibus Palatinis. Typis Bodonianis.* 1793. This is a beautifully printed and most sumptuous edition, with Greek text and Latin translation.

XIXth Century.

B. Weiske. *Dionysii Longini De Sublimitate, Graece et Latine. Denuo recensuit et animadversionibus virorum doctorum aliisque subsidiis instruxit B. Weiske. Lipsiae,* 1809.—In the English edition published in 1820 the most important part of this book—the contribution made by **Amati** to the elucidation of the problem of the authorship—is omitted.

Filinto Elysio (pseudonym of **Francisco Manoel do Nascimento**). *Obras Completas de Filinto Elysio. Tomo XI°, pp.* 298—387, *Tratado do Sublime de Longino : traduzido. Paris,* 1819.

G. Miller. Διονυσίου Λογγίνου περὶ ὕψους. *Dionysii Longini de Sublimitate commentarius.* Dublin, 1820 (*second edition*).

Anonymous. *A Literal Translation of Longinus on the Sublime. By a Graduate of Trinity College, Dublin.* Dublin, 1821.

Kowalewski. *Longina o Górności: przekładał z Greckiego Jozef Kowalewski. w Wilnie,* 1823.

Anonymous. *Longinus on the Sublime. A new translation, chiefly according to the improved edition of Weiske......By a Master of Arts of the University of Oxford.* London, 1830.

W. T. Spurdens. *Longinus on the Sublime in Writing. Translated with notes, original and selected, and three dissertations.* London, 1836.

D. B. Hickie. *Dionysius Longinus on the Sublime: chiefly from the text of Weiske.* London, 1838.

A. E. Egger. *Longini quae supersunt. Graece. Post edit. Lipsiensem a. MDCCCIX aucta et emendata. Parisiis,* 1837.

L. Spengel. *Rhetores Graeci. Lipsiae,* 1853. Contains the text of the Περὶ Ὕψους in the same volume (vol. 1.) as Aristotle's *Rhetoric.*

G. M. A. Pujol. *Traité du Sublime de Longin. Traduction nouvelle avec le texte grec en regard et des notes. Toulouse,* 1853.

L. Vaucher. *Études critiques sur le Traité du Sublime et sur les écrits de Longin. Genève,* 1854.

Otto Jahn. Διονυσίου ἢ Λογγίνου περὶ Ὕψους. *De Sublimitate libellus. In usum scholarum edidit O. Iahn. Bonnae,* 1867.

T. R. R. Stebbing. *Longinus on the Sublime. Oxford,* 1867. A translation with occasional notes.

H. A. Giles. *Longinus. An Essay on the Sublime. Translated by H. A. Giles. London,* 1870.

G. Canna. *Della Sublimità: libro attribuito a Cassio Longino. Tradotto da Giovanni Canna. Firenze,* 1871.

M. J. Moreno. *Tratado de la Sublimidad traducido fielmente del Griego de Dionisio Casio Longino: con notas históricas, críticas y biográficas, y con ejemplos sublimes Castellanos comparados con los Griegos citados por Longino. Sevilla,* 1882.

J. Vahlen. Διονυσίου ἢ Λογγίνου περὶ ὕψους: *edidit Otto Iahn a. MDCCCLXVII: iterum edidit a. MDCCCLXXXVII Ioannes Vahlen. Bonnae.*

Henry Morley. *Longinus on the Sublime. With an introduction by H. Morley.* 1889. Cassell's National Library, vol. 179.

H. L. Havell. *Longinus on the Sublime: translated into English. With an introduction by* **Andrew Lang.** *London,* 1890.

E. Janzon. *De Sublimitate Libellus in patrium sermonem conversus adnotationibusque instructus. Upsaliae,* 1894.

C. Hammer. *Rhetores Graeci ex recognitione Leonardi Spengel. Vol. I. pars II. Edidit C. Hammer. Lipsiae,* 1894.

G. Meinel. *Dionysios oder Longinos, Ueber das Erhabene. Uebersetzt und mit kritischen und exegetischen Bemerkungen versehen von G. Meinel. Kempten,* 1895.

In addition to the above editions and translations, the present editor has had the advantage of consulting, in the Library of the British Museum, MS. notes by **Isaac Casaubon** (in a copy of Robortello's edition, 1554), by **Richard Bentley** (in F. Portus' edition, 1569: Bentley mentions on the title-page that he had collated this edition with Robortello's and also with 'codice M^sto quem commodavit Joh. Moore Episc. Norvicensis,' the manuscript he thus refers to being without doubt the Eliensis: further on, in the margin ad loc., Bentley enters his own well-known emendation— 'leg. ἀπαστράπτει'), by **A. Dacier** (in the Greek-and-French edition of Boileau, 1694), and by **Charles Burney** (in the editions of Pearce 1752, of Morus 1769, and of Toup 1778).

II. Occasional and Periodical Publications.

XVIIIth Century.

Jean Boivin de Villeneuve. *Remarques sur Longin: par Monsieur Boivin, Garde de la Bibliothèque du Roy. Paris,* 1700.

Schurzfleisch. *C. S. Schurzfleischii animadversiones ad Dionysii Longini* Περὶ Ὕψους *commentationem. Vitembergae,* 1711.

Berger. *J. G. Bergeri de naturali pulchritudine orationis ad excelsam Longini disciplinam......commentarius. Lipsiae,* 1720.

Perrault. *Réponse aux réflexions critiques de Mr. Despréaux sur Longin. Par M. Perrault. Vol. I. pp.* 471—516 *of Mélanges curieux des meilleures pièces attribuées à Mr. de Saint-Evremond, et de quelques autres ouvrages rares ou nouveaux.* Amsterdam, 1726.

J. Holmes. *The Art of Rhetoric made easy: or, the Elements of Oratory. Being the substance of Dionysius Longinus's celebrated Treatise of the Sublime wrote in Greek about the year of Christ* 278. *With proper examples, ancient and modern.* London, 1739.

E. B. Greene. *Critical Essays :* the first of which is *Observations on the Sublime of Longinus with Examples of Modern Writers as of the Holy Scriptures to illustrate the several Figures remarked throughout the Work.* London, 1770.

R. Robinson. *Indices…vocum fere omnium quae occurrunt in Dionysii Longini commentario De Sublimitate, etc.* Oxonii, 1772.

P. J. Schardam. *Dissertatio philologica de vita et scriptis Longini.* (See p. 251 supra.)

XIXth Century.

Boissonade. Article **Longin** in *Biographie Universelle* XXIV. pp. 666—670 (year 1819).

Knox. *Remarks on the supposed Dionysius Longinus; with an attempt to restore the Treatise on Sublimity to its original state.* London, 1826.

Anonymous. *The Greek Philosophy of Taste. Edinburgh Review,* September, 1831. *Vol.* LIV. *pp.* 39—69.

J. Spongberg. *De Commentario Dionysii Casii Longini* περὶ ὕψους *expositio. Upsaliae,* 1833.

J. Naudet. *Longini quae supersunt, etc.* in *Journal des Savants,* Mars 1838, pp. 147—154.

G. Roeper. *Zur Bestimmung der Abfassungszeit der Schrift* Περὶ Ὕψους in *Philologus,* 1846, I. pp. 630, 631.

G. Buchenau. *De Scriptore Libri* Περὶ Ὕψους. *Marburgi Cattorum,* 1849.

A. E. Egger. *Longin est-il véritablement l'auteur du Traité du Sublime ?* In the first edition of Egger's *Essai sur l'histoire de la critique chez les Grecs* (*Paris,* 1849), *pp.* 524—533.

S. A. Cumanudes. *Specimen Emendationum in Longinum Apsinem Menandrum Aristidem aliosque artium scriptores. Athenis,* 1854.

L. Kayser. *Neue Jahrbücher für Philologie und Pädagogik,* 1854, LXX. pp. 271—296. 'L. Spengel: Rhetores Graeci. Vol. I.'

Nolte. *Zeitschrift für die Alterthumswissenschaft,* 1854, pp. 302—4, 447—8, 464.

Schück. *Commentarii περὶ ὕψους argumentum.* Breslau, 1855.

L. B. des Francs. *Utrum Dionysio Longino adscribendus sit liber qui* Περὶ Ὕψους *inscribitur.* Gratianopoli, 1862.

Aem. Winkler. *De Longini qui fertur libello* Περὶ Ὕψους. Halis, 1870.

M. Haupt. *Ind. lect. in Univ. Litt. Frid. Guil. habend.* Berolini, 1870. Reprinted in Haupt's *Opuscula,* II. pp. 428—433.

M. Schmidt. *Rheinisches Museum N. F.,* 1872, XXVII. pp. 481 —483. 'Eine Dekade Conjekturen.'

H. von Rohden. *Quas rationes in hiatu vitando scriptor de Sublimitate et Onesander secuti sint.* Forming a part of *Commentationes in honorem Francisci Buecheleri Hermanni Useneri.* Bonnae, 1873.

Ulrich von Wilamowitz-Möllendorff. *Hermes,* 1876, X. pp. 334—346. 'In libellum Περὶ Ὕψους coniectanea.'

L. Martens. *De libello* Περὶ Ὕψους, Bonnae, 1877.

H. Diels. *Hermes,* 1878, XIII. pp. 5, 6, 'Atacta.'

A. Reifferscheid. *Ind. Schol. in Univ. Litt. Vratisl. habend.,* Vrat., 1879.

A. Jannarakis. Εἰς τὸ Περὶ Ὕψους λεγόμενον βιβλίον Κριτικαὶ Σημειώσεις. Marburgi Cattorum, 1880.

J. Vahlen. *Ind. lect. in Univ. Litt. Frid. Guil. habend.* Berolini, 1880.

Erwin Rohde. *Rheinisches Museum N. F.,* 1880, XXXV. pp. 309—312. 'Zu der Schrift Περὶ Ὕψους.'

M. Hertz. *Ind. lect. in Univ. Litt. Vratislav. habend.* Vrat., 1881.

C. G. Cobet. *Mnemosyne N. S.,* 1882, X. pp. 319—323, 'De locis nonnullis apud Longinum περὶ ὕψους.'

R. Pessonneaux. *Annales de la Faculté des Lettres de Bordeaux*, 1883, v. pp. 291—303. 'De l'auteur du Traité du Sublime.'

H. Hersel. *Qua in citandis scriptorum et poetarum locis auctor libelli* Περὶ Ὕψους *usus sit ratione.* Berlin, 1884.

F. Buecheler. *Rheinisches Museum N. F.*, 1884, XXXIX. pp. 274, 5. 'Coniectanea.'

A. E. Egger. *Journal des Savants*, 1884, pp. 246—257. 'Publications Récentes sur Plutarque.'

M. Rothstein. *Hermes*, 1887, XXII. pp. 535—546. 'In libellum de Sublimitate coniectanea critica.'

J. B. Bury. *Classical Review*, 1887, I, pp. 300—302. 'Dionysios or Longinos on Sublimity of Style.'

B. Coblentz. *De libelli* Περὶ Ὕψους *auctore.* Argentorati, 1888.

M. Rothstein. *Hermes*, 1888, XXIII. pp. 1—20. 'Caecilius von Kalakte und die Schrift vom Erhabenen.'

T. Hultzsch. *Jahrbücher für Classische Philologie*, 1890, CXLI. pp. 369, 370. 'Zum Anonymus Περὶ Ὕψους.'

O. Immisch. *Rheinisches Museum N. F.*, 1893, XLVIII. pp. 512 —528. 'Ein sophokleischer Vers und das Urtheil über Klitarchs Stil in der Schrift vom Erhabenen.'

E. Brighentius. *De libelli* Περὶ Ὕψους *auctore dissertatio.* Patavii, 1895.

F. Nicolini. *Adnotationes in Longini* Περὶ Ὕψους *libellum.* Catinae, 1896.

Robinson Ellis. *Hermathena*, 1896, XXII. pp. 385—388. 'Notes on Longinus Περὶ Ὕψους.'

J. Freytag. *De Anonymi* Περὶ Ὕψους *sublimi genere dicendi.* Hildesheim, 1897.

W. Schmid. *Rheinisches Museum N. F.*, 1897, LII. p. 446. 'Zwei Vermuthungen zu der Schrift Περὶ Ὕψους.'

J. C. Vollgraff. *Mnemosyne N. S.*, 1898, XXVII. pp. 123, 124. 'Μωϋσῆς ὁ προφήτης καὶ νομοθέτης.'

T. G. Tucker. *Classical Review*, 1898, XII. pp. 23—27. 'Various Emendations.'

To this list may be added the following articles by the present editor :—

American Journal of Philology, 1897, vol. XVIII. 3, pp. 302 —312. 'Caecilius of Calacte : a contribution to the history of Greek Literary Criticism.'

Journal of Hellenic Studies, 1897, vol. XVII. Part 1, pp. 176 —188. 'The Greek Treatise on the Sublime : its Modern Interest.'

Journal of Hellenic Studies, 1897, vol. XVII. Part 2, pp. 189 —211. 'The Greek Treatise on the Sublime : its Authorship.'

Classical Review, 1897, vol. XI. pp. 431—436. 'The Quotation from *Genesis* in the *De Sublimitate*.'

Classical Review, 1898, vol. XII. pp. 299—301. 'Note on a Cambridge Manuscript of the *De Sublimitate*.'

Classical Review, 1899, vol. XIII. pp. 12—14. 'The Text of the *De Sublimitate*.'

Besides the above editions and other publications, all of which have been consulted during the preparation of this edition, there are other writings (chiefly translations) connected with the Περὶ Ὕψους which have not been accessible. Of these the authors' names in chronological order are : Tanneguy le Fèvre (Saumur, 1633); Pinelli (Patavii, 1639); Heineken (Dresdae, 1737); Valderrabano (Madrid, 1770); Henke (Halis Saxonum, 1774); Lancelot (Ratisbonne, 1775); G. Winter (Lipsiae, 1789); Blanti (1802); Glyky (Venice, 1805); Fiocchi (Vigeblani, 1812); Siegenbeck (Leyden, 1819); Accio (Mediolani, 1830); Tipaldo (Venice, 1834). The translation by Glyky is in Modern Greek ; and there is also said to be a Russian version. Egger (*Histoire de la Critique chez les Grecs*[3], p. 432) tells us that he knows of two unpublished French renderings. Another translation never published is that of Andrew Dudith made as early as 1570.

If proof were needed of the vogue and popularity of the treatise, it would be found in the fact that it has been translated into as many as twelve languages,—into Latin, Italian, French, Spanish, Portuguese, English, German, Dutch, Swedish, Polish, Russian, and Modern Greek. In some of these languages there exist several versions, of which some have been reprinted time after time.

Of Italy it has been said that 'before the end of the sixteenth century Greek had almost ceased to be studied there....All that was virile in humanism fled beyond the Alps[1].' But to the Περὶ Ὕψους, a work of literary criticism addressed to a Roman, the tribute of repeated translation has been paid by Italy, itself the birthplace of modern literary criticism. The latest Italian version is the excellent one in which Canna shows that the proverb 'traduttore traditore' does not always hold good. In Spain, which may be coupled with Italy, there is the even more recent version of Moreno, not to mention previous translations into Portuguese[2].

In France the great popularity of Boileau's translation made the treatise generally known. But it may be doubted whether the work has not suffered somewhat from its close association with the name of Boileau. Boileau's outlook was not a wide one. Neither as a scholar nor as a man of letters could he do full justice to the *De Sublimitate*, and it was as unfortunate as it was unjust that the treatise should come in any way to be identified with the formal and absolute in literature. One of its most marked characteristics is its exaltation of the freedom of the spirit. To this it owes a freshness which belongs exclusively neither to the 'Ancients' nor to the 'Moderns' but is perennial. In France Boileau's version still holds its ground, and it is possible that its prestige has discouraged attempts to produce a more exact translation. Be the reason what it may, France has during the present century contributed less to the elucidation of the treatise than might have been expected from a country of her literary gifts and scholarly tastes[3].

---

[1] J. A. Symonds, *Renaissance in Italy*, II. 543 (First Edition).

[2] An account of the leading features of the treatise has lately been given, from the Spanish standpoint, by Menéndez y Pelayo, *Historia de las Ideas Estéticas en España*, pp. 90—101 (edition of 1883).

[3] The translation of the treatise by Boileau, and remarks and reflexions by himself and other writers, will be found in vols. III. and IV. of M. de Saint-Marc's edition of the *Œuvres de M. Boileau Despréaux*.—Boileau's own *Esthétique* is characterised by M. Ferdinand Brunetière in the *Revue des Deux Mondes*, June 1889, pp. 662—685. Reference may also be made to the same writer's *L'Évolution des Genres dans l'histoire de la littérature*, cc. iii. and iv.—A suggestive comparison between the *Rhetoric* of Aristotle and the *De Sublimitate* is drawn by Fénelon in his *Premier Dialogue sur l'Éloquence*: 'Cette *Rhétorique*, quoique très belle, a beaucoup de préceptes secs et plus curieux qu'utiles dans la pratique ; ainsi elle sert bien plus à faire remarquer les règles de l'art à ceux qui sont déjà éloquents, qu'à inspirer l'éloquence et à former de vrais orateurs : mais le *Sublime* de Longin joint aux préceptes beaucoup d'exemples qui les rendent sensibles. Cet auteur traite le sublime d'une manière sublime, comme le traducteur (sc. Boileau) l'a

Germany, though late in the field, has (through its scholars) devoted much attention to the treatise. This is more particularly true of the latter half of the present century: in the earlier half less was accomplished. In the scientific treatment of the Greek text of the *De Sublimitate* German scholarship easily holds the foremost place; no other country has approached it. But it is worthy of note that translations of the book have been far rarer in Germany than in Italy, France, or England. The more or less professional interest taken in it by scholars does not seem to have been shared by a wider circle; and this indifference has not been without its ill effects upon scholars themselves, who have been apt to forget that the subject has its literary as well as its scientific side. In fact, it may perhaps be regarded as a weakness in Germany generally that interest in literature as literature, in style as style, is not more widely diffused. This may be partly explained by the fact that literary criticism has in Germany—the country where literature arrived late, during a period of reflexion and reason, and among a speculative people—been always intimately allied with philosophical criticism. So much is this the case that German scholars of the first rank (Theodor Mommsen being a conspicuous exception) have found it difficult to forgive the *De Sublimitate* because it is less philosophical than literary. And when a German scholar comes to treat of the attitude of the ancients in general towards literature, it is natural for him to write a *Geschichte der Theorie der Kunst bei den Alten*, whereas a French scholar, covering practically the same field, will entitle his book an *Essai sur l'histoire de la critique chez les Grecs*[1]. Even Schiller, if he produces a tract on the Sublime (his *Ueber das Erhabene*), casts it in a philosophical mould. When Edmund Burke, as a young man, issues his *Philosophical Inquiry into the Origin of our Ideas of the Sublime and Beautiful*, Lessing proposes to translate it into German[2]. And into German it

---

remarqué; il échauffe l'imagination, il élève l'esprit du lecteur, il lui forme le goût, et lui apprend à distinguer judicieusement le bien et le mal dans les orateurs célèbres de l'antiquité.'—What Fénelon says as to the inspiring nature of the book may be illustrated by the experience of Charles James Fox: 'I once heard him say that he was so idle at Eton that he verily believes he should have made but little comparative progress in the Greek language, had it not been for the intense pleasure he received on his first taking up Longinus,' C. C. Colton, *Lacon*, 11. 88.

[1] Eduard Müller and Émile Egger respectively.

[2] Émile Grucker, *Histoire des doctrines littéraires et esthétiques en Allemagne.* Vol. 11.: *Lessing*, p. 159.

is duly translated, though not by Lessing himself[1]. It is more than possible that England has lost by her neglect of *aesthetic* since Burke's time, but it is also quite possible that Germany might gain by paying more attention to the precepts, empirical though the study may be termed, of literary criticism in the narrower sense[2].

Burke's *Sublime and Beautiful* has no manner of connexion with the *De Sublimitate*, if indeed it contains a single reference to it. But its title has added to the confusion which already attended the use of the term *sublime* as an English representative of a Latin original. It is remarkable that Macaulay, in one of his earlier essays, should seem to base an attack upon a quibble of this kind. 'From Longinus we learn only that sublimity means height or elevation (ἀκρότης καὶ ἐξοχή τις λόγων ἐστὶ τὰ ὕψη). This name, so commodiously vague, is applied indifferently to the noble prayer of Ajax in the *Iliad*, and to a passage of Plato about the human body, as full of conceits as an ode of Cowley. Having no fixed standard, Longinus is right only by accident. He is rather a fancier than a critic[3].' But Macaulay was hard to satisfy. In the same essay he dismisses the plays of Euripides as 'inexhaustible mines of commonplaces,' a hasty judgment which he lived to repent[4]. And if he gives no quarter to Longinus, neither does he give any to Edmund Burke or Dugald Stewart. 'The origin of the sublime is one of the most curious and interesting subjects of inquiry that can occupy the attention of a critic. In our own country it has been discussed with great ability, and I think with very little success, by Burke and Dugald Stewart[5].'

By a singular coincidence of dates, the first critical treatise in the English language (Wilson's *Art of Rhetoric*) was published in 1553, a year before the reappearance (through Robortello's edition) of the last great work of literary criticism bequeathed to the modern world by Greek antiquity. Traces of the influence of the *De Sublimitate* are thus not to be expected in Wilson's book, but they are absent also from the works of the later Elizabethan critics, such as Sidney,

---

[1] A German translation appeared in 1773. The *Laocoon* was published in 1766, nine or ten years after Burke's treatise.

[2] In England the province of aesthetic has lately been occupied by Bosanquet's *History of Æsthetic* and Knight's *Philosophy of the Beautiful*, while contributions have been made to the history of literary criticism in J. Churton Collins' *Study of English Literature*, C. E. Vaughan's *English Literary Criticism*, and W. B. Worsfold's *Principles of Criticism*.

[3] *Works of Lord Macaulay*, VII. p. 662.   [4] *Ibid.* p. 661.   [5] *Ibid.* p. 662.

Webbe, and Puttenham. Nor does any mention of the Greek treatise occur in Ben Jonson's *Discoveries*.

The *De Sublimitate* was, however, edited by an Englishman as early as the year 1636; and it was translated into English in 1652, some twenty years before Boileau's version appeared in France[1]. This last point is important because it is often assumed that the *De Sublimitate* came to England by way of France. It is true, however, that in England, as well as in France, the influence of Boileau did much to popularise the treatise. Both the translator and the translated find a place in Pope's capacious gallery of critics, which includes Aristotle, Horace, Dionysius, Petronius, Quintilian, Longinus, Erasmus, Vida, Boileau. The days of Boileau and of Pope were the great days of the treatise. It was honoured, strangely enough, at a time and amid influences which might have seemed alien to its spirit. In our own century it has fallen upon days of neglect, in England no less than in France. To Pope and Boileau we must therefore revert for a worthy epilogue. It was the preface to Boileau's translation that suggested the last line in Pope's well-known tribute to Longinus:—

> Thee, bold Longinus! all the Nine inspire,
> And bless their critic with a poet's fire.
> An ardent judge, who zealous in his trust,
> With warmth gives sentence, yet is always just:
> Whose own example strengthens all his laws;
> And is himself that great sublime he draws.

Pope had in his mind the historical Longinus of the third century; but whatever the right view as to the authorship may be, the eulogy pronounced in the concluding words will not be considered extravagant if the term 'sublime' be understood to indicate that elevation which distinguishes the treatise (and its author) from its first page to its last.

---

[1] Milton, it need hardly be explained, used the Greek original. Towards the end of his *Tractate of Education* (first published in 1644) he has the following passage: 'And now lastly will be the time to read with them those organic arts which enable men to discourse and write perspicuously, elegantly, and according to the fitted style of lofty, mean, or lowly. Logic, therefore, so much as is useful, is to be referred to this due place with all her well-couched heads and topics, until it be time to open her contracted palm into a graceful and ornate rhetoric, taught out of the rule of Plato, Aristotle, Phalereus, Cicero, Hermogenes, Longinus.'

INDICES

See note as to Appendices and Indices on p. 163 supra.

I. INDEX RERUM

Accumulation of figures xx
Adjuration xvi
Alexandria 13, 21, 26
Amplification xi, xii
Analysis of contents 24 ff., 211—215
Apostrophe xvi. 2. Cp. p. 195
Aristotle's Poetics 30
Ars Poetica 215
Art and Nature ii, xxii. 1, xxxvi. 4
Asiatic rhetoric 186, 227
Asyndeton xix
Atticism 186, 227
Author, character and writings of 22 ff., 237
Authors quoted or named in the treatise 216 ff.
Authorship 1—23, 189—192, 245, 246, passim

Bibliography 247 ff.
Bombast iii
Bookishness iv. Cp. p. 34

Caecilius, relation of the author to 7, 220 ff.
Catholicity of the author 8, 26, 30, 216
Choice of words xxx
Climax xxiii. 1. Cp. p. 202
Codex Eliensis 164
Codex Parisinus 165 ff.
Comparative method in literary criticism 28 ff.
Composition xxxix

Conjunctions xxi
'Correctness' xxxiii, xxxvi. Cp. p. 28

Decline of Eloquence xliv. Cp. pp. 13, 14
Dialogus (of Tacitus) 15, 16
Diatyposis xx. 1. Cp. p. 197
Discoveries, recent classical—
    Bacchylides 219
    Euripides 225
    Hyperides 229
    Sappho 241

Editio princeps 1, 247
English study of the treatise 35, 249 ff., 260, 261

Familiar language xxxi
Figures xvi—xxix
French study of the treatise 31, 35, 168, 249 ff., 258
Frigidity iii
Future, bar of xiv

Gaps in the treatise 17, 166, 215
Genesis, quotation from 8, 231—237
German study of the treatise 35, 167, 168, 251 ff., 259, 260
'Grand style' 32
Great models, imitation of xiii, xiv

Hebrew affinities of the treatise 8, 12, 22, 31, 236, 237

Hyperbaton xxii
Hyperbole xxxviii

Imagery xv
Internationalism in literature 29 ff.,
247 ff.
Italian study of the treatise 3, 36, 164,
167, 247, 257, 258

Latin affinities of the treatise 10, 11,
14, 188
Literary criticism—
defined or described vi
exemplified in the treatise 26 ff.
Literature and art 13
Literature and life 34
Longinus, the historical 35, 245

Manuscripts 163 ff.
Metaphors xxxii

Novelty in expression iii
Number, singular and plural xxiii, xxiv

Passion viii. Cp. p. 204
Past, tribunal of xiv
Periphrasis xxviii, xxix
Persons, grammatical xxvi, xxvii
Plagiarism xiii. 4. Cp. p. 202
Platonic influence in the treatise 30,
187, 192

Puerility iii

Question and answer, rhetorical use of
xviii
Quotations, unidentified 244, 245

Rhythms xxxix. 4, xli. Cp. pp. 183,
184

Similes and comparisons xxxvii
Sources of the sublime viii
Spanish study of the treatise 35, 252
Standard of taste vii. 3, 4. Cp. pp. 28,
36
Stoicism 13, 36, 198
Style 25, 26, 32, 33, 34
'Sublimity' 23, 31, 32, 209, 210
Swedish study of the treatise 19, 36,
210, 253, 254

Tenses xxv
Text of the treatise 163 ff.
Titles in the manuscripts 3, 4. Cp.
the facsimiles
Tumidity iii

Vogue of the treatise 1, 35, 247 ff.

Words occurring only in this treatise
189
Worth of the treatise 36, 37

II. INDEX NOMINUM

The thick Arabic numerals refer to a special treatment of the name in question.

Achilles 88
Addison 1
Aelian 244
Aeschines 175
Aeschylus **217**
Actna 134. Cp. p. 238
Agathocles 52
Ahrens 173
Ajax 26, 60, 64
Alexander 50, 60
Alexandria 21, 27
Aloadae 58
Amati 3, 251
Ammonius 8, **217**
Amphicrates **217**
Amsel 183
Anacreon **217**
Antoninus 198
Apollonius Rhodius **218**
Aratus 27, **218**
Archagathus 220
Archilochus **218**
Arimaspi 218
Aristarchus 9
Aristeas **218**
Aristeides 14, 186
Aristophanes **219**
Aristotle 30, 32, 37, 194, 198 ff., **219**, 258 n. 3
Aristoxenus 184
Arnold, E. V., *Preface*
Arnold, Matthew, *Preface*, 33, 177
Arrian 215
Athenaeus 220, 231
Athenogenes 132, 229
Attici 130, 182, 245
Aurelian 245

Bacchylides 36, **219**
Bacon 183
Baudat 206, 226

Bayeux 204
Bentley 175, 253
Berger 253
Bergk 173, 218, 241
Bertrand 13
Blanti 257
Blass 17, 186, 208, 220
Boccaccio 247
Bodoni 251
Boileau 1, 210, 233, 249, 258
Boissonade 254
Boivin 168, 253
Bosanquet 260
Brandstaetter 206
Brighentius 246, 256
Brunetière 28, 258
Brzoska 13, 222
Bücheler 256
Buchenau 254
Burckhardt 222
Burke 32, 210, 224, 259, 260
Burkitt 237
Burney 253
Burns 33
Bury 176, 222, 256
Butcher 200, 208, 224

Caccialanza 222
Caecilius 7, 186, 209, **220**
Callisthenes **222**
Campbell, Lewis 239
Canna 252, 258
Caracalla 11
Carlyle 190
Casaubon 253
Cassandra 86
Catullus 240
Celsus 8
Ceyx 112

Chaeronea 90, 94
Christ, W. 16, 219 ff.
Cicero 9, 190, **222**
Circe 68
Cleitarchus **223**
Cobet 14, 255
Coblentz 256
Coleridge 196
Collins, J. C. 260
Colossus 10, 136
Colton 259
Courthope 196
Crusius 173
Cumanudes 255
Cyclops 66

Dacier 253
Dante 247
Danube 134
Demetrius 201, 209, 223
Demosthenes **223**
Diels 255
Dion Chrysostom 164, 186
Dion of Syracuse 50
Dionysius of Halicarnassus 16, 186, 193 ff., 224
Dionysius of Miletus 16
Dionysius Atticus of Pergamus 16
Dionysius of Phocaea 102
Dionysius II. of Syracuse 50
Dirce 146, 225
Domitian 10
Doryphorus 136
Dowden 204
Dudith 165, 257

Edwards, H. J. 165
Egger 252, 254, 256, 259

Ellis, Robinson 172 ff.,
256
Elwin 196
Elysio, Filinto 251
Epictetus 198
Erasmus 261
Eratosthenes 224
Erigone 128, 224
Erinnyes 88
Ernesti 183
Eupolis 224
Euripides 28, 225, 260
Eustathius 229

Faber 249
Fénelon 1, 258
Fèvre, Tanneguy le 257
Fiocchi 257
Fox, Charles James 259
Francs, L. B. des 255
Frazer 227
Freudenthal 235
Freytag 233, 256

Geddes 246
Gibbon, Edward 1, 14,
35, 229, 246
Giles 252
Glyky 257
Goetzeler 193
Gorgias 226
Gori 250
Gray, Thomas 177
Greene 254
Grenfell 184, 196, 217,
241
Grucker 259
Gudeman 16

Hadrian 10, 220
Hall 249
Hammer 206, 242, 244,
253
Hatch 196, 236
Haupt 255
Havell 253
Hecataeus 226
Hegesias 226

Heineken 257
Henke 257
Heracleides 50
Hermocrates 50
Hermogenes 6, 164, 197,
226
Hermon 50
Herodotus 227
Herondas 201
Hersel 256
Hertz 255
Hesiod 227
Hesychius 180
Hickie 252
Hiller 173, 224
Holm 203, 227, 243
Holmes 254
Homer 228
Horace 215
Hudson 250
Huet 233
Hultzsch 256
Hume 1
Hunt 184, 217, 241
Hurd 1
Hyperides 36, 229

Immisch 256
Ion of Chios 230
Isocrates 230

Jahn 252
Jannarakis 255
Jannaris 186
Janzon 253
Jebb 227
Johannes Siceliota 5
Johnson, Samuel 210, 224
Jonson, Ben 261
Josephus 12, 237
Jowett 33
Justus, Fabius 15, 18

Kaibel 20, 220
Kayser 255
Keats 33
Kenyon 219, 230
Kinkel 219

Knight 260
Knox 215, 254
Kock 225
Kowalewski 252

Laffetay 204
Laharpe 1
Lang, Andrew 253
Langbaine 248
Lange 18
Lascaris 165
Leclerc 233
Le Clercq 250
Lessing 259
Libanius 224
Lipsius 15
Livy 14
Longinus 35, 245, 246,
passim
Lowth 209
Lucian 174, 175, 186
Lucretius 240
Lutoslawski 196
Lycurgus of Thrace 86
Lysias 221, 230

Maass, 218, 224
Macaulay 260
Mahaffy 225
Manolesius 249
Manutius 247
Marathon 92
Martens 255
Mathews, *Preface*, 173,
184
Matris 231
Maurus 20
Maximus of Tyre 14
Meda 240
Megillus 52
Meidias 100
Meineke 225
Meinel 253
Meisterhans 181
Menander 244
Menéndez y Pelayo 258
Miletus 108
Miller 252

Milton 229, 261
Molière 224
Mommsen 237, 259
Moore 253
Morawski 222
Moreno 252
Morley, Henry 196, 253
Morley, John 224
Morus 251
Moses 8, **231**
Mozley 246
Müller, C. 220
Müller, Eduard 259
Müller-Strübing 174
Murray 242

Naudet 254
Neanthes 201
Nettleship, Henry 193
Nero 10
Newman 33
Nicolini 256
Nile 21, 134
Nolte 255

Oedipus 88
Oliveira 251
Omont 165
Orestes 88
Origen 8

Palmyra 245
Parmenio 60
Paul, St 218
Pauly-Wissowa 217 ff.
Pearce 250
Peloponnesus 108
Perrault 254
Pessonneaux 166, 256
Peterson 16
Petra, Gabriel de 248
Petrarch 247
Petrie 225
Petronius 14, 261
Philip of Macedon 118
Philistus **237**
Philo 12, 192, 236

Philodemus 223
Phryne 132, 229
Phrynichus 108
Pindar **238**
Pinelli 257
Plataea 92
Plato 30, 196 ff., **238**
Pliny the Elder 14
Pliny the Younger 14, 18
Plutarch 10, 16, 37, 189
    —192, 196 ff., 231, 240
Polybius 192
Polycleitus 136
Pope, Alexander 1, 195,
    261
Porphyry 2
Portus 231, 234, 248
Poste 218
Postgate 182, 185
Pujol 252
Pulteney 249
Puttenham 261
Pygmaei 10, 156, 203
Pythagoras 183, 244
Pythia 10, 80

Quintilian 9, 12, 14,
    194 ff.

Raspe 225
Reifferscheid 255
Reinach, T. 220, 235,
    236
Reuter 14
Rhine 134
Ridolfi 165
Robinson 254
Robortello 247, 248
Roeper 9, 235, 254
Rohde, Erwin 255
Rohden, H. von 255
Rollin 1
Rose 174
Rostgaard 4
Rothstein 256
Ruhnken 190, 245, 251
Rutherford 200
Ryle 236

Salamis 92
Sandys 194, 199
Sappho 27, 30, **239**
Schardam 251, 254
Schiller 210, 259
Schlosser 251
Schmid 186, 256
Schmidt 255
Schück 255
Schurzfleisch 234, 253
Scriblerus 195
Scriptor Incertus **244**
Seneca 14
Shakespeare 25
Shilleto 195
Sidney 260
Siegenbeck 257
Siegfried 193
Simonides **241**
Sirius 86, 177
Smith 251
Sonnenschein 179
Sophocles **241**
Spengel 231, 252
Spongberg 254
Spurdens 252
Starkie 172
Stebbing 252
Stephanus 181, 197
Stesichorus **242**
Stewart, Dugald 260
Stobaeus 241
Strabo 205
Striller 198
Suetonius 9
Suidas 2, 9, 218, 220
Susemihl 217 ff.
Symonds, J. A., *Preface*,
    71, 258

Tacitus 14, 15, 16, 18,
    35
Tennyson 33, 240
Terentianus 18 ff.
Themistius 164
Theocritus **242**
Theodorus 9, 237, **242**
Theon 16

Theophrastus **242**
Theopompus **242**
Thucydides **243**
Tiberius 9
Timaeus **243**
Tipaldo 257
Toll 249
Toup 251
Tropea 226
Tucker 181 ff., 256
Tyson 204

Usener 5

Vahlen 253, 255
Valderrabano 257
Varro, Terentius 20
Vaucher 252
Vaughan 260

Vauvenargues 204
Velleius Paterculus 14
Vendelin de Spira 15
Vespasian 10
Victorius 167
Vida 261
Virgil 33
Vitruvius 174
Vollgraff 231, 256
Voltaire 32, 243

Walz 6, 197
Way, *Preface*, 177, 199
Webbe 261
Weil 225
Weise 222
Weiske 251
Weissenberger 193
Welsted 250

Wetstein 250
Wharton 240
Wilamowitz - Möllendorff
    255
Wilson 260
Windle 204
Winkler 255
Winter 257
Wolf 8, 195, 232
Worsfold 260
Wyttenbach 231

Xenophon **243**
Xerxes 46

Young (Junius) 165

Zenobia 35, 245
Zoilus **243**

III. INDEX GRAECITATIS

The thick Arabic numerals refer to a special treatment of the word in question.

A

ἀβλεμὲς προσπίπτειν, *languescere, sine viribus concidere, nullis viribus tangere animum*, xxix. 1. Cp. p. 169.

ἄγαλμα, xxx. 1.

ἄγαν. τοῖς ἄγαν πλούτοις, xxxiii. 2. ἡ ἄγαν τῆς φράσεως συγκοπή, xlii. 1. Cp. p. 207.

ἀγανακτεῖν proprio sensu, xvii. 1, xxii. 1; metaphorice, xxi. 2.

ἀγγελία, *narratio*, xliii. 3.

ἄγειν, *abripere auditores*, xviii. 2, xxx. 1. ἄγειν ἀπ᾽ ἀλλήλων, *divellere*, xxii. 3. εἰς πειθὼ et ἔκστασιν, *evehere ad*, i. 4. εἰς τεχνικὰ παραγγέλματα, *in artis formam redigere*, ii. 1. δι᾽ ἀσφαλείας τὰ ὀνόματα, *vel vocabula caute usurpat*, xvi. 4. φυσικῶς ἀγόμενοι, *natura duce*, xxxv. 4.

ἀγεληδόν, *gregatim, catervatim*, xxiii. 4. Cp. p. 192.

ἀγεννὲς κακόν, iii. 4; φρόνημα, ix. 3; ζῷον, xxxv. 2; νόσημα, φιληδονία, xliv. 6.

ἀγχίνοια, *animi praesentia*, xxxiv. 4.

ἀγχίστροφος, ἀγχιστρόφως, 194.

ἀγών, ἀγωνιστικός, 194.

ἀγωνία, *contentio, anxietas*, xix. 2, xxii. 4.

ἀγώνισμα, *certamen* ingenii fictum, xiv. 2. Cp. ἀγωνιστής, xxxv. 2.

ἀγωνιστής, xxxv. 2. Cp. p. 183.

ἀδέκαστος (vocabulum a Tollio e cod. Vat. restitutum), *incorruptus*, xliv. 9.

ἀδιανέμητα, *quae non debent disiungi, inseparabilia*, xxii. 3. Cp. p. 189.

ἀδιάπτωτος, *errore vacuus*, xxxiii. 1 et 5, xxxvi. 4.

ἀδιάχυτος, *adstrictus, verbis non diffusus*, xxxiv. 3.

ἀδοξότερα τῆς ὕλης verba, *rei gravitate inferiora*, xliii. 1. Cp. ταπεινότερον τῆς ὅλης ὑποθέσεως, i. 1.

ἀδρεπήβολος, 194. Cp. p. 189.

ἁδρότερος, *amplior*, xl. 4.

ἁδὺ φωνεύσας (pro ἡδὺ φωνούσης) ὑπακούειν, e Sapphus carmine, x. 2.

ἀδύνατον (πᾶν τό), xv. 8. e Manutii coniectura: δυνατόν praebet P.

ἀεὶ vel αἰεί, 181.

ἄζηλος, *aemulatione indignus, neglectus*, xliv. 8.

ἄθεα, ix. 7.

ἀθρόα, *cuncta*, xxxiv. 4; ἀθρόα δύναμις, *magna oratoris vis vel facultas*, i. 4.

ἀθροισμός, 194.

αἱματοῦν. ἡματωμένον ὕδωρ, *aqua sanguine mixta*, e Thucyd., xxxviii. 3.

αἱρεῖν. ἔνθεν ἑλὼν ex Homero, xxxiv. 4. Cp. p. 198.

αἵρεσθαι ἀγῶνα, *certamen suscipere*, e Demosth., xvi. 2.

αἴσχη, *dedecora*, de verbis humilioribus, xliii. 3. Similiter αἰσχῦναι, i.q. *dehonestare*, xliii. 1.

αἰσχυντηλός, iv. 4. Cp. p. 191.

αἰτεῖσθαι φῶς, ix. 10. αἴτημα, ix. 10.

αἰτία μεγέθους (viii. 1), αἴτιον ὕψους (x. 1), *sublimitatis adiumentum*. τὰς μείζονας αἰτίας (sic P), xxxiii. 4.

αἰτιᾶσθαι, i. 2.

Αἴτνη, xxxv. 4. Cp. p. 238.

αἰὼν πᾶς ὁ μετ᾽ ἐμέ, *posteri*, xiv. 3; τοῦ παντὸς αἰῶνος ἄξιον, ix. 3.

ἄκαιρον πάθος, iii. 5.

ἀκατέργαστοι ἔννοιαι Aeschyli, xv. 5.

ἄκεντρον προσπίπτειν, sine vi corruere, xxi. 1.

ἀκμή. ἐπὶ ξυροῦ ἀκμῆς, ex Herodoto, xxii. 1.

ἀκόλαστος, immodicus, xliv. 7.

ἀκολουθία, rectus verborum ordo, xxii. 1.

ἀκονᾶν, tropice, xliv. 3.

ἄκουαι (ἄκουε P), i.q. ἀκοαί, in Sapphus fragmento, x. 2.

ἄκρα (ἡ). κατ᾽ ἄκρας, penitus, xliv. 6.

ἄκρατος, ix. 8, xxxii. 7.

ἀκρίβεια (xxxv. 2), τὸ ἀκριβές (xxxiii. 2, xxxvi. 3), summa cura et diligentia. Cp. ἀκριβῶς ἐκπεπονημένοι κρατῆρες, xliii. 2.

ἄκριτον πάθος, adfectus immoderatus, xxxii. 8.

ἄκρος. ἐπ᾽ ἄκρον, summe, xxxiv. 4; cp. κατ᾽ ἄκρον, xxx. 1. τῶν ἄκρων ἐφίεσθαι, alta petere, xxxiii. 2. τὰ ἄκρα καὶ ὑπερτεταμένα, x. 1.

ἀκροσφαλές (τό), ad lapsum proclivitas, xxii. 4.

ἀκρότης καὶ ἐξοχή τις λόγων, summa orationis virtus, i. 3.

ἄκρως, xv. 7, xx. 1, xxxiv. 2.

ἀκρωτηριάζειν, metaphorice, xxxix. 4; itemque e Demosthene, xxxii. 2. Cp. pp. 179, 184.

ἀλγηδόνες ὀφθαλμῶν dicuntur formosae mulieres ab Herodoto, iv. 7.

ἀλέξημα in figurarum usu, xvii. 2.

ἀλεξιφάρμακος λόγος, xvi. 2. ἀλεξιφάρμακα πλήθους καὶ τόλμης μεταφορῶν, xxxii. 4.

ἀληθινὸς λόγος opponitur fabulae, iii. 1. Cp. ἀλήθεια (x. 1), τὸ ἀληθές (xxxiv. 1).

ἀλληγορία, 190, 194. ἀλληγορικὸς στόμφος Platonis, xxxii. 7.

ἀλληλουχία, mutua coniunctio, xxxvi. 4.

ἀλλότριον πνεῦμα, xiii. 2.

ἀλλόφυλος τάξις, locus alienus, xxii. 4.

ἄλλως, vii. 1, ix. 7.

ἀλογιστεῖν, ratione carere, x. 3.

ἀλόγως, temere, xxii. 1, xxxv. 5.

ἀλουργής, e Theopompo, xliii. 2.

ἁλῶναι παρανοίας, xxxvi. 2.

ἀμαθὴς τόλμα, ii. 2.

ἀμάλακτοι ἔννοιαι Aeschyli, xv. 5.

ἁμαρτάνειν. ἡμαρτημένος, vitiosus, xxxvi. 3.

ἁμαρτήματι opponitur ἀρετή, xxxv. 1.

ἄμαχος βία, i. 4. ἄμαχος ἔρως, xxxv. 2.

ἀμβλοῦσθαι, metaphorice, xiv. 3.

ἀμεγέθης, ad sublimitatem non factus, xxxiv. 4, xl. 2, et alibi.

ἀμέθοδος, nulla lege constrictus, ii. 2.

ἀμέλει, 195.

ἄμετρον πάθος, iii. 5.

ἀμίμητος, xxviii. 4, xxxiv. 2.

ἄμοιρος, xxxiv. 3.

ἄμουσος, xxviii. 1, xxxix. 2. Cp. p. 226.

ἀμπώτιδες τοῦ μεγέθους, sc. Ὠκεανοῦ, ix. 13.

ἀμυδρὰ φέγγη, xvii. 2.

ἀμφιλαφὴς ἐμπρησμός, late fusum incendium, xii. 4.

ἀμώμητος, vitio immunis, xxxiii. 5.

ἀναβαλλόμενα σπλάγχνα ex Arimaspeis, x. 4. Cp. p. 219.

ἀναβλέπειν, suspicere, xiii. 1, xliv. 8.

ἀνάγεσθαι, xv. 7.

ἀναγκάζειν. ἠναγκασμένα, quae necessitas dicere iussit ex tempore, xxii. 2.

ἀναγκοφαγεῖν πράγματα, e Theopompo, xxxi. 1. Cp. pp. 221, 242.

ἀναγράφειν, xiii. 3.

ἀνάγωγα σκώμματα, xxxiv. 2.

ἀναξεῖν, xliv. 4.

ἀναζωγραφεῖν, xxxii. 5.

ἀναθεωρεῖν, vii. 3. ἀναθεώρησις, vii. 3, xxiii. 2.

ἀναιρεῖν τὴν ὑπερβολήν, vim hyperboles omnem tollere, xxxviii. 1.

ἀνακαλεῖσθαι (si lectio sana est), xlii. 2, 184.

ἀνακαλυπτήρια, e Timaeo, iv. 5. intell. diem (tertium a nuptiis) quo novam nuptam facie retecta prodire mos erat.

ἀνακάμπτειν, xxxvi. 4.

ἀνακίρνασθαι, xx. 1.

ἀνακρεμάσας τὸν νοῦν, xxii. 4.

ἀνακυκλοῦν, per anfractum redire, xxii. 1.

ἀναλαμβάνειν, 195.

ἀναλήθης, iii. 4.

ἀναλλάττειν, xxxviii. 2.

ἀναλογεῖν, xl. 3. ἀνάλογον (τό), xxxi. 1.

ἀναμάρτητος, xxxii. 8, xxxiii. 2, xxxvi. 1.

ἄναμμα τῶν φλεβῶν, e Platone, xxxii. 5.

ἀναμφίλεκτος πίστις, vii. 4.

ἀνάπαυλα, opp. ἀρχή, xi. 1.

ἀναπετανννύναι. ἀναπεπταμένον μέγεθος, xii. 2.

ἀναπλάττεσθαι τῇ ψυχῇ, xiv. 1.

ἀναπνεῖν, xiii. 2.

ἀναπτύσσειν, vii. 1.

ἀναρρηγνυμένη ἐκ βάθρων γῆ, ix. 6.

ἀνασκοπεῖν πρὸς αὐγάς, iii. 1. ἀνασκοπεῖσθαι, *legendo diiudicare*, i. 1.

ἀνάστημα, h. e. ὕψωμα, vii. 2.

ἀνατέτροφα, e Demosth., xxxii. 2.

ἀνατομή, xxxii. 5.

ἀνατρέφειν τὰς ψυχὰς πρὸς τὰ μεγέθη, ix. 1. ἀνατρέφεσθαι, de flammis incendii, xii. 4.

ἀνατροπὴν λαμβάνειν, *everti*, ix. 6.

ἀναφαίρετος, xxxvi. 2.

ἀναφέρειν, xiii. 1 (e Platone), xiv. 1, xxxv. 4.

ἀναφορά, **195.**

ἀναχοαί, *flammarum eructatio*, de Aetna, xxxv. 4. Cp. p. 189.

ἀνδραποδίζειν, metaphorice, xliv. 9.

ἀνέγκλητος συγγραφεύς, xxxiii. 1.

ἀνειδωλοποιούμενα μέτρα, xiv. 1. Cp. p. 197.

ἀνειλεῖσθαι, xii. 4.

ἀνεξάλειπτος μνήμη, *memoria indelebilis*, xxxiii. 3.

ἀνεπαίσθητος, active, iv. 1.

ἀνεπιστάτως, xxxiii. 4. Cp. p. 192.

ἀνερμάτιστος, ii. 2. Cp. p. 192.

ἀνηθοποίητος, xxxiv. 3. Cp. p. 200.

ἀνθρωπεία φύσις, xxxix. 3. τὰ ἀνθρώπεια, xxxiii. 3. τὰ ἀνθρώπινα, ix. 10.

ἀνθυπαντᾶν, *vicissim aliquod dictum reponere*, xviii. 1, 2. Cp. p. 189.

ἀνοίκειον, xliii. 1.

ἀνοικονόμητα, xxxiii. 5.

ἀνταγωνιστής, xiii. 4.

ἀντανοῖξαι τὰ ὄμματα τοῖς κεραυνοῖς, xxxiv. 4. Cp. p. 189.

ἀντιδιατίθεσθαι πρὸς τὴν πειθώ, xvii. 1.

ἄντικρυς, *plane*, iii. 4.

ἀντιμεθίστασθαι εἰς πρόσωπον, *mutata persona induere aliam*, xxvii. 1.

ἀντιμετάθεσις προσώπων, xxvi. 1.

ἀντιπεριΐστασθαι, xxxviii. 1.

ἀντισπᾶσθαι τῇδε κἀκεῖσε, xxii. 1. Cp. pp. 192, 236.

ἀντισυμμαχεῖσθαι, *vicissim iuvari*, xvii. 1. Cp. p. 189.

ἀντιτάττεσθαι, ix. 10.

ἀντιτιμᾶσθαι, xxxiii. 5.

ἀντοφθαλμεῖν πάθεσι, *oculos* (*animi*) *obvertere adfectibus*, xxxiv. 4.

ἀντωθεῖν. λόφους ἀντωθουμένους, xliii. 2.

ἀξία. κατὰ τὴν ἀξίαν, ix. 9.

ἀξιοθαύμαστος, xxxv. 4.

ἀξιόνικος ἀγών, xiii. 4.

ἀξιοπιστία, xvi. 2.

ἀξίωμα fere idem quod ὕψος, viii. 1, xxxix. 3.

ἀόριστος πλοῦτος, xliv. 7.

ἀπάγειν, xviii. 2.

ἀπαθανατίζειν, xvi. 3.

ἀπαθέστατα, positum adverbialiter, xli. 1.

ἀπαιτεῖσθαι, *posci*, i. 1.

ἀπακμή, ix. 15 et (e coniect. Manutii) ix. 14. Cp. p. 189.

ἀπαλλάττεσθαι, i. 3.

ἁπαλός. ἐξ ἁπαλῶν ἔτι φρονημάτων, *iam inde usque a pueritia* (ut Terentii verbis utamur), xliv. 3.

ἀπαρρησίαστον, τό, *servilis formido et taciturnitas*, xliv. 4.

ἅπας. ἐξ ἅπαντος, viii. 3, xxxiii. 1. Cp. p. 188.

ἀπαστράπτει, xii. 3 (e coniect. Bentl.). Cp. p. 175.

ἀπαύξησις, vii. 3. Cp. p. 189.

ἀπείκειν. ἀπεοικυῖα τάξις, *locus incommodus*, xxii. 4.

ἀπεικότως, xv. 11.

ἀπείργειν, x. 6. Cp. p. 173.

ἀπείρων, *immensus*, xxiii. 2 (e scr. quod. inc.).

ἀπεργάζεσθαι τὴν ἐξοχήν, x. 3. ἀπειργασμένος χρυσός, xliii. 2 (e Theopompo).

ἀπερείδειν πρὸς αὐτὰ τὰ πρόσωπα, xxvi. 2.

ἀπεριόριστος, xvi. 1, xliv. 6.

ἀπηνὴς μεταφορά, dura metaphora, xxxii. 7.

ἀπήχημα μεγαλοφροσύνης, ix. 2.

ἀπίθανα, ix. 14.

ἀπιστία ἡ καθ᾽ αὑτοῦ, xxxviii. 2.

ἀπλανὴς ἄσκησις καὶ χρῆσις, ii. 2.

ἀπλῶς, xviii. 1, xxxix. 2.

ἀπό, iv. 3, vii. 4, ix. 13, x. 5, xii. 2, et passim.

ἀπογεννᾶν, metaphorice, xv. 11.

ἀποδεικτικόν, τό, xv. 11.

ἀπόδειξιν εἰσφέρειν ὑπέρ, xvi. 2.

ἀποδέχεσθαι, xxxii. 4.

ἀποδιδόναι, xxxix. 1.

ἀποδιδράσκειν ἐκ τῶν ὑψηλοτέρων εἰς τὰ ταπεινότερα, xliii. 3.

ἀποθαρρεῖν, magna confidentia uti, xxxii. 8.

ἀποθεοῦν, in deorum numerum referre, xvi. 2.

ἀποθηριοῦσθαι, efferari, xvii. 1.

ἀποίχεσθαι (pro imper. ἀποίχεσθε), ex Hecateo, xxvii. 2.

ἀποκεῖσθαι, iii. 5.

ἀποκρύπτειν τι τῷ φωτὶ αὐτῷ, xvii. 2.

ἀποκύλισμα, xl. 4. Cp. p. 189.

ἀπόλαυσις τραπεζῶν, xliii. 4.

ἀπολισθαίνειν μεγάλων, iii. 3. Cp. p. 245.

ἀπολύειν, verbum dubium, xxi. 2. fort. leg. ἀπολλύει. Cp. p. 179.

ἀπόπλους, sc. Graecorum a Troia, xv. 7.

ἄπορος νύξ, ix. 10.

ἀπορρεῖν, e memoria effluere, xxxiii. 3.

ἀπόρρητα μέρη, sc. τοῦ σώματος, xliii. 5.

ἀπόρροιαι, effluvia, xiii. 2.

ἀποσκιάζειν, xvii. 3. Cp. p. 191.

ἀποστρέφειν, xxii. 2, xxvii. 3. Cp. p. 175.

ἀποστροφή, 195.

ἀποτελεῖν, fere i.q. ποιεῖν, xxvi. 3, xxviii. 1, xxix. 2, xxxix. 2. Cp. ἀποτελεστικὰ μεγαληγορίας, xvi. 1.

ἀπότομος, xii. 4, xxvii. 1, xxxix. 4.

ἀποτραχυνόμενον, τό, asperitas et vehementia, xxi. 1.

ἀποτύπωσις, xiii. 4.

ἀποφαίνεσθαι, i. 2, ii. 3, xxxii. 8.

ἀποχετεύεσθαι, xiii. 3. Cp. p. 191.

ἀπόχρη, xxxii. 6.

ἀποχρώντως ἀποδιδόναι ὑπέρ τινος, xxxix. 1.

ἀποχρῶσα πίστις, xxxix. 3.

ἀπόψυχος, xlii. 3. Cp. p. 189.

ἄπρακτον σκότος, ix. 10.

ἀπρεπὲς τῇ προσόψει, indecorum adspectu, xliii. 3.

ἀπρίξ, xiii. 2.

ἀπρόσιτος δεινότης, inaccessa vis et vehementia, xxxiv. 4.

ἀραιὸς αὐλών, xxxii. 5 (e Platone).

ἀραιώματα, x. 7. Cp. p. 174.

ἀργεῖν πρός τι, ix. 10.

ἀργός, xxxiv. 4.

ἀρέσκεσθαι, xxxiii. 4.

ἀρετή, virtus orationis quaevis, xi. 1, xxxv. 1, et alibi; summa excellentia, x. 1.

ἀριστεύς, xvi. 2.

ἀριστίνδην ἐκκαθαίρειν, x. 7.

ἀρκεῖν. ἠρκέσθην, contentus essem, ix. 4.

ἁρμόδιος, xii. 5.

ἁρμονία λόγων, verborum lenis compositio, xxxix. 1, 3.

ἀρτίως, paulo ante, xi. 3.

ἀρχέτυπον γενέσεως στοιχεῖον, ii. 2.

ἀσεβεῖν εἰς τὸν Ἑρμῆν, iv. 3.

ἄσεμνος, v. 1, x. 7, xliii. 1.

ἀσκός. τὰ περὶ ἀσκὸν apud Homerum, ix. 14.

ἄστατον πνεῦμα, ventus instabilis, xxi. 1.

ἀστεῖος, xxxiv. 3. ἀστεϊσμοί, xxxiv. 2.

ἀστήρικτος, ii. 2.

ἀσύγγνωστος, iii. 1.

ἀσύμφωνος, vii. 4.

ἀσύνδετα, 195.

ἀσύνθετος, x. 6.

ἀσφαλής, xxxiii. 2. Similiter ἀσφάλεια s.v. ἄγειν supra.

ἀσχημονεῖν, iii. 5, iv. 17. Cp. p. 191.

ἀσχήμων λόγος, xliii. 6.

ἀταξία, xx. 2, 3.

ἀτὰρ δὴ καί, ix. 12.

ἀτελής, xiv. 3, xxvii. 3.

ἀτμὸς ἔνθεος, de oraculo Delphico, xiii. 2.

ἄτολμος, xv. 3.

ἀτονεῖν, xi. 2.

ἄττα. μυρί ἄττα, xxxii. 6.

Ἀττικοί, xxxiv. 2. Cp. pp. 182, 245.

ἀτυχέστατα, adverbialiter positum, xxxiii. 5.

ἀτυχία, ix. 7.

αὐγή. πρὸς αὐγὰς ἀνασκοπεῖν, iii. 1.

αὐθάδης, *audax, insolens* (in hyperbatis): xxii. 3.

αὐθιγενὴς σύστασις, viii. 1.

αὔξησις, 195. Cp. p. 179.

αὐξητικά, xi. 2.

αὐξητικῶς λέγειν, xxxviii. 2.

αὔτανδρος, xliv. 6.

αὐτάρκης, xliii. 4.

αὐτίκα, 195.

αὐτόθεν, 195.

αὐτόθι, *hoc ipso loco* s. *non multo postea*, xvi. 1.

αὐτόνομος, ii. 2.

ἀφαιρεῖν, iv. 3, xxi. 2.

ἄφατος, xxxiv. 2.

ἀφέλεια, 195.

ἄφετοι, *beluae e claustris emissae*, xliv. 10. Cp. ἀφεθεῖσαι *ibid.*

ἀφίστασθαι, xxxiv. 3.

ἀφορία, xliv. 1.

ἀφορίζεσθαι, *pronuntiare, asseverare*, viii. 4.

ἄφορος πρός τι, iv. 1.

ἄχαρι τέλος ex Herodoto, xliii. 1.

ἀχλύς, *caligo*, ix. 10; *Tristitia*, persona ap. Hesiodum in Sc. H., ix. 5.

ἄχραντος, de divino numine, ix. 8.

ἄχρι νῦν, xxxvi. 2.

ἀψοφητί, xxiii. 1. Cp. p. 192 n.

ἄψυχος, xvi. 3.

B

βάθος, 171, 195.

βάθρον. ἐκ βάθρων, *ex imis fundamentis*, ix. 6.

βαίνειν ἐν ῥυθμῷ, xxxix. 2; ἐπὶ μακροῦ τοῦ πρώτου ῥυθμοῦ βέβηκε, xxxix. 4.

βακχεία τῶν λόγων, xxxii. 7. Cp. p. 191.

βακχεύειν proprie ap. Aeschylum, xv. 6; tropice, iii. 2.

βάκχευμα. κἄν βακχεύμασι νήφειν ἀναγκαῖον, xvi. 4. Cp. p. 226.

βάρος coniunctum cum ἰσχύς, κράτος et similibus, xxx. 1.

βασανίζειν, *torquere, vim inferre*, de dura compositione verbi, x. 6.

βάσις ῥυθμοῦ, xxxix. 2.

βιάζεσθαι, xxxiv. 3, xli. 2.

βιολογεῖν, *narrare de rebus e vita communi petitis*, ix. 15. Cp. p. 189.

βίος, vii. 1, xxxvi. 2, xliv. 6.

βόειος πλοῦτος, periphrasis ad ridendum Platonem facta, xxix. 1.

βραβεύειν, *gubernare*, xliv. 9.

βραχυσύλλαβα, xli. 3.

Γ

γαῦρόν τι ἀνάστημα, vii. 2.

γειτνιᾶν τινι, xxxvii. 1.

γελοῖος, xxxiv. 3.

γέλως, eius definitio, xxxviii. 5.

γενναῖος, viii. 1, 4; ix. 1; xv. 8; xxxii. 4.

γεννᾶν, ii. 1, v. 1, vii. 2, xviii. 2, xliii. 2.

γεννητικὸν λόγου ἐννόημα, xv. 1.

γένος: ἐν τῷ γένει τούτῳ, ut Lat. *in hoc genere*, xiii. 3.

γίνεσθαι. γενέσθω φῶς, e Moyse, ix. 9.

γινώσκειν, *iudicare*, xii. 4.

γλαφυρός, 193, 196, 209.

γλυκύτης, xxxiv. 2.

γλωττόκομον, 196.

γνήσιος, opp. νόθος: xxxix. 3, xliv. 7.

γόνιμος, viii. 1, xxxi. 1, xliv. 2.

γοῦν, 196.

γυμνούμενος τάρταρος, ix. 6.

γὺψ ἔμψυχος τάφος, e Gorgiae dicto, iii. 2. Cp. p. 226.

Δ

δαιμόνιος, ix. 5, 8; xxxiii. 5; xxxv. 2.

δαιμονίως, *praeclare*, xliii. 1.

δακτυλικὸς ῥυθμός, xxxix. 4. Cp. p. 183.

δαπάνη, xliv. 11.

δὲ pleonast. in οὕτω δὲ post ὡς s. ὥσπερ, ii. 2 ; post complura verba arcte cohaerentia, xl. 2.

δέδυκε, xvii. 2.

δειλός, ii. 1. Cp. p. 187.

δεῖν ὀλίγου, xix. 1, xxxii. 8; δεῖν μικροῦ, xv. 2.

δεινός, ix. 5 ; x. 1, 4, 6; xv. 8; xxii. 3; xxvii. 2.

δεινότης, δεινοῦν, δείνωσις, 196. Cp. p. 191.

δεκάζεσθαι, δεκασμοί, xliv. 9.

δέος (e coniect. Victorii), x. 4.

δεσμὸς περικείμενος τοῖς σώμασι (τῶν Πυγμαίων), xliv. 5. δεσμῷ τῆς ἁρμονίας, xl. 1.

δεσμωτήριον ψυχῆς philosophus quidam dicebat servitutem : xliv. 5.

δεύτερος. τὸ δεύτερον, xxxiii. 5.

δηλοῦν. τὰ δεδηλωμένα, quae hactenus exposita sunt, xxxii. 6.

δημιούργημα, xiii. 4.

Δημοσθενικὸς et Δημοσθένειος, xii. 5, xxxiv. 2.

δημώδης, 191, 196.

διαβαίνειν, xl. 4.

διαβάλλειν, xliii. 2.

διάγνωσις, vi. 2.

διαγραφή, descriptio, xxxii. 5.

διαδορατίζεσθαι, xiii. 4.

διαδοχὰς (κατά), per vices, xii. 4.

διαίρειν, δίαρμα, δίαρσις, 196.

διακλέπτειν, xvi. 4.

διακληρονομεῖσθαι, xii. 4. Cp. p. 189.

διακόπτειν, xix. 2.

διακριβοῦν, xvi. 1. Cp. p. 191.

διαλανθάνειν, xvii. 1, xxxviii. 3. Cp. p. 191.

διαλείπειν, xxxviii. 5.

διαλλάττειν, xxvii. 3.

διαμαρτάνειν, viii. 2, xxxii. 8.

διαμέλλειν, xxvii. 2.

διάνοια, xxxv. 3, xxxix. 4.

διαπατᾶσθαι, ii. 1, viii. 4.

διαπονεῖν, elaborare, xiv. 1.

διαπορεῖν, ii. 1, v. 1, xxxiii. 1, xxxix. 3.

διαπρέπειν, xiv. 1.

διαπτύσσειν, xxx. 1. Cp. pp. 191, 2.

διάπτωσις τοῦ λόγου, xxii. 4.

διάπυρον (τό), ardor, vehementia, xii. 3.

διαριστεύεσθαι, contendere, certare, xiii. 4. Cp. p. 189.

διαρπάζειν, xii. 4.

διασπᾶν, xxvii. 3.

διάστασιν λαμβάνειν, scindi, ix. 6.

διάστημα, ix. 4, 5 ; xl. 2. Cp. διαίρειν.

διασυρμός, 197. διασύρειν, xxxii. 7.

διατίθεναι, ix. 10, xiv. 2, xxxiv. 2.

διατύπωσις, 197.

διαυγὲς ῥεῖθρον, xxxv. 4.

διαφέρειν πρός τι, xliii. 4.

διαφορεῖν, i. 4.

διαχαλᾶν, xxxix. 4.

διαχλευάζειν, xxix. 4.

διδάσκειν δρᾶμα, ex Herodoto, xxiv. 1.

διδόναι, permittere, xxvii. 2.

διεξιέναι, diligenter pertractare, xvi. 1.

διεξοδεύειν, a re proposita dicendo aberrare, xxxiv. 2.

διηγηματικὴ est Odyssea, Ilias δραματική : ix. 13.

διήκειν πρὸς τὸν αἰῶνα, xliv. 9. Cp. p. 191.

διϊστάναι, viii. 2, xxiii. 2, xxiv. 1.

δίκαιος. δικαία δουλεία, xliv. 3, 5.

δικαστήριον, tropice : xiv. 2.

δίκην (modo, ritu), i. 4, xxxii. 1. Cp. p. 187.

διό, xii. 1. Cp. p. 175.

διοίχεσθαι, x. 3.

διομαλίζειν, intransitive, xxxiii. 4.

διοσημεία, xv. 7.

διότι pro ὅτι, vii. 1.

διοχετεύειν, xxxii. 5.

διστάζειν, xxviii. 1. Cp. p. 191.

διχόρειοι, xli. 1.

δοκίμιον γεύσεως, e Platone, xxxii. 5.

δοξοκοπεῖν, 197. Cp. p. 169.

δορυφορικὴ οἴκησις, e Platone, xxxii. 5.

δουλαγωγεῖν, metaphorice, xliv. 6.

δουλοπρεπῆ φρονεῖν καὶ ἐπιτηδεύειν, ix. 3. Cp. p. 191.

δουλοῦσθαι, xv. 9.

δραματικὸν καὶ ἐναγώνιον opponitur διηγηματικῷ, ix. 13.

δράσσεσθαι, ex Herodoto, xliii. 1.

δριμύς, xliv. 1.
δυεῖν, i. 1.
δύναμις, viii. 1, xxxiv. 4.
δυσδαιμονεῖν, ix. 7. Cp. p. 189.
δυσεξάλειπτος μνήμη, vii. 3.
δύσκολος κατεξανάστασις, vii. 3.
δύσληπτον, vi. 1.
δυσσεβὴς εἰς, iv. 3.
δυσφυλακτότατος, iii. 3.
δωρητός, ix. 1.

E

ἐγγὺς ἐκστάσεως, τά, xxxviii. 5.
ἐγκαταβιοῦν τῇ ῥαθυμίᾳ, xliv. 11.
ἐγκαταλείπειν τῇ διανοίᾳ, vii. 3.
ἐγκατατάττειν, x. 7, xliii. 3.
ἐγκελεύεσθαι, i. 2.
ἐγκλείειν, xliv. 5.
ἐγκοπή, xli. 3. Cp. p. 184.
ἐγκρύπτειν, xv. 11.
ἐγκύμων, ix. 1, xiii. 2. Cp. p. 191.
ἐγκωμιαστικός, viii. 3.
ἐγκώμιον, viii. 3, xvi. 3, xxxviii. 2.
ἔδαφος, metaphorice, viii. 1.
ἑδραῖον μέγεθος, xl. 4. Cp. p. 191.
ἐθίζειν, solere, ix. 10. Cp. p. 179.
εἴγε, i. 4.
εἰδοποιΐα, xviii. 1. Cp. pp. 192, 197.
εἶδος, 197. Cp. p. 176.
εἴδωλον, ix. 5, xxxix. 3.
εἰδωλοποιεῖν, εἰδωλοποιΐα, 197. Cp. p. 191.
εἰκαῖος, ii. 2.
εἰκῇ, xliv. 12.
εἰκονογραφεῖν, x. 6. Cp. p. 192.
εἰκός, τό, xliv. 3.
εἰκότως, iii. 5.
εἰκών, 197.
εἰρήνη, ἡ τῆς οἰκουμένης, xliv. 6. Cp. p. 14.
εἱρμός, xxii. 1. Cp. p. 192.
εἰσβολή, ix. 9, xxviii. 2, xxxviii. 2.
εἰσπράττεσθαι, xxxii. 4.
εἰσφέρειν, xvi. 2.
εἶτα, i. 1, iii. 5, xvi. 4, xx. 3.
ἐκ, 188.
ἐκβαίνειν, xliv. 3.
ἐκβολή, xxxiii. 5.

ἐκθαυμάζειν, xliv. 8.
ἐκθειάζειν, xliv. 7.
ἐκκαθαίρειν ἀριστίνδην, x. 7.
ἐκλαμβάνειν, x. 3.
ἐκλέγειν, x. 1, xiii. 3.
ἐκλογή, viii. 1, x. 1, xxx. 1.
ἐκλύεσθαι εἴς τι, ix. 15. Cp. p. 188.
ἐκμαθεῖν παρά τινος, ii. 3.
ἑκούσια ἁμαρτήματα, xxxiii. 4.
ἐκπάθεια, xxxviii. 3. Cp. p. 189.
ἐκπίπτειν, iv. 1, xix. 1, xxxviii. 5.
ἐκπληκτικός, xv. 11.
ἔκπληξις, i. 4, xv. 2.
ἐκπληροῦν, xl. 4. Cp. p. 191.
ἐκπλήττειν, xii. 5, xxxv. 4.
ἐκπνεῖν, viii. 4.
ἐκπονεῖν. ἐκπεπονημένοι κρατῆρες, e Theopompo, xliii. 2.
ἐκτιθέναι, xxxviii. 2.
ἐκτιμᾶν, xliv. 7. Cp. p. 192.
ἐκτραγῳδεῖν, xv. 3.
ἐκτρίβειν, xliv. 3.
ἐκφαίνειν, ix. 9.
ἐκφέρειν, i. 4, ix. 3, xix. 2, xxxii. 7.
ἐκφλέγεσθαι, xii. 3.
ἔκφρων, xxxix. 2. Cp. p. 191.
ἔκφυλος, xv. 8.
ἐλάττωμα, xxxii. 8.
ἐλαύνειν, xxxii. 1.
ἐλεγκτικός, i. 4.
ἐλέγχειν, ii. 2, xxxvi. 1.
ἔλεγχος, xxxii. 4.
ἐλευθερία (lectio fortasse vera), xxxix. 1. Cp. p. 183.
ἐλεύθερος, xliv. 9.
ἐμβολή, xx. 3.
ἐμβριθεῖς ἔννοιαι, ix. 3.
ἐμπαθής, viii. 4, xv. 9.
ἔμπαλιν, xliii. 3.
ἐμπειρία, i. 4.
ἔμπειρος, vii. 3.
ἐμπεριεχόμενα, viii. 1.
ἐμπίπτειν εἴς τινα, cadere in aliquem, inesse posse alicui, ix. 4. Cp. p. 191.
ἔμπλεως ἀγῶνος, xxvi. 3. Cp. p. 194.
ἐμπνεῖν, xv. 2.
ἐμποδίζειν, xix. 2, xxi. 2.

ἐμποιεῖν, x. 7. Cp. p. 174.

ἔμπρακτος, 197.

ἔμπροσθεν, xxii. 2.

ἐμφανιστικός, xxxi. 1.

ἔμφασις, xix. 2.

ἐμφερόμενα, 197.

ἔμφρουρον, τό, xliv. 4.

ἔμφρων, vii. 3.

ἐμφύειν, v. 1, xxxv. 2.

ἔμφυτοι ἀνθρώποις λόγοι, xxxix. 3.

ἔμψυχος, iii. 2 (dictum Gorgiae), xxxiv. 4.

ἐν, viii. 1, xxxiii. 1. Cp. p. 188.

ἐναγώνιος, ἐναγωνίως, 194.

ἐναληθές, τό, xv. 8. Cp. p. 189.

ἐνάλλαξις, xxiii. 1.

ἐναλλάττειν, xxii. 1, xxxviii. 2.

ἐνάργεια, 191, 197.

ἐναργής, xv. 7, xxxi. 1.

ἐναφανίζεσθαι, xvii. 2.

ἐνδείκνυσθαι, xiii. 2.

ἐνδιδόναι, xxxix. 2, xli. 2.

ἐνέδραι διαθηκῶν, xliv. 9.

ἐνεῖναι. ὡς ἐνῆν, *quantum fieri poterat*, xliii. 5.

ἐνέργημα, 198.

ἐνεργούμενα, xxvi. 2.

ἔνθεν ἐλών, 198.

ἐνθένδε, i. 3.

ἔνθεος, xiii. 2, xviii. 1.

ἐνθουσιᾶν, iii. 2. Cp. p. 192.

ἐνθουσιασμός, xv. 1.

ἐνθουσιαστικός, viii. 1, 4.

ἐνικά, *singularia* numero grammatico, xxiii. 2, xxiv. 1.

ἐννόημα, xv. 1.

ἔννοια, ix. 2, xv. 5, xxviii. 3.

ἑνότης, xi. 3.

ἑνοῦν, xxii. 3, xxiv. 1.

ἐνσημαίνειν, iv. 4.

ἐνσπαργανοῦν, 198.

ἐντάφιον, 198.

ἐντιθέναι, xvi. 3, xxx. 1, xxxix. 2.

ἐντίκτειν, xvi. 3, xliv. 7.

ἐντρεχής, xliv. 1.

ἔντροφος, xxxix. 3.

ἐντυγχάνειν, i. 1.

ἐντυποῦν, x. 6.

ἐνύπνια Διὸς dicuntur *nugae optimi scriptoris*: ix. 14.

ἐξαιρεῖν, xi. 2.

ἐξακούειν, xxiii. 4.

ἐξαμαυροῦν, xvii. 2.

ἐξάπτεσθαι κώδωνας, *adnexa tintinnabula habere*, xxiii. 4 (cp. p. 202).

ἐξεγείρεσθαι, xxvi. 3.

ἐξεμεῖν πρὸς οὐρανόν, e fragm. Aeschyli: iii. 1.

ἐξεργάζεσθαι. ἐξείργασται ὁ τόπος, *tractatus et diiudicatus est locus*, ix. 8. Cp. p. 229.

ἐξέρεισμα, xl. 4. Cp. p. 189.

ἑξῆς, xxxiii. 5.

ἕξις, xliv. 4.

ἐξιστάναι, iii. 5, xx. 3 (e Demosth.).

ἐξομαλίζειν, ix. 13, xxi. 1.

ἐξοχή, i. 3, x. 7.

ἔξοχος, xvii. 3.

ἐξυβρισμένα, xliii. 5. Cp. p. 191.

ἔξωθεν, vii. 1, xxii. 4, xxxiii. 4.

ἐξωνεῖσθαι, xxxvi. 2.

ἐπάγειν, xxxv. 2, xxxix. 2, xl. 2.

ἔπαθλον, xliv. 3.

ἐπαινετικός, viii. 3.

ἐπαινετός, xxxi. 1.

ἐπαίρεσθαι, vii. 2.

ἐπακμάσαι, xiii. 4.

ἐπάλληλος, ix. 13, xx. 2, xxxii. 5, xxxiv. 4, xli. 3. Cp. p. 193.

ἐπαναγκάζειν, xxvii. 1.

ἐπαναφορά, xx. 2, 3 (cp. p. 195).

ἐπανθεῖν, xxx. 1.

ἐπανιέναι, xiii. 1, xxxvii. 1.

ἐπάνω, i. 4.

ἐπαφρόδιτος, xxxiv. 2.

ἐπεγείρειν, xxiii. 1.

ἐπείγει, 198.

ἐπεισάγειν, xi. 1.

ἐπεισιέναι, xliv. 7.

ἐπεισκυκλεῖσθαι, xi. 1.

ἐπεισόδια, ix. 12.

ἐπεκτείνειν, xxviii. 3, xxxix. 4.

ἐπελπίζειν, xliv. 2.

ἐπέρχεσθαι, xliii. 4.

ἐπέχειν, 198.

ἐπί, i. 2, xxxix. 4, xliii. 6, etc.

ἐπίβασις, xi. 1.
ἐπιβλέπειν, ix. 6.
ἐπιβολή, xxxv. 3.
ἐπιβουλή, xvii. 1.
ἐπιγέννημα, 198.
ἐπιγινώσκειν, xxxi. 1, xxxiii. 3.
ἐπιδεικτικός, viii. 3, xii. 5, xxxiv. 3 (cp. p. 198).
ἐπιδέξιος, xxxiv. 2.
ἐπιδέχεσθαι, iii. 1, xxii. 2.
ἐπίδοσις, i. 1.
ἐπιζητεῖν, x. 3, xv. 2.
ἐπικαίειν, xliv. 10. Cp. p. 185.
ἐπίκαιρος, xviii. 2.
ἐπικείμενα, sc. σκώμματα, xxxiv. 2. Cp. p. 182.
ἐπίκηρος, xxix. 1. Cp. p. 191.
ἐπικίνδυνος, ii. 2. Cp. p. 191.
ἐπικουρία, xvii. 2.
ἐπικρατεῖν, xvii. 1, xxxix. 3. Cp. p. 191.
ἐπικρίνειν, xii. 4, xxxvi. 4. Cp. p. 191.
ἐπίκρισις, vi. 1, xxxiii. 1.
ἐπιλογίζεσθαι, ii. 3.
ἐπίλογος, ix. 12, xii. 5 (cp. p. 199).
ἐπιμονή, 199.
ἐπίμονος, xii. 4.
ἐπινοητικός, iv. 1.
ἐπίνοια, i. 2, xxxv. 3.
ἐπίπεδον, xvii. 3.
ἐπιπνεῖσθαι, xlii. 2.
ἐπίπνοια, xiii. 2.
ἐπιπολάζειν, xli. 1.
ἐπιπροσθεῖν τινι, *obtegere*, xxxii. 2. Cp. p. 193.
ἐπιπροστιθέναι, xliv. 1.
ἐπίρρωσις, ii. 2.
ἐπισκέπτεσθαι, ii. 2, vii. 1.
ἐπισκοπεῖν, vii. 3.
ἐπισκοτεῖσθαι, xxxv. 4.
ἐπιστήμη καθαρά, vi. 1.
ἐπιστολή, *epistula Laconica*, e poeta quodam, xxxviii. 5. Cp. p. 244.
ἐπιστρέφειν, xii. 3, xxvii. 3, xxxi. 1. Cp. p. 175.
ἐπισυνάγεσθαι, xxiv. 1.
ἐπισυνδεδεμένα, xli. 3.

ἐπισύνθεσις, x. 1, xl. 1.
ἐπισυντιθέναι, x. 7, xxxiii. 4.
ἐπισυστρέφειν, *cogere in unum*, xxiv. 1.
ἐπισφαλής, xxxiii. 2. Cp. p. 191.
ἐπίτασις, *exaggeratio*, xxxviii. 5.
ἐπιτηδεύειν, ix. 3, xviii. 2.
ἐπιτήδευμα, xxx. 1.
ἐπιτίθεσθαι, xv. 3.
ἐπιτολμᾶν, xv. 5.
ἐπιτυχής, xv. 3, xxii. 1, xxxiii. 4.
ἐπιτυχία, v. 1.
ἐπιφάνεια, xv. 6.
ἐπιφέρειν, viii. 2, xxxix. 4.
ἐπιφθέγγεσθαι, ix. 5.
ἐπιφλέγειν, xxxv. 5.
ἐπίφορον εἴς τι, *quod ad rem conducit*, v. 1.
ἐπιφωνεῖν, iv. 3.
ἐπίχαρις, xxxiv. 3. Cp. p. 191.
ἐπιχειρεῖν, x. 6, xxxiv. 3.
ἐπιχείρησις, 199.
ἐποικοδόμησις, xxxix. 3.
ἐποικονομία, xi. 2. Cp. p. 189.
ἐποκέλλειν, iii. 4.
ἐπορέγεσθαι, xxxiv. 2.
ἔπος, *versus metricus*, x. 6.
ἔρανος, 191, 199. ἐρανίζειν, xx. 1.
ἔργα, xxii. 1, xxiii. 3, xxxviii. 5.
ἐργάζεσθαι, xliii. 6.
ἐρημοῦσθαι, de mari recedente, ix. 13.
ἑρμηνεία, *elocutio*, v. 1, xliii. 3.
ἑρμηνευτικά, τά, xxiii. 1.
ἐρύκειν, x. 6. Cp. p. 173.
ἐρώτησις, 199.
ἐρωτικαὶ μανίαι, x. 1.
ἑτέρωθι, ix. 2.
εὐβουλία, ii. 3. Cp. p. 191.
εὐγένεια, *urbanitas et elegantia*, xxxiv. 2.
εὐγενής, iii. 3, xxxix. 4, xliii. 6.
εὐεργεσία, *beneficentia*, i. 2.
εὐεργετεῖν, i. 2. Cp. p. 244.
εὔηχος, xxiv. 2.
εὐθύνας ὑπέχειν, xiv. 2.
εὐθύς, xxix. 4, xli. 1, xlii. 2.
εὐκαμπής, xxxiv. 2.
εὐκαταφρόνητον, τό, iii. 2.
εὔκλεια, xiii. 4. Cp. p. 226.
εὐλόγως, xxxviii. 4.

εὐμέλεια, xxviii. 2, xxxix. 3.

εὐπάλαιστρον, τό, xxxiv. 2. Cp. p. 189.

εὐπίνεια, 189, 199. Cp. p. 193.

εὐπόριστος, xxxv. 5.

εὔστοχος, xxxiv. 2.

εὐτελισμός, extenuatio rerum, xi. 2.

εὔφορος πρός τι, xliv. 1.

ἐφάπτεσθαι, i. 1, iv. 5, xxxix. 3.

ἐφεστώς, xxii. 2. Cp. p. 179.

ἐφηδύνειν, 199.

ἐφιέναι, permittere, xii. 4.

ἐφικτός, xxxix. 1. Cp. p. 191.

ἐφορμᾶν, ix. 5.

ἔχει με θαῦμα, xliv. 1. ἔχω εὑρεῖν, xliv. 7. λόγος ἔχει, fama tenet, fertur : xiii. 2. ἔχεσθαι σκοποῦ, xiii. 2.

Z

ζεῖν. ζεσάσης τῆς θαλάσσης, ex Herodoto, xliii. 1.

ζῆλος, ζηλοῦν, ζήλωσις, vii. 4, xiii. 2. Cp. p. 201.

ζηλοτυπία, xxii. 1.

ζωγραφία, xvii. 3. Cp. p. 191.

H

ἡγεμὼν ἐν ὑπεροχῇ, xvii. 1. Cp. (auct. Hammero) Demetr. π. ἑρμ. § 289.

ἡδονή, v. 1, xxix. 2, xxxix. 1, xliv. 1.

ἡδύς. Τερεντιανὲ ἥδιστε: i. 4, iv. 3. τὸ ἡδύ, iii. 4.

ἡδύσματα, xliii. 4. Cp. p. 191.

ἦθος, ἠθικός, κ.τ.λ., 200.

ἡλικία, xliv. 7.

ἡνίκα, xxvii. 2. Cp. p. 180.

ἠρεμεῖν, xx. 2, xxxiv. 4. Cp. pp. 191, 193.

ἡρωϊκός, ix. 10, xv. 5.

ἥρως, 200.

ἧσσον, xix. 2. Cp. p. 179.

Θ

θάλλειν. ἔστ᾽ ἂν τεθήλῃ, e vetere quodam poeta : xxxvi. 2. Cp. p. 244.

θαρρεῖν, viii. 4.

θαυμάζειν. τεθαυμασμένος, xiii. 4.

θ αυμαστός, iv. 1.

θέατρον, metaphorice, xiv. 2.

θεῖος, iv. 6, ix. 9.

θέλγητρον, oblectamentum, xxxix. 2.

θέμα, postulatum sive principium, xxxii. 8.

θεμιτός, xxxiv. 4.

θεομαχία apud Homerum, ix. 6.

θεόπεμπτος, xxxiv. 4.

θεοφορεῖσθαι, 200.

θεσμοθέτης, ὁ τῶν Ἰουδαίων : ix. 9. Cp. pp. 64, 236.

θεωρεῖν, i. 2, xvii. 1.

θεωρία, ii. 3, xxx. 3, xxxix. 1.

θήλεια νόσος, ex Herodoto, xxviii. 4.

θῆραι ἀλλοτρίων θανάτων, xliv. 9.

θολοῦν τῇ φράσει, iii. 1.

θορυβεῖν, iii. 1.

θρασεῖαι μεταφοραί, metaphorae audaces, xxxii. 3.

θρεπτικός, xxxi. 1. Cp. p. 191.

θρυλούμενον, τό, decantatum illud, xliv. 2. Cp. p. 14.

θυμικῶς ἐκφλέγεσθαι, xii. 3.

θυμός, xiii. 4, xxvii. 3, xxxii. 2.

θύννος, e poeta incerto, xxiii. 2. Cp. p. 245.

I

ἰᾶσθαι τὰ τολμηρά, xxxii. 3. Cp. p. 219.

ἰδέα, viii. 1, xi. 2, xxii. 1, xxxii. 5, xxxix. 3.

ἴδιος, iii. 5, xliv. 12, etc.

ἰδίωμα κινδύνου, natura periculi, quod proprium erat periculo, x. 6.

ἰδιώτης, ἰδιωτικός, ἰδιωτισμός, 200.

ἰδιωτεύειν, xxxi. 2. Cp. p. 191.

ἰδρώς, e Sapphus carmine, x. 2. Cp. p. 173.

ἱερεῖα πρὸς κατακοπήν, xliii. 2.

ἴζημα, ix. 13.

ἱκανός, iv. 1.

Ἰλιάς, Ἰλιακός: ix. 7, 12, etc.

ἴσα βαίνειν, xliv. 7.

ἰσοδρομεῖν, xv. 4.

ἰσόθεοι ἐκεῖνοι, praestantissimi illi scriptores, xxxv. 2. Cp. ἥρως supra.

ἱστορία, xii. 5.

ἰσχυρὰ μνήμη, vii. 3.

ἰσχυροποιεῖν, xii. 2. Cp. p. 192.
ἰσχύς, de oratione, xxx. 1.
ἰταμός, 50, 172.

K

καθάπερ, v. 1, vii. 1.
καθαρός, xxxii. 8 et xxxiii. 1, 2 (scriptor),
vi. 1 (ἐπιστήμη), xxxv. 4 (φέγγος).
καθεύδειν, e Platone, iv. 6.
καθιέναι, xvi. 2.
καθίστασθαι, i. 4, ii. 1, etc.
καθολικῶς, xxxiii. 1.
καθόλου, xi. 3.
καίειν, x. 3, xii. 4.
καινόσπουδος, 189, 200.
καίριος, i. 1, x. 1.
καιρός, ii. 2, xii. 5, xliii. 3.
καίτοι, καίτοιγε, 188.
κακία, iii. 5, v. 1.
κακόζηλος, 201.
κακόστομος, xliii. 1.
καλλιγραφεῖν, xxxiii. 5.
κάλλος, v. 1, xxx. 1.
κακονίζειν, 201.
καρδίη νήφων, e vet. fort. poeta s. proverbio, xxxiv. 4. Cp. p. 182.
καταβροντᾶν, xxxiv. 4.
καταβυθίζειν, xliv. 6.
καταγνύναι. κἀμ μὲν γλῶσσα ἔαγε, e Sapphus carmine, x. 2.
κατάγνωσις, iii. 3.
καταδεής, xviii. 1.
καταδυόμενος, ix. 13.
καταιγίς, xx. 3.
καταισχύνειν, xliii. 5. Cp. p. 191.
κατακάλυψις, xvii. 3. Cp. pp. 178, 188.
κατακερματίζειν, 201.
κατακηλεῖν, xxx. 1.
κατακίρνασθαι, xv. 9.
κατακορής, 201.
κατακρεουργεῖν, ex Herodoto, xxxi. 2.
κατάληξις, xli. 2.
καταμέμφεσθαι, xxxi. 1.
καταμετρεῖν, ix. 5, xxxix. 4.
κατανθρακοῦσθαι, ex Aeschyli fragmento,
iii. 1.
καταντᾶν, xliii. 5.
καταντλεῖν, xii. 5. Cp. p. 192 n.

καταποικίλλειν, xxiii. 1.
καταπυκνοῦσθαι, ix. 13.
καταρρυθμίζειν, xli. 2.
κατάρυθμα, τά, xli. 1. Cp. p. 189.
καταρχαιρεσιάζειν, 201.
κατασημαντικός, xxxii. 5. Cp. p. 189.
κατασκελετεύειν, 193, 201.
κατασκευάζειν, xii. 2.
κατασκευή, xi. 2.
κατασοφίζεσθαι, xvii. 1.
κατασπεύδειν, xix. 2, xl. 4.
καταφέγγειν, xxxiv. 4. Cp. p. 189.
καταφρόνησις, xvii. 1. Cp. p. 188.
καταχορδεύειν, ex Herodoto : xxxi. 2.
καταχῶσαι, ex eodem, xxxviii. 4 (ubi
auctor κατακεχῶσθαι).
κατεξανάστασις, vii. 3.
κατέχειν, xliv. 6.
κατολιγωρεῖν, xiii. 2.
κατορθοῦν, xvi. 4 (e Demosth.), xxxvi. 2.
κατόρθωμα, κατόρθωσις, 202.
κεῖνο, xii. 1. Cp. p. 175.
κεῖσθαι ἔν τινι, consistere in aliqua re,
xii. 1.
κεκλασμένος, xli. 1.
κεκραμένος, xxviii. 1.
κενός, v. 1.
κενοῦσθαι, languescere, xi. 2.
κέντρον, ii. 2, xxxiv. 2.
κεραυνός, xii. 4.
κηλεῖν, xxxix. 3. Cp. p. 191.
κιθάρα, xxxix. 1.
κίνδυνος, xxii. 3, xxxiii. 2.
κινεῖν, iv. 1, xviii. 2, xx. 1, xxxiv. 3.
κλῖμαξ, 202.
κλοπή, 202.
κοῖλος ἄργυρος, e Theopompo, xliii. 2.
κοινός, ii. 3, vii. 1, xxxi. 1, xl. 2.
κοινῶς, xv. 1.
κολούει τὸν νοῦν, xlii. 1.
κομπώδης, xxiii. 4.
κομψός, xli. 1.
κονδυλίζειν, xliv. 4. Cp. pp. 13, 193.
κοπάζειν, de vento, reprehenditur: xliii.
1.
κόραι, pupillae oculorum, iv. 4.
κορυβαντιᾶν περί τι, v. 1.
κορυβαντισμοῦ πλήρης, xxxix. 2.

κοσμικὴ ἀφορία, xliv. 1 (cp. p. 244).
κοσμικὸν διάστημα, ix. 5.
κόσμος, *oratio elegans et urbana,* cui verbum contrarium est ἰδιωτισμός: xxxi. 1. *mundus, totum universum,* ix. 5.
κουφίζεσθαι, xvi. 2.
κουφολογία, xxix. 1.
κρατεῖν, i. 4, ix. 14, xv. 1.
κρατῆρες τῆς Αἴτνης, xxxv. 4.
κράτος, xxx. 1.
κρίνειν, xvi. 2, xxxv. 2.
κρίσις, vi. 1, xliv. 9.
κριτής, xiv. 2.
κροῦσις, xxxix. 2.
κύκλος, xl. 1.
κυπαρίττιναι μνῆμαι, pro δέλτοι, e Platone: iv. 6.
κυριολογία, 202.
κύριος, i. 1, ii. 3, xvii. 1, xxx. 1, xxxiv. 4, xxxvi. 2.
κώδωνας ἐξάπτεσθαι, 202.
κωμικός, xxxiv. 2.
κωμῳδία ἠθολογουμένη, 200.

Λ

λαμβάνειν, vii. 2, 4, ix. 6, 7, 13, xvii. 1, xxix. 1. Cp. p. 188.
λανθάνειν, xv. 2, xxii. 1.
λαός, *multitudo,* de piscibus, e poeta incerto: xxiv. 2.
λέγειν, viii. 1, ix. 1.
λειότης, xxi. 1.
λείπεσθαι, *superari,* iv. 2, xxxiv. 1.
λείψανα, ix. 12. Cp. p. 191.
λεκτικός, xxxviii. 5.
λέξις, viii. 1, xxvii. 3.
λήγειν εἴς τι, iii. 4.
λῆμμα, 202.
λῆψις, x. 3. Cp. p. 191.
λιθοκόλλητοι κρατῆρες, e Theopompo, xliii. 3.
λιμὴν κακῶν ὁ θάνατος, ix. 7.
λιτῶς ἐφηδύνειν, xxxiv. 2.
λογίδιον, xxxiv. 3.
λογίζεσθαι, xliv. 7.
λογικός, xxxvi. 3.
λόγοι, 203.

λοιμικὴ διαφθορά, xliv. 9.
λοιπόν, τό, *in posterum,* ix. 13, xvii. 2.
λυμαίνεσθαι, x. 7.
λύσις τολμήματος λεκτικοῦ, xxxviii. 5.

Μ

μαγεῖον, xxxii. 5. Cp. Plat. *Tim.* 72 C.
μαγειρεῖον, xliii. 3. Cp. p. 193.
μάλαγμα, xxxii. 5. Cp. Plat. *Tim.* 70 C.
μανία, viii. 4, x. 1.
μεγαλαυχία, vii. 2. Cp. p. 191.
μεγαληγορία, xv. 1, xvi. 1, et (e coniect. Toll.) xxxix. 1.
μεγαλήγορος, viii. 4.
μεγαλοπρεπής, xii. 3, xxx. 1. Cp. p. 191.
μεγαλορρημονέστερα, xxiii. 2.
μεγαλοφροσύνη, 191, 203.
μεγαλόφρων, ix. 2, xliv. 2. Cp. p. 191.
μεγαλοφυής, ii. 1, ix. 1, 14, xv. 3, xxxvi. 1, xliv. 3.
μεγαλοφυΐα, xiii. 2, xxxiii. 4, xxxvi. 4.
μεγαλοψυχία, vii. 1. Cp. p. 191.
μέγα, τό, xvi. 3, xxx. 2, xxxv. 2, xliv. 2.
μεγεθοποιεῖν, 203.
μεγεθοποιός, xxxix. 4. Cp. p. 189.
μέγεθος, i. 1, iv. 1, xi. 1, xiii. 2, xxxiii. 2. Cp. pp. 174, 210.
μεγεθύνειν, ix. 5, xiii. 1.
μεθάλλεσθαι, xx. 2.
μέθη, iii. 5, iv. 7.
μεθιστάναι, xvi. 2. Cp. p. 178.
μέθοδος, ii. 2.
μειλίγματα, xxxii. 3.
μειρακιῶδες, τό, iii. 4.
μειωτικὸν ὕψους, xlii. 1.
μέλος, iii. 1, xxxiii. 5, xl. 1. Cp. p. 203.
μερίς, xvi. 1.
μέρος, xii. 5.
μέση φύσις, xxxiii. 2.
μεταβαίνειν, μετάβασις, xxvii. 1, 2.
μεταβολή, 203.
μεταμόρφωσις, xxiv. 2.
μεταξύ, xxii. 4, xxxii. 5.
μεταπηδᾶν, xxii. 1.
μετατιθέναι, xxxix. 4.
μεταφέρειν, x. 6.

μεταφοραί, xxxii. 1–6.
μετέωρα in oratione, iii. 2.
μετουσία, xxxix. 3.
μέτριος, iii. 5. μετρίως, xxviii. 2.
μέτρον, ix. 4, 13, xiv. 1.
μέχρι ἀκοῆς, *tantummodo inter audiendum*, vii. 3.
μηδείς. εἰ μὴ δι' ἑνὸς ἑτέρου, tmesis: xxxiii. 4.
μήποτε, **203.**
μικρὸν καὶ γλαφυρόν, x. 6.
μικροποιεῖν, *sublimitatem minuere*, xli. 1. Cp. p. 189.
μικροποιός, xliii. 6, xliv. 6. Cp. p. 189.
μικρότης τῶν ὀνομάτων, xliii. 1.
μικροχαρής, ix. 4, xli. 1.
μικρόψυχος, iii. 4. μικροψυχία, iv. 7.
μίμημα, xxxix. 3.
μίμησις, xiii. 2.
μῖξις, xxxix. 2, 3.
μισητός, ix. 5.
μνῆμαι, e Platone, iv. 6.
μνηστηροφονία, ix. 14.
μοῖρα, ix. 1, xxxix. 1.
μόνον οὐκ et μόνον οὐχί, *tantum non*, x. 6.
μονοτόνως, xxxiv. 2.
μόριον, viii. 1, x. 1, xii. 2.
μυθικός, ix. 4.
μυθολογεῖν, xxxiv. 2. Cp. p. 191.
μυθώδης, ix. 13. Cp. p. 191.
μυκτήρ, **203.**
μύξαι, ex Hesiodo, ix. 5. Cp. p. 227.

N

νᾶμα, xiii. 3.
νᾶνοι, **203.**
ναυάγιον, x. 7.
νεανίας, xv. 1. Cp. p. 19.
νεκυία, ix. 2.
νέμεσθαι, xii. 4.
νεοσσός, ix. 14. Cp. p. 179.
νεοττοποιεῖσθαι, xliv. 7. Cp. pp. 193, 239.
νήπιος παῖς, xxx. 2.
νήφειν, xvi. 4, xxxii. 7, xxxiv. 4. Cp. p. 182.
νικητήρια, xvi. 2, xxxvi. 2. Cp. p. 191.
νόημα, xii. 1. Cp. p. 191.

νόησις, viii. 1, xxviii. 2. Cp. pp. 191, 204.
νόθος, xxxix. 3.
νομιζόμενα, xxviii. 2.
νομοθετεῖν, xxii. 1.
νοσεῖν πρός, xliv. 6.
νοῦς, **204.**

Ξ

ξένος, xvi. 2.
ξηρός, iii. 4.
ξηρότης, iii. 3. Cp. p. 191.
ξυμφέρεσθαί τινι, e Platone, iv. 6.
ξυστίς, e Theopompo, xliii. 2.

O

ὄγκος, ὀγκηρός, **204.**
ὀγκοῦν, xxviii. 2.
ὄζειν τινός, xxix. 1.
οἰδεῖν, iii. 1. Cp. p. 191.
οἰκεῖος, xxxiii. 1, xliv. 9.
οἰκονομία, i. 4.
οἰκουμένη, ἡ, xliv. 6.
οἰκτίζεσθαι, xxxiv. 2.
οἶκτοι, ix. 12.
οἴχεσθαι, xvi. 2.
ὀλισθαίνειν εἰς, iii. 4.
ὅλος, i. 1, iii. 4, viii. 4, x. 7, xxxv. 2. Cp. pp. 183, 188.
ὀλοσχερῶς, xliii. 4.
ὀλοφύρσεις, ix. 12.
ὁμοειδία, xli. 1.
ὁμολογούμενα, xxxii. 8, xxxix. 3.
ὁμοτικὸν σχῆμα, xvi. 2.
ὁμότονος, xxxvi. 4.
ὀνομάζειν, xliii. 4.
ὀνόματα, xxx. 1, xliii. 1.
ὀνομάτια, xliii. 2. Cp. p. 189.
ὀξύρροπος, xviii. 1. Cp. p. 191.
ὀξὺς καιρός, xxvii. 2.
ὁπωσοῦν, xv. 1, xvi. 3.
ὄργανον, xxi. 2, xxxix. 1.
ὁρίζεσθαι, viii. 1.
ὁρμή, ix. 5.
ὅρος, xxxii. 1 et (e coniect. Postg.) xxxiv. 1.
ὀρχηστικός, xli. 1. Cp. p. 191.
οὐράνιος, xxxv. 4.

οὔριος, ix. 11.
οὕτως, ii. 2, xv. 1.
ὄχθος, xxxv. 4.
ὀχληρός, ix. 10. Cp. p. 191.
ὄχλος, xxiii. 2.
ὄψις, x. 3, xv. 1, 7, xvii. 3. Cp. p. 188.
ὀψοποιΐα, xliii. 4. Cp. p. 191.

Π

παθήματα, ix. 12.
παθητικός, ii. 2, iii. 5, viii. 2, xii. 3, xviii. 2, xxix. 2, xxxii. 6.
πάθος, ix. 7, xliii. 1, xliv. 6. Cp. p. 204.
παιδαριώδης, iv. 1. Cp. p. 191.
παιδείας ἐπιστήμων, doctus, i. 3.
παιδιὰ εὔστοχος, xxxiv. 2.
παιδομαθής, xliv. 3. Cp. p. 192.
παίζειν. πεπαῖχθαι, xiv. 2. Cp. p. 176.
παιώνειος λόγος, xvi. 2.
παλαίστρα, metaphorice, iv. 4.
πάμφυρτα πάθη, ix. 7. Cp. p. 193.
πανάκεια, xxxviii. 5.
πανηγυρικός, iv. 2, xxxviii. 2.
πανήγυρις, xxxv. 2.
πανουργεῖν, de oratore, xvii. 1, 2.
παντελής, xxii. 4. Cp. p. 191.
πάντη, 191, 204.
πάντως, 191, 204.
πάνυ, viii. 4.
παράβασις, 204.
παραβολαί, xxxvii. 1. Cp. p. 191.
παράβολος, xxii. 4, xxxii. 4.
παραγγέλλειν, xi. 3.
παράγγελμα, 205.
παραγίνεσθαι, ii. 1.
παραγράφειν, xxi. 1.
παραδιδόναι, ix. 7.
παράδοξος, xxxv. 5. παραδόξως, xv. 6.
παραίνεσις, xxxvi. 4.
παρακεῖσθαι, iii. 5, xxxvi. 3, xliii. 4.
παρακινδυνεύειν, xxxiii. 2.
παρακινδυνευτικός, xxxiii. 2.
παρακολουθοῦντα, τά, x. 3.
παραλαμβάνειν, iv. 2, xvii. 2, xxxi. 8, xxxviii. 4. Cp. p. 178.

παραλλάττειν, xi. 3, xii. 1, 4. Cp. p. 191.
παράλληλα, xvii. 3.
παραλογίζεσθαι, xviii. 2.
παραλογισμός, xvii. 1.
παραλόγῳ (ἐν τῷ), xxiv. 2.
παραλόγως, xxii. 4.
παραμένειν, xxiii. 3.
παραμίξας, xliii. 3.
παραμυθία, iv. 7.
παράνοια, xxxvi. 2.
παρανομηθείς, iv. 3.
παραξύειν, xxxi. 2.
παραπίπτειν, xxii. 1.
παράπτωμα, xxxvi. 2. Cp. p. 192.
παρασκευαστικός, xv. 1.
παράστημα, 193, 205.
παρασύρειν, xxxii. 4, xxxiii. 5.
παρατήρησις, xxiv. 2.
παρατίθεσθαι, afferre (exempli gratia), iv. 2, ix. 10, xv. 7.
παρατετολμημένα, viii. 2.
παρατράγῳδα, 205.
παρατρέπεσθαι εἰς, ix. 14.
παρατρέφεσθαι, ix. 14.
παρατροπαί, xiii. 3.
παραυτίκα, xiii. 2.
παραφέρεσθαι, xxvii. 1.
παράφωνοι φθόγγοι, xxviii. 1.
παρεικάζειν, ix. 13, xii. 4. Cp. p. 191.
παρεῖναι, xvi. 1, xxxix. 1.
παρείρειν, iii. 1.
παρεισάγειν, xxxix. 3.
παρεκβαίνειν, ix. 14.
παρεμβάλλειν, xxii. 1.
παρενθήκη, xxix. 2.
παρένθυρσος, 205.
παρεντιθέναι, xxvii. 1.
παρέπεσθαι, x. 1.
παριστάναι, ix. 8, xv. 1, xvi. 2, xxvii. 3, xxxix. 3. Cp. pp. 178, 179.
παρολιγωρεῖν, xxxiii. 2. Cp. p. 191.
παροξυνθέντες (παροξύνοντες P), xviii. 2. Cp. p. 179.
παρόραμα, xxxiii. 4.
παρορίζειν, ii. 2, x. 6, xxxviii. 1.
παρορμητικός, xiv. 3.
πᾶς. ἐκ παντός, ii. 2. Cp. p. 188.

πάσχειν, iii. 5, ix. 11, xxxviii. 2.
πέλαγος, xii. 2. Cp. p. 191.
πειθώ, i. 4, xxxix. 1.
πεῖρα, i. 4, v. 1, xxxix. 3.
πένταθλος, xxxiv. 1. Cp. p. 229.
περιαυγούμενα τῷ ἡλίῳ, xvii. 2. Cp. p. 169.
περιβάλλειν, i. 3. περιβάλλεσθαι, xl. 2.
περιβλέπεσθαι, xxxv. 3.
περιγραφή, xiii. 3.
περιέλκεσθαι, xv. 1.
περιεργασία, iii. 4.
περιέχειν, xxii. 1, xliii. 1. Cp. p. 205.
περιηθήματα, xliii. 5.
περιΰστάναι, iii. 4.
περικείμενος, xliv. 5.
περικόπτειν, iv. 3.
περιλαμβάνειν, xii. 2, xx. 3, xxxiv. 2, xxxix. 3.
περιλάμπεσθαι, xv. 11. Cp. p. 193.
περιμάχητος, xxxviii. 3. Cp. p. 191.
περίοδος, 205.
περιουσία, xxxiv. 4. Cp. p. 191.
περιπαθής, viii. 3.
περιποιεῖν, i. 1. περιποιεῖσθαι, vi. 1.
περισπᾶν, xv. 11, xliii. 1.
περίστασις, 206.
περιτιθέναι, xii. 1, xxvii. 1.
περιττεύειν, xxxv. 1. Cp. p. 191.
περιττός, iii. 4, xxx. 1, xxxiv. 2, xxxv. 3, xl. 2.
περίφρασις, 206.
περιφρονεῖν, vii. 1. Cp. p. 191.
περιχεῖν, xvii. 2, xxviii. 2.
πεῦσις, xviii. 1.
πηγαὶ τῆς ὑψηγορίας, viii. 1.
πηροῦν, xlii. 1. Cp. p. 192.
πιθαναὶ φύσεις, xliv. 1.
πίπτειν, vii. 3, xxxiii. 5, xxxvi. 1, xliv. 4. Cp. p. 206.
πίστις, xii. 2, xvi. 3, xxix. 3.
πιστότερος, xxxi. 1.
πιστοῦσθαι, xvi. 1.
πλάνος, ix. 13.
πλάσις, viii. 1, xl. 3.
πλάσμα, xiii. 4, xv. 8.
πλεονάζεσθαι, xxiii. 3.
πληθυντικά, xxiii. 2.

πλήν, iv. 1, ix. 7, xi. 2.
πληροῦσθαι, vii. 2.
πλήττειν, xx. 2.
πλουσιώτατα, xii. 3.
πνεῦμα, ix. 3, xiii. 2, xxxiii. 5.
ποιεῖν, iii. 4, viii. 1.
ποιητής, ὁ, *Homerus*, ix. 10 et alibi.
ποικίλται χλανίδες, e Theopompo, xliii. 2.
ποιός, viii. 1, xii. 1, xx. 3.
ποκοειδής, xv. 5. Cp. p. 189.
πόλεμος, tropice, xliv. 6.
πολιτεία, xiii. 1, xliv. 3.
πολιτεύειν, xvi. 2, 4.
πολιτικός, 206.
πολλαχῇ, xii. 3.
πολλοστημόριον, xxxvi. 2.
πολύεργον, xvi. 1.
πολυΐστωρ, iv. 1.
πολυμορφία, xxxix. 3.
πολυπλήθεια, xxxii. 1.
πολυπρόσωπον, τό, xxvii. 3.
πολύπτωτος, 206.
πολυτέλεια, xliv. 7.
πολύφωνος, 206.
πομπικός, viii. 3. πομπικῶς, xxxii. 5.
πορίζεσθαι, vi. 1, xxxvi. 4.
πόρναι, e Timaeo, iv. 5.
πόροι, e Platone, xxxii. 5.
πόρρω, iv. 7, xvii. 3.
ποσότης, ii. 2, xii. 1.
ποταμοὶ πυρός, xxxv. 4.
πρᾶγμα, i. 4, iii. 1, xi. 1, xxxviii. 4, xli. 2.
πραγματεύεσθαι. πεπραγμάτευται, xvi. 3.
πραγμάτια μικρά, xxx. 2.
πραγματικός, 206.
πρακτικόν, opponitur μυθικῷ: ix. 14.
πρέπουσαν, xxvii. 1. Cp. p. 180.
προάγειν, i. 1.
προαγωγός, xxxii. 7.
προαποδιδόναι, xli. 2.
προβάτειος πλοῦτος, dictum ad Platonem ridendum, xxix. 1.
προγενέστεροι, xiii. 4.
προγινώσκειν, ix. 12.
προεισβάλλειν ἀπό τινος, *initium facere ab aliqua re*, xxii. 2.

προεκκείμενος, *ante expositus*, xi. 1.
προεκπίπτειν, xv. 8, xxxviii. 1.
προεμφανίζεσθαι, xvii. 3.   Cp. p. 189.
προέχειν, xxxiv. 1.
προηγουμένως, **206.**
πρόθεσις, x. 6.
πρόθυμον, τό, xliv. 2.
προκείμενον, τό, ii. 3, xvi. 1.
προκινδυνεύειν, xvi. 3, 4.
προκόσμημα, xliii. 3.   Cp. p. 193.
προλαμβάνειν, iv. 2.
προοίμιον, xxxviii. 2.
προπομπή, e Platone, xxviii. 2.
πρός, i. 4, iv. 2, xxii. 2, xxxvi. 3.
προσαγγελία, x. 7.
προσάγεσθαι, x. 1.
προσαναγκάζειν, xv. 3.
προσαποδιδόναι, ix. 12, xxii. 4.
προσάπτειν, xxvii. 1.
προσβάλλειν ὑπόνοιαν, *movere suspicionem*, xvii. 1.
προσβιβάζειν, xv. 5.
προσεισφέρειν, xv. 9.
προσεκτικός, *attentus*, xxvi. 3.
προσέναγχος, xliv. 1.   Cp. pp. 184, 189.
προσεπεισφέρειν, ix. 12.
προσεπιθεᾶσθαι, xxx. 1.   Cp. p. 189.
προσεπιθεωρεῖν, ix. 11.
προσθήκη, xxi. 2.
προσκεῖσθαι, vii. 1.
προσόψει (τῇ) ἀπρεπές, *indecorum adspectu*, xliii. 3.
προσπεριορίζεσθαι, xxviii. 3.   Cp. p. 189.
προσπίπτειν, **206.**
προστραγῳδούμενον, vii. 1.
προσυπογράφειν, xiv. 2.   Cp. p. 193.
προσφέρειν, i. 4.
προσφυής, xxxiv. 2.
προσφώνησις, xxvi. 3.
προσωπεῖον τραγικόν, xxx. 2.
πρόσωπον, iv. 7, xiv. 1, xxvi. 1, xxvii. 1.
προτερήματα ψυχικά, xliv. 3.
προτίθεσθαι, xxii. 1, xxxvi. 4, xxxix. 1.
προτροπή, xvi. 3.
προϋπαντᾶν, xvii. 3.
προϋποδεικνύναι, xliii. 6.
προϋποκεῖσθαι, viii. 1.   Cp. p. 193.

προϋποτίθεσθαι, i. 3, ix. 3.
προφαίνεσθαι, xv. 7.
προφέρειν, xxxii. 8.
προχεῖν, xix. 1.
πρόχρησις, xxvii. 2.   Cp. pp. 180, 189.
πρόχυσις, ix. 13.
προωθεῖν, xxxii. 4.
πρωτεῖον, xiii. 4, xxxiii. 1, 4, xxxiv. 1.   Cp. p. 192.
πταῖσμα, xxxiii. 4.
πτοεῖν. ἐπτόασεν, e Sapphus carmine: x. 2.
Πυγμαῖοι, **203.**   Cp. p. 10.
πύκνωσις, x. 1.
πυρρίχιοι, xli. 1.
πῶλος, ex Anacr., xxxi. 1.   Cp. p. 218.

Ρ

ῥᾳθυμία, xliv. 11.
ῥῆγμα, xiii. 2.
ῥήτωρ, **207.**
ῥόθιον, τό, xxxii. 4.
ῥυθμός, xxxix. 4.
ῥυπαρός, xxxi. 1, xliii. 5.
ῥώμη in oratione Demosthenis, xii. 4.   Cp. p. 193.
ῥωπικός, 192, **207.**

Σ

σβέννυσθαι, metaphorice, xxi. 1, xxxiii. 5.
σεμνὰ ὀνόματα, xxx. 2.
σεμνότης μεγαλοπρεπής, xii. 3.
σημαίνειν, xxxix. 2.
σημαντικός, xxxi. 1, 2.   Cp. p. 181.
σιωπὴ τοῦ Αἴαντος μέγα, ix. 2.
σκεδασθέντα, xl. 1.
σκέμμα, xxxiii. 1, xxxvi. 4.
σκέπτεσθαι. ἐσκεμμένα, quae *meditata et cogitata* dicuntur, xviii. 2, xxii. 2.
σκευάζειν, xvi. 1, xliii. 2.
σκῆνος ἀνθρώπινον, *corpus humanum*, xxxii. 5.
σκηπτός, xii. 4.
σκληρότης, xli. 3.   Cp. p. 184.
σκοπός, xiii. 2.
σοβαρός, xviii. 1.
σοβεῖν, xli. 1.

σοφίσματα τῆς ῥητορικῆς, xvii. 2.
σοφιστής, σοφιστικός, **207**.
σοφοί. κατὰ τοὺς σοφούς: fortasse unus
Plato intellegendus: xliv. 7.
σπᾶν εἰς ἑαυτόν, xxxiv. 4.
σπάνιος, xliv. 1.
σπέρμα, xvi. 3, xliii. 4.
στέφανος, xiii. 4. Cp. p. 226.
στηριγμός, xl. 4.
στίγματα, xliii. 3.
στοιχεῖον, ii. 2.
στόμια ἱερά, *antrum sacrum* oraculi
Delphici, xiii. 2.
στόμφος, **207**.
στοχάζεσθαί τινος, i. 1.
στρέφεσθαι ἐν μέσοις τοῖς κινδύνοις, xxvi.
1.
συγγενής, xxxix. 3.
σύγγραμμα, xxxii. 8. Cp. p. 221.
συγγραμμάτιον, **207**.
συγγραφεύς, **207**.
συγκατάθεσις, **207**.
συγκατατίθεσθαι, xxxii. 1.
συγκείμενα (λίαν), *coartata*, xli. 3.
συγκινδυνεύειν, ix. 6. Cp. p. 192.
συγκινεῖν, xv. 2, xxix. 2.
συγκίνησις, xx. 2.
συγκλείειν, viii. 1.
συγκοπή, **207**.
συγκόπτειν, xli. 3.
συγκορυφοῦν, xxiv. 2.
σύγκρισις, iv. 2.
συγχρῆσθαι, xl. 2.
συλλαμβάνεσθαι, xiv. 3.
συμβαίνειν, x. 1, xvii. 3.
συμβάλλειν, xliii. 4.
συμβιάζεσθαι, x. 6.
συμμαχεῖ τῷ ὕψει τὰ σχήματα, xv. 1.
σύμμετρον, τό, xxxiii. 1.
συμμέτρως (si vera lectio), xxix. 1.
συμμορία, **207**.
συμπεφυκέναι, viii. 2.
συμπληθύνειν, xxiii. 3.
συμπλήρωσις, xii. 2.
συμπολεμεῖν, ix. 6.
συμπτεροῦσθαι, xv. 4.
συμφέρειν, ii. 2.
συμφθέγγεσθαι, xxviii. 1.

συμφυής, xliv. 7.
συμφωνία, xxxix. 2.
συνάγειν εἰς λίαν βραχύ, xlii. 1.
συναθροίζειν, xxxvi. 2.
συναίρεσις, x. 3.
συναναγκάζειν, x. 6, xxii. 4.
συναναιρεῖν, ii. 3.
συναναπλέκεσθαι, xx. 1.
συναποκινδυνεύειν, xxii. 4.
συνάπτειν, xliv. 7.
συναραιοῖ, 185.
συναρμόζειν, xxxix. 3, xl. 3.
συναρπάσας ᾤχετο, xvi. 2.
συνδεῖν, xxi. 2.
σύνδεσμος, *coniunctio*, quam gramma-
tici appellant: xxi. 1.
συνδιατιθέναι, vii. 3.
συνδιαφορεῖν, xl. 1.
συνδιώκειν, xxi. 1, xliii. 5.
συνεδρεύειν, x. 1.
σύνεδρος, xi. 1.
συνεκλύεσθαι, xxxix. 4.
συνεκπίπτειν, xli. 1. Cp. p. 192.
συνεκφωνεῖν, xxxviii. 3.
συνεμβαίνειν, ix. 10, xiii. 4.
συνεμπίπτειν, x. 6.
συνεμπνεῖν, ix. 11. Cp. p. 189.
συνεμφαίνειν, xxii. 3.
συνενθουσιᾶν, xiii. 2, xxxii. 4.
συνεξομοιοῦσθαι, xxxix. 2.
συνεπιβαίνειν, xv. 4.
συνεπικρίνειν, i. 2. Cp. p. 192.
συνεπιρρώνυσθαι, xi. 2.
συνεπισπᾶσθαι, xxii. 3. Cp. p. 192.
συνεργὸν κόσμου, *quod ad ornatum conducit*, xxiii. 1.
συνεφέλκεσθαι, *secum rapere*, xxxii. 1.
συνεχής, vii. 3, xx. 3, xxxii. 5.
σύνηθες, τό, xxxi. 1.
συνηχεῖν, xxviii. 1, xxxix. 4.
σύνθεσις, viii. 1, xxxix. 1.
σύνθλιψις, x. 6.
συνιστάναι, xi. 2, xxxiv. 3, xxxix. 4.
σύνοδος, x. 3, xx. 1.
συνοικίζεσθαι, xliv. 7.
συνοικονομούμενα, x. 7. Cp. p. 174.
σύνολον, τό, **207**.
σύνταγμα, v. 1.

σύνταξις, xii. 3.
συντάττεσθαι, *conscribere* librum : i. 1,
iv. 2. συντάττεσθαι ὑφ' ἕν, *in unum
coniungi*, xv. 11.
συντείνειν, xviii. 1.
συντειχίζειν, x. 7.
συντελεῖν, viii. 4, xxxiv. 4, xxxix. 1.
Cp. p. 172.
συντομία, xlii. 1.
συνυπάρχειν, viii. 2, x. 1.
συοφορβουμένους, ix. 14. Cp. pp. 172,
189.
σύστασις, 208.
σύστημα, xl. 1.
συστρέφειν, xlii. 1.
σφάλματα, xxxvi. 2.
σφοδρὸν πάθος, viii. 1.
σφοδρότης, ix. 13.
σχεδόν, xvii. 2.
σχέσις, x. 7.
σχῆμα, xvi. 1.
σχημάτια, *figurae* cum significatione
contemptus, xvii. 1.
σχηματισμός, xvi. 2, xviii. 1.
σχολαστικός, 208.
σχολικός, 208.
σῴζεσθαι, vii. 3.
σωμάτιον ὅλον τῆς Ἰλιάδος, ix. 13.
σωματοειδέστερον, xxiv. 1. Cp. p. 191.
σωματοποιεῖσθαι, xl. 1.

T

τάξις, i. 4, ii. 3, xx. 2, xxii. 1, 2.
ταπεινός, iii. 4, ix. 10, xxxiii. 2, xxxv.
2, xliii. 3.
τάττειν ὑπὸ νόμον, xxxiii. 5.
τάχος, xii. 4, xxxiv. 4.
τείνει ὁδὸς ἐπὶ τὰ ὑψηλά, xiii. 2.
τεκμηριοῦν, xxviii. 2. Cp. p. 193.
τέλεον, xli. 1. Cp. p. 208.
τελεσιουργεῖσθαι, xliv. 8.
τελεσφορούμενα, xiv. 3.
τέχνη, ii. 1, xxii. 1, xxxvi. 4.
τεχνίτης ῥήτωρ, xvii. 1. Cp. p. 192.
τεχνογράφος, xii. 1. Cp. p. 244.
τεχνολογία, 208.
τηρεῖν ἐν κατακαλύψει, xvii. 3. Cp.
pp. 178, 188.

τλημόνως, xxxi. 1.
τοῖα καὶ τοῖα ἔλεγε, xxvii. 1.
τόλμα μεταφορῶν, xxxii. 4.
τόλμημα λεκτικόν, xxxviii. 5.
τολμηρά, τά, xxxii. 3.
τόνος, ix. 13, xxxiv. 4.
τοπηγορία, 189, 208.
τόπος, iii. 5, ix. 8, xii. 2, xxxii. 6.
τραγικὴ φύσις, xv. 3.
τρέφειν, xliv. 2.
τρόποι, τροπικός, 208.
τροχαῖοι, xli. 1.
τυγχάνειν. οὐχ ὁ τυχών, ix. 9. Cp.
xvi. 1.
τύπος, 208.

Υ

ὑγιής, xxxiii. 1, xliv. 9.
ὑγρός, de oratore, xxxiv. 2, 3.
ὑδρωπικοῦ οὐδὲν ξηρότερον, iii. 4.
ὕλη, x. 1, xiii. 4, xliii. 1.
ὕπακρος, xxxiv. 1. Cp. p. 192 n.
ὑπαντᾶν, xvi. 4.
ὑπέκ, ex Homero, x. 6.
ὑπεναντίος, iii. 4. Cp. p. 192.
ὑπεναντιώσεις, κατά, xxxviii. 1.
ὑπέρ, 188.
ὑπεραίρειν, iii. 4, xv. 8, xxxvi. 3. Cp.
p. 192.
ὑπερβαίνειν, xv. 10.
ὑπερβάλλειν, vii. 1, xvi. 2.
ὑπέρβασις, ὑπερβατόν, xxii. 1, 3.
ὑπερβιβάζειν, xxii. 2.
ὑπερβολή, ix. 5, xxiii. 4, xxxviii. 1.
ὑπερέκπτωσις, xv. 8.
ὑπερήμερος, xiv. 3. Cp. p. 176.
ὑπερμεγέθης, xxxiii. 2, xliv. 1.
ὑπερορᾶν, vii. 1.
ὑπεροχή, xvii. 1, xxxvi. 4, xxxviii. 3.
Cp. p. 192.
ὑπερτείνειν, x. 1, xii. 5, xxxviii. 3.
Cp. p. 210.
ὑπερφρονεῖν, xxxv. 2.
ὑπερφυής, i. 4, ix. 4, xvi. 2.
ὑπερφυῶς, xliii. 2. Cp. p. 192.
ὑπογύου (ἐξ), *ex tempore*, xviii. 2, xxii.
3. Cp. p. 192.

ὑπόθεσις, i. 1, v. 1, ix. 12, xxxviii. 2, xxxix. 1.

ὑποκείμενον (τό), i. 1, xxiii. 4.

ὑποκρούειν, *pedem supplodere*, xli. 2.

ὑπολαμβάνειν, xliv. 6.

ὑπόμνημα, ὑπομνηματίζεσθαι, 208.

ὑπόνοια, xvii. 1, 2.

ὑπονοπτεῖν, iii. 1.

ὕποπτος, xvii. 1.

ὑποτίθεσθαι, v. 1, xiv. 2.

ὑποτίμησις, xxxii. 3. Cp. p. 181.

ὑποφέρειν, iii. 3, ix. 11, xvi. 4. Cp. p. 209.

ὑποχωρεῖν, ix. 13.

ὑστεροφημία, xiv. 3. Cp. p. 185.

ὑφηγεῖσθαι, i. 4.

ὑφιστάναι, ii. 2, xii. 1.

ὕφος, i. 4.

ὑψηγορία, viii. 1, xiv. 1.

ὑψηλόν, τό, i. 1, xliii. 3, xliv. 1. Cp. p. 209.

ὑψηλοποιός, xxviii. 1, xxxii. 6. Cp. p. 189.

ὑψηλοφανής, xxiv. 1. Cp. p. 189.

ὕψος, ὑψόω, 209, 210.

Φ

φαντάζεσθαι, xv. 2.

φαντασία, vii. 1, xv. 1, xliii. 3. Cp. p. 210.

φάντασμα, ix. 6.

φέρειν, xix. 2, xxxiii. 1, xxxiv. 4, xliii. 3.

φησίν, ii. 1, xxix. 1. Cp. pp. 171, 180, 222.

φθάνειν, xvi. 4, xix. 1, xxvii. 1.

φθέγγεσθαι, de scriptore, xiv. 3.

φιλεῖ, *amat, solet*, v. 1, xxi. 1.

φιληδονία, xliv. 6.

φιλολογεῖσθαι, xxix. 2.

φιλόμυθον, τό, ix. 11.

φιλονεικία, xxxii. 8. Cp. p. 181.

φιλονεικότερον, adverbialiter, xiii. 4. Cp. p. 192.

φιλόπονος, cum infinitivo, xv. 3.

φιλοχρηματία, xliv. 6. Cp. p. 192.

φλογίον, xxxv. 4.

φλοιώδης, 211.

φοβερός, iii. 1, ix. 7.

φοιβάζειν, viii. 4.

φοιβαστικός, xiii. 2.

φοιβόληπτος, xvi. 2.

φορά, ii. 2, xx. 2, xxi. 2, xxxii. 4.

φορβειά. φορβειᾶς ἄτερ, e Soph., iii. 2; *sine capistro*, vel (ut poeta noster) *not in government*.

φορταγωγεῖν, xliii. 4. Cp. p. 189.

φράζειν. πέφρασται, xliii. 1.

φράσις, iii. 1, viii. 1, xiii. 4, xxx. 1.

φραστικός, xii. 5, xxx. 1, xxxii. 6.

φρονεῖν, ix. 3, x. 3, xvi. 2.

φρόνημα, ix. 3, xliv. 2, 3.

φρονηματίας, ix. 4.

φρουρεῖν, xliv. 6.

φυσικῶς, xxxv. 4.

φυσιολογίαι, *disputationes de rerum natura*, xii. 5.

φύσις, ix. 7, xv. 3, xvi. 2, xxii. 1, xxiii. 4.

φυσώδης, xxviii. 1.

φωναί, *verba*, xliii. 5.

φωνεῖν. πεφώνηται, xxxix. 4.

φωνήεις, xl. 1.

φωνητικὴ ψυχή, xxx. 1.

φώριόν τι, iv. 5. Cp. Ael. *de Nat. Anim.* xiv. 5.

φῶς, *lumen*, xxx. 2.

X

χαίρειν, xxxii. 6, xxxvi. 4.

χαλᾶν, xxxviii. 1.

χαλινός, metaphorice, ii. 2. Cp. p. 245.

χαρακτὴρ πάθους ἀληθέστατος, xxii. 1.

χάρις, i. 2, xxxiv. 2. Cp. p. 193.

χάρται βυβλίων, e Theopompo, xliii. 2.

χαῦνος, *inanis*, iii. 4, vii. 1. Cp. p. 192.

χειμάρρους, xxxii. 1. Cp. p. 192.

χεῖν, xii. 3, xxiii. 3, xxxiv. 2.

χεῦμα, xiii. 1.

χηρεύειν, viii. 3.

χοιρίδια κλαίοντα, e Zoili dicto, ix. 14.

χορηγήματα πρὸς τρυφήν, xliii. 4.

χρειώδης, xxx. 2.

χρησμῳδεῖν, xiii. 2. Cp. p. 192.

χρηστομαθεῖν, χρηστομάθεια, 211.

χρόνος, verbum artis metricae, xxxix. 4, xl. 4.

χύσις, de Ciceronis dictione, xii. 4, 5.

χωρεῖν, *animo concipere,* ix. 9. Cp. p. 172.

Ψ

ψιλὴ καθ' ἑαυτὴν ἔννοια, *sententia ipsa per se sine voce,* ix. 2; ψιλὴ νόησις, *tenuis sententia,* xxviii. 2.

ψύγματα, *spiramenta,* x. 7. Cp. p. **174.**

ψύχεσθαι, x. 3, xii. 3, xxvii. 1.

ψυχρόν, τό, iii. 3, v. 1.

ψυχρότης, iii. 4.

Ω

ᾠδάριον, *cantiuncula,* xli. 2.

ὠνεῖσθαι τῆς ψυχῆς, xliv. 9.

CAMBRIDGE: PRINTED BY JOHN CLAY, M.A. AT THE UNIVERSITY PRESS.

BY THE SAME AUTHOR.

The Ancient Boeotians: their Character and Culture, and
their Reputation. With a Map, a Table of Dates, and a List
of Authorities. Cambridge University Press. Demy 8vo. 5*s.*

Dionysius of Halicarnassus: the Three Literary Letters.
The Greek Text edited with English Translation, Facsimile,
Notes, Glossary of Rhetorical Terms, Bibliography, and In-
troductory Essay on Dionysius as a Literary Critic. Cambridge
University Press. Demy 8vo. 9*s.*

Demetrius on Style. The Greek text of Demetrius
de Elocutione, edited after the Paris Manuscript, with Translation,
Facsimiles, Glossary, etc., and Introductory Essay on the Greek
Study of Prose Style. Cambridge University Press. Demy 8vo.
9*s.* net.